Israel's First Fifty Years

Edited by Robert O. Freedman

University Press of Florida
Gainesville · Tallahassee · Tampa · Boca Raton
Pensacola · Orlando · Miami · Jacksonville · Ft. Myers

Copyright 2000 by the Board of Regents of the State of Florida
Printed in the United States of America on acid-free paper
All rights reserved

05 04 03 02 01 00   6 5 4 3 2 1

Library of Congress Cataloging-in-Publication Data
Israel's first fifty years / edited by Robert O. Freedman
p. cm.
ISBN 0-8130-1819-6 (alk. paper)
1. Israel—Foreign relations. 2. Israel—Politics and government—20th century.
I. Freedman, Robert Owen.
DS119.6.I778   2000
956.9405—dc21   00-024427

The University Press of Florida is the scholarly publishing agency for the State University System of Florida, comprising Florida A&M University, Florida Atlantic University, Florida Gulf Coast University, Florida International University, Florida State University, University of Central Florida, University of Florida, University of North Florida, University of South Florida, and University of West Florida.

University Press of Florida
15 Northwest 15th Street
Gainesville, FL 32611-2079
http://www.upf.com

Israel's First Fifty Years

DS 119.6 .I778 2000
Israel's first fifty years

University of Central Florida, Orlando
University of Florida, Gainesville
University of North Florida, Jacksonville
University of South Florida, Tampa
University of West Florida, Pensacola

**NEW ENGLAND INSTITUTE
OF TECHNOLOGY
LEARNING RESOURCES CENTER**

To my wife, Sharon, who adds a special sparkle to my life

Contents

Preface ix
Introduction xi

1. Moscow and Israel: The Ups and Downs of a Fifty-Year Relationship
   Robert O. Freedman   1
2. U.S.-Israeli Relations since 1948
   Robert J. Lieber   16
3. Israel and the American Jewish Community: Changing Realities Test Traditional Ties
   George E. Gruen   29
4. Israel and the Arab States: The Long Road to Normalization
   Malik Mufti   67
5. Israeli Thinking about the Palestinians: A Historical Survey
   Mark Tessler   95
6. Labor during Fifty Years of Israeli Politics
   Myron J. Aronoff   119
7. The Right in Israeli Politics: The Nationalist Ethos in the Jewish Democracy
   Ilan Peleg   139
8. Religio-Politics and Social Unity in Israel: Israel's Religious Parties
   Chaim I. Waxman   162
9. The Arab Parties
   Elie Rekhess   180
10. The Changing Political Economy of Israel: From Agricultural Pioneers to the "Silicon Valley" of the Middle East
    Ofira Seliktar   197
11. The Press and Civil Society in Israel
    Michael Keren   219
12. Epilogue: The 1999 Elections and the Victory of Ehud Barak
    Mark Rosenblum   236

Bibliography   273
Contributors List   281
Index   283

Preface

In its first fifty years, Israel has undergone radical transformation economically and militarily as it has moved from an agriculturally based state of 600,000 people with a weak and ill-equipped army to an industrialized high-tech state of more than 6 million people with an army that is one of the strongest in the world. Yet as Israel has forged ahead economically and militarily, basic questions about its identity and social structure remain. Should Israel be a Western-style secular democracy, or should its legal system and daily rhythms be based on Jewish law and tradition? Will there ever be economic and social equality between Ashkenazi and Sephardi citizens in Israel? Will Israel ever be able to make peace with its Arab neighbors, especially with the Palestinians, and integrate into the Middle East, or will it forever be a state that "dwells apart," to use the biblical terminology? And what of the Arab citizens of Israel who now number almost one million? Will they be successfully integrated in Israeli life, on the basis of genuine civic and social equality, or will they become a fifth column threatening Israel's security?

In the foreign arena, there remain a number of questions as well. Will Israel's alliance with the United States remain strong, or will the fissures that emerged following the election of Binyamin Netanyahu widen? Similarly, will Israel's relations with Russia, which initially looked so promising after the collapse of the Soviet Union, again begin to deteriorate, thus repeating the pattern of Israeli-Soviet relations after the State of Israel was established in 1948? Finally, what of the future of relations between Israel and American Jewry, which reached a high point during the prime ministerships of Yitzhak Rabin and Shimon Peres from 1992 to 1996, only to deteriorate seriously afterward? Will these relations recover, or will the differences over issues such as religion and the peace process intensify and cause a major rift between the two largest segments of world Jewry?

These are some of the questions that were dealt with at a conference, "Israel at Fifty," held at Baltimore Hebrew University in May 1998, the fiftieth anniversary of Israel's independence. The conference, attended by scholars from around the world who brought with them differing perspectives, was held under the auspices of BHU's Center for the Study of Israel and the Contemporary Middle East, which celebrated its twentieth anniversary in May 1998. The center's first conference, "The Middle East and the Arab-Israeli Conflict," was held in May 1978; subsequent conferences have been held on such topics as "The Middle East after Camp David"; "Israel in the Begin Era"; "The Middle East after the Israeli Invasion of Lebanon"; "The Middle East from the Iran Contra Affair to the Intifada"; "The Intifada: Its Impact on Israel, the Arab World, and the Superpowers"; "The Middle East after the Iraqi Invasion of Kuwait"; "Israel under Rabin"; and "The Middle East and the Peace Process." The proceedings of each of the conferences were published in book form, after being edited by the director of the center, Robert O. Freedman. This book, *Israel's First Fifty Years,* also edited by Freedman, is the tenth in the center's series.

In preparing a book of this type, I received help from many sources. My secretary, Jean Bernstein, helped insulate me from the hubbub of running our university while I completed the editing of the book; Elise Baron, secretary of the Graduate School, prepared the manuscript; Bruce Mendelsohn, director of University Communications, helped publicize the conference from which this book emerged; Steven Fine and his able staff in the BHU Library—Barbara Salit-Mischel, Andrew Johnson, and Elaine Mael—provided invaluable computer and research assistance; and Liya Slobodsky helped maintain my research files. I would also like to thank George Hess, then chairman of the Board of Trustees of Baltimore Hebrew University, for his strong support of the Center for the Study of Israel and the Contemporary Middle East, as well as his successor, current board chairman, Michael Hettleman; Richard Pearlstone whose generous contribution, through the Jack Pearlstone Institute for Living Judaism, provided the bulk of the funding for the conference; and Arthur Abramson, Lynne Katzen, and Stacey Steinberger of the Baltimore Jewish Council who were Baltimore Hebrew University's partners in convening the conference. Finally I would like to thank my wife, Sharon, who has always showed gracious understanding as I seek to juggle the responsibilities of directing a university while at the same time continuing my scholarly research. It is to my wife that this book is dedicated.

Robert O. Freedman

Introduction

In the fifty years since its birth, Israel has developed at an extraordinary pace. Its population has increased sixfold, from 600,000 to 6 million, and in the process Israel has resettled millions of immigrants from all over the world, with the majority coming from the Arab world, the former Soviet Union, Romania, and post-Holocaust Europe. Israel's economic base has been transformed from agriculture to industry, with a significant portion of the industry being high tech. Universities have appeared in Tel Aviv, Haifa, and Beersheva to compete with The Hebrew University of Jerusalem. The per capita standard of living has risen from near poverty after Israel's War of Independence to the level of Western Europe by 1998. Finally, Israel's army has also been transformed from what could basically be called a citizen militia in 1948 to one of the top professional armies in the world.

In the political sphere Israel has also developed, although the direction of its development has been hotly debated. It has moved from a dominant party system in the 1948–77 period, with Labor in the dominant position, to a system of two major contending parties, courting a number of smaller parties, from 1977 to 1998. Some feel that, as a result of the change in Israel's electoral system in 1996, which established separate voting for the Knesset and the prime minister, the two-party competitive system may itself erode as smaller parties make electoral gains at the expense of the two major parties. This certainly proved to be the case in the 1999 elections. In the social sphere, the once-dominant secular socialist Ashkenazi leadership has been challenged, first by Sephardi immigrants, then by religious parties, and most recently by Russian immigrants, even as the socialist ideology, held so tightly by the generations that founded Israel, has greatly eroded. In addition, the Arab citizens of Israel, now one-sixth of the population, have become increasingly assertive and are demanding political and economic equality with the Jewish citizens of the state.

In foreign policy, Israel's alliance with the United States, which took form after the 1967 war (when the United States began a major program of economic and military aid to Israel) and which significantly increased after the signing of the Egyptian-Israeli Peace Treaty in 1979, remains strong. So does the relationship between Israel and American Jewry. Both relationships became problematic following the election of Binyamin Netanyahu as prime minister in 1996, although they improved when Ehud

Barak was elected prime minister in 1999. Meanwhile, Israel's relations with the Soviet Union and then Russia have gone through a series of ups and downs, although the presence of almost one million Russian-speaking immigrants in Israel forms a major cultural bond between the two countries. Perhaps the most important foreign policy change Israel has undergone in the past fifty years has been in its relations with the Arab world. In 1948 the Arab world was united in its opposition to Israel's very existence (although its lack of unity on the battlefield against Israel was one of the factors enabling Israel to win its War of Independence). By 1999 Israel had signed peace treaties with Egypt (1979) and Jordan (1994), had low-level diplomatic relations with other Arab states, was involved in a tortuous peace process with the Palestinians, and had resumed peace talks with Syria. All but the most extreme Arab states, such as Libya and Iraq, now recognize Israel's right to exist and even are developing commercial contacts with the Jewish state, albeit slowly.

It is difficult to cover all of these developments in a single volume, even a multiauthored one, but the authors selected for this task, all experts in their fields, have been asked to focus on the central trends of the last fifty years so that the reader will understand not only what has happened since Israel was born in 1948 but also where it may be going in the future.

Robert O. Freedman, Peggy Meyerhoff Pearlstone Professor of Political Science and president of Baltimore Hebrew University, begins the book with an analysis of the ups and downs of the relationship between Moscow and Jerusalem from 1948 to 1999. He argues that there were three central issues in the relationship that had to be taken into consideration: (1) the exodus of Soviet Jewry, which caused problems in Soviet-Israeli relations from 1948 until Mikhail Gorbachev threw open the gates to allow hundreds of thousands of Jews to emigrate from the USSR in the 1989–91 period; (2) the strategic relationship between Israel and the United States, which led both Soviet and Russian leaders to seek to improve relations with the United States by first improving ties with Israel; and (3) the security needs of the USSR, which led Moscow first to back Israel against the British-supported Arab bloc in 1948 and then to back Israel's enemy, Egypt, which opposed another British-supported Arab bloc (the Baghdad Pact) in 1955. Soviet efforts to increase its influence in the Middle East helped precipitate the 1967 Arab-Israeli war, while Soviet aid to the Arabs in the 1973 war was to prove insufficient to prevent the United States from becoming the dominant external power in the region, something ultimately acknowledged by Gorbachev at the end of his rule. In the Yeltsin era, Freedman asserts, issues of trade, cultural relations, and even military cooperation have dominated Russian-Israeli relations, although following the advent of Yevgeny Primakov to the post of foreign minister and then to prime minister, a chill developed in Russian-Israeli diplomatic relations.

While relations between Moscow and Jerusalem experienced a series of fluctuations in the 1948–98 period, relations between Washington and Jerusalem have been marked by increasingly close ties. These are discussed by Robert J. Lieber of Georgetown University in "U.S.-Israeli Relations since 1948." He states that the relationship developed slowly and even encountered some serious problems, as in the Suez crisis of 1956–57 when the United States pressured Israel to withdraw from the captured Sinai Peninsula. Beginning in 1958, however, following the overthrow of the pro-Western regime in Iraq, the United States began to appreciate Israel's important strategic role in the region as a stable pro-Western state. The relationship began to expand after that, although it was not to solidify until after the 1967 war when the United States replaced France as Israel's main supplier of military equipment. In addition, as the author points out, Israel had become by the late 1970s the largest single recipient of American foreign aid. But it is not only common strategic interests that tie the two countries together (interests that have outlived the end of the Cold War, as he notes), but also a combination of historical, moral, ethnic, political, and institutional factors. Lieber also asserts that without a close U.S.-Israeli relationship, the achievements of the Middle East peace process would not have taken place. He contends that the underlying ties between the two countries are so deep that they can outlast any personal antagonism among leaders such as what occurred between President George Bush and Prime Minister Yitzhak Shamir or between President Bill Clinton and Prime Minister Binyamin Netanyahu.

Underlying the close tie between Israel and the United States is a strong relationship between the State of Israel and American Jewry. It became even closer after the Six-Day War in 1967, as George E. Gruen of Columbia University notes in "Israel and the American Jewish Community: Changing Realities Test Traditional Ties." Basing his research on a number of polls of the American and Israeli Jewish communities, he states that despite overall support for Israel, issues of religious pluralism and the peace process have created serious problems in the relationship. Segregating American Jews by age and religious affiliation, Gruen argues that, in general, younger Jews and non-Orthodox Jews tend to be less supportive of Israel, are less likely to have visited Israel, and are more willing to criticize the policies of an Israeli government. Gruen also expresses some skepticism about suggested gimmicks such as guaranteeing a free trip to Israel to all Jewish teenagers.

While American Jews have tended to be supportive of the State of Israel, the Arab states were for many years in strong opposition to it. Malik Mufti of Tufts University, in "Israel and the Arab States: The Long Road to Normalization," analyzes the diplomatic and military interactions of Israel and the Arab world from 1948 until 1998. He notes that while Israel may have seen its survival at stake during this period, the question of Israel remained subordinate, for the Arab states, to their own inter-Arab ambitions and rivalries, particularly from 1948 to 1967. Relying heavily on Israeli revisionist historians such as Avi Shlaim, Mufti also suggests that Israel was considerably stronger and that the Arabs were more willing to reach at least a partial accommodation with Israel in the 1948–52 period than is generally assumed. However, following the rise of Nasser (who Mufti feels was never serious about making peace with Israel), conflict between Israel and its Arab neighbors escalated, resulting in war in 1956. Mufti sees that war as a military victory for Israel but a political victory for Nasser and the 1967 war as both a military victory for Israel and a political disaster for Nasser (he calls it the Egyptian leader's "momentous blunder"). Yet an overconfident Israel ran into serious problems during the Yom Kippur War of 1973 and, despite its peace treaty with Egypt in 1979, during its invasion of Lebanon in 1982 and the *intifada* of 1987–93. These events, combined with a weakened PLO because of its backing of Iraq during its occupation of Kuwait, made Israel and the PLO ready to negotiate seriously in 1993 (although Mufti contends that the Oslo Agreement of 1993 benefited Israel far more than it did the PLO). The Oslo Agreement, in turn, enabled King Hussein of Jordan to sign a peace treaty with Israel in 1994, leaving Syria's president, Hafez Assad, isolated. The result of the process, Mufti contends, is that Israel now feels secure enough to view relations with its Arab neighbors as other than a zero-sum game: it no longer feels threatened if one of them gains in strength or if another draws closer to the United States. Ironically, contends Mufti, given its virtual alliance with Jordan, Israel has finally become integrated into the region, albeit as one more player in inter-Arab conflicts.

While Egypt, Syria, Lebanon, and Jordan have been important factors in Israeli foreign policy, the Palestinians have been the most important, as the Israeli leadership somewhat belatedly acknowledged. Mark Tessler, of the University of Wisconsin, Milwaukee, analyzes Israel's changing relationship with the Palestinians in "Israeli Thinking about the Palestinians: A Historical Survey." He begins with a detailed examination of Zionist thinking about the Palestinians prior to the establishment of the State of Israel, noting that, for the most part, early Zionists were unwilling to recognize the nationalist aspirations of the Palestinians, an attitude that the Palestinians themselves reciprocated. Following Israel's War of Independence in 1948, which resulted in the exodus of 750,000 Palestinians (how and why the Palestinians left remains a contentious issue among Israelis), what Tessler describes as the "blind spot" of Israeli thinking toward the Palestinians continued. The Labor party, in power until 1977, sought to trade land—conquered in the 1967 war and populated by Palestinians—with neighboring Arab states in return for peace, but the effort was unsuccessful. When Likud came to power in 1977, it tried, through the construction of a network of settlements, to tie the conquered land (which it termed "liberated land") directly to Israel while trying (unsuccessfully) to administer the West Bank through so-called village leagues. The *intifada*, however, underlined for the majority of Israelis the high cost of occupation, and Tessler notes that there was popular support in Israel for Prime Minister Yitzhak Rabin's recognition of Palestinian national aspirations in the Oslo Agreements.

Although foreign policy and security considerations have dominated Israeli thinking since 1948, internal political developments have been no less important and, indeed, have often shaped how Israelis have viewed the outside world. The party that dominated Israeli politics for three decades following the War of Independence (and that, in the two decades before the war, had dominated Jewish politics in the Yishuv) was the Labor party. Myron J. Aronoff of Rutgers University analyzes that party in "Labor during Fifty Years of Israeli Politics." Drawing on his previous analyses of the Labor party, he notes that it lost its position of domination because its elite became a self-perpetuating oligarchy who took their positions for granted and who came to assume that they had a natural right to rule. As a result, they were unresponsive to the social, economic, cultural, and political changes in Israel, particularly the rise of the Sephardim, who were poorly represented in the party's institutions. This led to the party's defeats in 1977 and 1981, and it was not until 1992 that Labor returned to power under the leadership of Yitzhak Rabin as the head of a coalition government. Aronoff notes that not only did Rabin begin the process of making peace with the Palestinians, he also brought about a "fundamental ideological reorientation" away from the emphasis on the Holocaust and Israel's isolation in the world that had been the motif of the Likud's government. He criticizes Rabin, however, for not using the "bully pulpit" to educate the Israeli public better on the benefits of Oslo. Aronoff also raises questions about the political competence of the Labor party's new leader, former general Ehud Barak, who was elected prime minister in 1999. Aronoff notes that for Barak to succeed, he must listen to the advice of experienced Labor party leaders such as Yossi Beilin and Chaim Ramon.

While the Labor party has lost most of its ideological élan since 1948, Ilan Peleg of Lafayette College contends, in "The Right in Israeli Politics: The Nationalist Ethos in the Jewish Democracy," that Likud leaders from Begin to Netanyahu have remained true to the ideological precepts of Vladimir Jabotinsky, the founder of the Revisionist movement from which Likud was to evolve. While the Labor Zionists, in the 1920s and 1930s, supported the establishment of a society based on equality, self-reliance, physical work, and social justice, Peleg asserts that Jabotinsky and the Revisionists introduced a model of military power, national pride, grandeur, conquest, and domination. Peleg sees six characteristics of the Israeli rightist ideology: (1) emphasizing the power of the nation as the metavalue to the exclusion of all other values, including peace and compromise with other national groups; (2) presenting the outside, non-Jewish world as not only attitudinally hostile but actively involved in efforts to destroy Israel; (3) emphasizing military power as the sole instrument in relations between nations; (4) dehumanizing all opponents of Israel, particularly the Palestinians and other Arabs; (5) emphasizing maximal territorial expansion; and (6) identifying Jewish opponents of Likud policies as "enemies of the people and non-patriotic traitors." From this perspective, Begin's invasion of Lebanon can be seen as a reflection of Likud's overemphasis on the use of military force, and Netanyahu's pre-1996 opposition to the Oslo Agreements can be seen as flowing from his desire for Israel to hold on to the maximum amount of territory. Peleg concludes that "for Netanyahu, the nationalist values of Greater Israel are more important than the alternative values of strengthening Israel's Jewishness (by withdrawal from all Arab-inhabited territories), promoting democracy and human rights, and making peace a reality" but that his policies helped contribute to Likud's electoral disaster in 1999.

While Israel's two main political parties have struggled for leadership in Israel since 1977, the post-1977 era has also seen another important political development—the rise in influence and political power of Israel's three religious parties, which together won 23 of the Knesset's 120 seats in 1996: Mafdal, the National Religious party (9 seats); United Torah Judaism, the Ashkenazi ultra-Orthodox or Haredi party (4 seats); and Shas, the Sephardi ultra-Orthodox party (10 seats). These parties did even better in the 1999 elections with Shas capturing 17 seats, and United Torah

Judaism 5 seats, although Mafdal fell from 9 to 5 seats. These developments are described by Chaim I. Waxman of Rutgers University in "Religio-Politics and Social Unity in Israel: Israel's Religious Parties." During this period, Shas played the ethnic card, attracting traditional, nonreligious Sephardim to its ranks, while the National Religious party became intensely ideological, seeing Israel's continuing occupation of the West Bank as a messianic obligation. Since the Likud was traditionally more sensitive to the needs of the religious parties than was Labor, its alliance with the ultra-Orthodox parties was a natural one (although the more pragmatic Shas was briefly part of Rabin's governing coalition from 1992 to 1993 and joined Barak's government in 1999, as did Mafdal and, initially, United Torah Judaism), while Likud's nationalist and historical attachment to the West Bank dovetailed closely with the National Religious party's religious attachment to it. Waxman also notes that in recent years even the Haredi ultra-Orthodox parties have become more supportive of holding on to the West Bank, and this has strengthened their alignment with Likud. Waxman concludes that with two-thirds of the religious voters supporting them, and with an easily mobilizable political base, the ultra-Orthodox parties have become a significant political force in Israeli politics, and he speculates on whether the growing political conflict between the ultra-Orthodox and secular forces will end in a real Kulturkampf.

While Israel's religious parties increasingly advocate holding on to the West Bank and preventing the emergence of an independent Palestinian state, Israel's Arab parties take the opposite position. In "The Arab Parties," Elie Rekhess, of Tel-Aviv University's Dayan Center, traces the evolution of Israeli-Arab political participation in Israeli politics. He notes that, historically, Israel adopted a dual policy toward its Arab minority that was underlined by two contradictory considerations: one that was security-oriented and viewed the Arabs as a potentially enemy-affiliated minority, and another, drawing upon the liberal and democratic principles established in Israel's declaration of independence, that argued for the integration of the Arab minority into Israeli life. While the security orientation dominated Israeli life for most of the state's history (there was a military government in Arab areas until 1966), Israel's occupation of the West Bank and Gaza in 1967 led to what Rekhess calls a growing Palestinization of the consciousness of the Israeli Arabs. Ironically, once Israel signed the Oslo Accords and recognized the national rights of the Palestinians, the process of Palestinization of the Israeli Arabs lessened, and the Arab citizens of Israel concentrated their efforts on gaining full equality with their Jewish fellow citizens. Indeed, Rekhess cites recent polls indicating that the vast majority of Israeli Arabs have no desire to resettle in a future Palestinian state. Instead, they have become more active in Israeli politics, spurred by the rise of the Islamic movement, with a record nine Arabs sitting in the Knesset in 1996 in Arab parties, two in Labor, and one in Meretz. In addition, the percentage of Arabs participating in the Israeli national elections shot up to a point that nearly equaled the Jewish percentage.

Despite these developments, as Rekhess points out, genuine equality with Jewish Israelis is still far from being achieved, and the modest gains that occurred during the Rabin-Peres era (1992–96) were in many ways undermined by Netanyahu. Nonetheless, Rekhess concludes that the Israeli Arabs will be an increasingly important factor on the Israeli political scene in years to come.

Israel's economic development is a major factor influencing the lives of both its Jewish and its Arab citizens, and Ofira Seliktar, in "The Changing Political Economy of Israel: From Agricultural Pioneers to the 'Silicon Valley' of the Middle East," describes how Israel's economy has evolved since 1948. Beginning as an agriculturally based economy that was heavily subsidized by the government, it has changed considerably since 1948, albeit not without numerous problems, including government mismanagement, the misallocation of resources, and ideological approaches that were divorced from good economic management principles. Thus in the early years of the state, as the Labor party grappled with the twin challenges of security and the resettlement of millions of refugees, Seliktar describes a network of government interventions in the economy that included controls on capital markets, wages, prices, and foreign exchange, along with micromanagement of agriculture (which received major government subsidies), industry, and the service sector of the economy. Indeed, Seliktar asserts, "Israel had created the most advanced socialist economy outside the Soviet bloc." When the Labor government sought to shift its priority to industry, it also ran into economic trouble by creating a number of industrial enterprises, such as textiles, that had to be repeatedly bailed out, and an import-substitute car industry that proved to be an embarrassing white elephant. Fortunately for Israel, it was able to muddle through this period because of transfers of funds from abroad, especially German reparations, American grants, and the contributions of world Jewry.

When Likud took over from Labor in 1977, following the political and economic shock of the Yom Kippur War of 1973, it did little better. Indeed, thanks to Likud policies which its opponents branded "voodoo economics," Israel's inflation rate soared and its foreign currency reserves shrank to dangerous levels as Likud's populist perspective undermined attempts at rational economic management. A major reform effort emerged only after U.S. prodding—and an emergency U.S. aid package of $1.5 billion—in 1985 that managed to halt the runaway inflation, although many of the underlying structural problems of Israel's economy remained. The economy was to take off only in the 1990s following the immigration of hundreds of thousands of highly skilled Soviet Jews who, with their skilled knowledge and low labor costs, attracted numerous high-tech investors from abroad. The result was that Israel's unusual growth since 1990 has been about 6 percent, and its GDP per capita has climbed to $17,000, the level of Western Europe. However as the peace process encountered problems following the election of Netanyahu in 1996, so too did the Israeli economy. By 1998, as Seliktar notes, economic growth had dropped off sharply while unemployment had begun to rise. She concludes that continued economic reform and rationalization is needed, along with the dropping of ideological constraints if Israel's economy is to be internationally competitive in the twenty-first century.

While Israel has made great strides economically, there is a question as to how far it has developed as a civil society, with a large number of nongovernmental organizations insulating the Israeli citizen from the government. Within a civil society, the free press plays a critical role, and in "The Press and Civil Society in Israel" Michael Keren, of Tel Aviv University, discusses the evolution of the Israeli press from the early pre-state period to the present. He notes that while the Israeli press as a whole has moved a long way from its ideological origins, with only the religious parties today having newspapers of their own, there has been too much of a concentration on the Arab-Israeli conflict in the press and not enough on human rights issues. Keren concludes that the press must play a more vigorous and balanced role if Israel is to have a truly civil society.

These chapters, along with the epilogue by Mark Rosenblum of Queens College, describing the reasons for Barak's victory and Netanyahu's defeat in the 1999 elections, will, it is hoped, provide the reader with a balanced overview of political, societal, and economic developments in Israel since the state was born in 1948. It has been an interesting fifty years, and as these authors indicate, the next fifty should be at least as interesting.

1

Moscow and Israel
The Ups and Downs of a Fifty-Year Relationship

Robert O. Freedman

In the fifty years since the State of Israel was established, relations between Israel and the Soviet Union (until 1991) and then Russia have been decidedly mixed. Initially, in May 1948, the Soviet Union was Israel's strongest supporter, only to break diplomatic relations with it in February 1953 in the bleakest period of the Stalinist era. While diplomatic relations were restored during the thaw that followed Stalin's death, they were again broken by Moscow during the Six-Day War in 1967 and were not fully restored until the end of the Gorbachev era in September 1991. When Russia established itself as an independent state in December 1991 under Boris Yeltsin, a honeymoon relationship with Israel prevailed, but it was replaced by a new chill when Yevgeny Primakov became Russia's foreign minister in January 1996.

In order to understand the twists and turns of the relationship between Moscow and Israel, three central factors need to be taken into consideration: the exodus of Soviet Jewry, the strategic relationship between Israel and the United States, and the security of the Soviet Union. These were the dominant issues in the 1948–91 period; in the post-Soviet period, issues of trade, cultural relations, and even military cooperation between Russia and Israel became increasingly important.

The Stalinist Period, 1948–1953

One of the major surprises in international politics in the late 1940s was the USSR's decision—despite its ideological hostility to Zionism and Stalin's personal anti-Semitism—not only to vote in the United Nations in 1947 for the partition of Palestine into Jewish and Arab states but also to give strong diplomatic support to the State of Israel when it was proclaimed in May 1948, as well as military support (via communist Czechoslovakia), even before it was invaded by its Arab neighbors after declaring its independence.[1] The central reason for this appears to have been the security concerns of the USSR.[2] With Britain seeking to establish a bloc of Arab states allied to London, from Egypt to Iraq, and the Jewish leadership in Palestine engaged in guerrilla warfare against the British who were preventing Jewish survivors of the Holocaust from entering, Stalin saw the Jewish community in Palestine as an ally in preventing the British from creating a contiguous Arab alliance near the southern periphery of the USSR. Indeed, in a frank comment to a Zionist official prior to the establishment of the State of Israel, a Russian diplomat openly acknowledged that the socialism of the Yishuv (the Jewish community of Palestine) was not the socialism of the Soviet Union but that, nevertheless, Moscow was prepared to support the Yishuv if it promised not to allow either Britain or the United States to have military bases in it.[3]

Following the initial period of Soviet-Israeli harmony, relations began to deteriorate. The triumphant visit of Golda Meir, Israel's first ambassador to the Soviet Union, which led to a major rally of Moscow Jews, may have unnerved Stalin, as did Israel's request to allow Soviet Jews to emigrate. In any case, a major crackdown on Jews in the USSR was already under way before the Meir visit, and, although relations between Israel and the USSR were not to be negatively affected by it until several years later, the question of Jewish emigration was already being felt and would be a central motif in the Soviet-Israeli relationship until 1991.[4] But diplomatic relations between Moscow and Jerusalem did not really begin to chill until June 1950, when Israel sided with the United States (which had given it a major loan in 1949) and against the USSR over the North Korean invasion of South Korea. From then on, relations quickly deteriorated, the situation made worse by Stalin's murder of Soviet Jews after a series of show trials in Prague and Kiev and the threat of a major pogrom against Soviet Jews during the so-called Doctor's Plot, which led to a strong Israeli denunciation in January 1953 of Stalin's policy toward Soviet Jews. Diplomatic relations were finally broken off, by Moscow, following the explosion of a bomb in the garden of the Soviet Legation in Tel Aviv in February 1953, possibly thrown by an Israeli protesting Stalin's treatment of Soviet Jews. Thus, in the month before Stalin's death, not only were Soviet Jews who had no hopes of emigrating to Israel being severely persecuted, but relations between Moscow and Israel, begun so promisingly in May 1948, hit rock bottom.

The Malenkov-Khrushchev Period, 1953–1964

During the period following the death of Stalin, a brief thaw in Russian foreign policy took place. The war in Korea ended, Moscow ceased making threats against Turkey, Iran, and Yugoslavia, and on July 20 it resumed diplomatic relations with Israel. Yet strategic questions were soon to cause difficulties in the Israeli-Soviet relationship. Britain was again seeking to create an alliance in the Middle East, this one called the Baghdad Pact which, backed by the United States, was seen as linking the North Atlantic Treaty Organization (NATO) with the Southeast Asia Treaty Organization (SEATO), thus encircling what was seen as a hostile Sino-Soviet bloc. Leading the Arab opposition to the Baghdad Pact was Egyptian leader Gamal Nasser, whose main Arab rival, Nuri Said, prime minister of Iraq, was a primary supporter of the Baghdad Pact—and the Western military and economic aid that went with it.

Nikita Khrushchev, who by 1955 had succeeded Georgi Malenkov as the leader of the USSR, saw Egypt as an ally against the West. The fact that Nasser was also an enemy of Israel was less important to Moscow than the chance to score a major victory in the competition with the United States for influence in what was now being called the Third World. Consequently, Khrushchev agreed to supply Egypt with a significant shipment of arms (planes and tanks) which were seen as a strategic threat by Israel. Egyptian-Israeli relations rapidly deteriorated. In October 1956, with the support of France and England, which had their own serious problems with Egypt (France because of Nasser's support for the Algerian revolt and Britain because of Nasser's nationalization of the Suez Canal and his opposition to the Baghdad Pact), Israel launched an attack against Egypt. Not only was it seeking to destroy the arms supplied by Moscow (again via Czechoslovakia), but it also wanted to end Egyptian-backed terrorist attacks across Israel's western border and to open the Straits of Tiran (which had been blockaded by Egypt) to Israeli shipping. Both the United States and the Soviet Union denounced the Israeli attack and the subsequent landing of British and French troops in Egypt. Moscow, initially bogged down by the rebellion in Hungary, subsequently issued threats against Britain, France, and Israel, albeit only when the crisis was already over due to U.S. pressure, as Khrushchev sought "on the cheap" to win support in the Arab world.[5]

Following the 1956 war, Moscow increasingly aligned itself with the Arab world against Israel, although Khrushchev was soon to find himself caught in a bitter intra-Arab struggle between Nasser and Abdul Karim

Kassem, who had overthrown Nuri Said in July 1958. Nonetheless, until he himself was ousted in October 1964, Khrushchev maintained diplomatic relations with Israel and even began to improve somewhat the internal situation of Soviet Jews as he sought support in the West for his growing confrontation with China.[6]

The Brezhnev Era, 1964–1982

Of all the periods of Soviet-Israeli relations, the Brezhnev era was perhaps the most contradictory. On the one hand, diplomatic relations between Israel and the USSR, broken during the Six-Day War, remained severed. On the other hand, the emigration of Soviet Jews to Israel, a policy goal of successive Israeli prime ministers since the birth of Israel in 1948, began in earnest. The purpose of Brezhnev's emigration strategy, however, was to improve ties not with Israel but rather with the United States, from which Moscow hoped for major trade and strategic arms agreements. Indeed, when after the Soviet invasion of Afghanistan there was a sharp deterioration in Soviet-American relations, there was a correspondingly sharp drop-off in Soviet Jewish emigration as well.

The slight warming of Soviet-Israeli state-to-state relations that had begun under Khrushchev ended abruptly with Israel's decisive victory in the Six-Day War in June 1967, which torpedoed Moscow's efforts to create an "anti-imperialist" alignment in the Middle East directed against the United States. From a strategic point of view, despite its lack of active aid to the Arabs, Moscow fared rather well as a result of the Six-Day War, at least initially. Egypt, Syria, and Iraq, the leading states in the Arab world, all broke diplomatic relations with the United States. In return for additional military supplies and aid against Israeli deep penetration raids during the 1969–70 Canal war, Moscow acquired control over five Egyptian air bases and Egypt's naval base in Alexandria. This enabled Moscow, which at the time had no aircraft carriers of its own, to balance the U.S. Sixth Fleet in the Mediterranean. Unfortunately for Moscow, however, the "no war, no peace" situation between Israel and the Arab world which provided the USSR with important strategic benefits was not to last. When Nasser died in September 1970, he was replaced by Anwar Sadat, who saw Washington, not Moscow, as the key to regaining the Sinai Peninsula which had been lost to Israel in 1967. Sadat began a gradual rapprochement with the United States in 1971 which hit a high point with the expulsion of Soviet advisers and the reestablishment of Egyptian control over its air and naval bases in 1972. Although the United States did not immediately move on that signal, once Sadat successfully organized an Arab coalition—together with the oil weapon—to confront Israel during the 1973 Yom Kippur War, the United States did pay attention. Indeed, despite massive Soviet aid to the Syrians and Egyptians during the war, and even more massive U.S. aid to Israel, it was the United States, not the USSR, that emerged victorious in the competition for influence in the Arab world following the Yom Kippur War. First Egypt and then Syria resumed diplomatic relations with the United States (Iraq was not to do so until 1984), as Secretary of State Henry Kissinger helped negotiate a series of agreements between Israel and both Egypt and Syria in the 1974–75 period, and President Richard Nixon made a triumphant tour of the region. It slowly became clear to the Soviet leaders that the United States could talk to both sides of the Arab-Israeli conflict and that Moscow could talk only to the Arab states, but Moscow was not yet ready to reestablish diplomatic relations with Israel. It was therefore excluded from a role in Middle East peacekeeping, which had its first major success in March 1979 when Israel and Egypt signed their peace treaty, the first between Israel and an Arab state. The U.S. position improved further following the Soviet invasion of Afghanistan in 1979, which alienated much of the Arab world, and the outbreak of the Iran-Iraq war in 1980, which was to lead to an Arab rapprochement with Egypt despite its peace treaty with Israel.[7]

Although there were no formal relations between the USSR and Israel during the Brezhnev era after 1967, there were contacts between the two countries, albeit not particularly substantive ones. Thus the Soviet and Israeli foreign ministers occasionally held discussions at the United Nations during its annual fall meetings, and there were infrequent visits back and forth of representatives of (usually left-wing) organizations of the two countries. Far more important than these contacts, however, was the mass emigration of Soviet Jews that Brezhnev allowed during most of his period of rule (1971–80)—ironically despite the 1975 UN General Assembly resolution "Zionism Is Racism," which the USSR spearheaded. Initially, most of these Jews went to Israel, thus strengthening the Jewish state's scientific and defense potential, since many of the emigrants were scientists and engineers. Needless to say, this development was not greeted positively by the Arab states in conflict with Israel, but Brezhnev continued to allow the emigration although it tended to fluctuate with the ups and downs of Soviet-American relations. Essentially emigration rose when Moscow (1) felt it was close to signing a strategic arms agreement with the United States, (2) sought trade benefits from the United States, and (3) sought to avert an anti-Soviet entente between the United States and China. When all three factors were present as in 1971–73 and 1978–79, emigration shot up; when one or more were missing, as in 1974–77, emigration dropped. Finally, when Soviet-American relations fell into a deep freeze following the Soviet invasion of Afghanistan and the election of Ronald Reagan in November 1980, emigration plummeted.[8] Complicating the Soviet-American relationship during this period was what became known as the Jackson-Vanik amendment to the Soviet-American trade bill. It penalized the USSR if it blocked free emigration, as in the case of the exit tax that was imposed by the USSR in August 1972 but that fell into disuse, under heavy U.S. pressure, in subsequent years. There was also an ironic development relating to emigration in the late 1970s. By 1976, more emigrating Soviet Jews were choosing to go to the United States than to Israel. This was to cause serious friction between the American Jewish community and the State of Israel, which was exacerbated as emigration plummeted during the early 1980s.[9]

The Gorbachev Era, 1985–1991

The Gorbachev era can be divided roughly into three parts. During the first period, 1985–86, the Soviet leader essentially continued the domestic and foreign policies of his predecessors while actively considering alternative strategies to solve the USSR's increasingly severe economic problems. During the second period, 1987–88, he began to implement a series of domestic and foreign policy reforms. The third period, 1989–91, was characterized by the collapse of the USSR as Gorbachev, who never was able to understand the phenomena of nationalism and religion, saw his reforms prove increasingly unable to solve the problems of the USSR. As a result, it became increasingly dependent on aid from the United States.

As far as Israel was concerned, while there were some hints of an improvement in Soviet-Israeli relations as early as August 1985, it was not until after the Soviet Union suffered the double blows in the spring of 1986 of the Chernobyl atomic power plant disaster and the plummeting of world oil and natural gas prices (Moscow's main means of earning foreign exchange was the sale of oil and natural gas) that relations began to improve. Thus in August 1986, in Helsinki, Finland, there were discussions between Israeli and Soviet diplomats on the resumption of diplomatic relations, although the discussions did not produce the results either side said it wanted.[10]

This improvement of Soviet-Israeli relations accelerated rapidly in the second period of Gorbachev's rule, 1987–88. During this time he proclaimed his domestic policy initiatives of glasnost (openness and truthfulness) and perestroika (reconstruction) in an effort to reinvigorate the weakening Soviet economy. In foreign affairs, he proclaimed the doctrine of "New Thinking," which involved Soviet-American cooperation (rather than the earlier competition) in solving the problems of the Third World, respect for interests of Third World countries as well as the superpowers, and superpower cooperation in limiting nuclear weapons.[11] These actions were clearly aimed at winning U.S. agreement to nuclear arms limitation and trade agreements, since the weakening Soviet economy could no longer provide the resources to compete with the planned U.S. Star Wars (Strategic Defense Initiative) Anti-Missile Deployment. Gorbachev was to follow his words with deeds, especially in announcing Moscow's departure from Afghanistan. Moscow was also forthcoming as far as Israel was concerned, and, given President Ronald Reagan's continued emphasis on the issue of Soviet Jewry in his summit meetings with Gorbachev, the Soviet leader made major concessions in this area as well.

Beginning in February 1987, Gorbachev began to increase Jewish emigration. The exodus of Soviet Jews reached 8,155 by the end of the year and rose to 18,965 by the end of 1988. As far as Israel was concerned, Gorbachev promised that an international conference (which the Soviet leader had long wanted since Moscow would play a coequal role in it with the United States) would not impose a settlement on Israel (April 1987); he urged Israel's main enemy, Syrian President Hafiz Assad, to settle his country's conflict with Israel politically and not by war (April 1987); he dispatched a consular delegation to Israel in July 1987 and accepted an Israeli consular mission in return (July 1988); and he told PLO leader Yasser Arafat in April 1988, with the *intifada* in full swing, that Israel's security had to be part of any Middle East settlement. Gorbachev was not yet ready, however, to allow direct flights (primarily for emigrating Soviet Jews) between the USSR and Israel, or to repeal the "Zionism Is Racism" declaration at the United Nations, or to restore full diplomatic relations with Israel.[12]

As the Soviet economy weakened, in 1989 Gorbachev permitted a rapid increase in Soviet Jewish emigration, which reached 213,042 per year by 1990 (of whom 181,759 went to Israel), as well as a flowering of cultural relations between the Soviet Union and Israel which included a January 1990 visit to Moscow by Israel's Habimah Theatre, which had originated in the early years of the USSR.[13] These moves were calculated to win favor in the United States at a time when the Soviet Union's world position was weakening, following the Soviet withdrawal from Afghanistan in February 1989 and the USSR's loss of its East European empire as one after another of Moscow's erstwhile Warsaw Pact allies broke away later that year.

The Gulf War, during which Moscow was on the diplomatic sidelines, accelerated the decline of Soviet influence in the Middle East, and the abortive coup against Gorbachev in August 1991 made things even worse. In a weakened political position and far more desirous of American support than ever before, Gorbachev finally agreed not only to support repeal of the UN's "Zionism Is Racism" resolution but also to allow direct flights to Israel and restore full diplomatic relations with Israel, which enabled the USSR to formally cosponsor the Madrid Middle East Peace Conference in October 1991. Unfortunately for Gorbachev, he would not be in power long enough to benefit from these political moves; less than two months after the Madrid Conference, the Soviet Union disintegrated, leaving Gorbachev without a formal role in the new political structure, which now included fifteen independent states in the territory of the former Soviet Union.

The Yeltsin Era, 1991–1999

Following the collapse of the Soviet Union, Russia emerged as the most important of the successor states, and its president, Boris Yeltsin, took an active role in formulating Russian foreign policy. Yeltsin's term of service, as far as Russia's policy toward Israel was concerned, can be divided into two periods. The first, 1992–95, was perhaps the warmest and most positive since 1948. Emigration flowed freely, cultural and economic ties blossomed, and diplomatic relations were almost halcyon in nature. When Yevgeny Primakov became Russia's foreign minister in 1996, however, Russian-Israeli diplomatic relations chilled, although trade and cultural and even military cooperation expanded as Russian-Israeli relations became increasingly complex.

When Yeltsin took power, Russia had four basic interests in Israel. The primary interest was an economic one as Yeltsin sought help for his hard-pressed economy. In this he proved successful, at least until the Russian economic collapse during the summer of 1998, with trade rising to $650 million in 1996, which made Israel the second largest Russian trade partner in the Middle East after Turkey. The trade included Israeli supplies of agricultural and high-tech goods to Russia and cooperation in military technology. The second major Russian interest was a diplomatic one. Especially during Yeltsin's first period, when Yitzhak Rabin, who was particularly close to U.S. President Bill Clinton, was Israel's prime minister, Yeltsin apparently hoped to keep a door open to the White House through good ties with Israel, as Russian-American relations became increasingly strained during the 1994–95 period. A close tie with Israel enabled Russia to play, or at least appear to play, a major role in the Arab-Israeli peace process, and this, in turn, enabled Yeltsin to demonstrate to his increasingly vociferous opposition—made up of old line communists and ultranationalists—that Russia was still playing a significant role in world affairs. Consequently, Russia strongly endorsed the Oslo I and Oslo II Agreements as well as the Israeli peace treaty with Jordan. In addition, when conflict broke out between Israel and Lebanon in the summer of 1993 and the Israelis deported 400 Hamas activists to Lebanon in December of that year, Russia took an evenhanded position, calling for "maximum restraint on both sides"—a major departure from Soviet times when Moscow was usually one-sided in its condemnation of Israel.[14]

A third Russian interest in Israel that continued through both periods of Yeltsin's rule was a cultural one. With almost a million immigrants from the former Soviet Union having arrived in Israel by 1995, the country had the largest Russian-speaking diaspora outside the former Soviet Union. Extensive cultural ties developed between the two countries, with Israel hosting a large number of Russian artists, pop singers, newspapers, and even cable television programs, as well as numerous Russian tourists who found both the sights and the Russian-language atmosphere of Israel appealing.

Israel had four central interests in Russia when Yeltsin took power. The first was to maintain the steady flow of immigrants that had provided Israel with a large number of scientists and engineers. Emigration to Israel remained steady, although not as large as in the early 1990s, as more Russian Jews stayed in Russia to pursue newly available business careers, with an average of 63,000 emigrating to Israel per year in the 1993–96 period. The second Israeli interest was to prevent Russia from exporting nuclear weapons or nuclear materials to Israel's Middle East enemies, such as Libya, Syria, Iran, and Iraq, and to limit the supply of conventional weapons to these countries. In this effort, Israel's experience was mixed. While Libya and Iraq were under UN sanctions, Moscow not only supplied sophisticated jet fighters and submarines to Iran but also began to supply it with nuclear reactors in 1995, a development Israel feared would speed Iran's acquisition of nuclear weapons. Israel also wanted trade with Russia, which soon began to supply Israel with such products as uncut diamonds, metals, and timber, and Soviet Jewish emigrants helped establish joint ventures in Russia. Finally, Israel also wanted, at a minimum, an evenhanded diplomatic policy in the Middle East, and, as noted, it was successful in this effort during Yeltsin's first period. Unfortunately for Israel, diplomatic relations were to chill during Yeltsin's second period from 1996 to 1998.

Under heavy pressure from the communists and ultranationalists in his Duma (Parliament), who had scored a major victory in the December 1995 elections, Yeltsin fired his pro-Western foreign minister, Andrei Kozyrev, and replaced him with hard-liner Yevgeny Primakov, who had extensive experience in the Middle East during the Brezhnev era. Although economic and cultural relations continued to develop while Primakov was foreign minister (the development of close ties between the Russian and Israeli Mafias, for example), and military cooperation actually increased as the two countries cooperated on building an AWACS plane, the Russian foreign minister had to struggle with other groups in the apparatus involved in making policy toward Israel; in the area of Middle East diplomacy, which Primakov dominated, Russian-Israeli relations cooled sharply.[15] Unlike 1993, when, during the fighting between Israel and Hezbollah forces, Russia took an evenhanded position, in 1996, when fighting erupted again, Primakov sharply condemned Israel. Relations improved somewhat with Yeltsin's reelection in June 1996, and former Refusnik Natan Sharansky, whose political party, Yisrael b'Aliyah, advocated an improvement in Russian-Israeli relations, made a triumphant visit to Moscow in January 1997. Relations worsened later that year when Israeli Prime Minister Benjamin Netanyahu, who had made a trip to Moscow in March 1997, unilaterally canceled a proposed Russian natural gas sale to Israel because of Russian aid in Iranian missile development, and Primakov again strongly criticized Israeli policy toward the Palestinians. When Primakov was elevated by Yeltsin to the position of prime minister in September 1998, it appeared that Russian-Israeli relations were headed for further deterioration especially since there was a resurgence in anti-Semitism in Russia, a phenomenon worrying to Israeli leaders, although it was to spark an increase in Russian Jewish emigration to Israel. In any case, the appointment of Primakov as Russia's prime minister is a useful point of departure for analyzing the ups and downs of Russian-Israeli relations in Israel's first fifty years.

Conclusions

Several conclusions can be drawn about the first fifty years of relations between Moscow and Israel. First, with perhaps no other country in the world have Israel's relations fluctuated to such a major degree. Initially, the Soviet Union was Israel's major external ally during its 1948 War of Independence, as Moscow supplied it with both military and diplomatic support. Less than five years later, however, Stalin severed relations. Although they were restored following Stalin's death in 1953, they were again broken off by Moscow in 1967 during the Six-Day War and were not fully restored until late 1991 at the end of the Gorbachev era. Relations hit another high point during the early years of Yeltsin's presidency but began to chill again once Yevgeny Primakov, an old foe of Israel, was appointed Russia's foreign minister.

In explaining the fluctuations of Israel's relations with first the USSR and then Russia, perhaps the major factor was the attitude of successive Soviet leaders about how Israel affected Moscow's security position in the Middle East. In 1948, Stalin saw Israel as a useful ally in helping to thwart a British plan to create an alliance of Arab states on Moscow's southern periphery. Seven years later, Khrushchev saw Egypt, Israel's enemy, as an ally in a similar effort, preventing the U.S.-backed Baghdad Pact from recruiting additional Arab members in an alliance linking NATO and SEATO. The Soviet leader was willing to supply Egypt with sophisticated arms that could be used in a confrontation with Israel, and the arms became a factor in the outbreak of the 1956 war. In 1966, with Moscow and Washington engaged in a zero-sum competition for influence in the Arab world, Brezhnev sought to exclude the United States from the oil-rich area by seeking to create an "anti-imperialist" Arab alliance based on Arab hostility to what the USSR called the "linchpin" of U.S. imperialism in the Middle East—Israel. When an Arab-Israel war broke out in 1967, in large part because of Soviet maneuvering, the USSR, checked by the United States, proved unable to intervene in the war and limited itself to breaking diplomatic relations with Israel again. Following the war, U.S.-Israeli relations grew warmer while Moscow again championed the Arab world, and the two superpowers found themselves on opposite sides during the 1973 Yom Kippur War, supplying weaponry to their respective clients but again not intervening directly. Following the 1973 war, however, the United States gradually became the dominant outside power in the Middle East, a process reinforced by the Soviet invasion of Afghanistan and the outbreak of the Iran-Iraq war. By the time Gorbachev took power, Moscow was for all intents and purposes marginalized in the Middle East, as only the United States proved able to talk to both sides of the Arab-Israeli conflict.

As the USSR's economic situation worsened, Gorbachev saw the necessity of improving ties with the United States, and one way he chose to do this was to improve ties with Israel (thus enabling Moscow to play a diplomatic role in the Arab-Israeli conflict) as well as to allow Soviet Jews to emigrate in ever larger numbers. Initially Yeltsin's strategy was similar to that of Gorbachev, but when Primakov became foreign minister, an element of the Brezhnev-era zero-sum competition in the Middle East crept back into Russian foreign policy, and Russian-Israel relations again chilled, as Primakov favored the Arab states over Israel.

A second major conclusion that can be drawn from this study is that the issue of Soviet Jewry has been an important one in relations between Moscow and Jerusalem. Initially, in part for ideological reasons, both Stalin and Khrushchev opposed the exodus of Jews from the USSR. Brezhnev by contrast, despite spearheading the UN General Assembly's anti-Zionist resolution, employed the exodus of Soviet Jews as a tool to improve Soviet-American relations. However, once Moscow's relations with Washington had deteriorated sharply following the Soviet invasion of Afghanistan, the exodus dropped from a high of 50,000 to less than 1,000 a few years later. Gorbachev also used the exodus of Soviet Jews to Israel as a means to improve U.S.-Soviet relations, but, unlike Brezhnev, he opened the floodgates so that hundreds of thousands of Soviet Jews left in his final two years in office. The vast majority of them went to Israel, thereby greatly strengthening its scientific and defense capabilities. Yeltsin continued to allow free emigration, but the elevation of Yevgeny Primakov to the post of prime minister in September 1998 may foreshadow a toughening of Russian policy on the emigration question, particularly if Russian-American relations chill further.

In sum, the relationship between Moscow and Jerusalem over the last fifty years is in reality a triangular one, with Washington's relations with both Moscow and Jerusalem, especially after 1967, playing a highly significant role first in Israel's relations with the Soviet Union and, more recently, in Israel's relations with Russia.

Epilogue: The 1999 Elections

Despite the conflict between Netanyahu and Yeltsin over the issue of Russian military technology sales to Iran and the sharp rise in anti-Semitism in

Russia following Primakov's elevation to prime minister in September 1998, the Israeli prime minister suddenly reversed his position toward Russia in the spring of 1999, following the announcement of the Israeli elections. It was the opinion of both Netanyahu and Israeli Foreign Minister Ariel Sharon—erroneous, as it turned out—that if the one million immigrants from the former Soviet Union living in Israel saw a marked improvement in Russian-Israeli relations, that would be the decisive factor in persuading them to vote for Netanyahu over his opponent, Ehud Barak.

During the spring of 1999, both Netanyahu and Sharon journeyed to Moscow, as did a number of Israeli cabinet members. Sharon had delighted his Russian hosts and angered the United States (and a number of Israelis) by questioning NATO's intervention in Kosovo, and Netanyahu supported the Russian quest for additional IMF support.[16] In March, Prime Minister Primakov (who was to be deposed by Yeltsin soon thereafter) responded to the Israeli initiative by letting it be known that he was hoping for a Netanyahu victory.[17] Subsequently, the Russian foreign minister advised Arafat against proclaiming a Palestinian state on May 4, 1999, a major concern of Israel at the time.[18]

However much the Russian-speaking immigrants genuinely wanted an improvement in Russian-Israeli relations (and there were clear indications that this was the case), they were far more concerned about their status in Israel. There was a major conflict between the Russian immigrant community and the Sephardi ultra-Orthodox Shas party. The party had control of the Ministry of the Interior, which had a direct impact on the lives of Israelis and which had sought to deport the spouses of a number of immigrants who were not considered "properly Jewish." Barak cleverly seized on this unhappiness and promised to move the Ministry of the Interior from Shas control to that of the Russian Immigrant party, Yisrael b'Aliyah. The promise coincided with the campaign slogan of Yisrael b'Aliyah calling for such a transfer of the ministry to its control. The result of the process was that despite Netanyahu's moves to improve relations with Russia, more than half of the immigrants voted for Barak.[19]

Three months after the elections, Barak journeyed to Moscow to meet Yeltsin. He was warmly received by the Kremlin, although he reiterated earlier Israeli concerns about the supply of Russian military technology to Iran and urged Yeltsin to deal with the rising threat of Russian anti-Semitism. Yeltsin pledged that the Russian government would do everything possible to stop the technology leaks, and he denounced the recent acts of anti-Semitism in Russia, stating that "there will be no leniency toward those who foment anti-Semitism" and that "the culprits will be found and brought to justice."[20] The Israeli and Russian leaders also discussed the possibility of Russian help in achieving a Syrian-Israeli peace agreement, although given Russia's weakened economic, military, and diplomatic position in the world, it was an open question whether Moscow could be of much help in this effort.[21]

Notes

1. See Louis Rapoport, *Stalin's War against the Jews*.
2. See Robert O. Freedman, "The Partition of Palestine."
3. Ibid., 204. See also Yaacov Ro'i, *Soviet Decision Making in Practice*. The documents on which this analysis are based are found in the Central Zionist Archives, Jerusalem, Document nos. S/25/9299 (September 11, 1947), S/25/486 (September 9, 1947), and S/25/6600 (April 5, 1947).
4. See Avigdor Dagan, *Moscow and Jerusalem*, 37–38.
5. See Robert O. Freedman, *Soviet Policy toward the Middle East since 1970*.
6. See Robert O. Freedman, "Soviet Jewry and Soviet-American Relations," 40–41.
7. See Robert O. Freedman, *Moscow and the Middle East*.
8. These issues are discussed in detail in Freedman, "Soviet Jewry and Soviet-American Relations." Immigration figures during the 1970s were 1971, 13,022; 1972, 31,681; 1973, 34,733; 1974, 20,628; 1975, 13,221; 1976, 14,261; 1977, 16,736; 1978, 28,864; 1979, 51,320; 1980, 21,471 (data from Research Bureau, National Conference on Soviet Jewry, New York).
9. This issue is discussed in Robert O. Freedman, "Soviet Jewry as a Factor in Soviet-Israeli Relations," 80–81.
10. See Robert O. Freedman, *Soviet Policy toward Israel under Gorbachev*, 29.
11. Ibid., 10–11.
12. These events are discussed in Robert O. Freedman, "Soviet-Israel Relations in the Gorbachev Era."
13. Ibid., 230. Because of U.S. immigration restrictions, the vast majority of exiting Soviet Jews now went to Israel (181,759 of 213,042 in 1990 and 145,005 of 179,720 in 1991).
14. These events are discussed in Robert O. Freedman, "Russia and Israel under Yeltsin."
15. See Robert O. Freedman, "Russia's Middle East Ambitions."
16. Akiva Eldar, "Netanyahu asked IMF to give Russia $4.8 billion loan: In Washington, Sharon calls Russian Israelis 'key to vote,'" *Haaretz*, April 9, 1999. See also Ze'ev Schiff, "Israel's dangerous dance with Russia," *Haaretz*, April 9, 1999, and Leonid Gankin, "Israel will help Russia get IMF loan," *Kommersant* (Moscow), March 23, 1999 (*CDSP*, vol. 51, no. 12, 24).
17. Eldar, "Netanyahu asked IMF to give Russia $4.8 billion loan."

18. Yelena Suponina, "Russia tells Palestinians to hold off," *Vremya*, April 7, 1999 (*CDSP*, vol. 51, no. 14, 22).

19. For an excellent analysis of this issue, see Oded Eran, "Russian Immigrants, Russia, and the Elections in Israel," *Analysis of Current Events (ACE)* 11, nos. 5–6 (May–June 1999): 13–15.

20. Cited in Michael Wines, "Russia pressed by Barak on technology to Iran and Iraq: Moscow talks center on peace efforts in the Middle East," *New York Times*, August 3, 1999. See also Danna Harman, "Barak hopes Russia can break the ice with Syria," *Jerusalem Post*, August 3, 1999.

21. On this issue, see Robert O. Freedman, "Russia, Syria, and a Syrian-Israeli Peace Agreement," *Middle East Insight*, November–December 1999.

2

U.S.-Israeli Relations since 1948
Robert J. Lieber

Any analysis of the U.S.-Israeli relationship should begin with recognition of the uniqueness of both parties. For its part, Israel (as its founding father, David Ben-Gurion, is said to have remarked) was meant to be just an ordinary *Jewish* country. Fifty years after its creation, the modern state of Israel has become well established in world affairs—a phenomenon that might not otherwise seem remarkable, except that this has taken place after a hiatus of nearly 2,000 years. Moreover, Israel has acquired an importance far beyond its size. What other country of 6 million people figures so large in the eyes of its friends and foes? Of how many other countries can most well-informed observers name even two leading political figures? The point is made more tellingly if we ask ourselves quickly to name the prime ministers of Japan, or Italy, or Spain, or are challenged to identify the second most important political figure in Germany. These are countries with populations ten or more times the size of Israel's and with tumultuous and important twentieth-century histories, yet most members of the informed public, and even many with a special interest in foreign affairs, are more likely to possess some degree of basic information about Israeli politics.

As for the United States, despite the title of Richard Rosecrance's book of some two decades ago, America is *not* an "ordinary country."[1] This is evident not only in terms of its origins and the aspirations of its founders as an escape from European decadence, but this same sense of uniqueness is reflected centuries later. It can be found in the lofty aspirations of John F. Kennedy's 1961 inaugural address, which called upon Americans to "pay any price" and "bear any burden," as well as in Ronald Reagan's 1981 inaugural with its invocation of America as a "shining city on a hill." More recently, echoes of these ideals remain evident, for example, in the foreign policy impulses of the Clinton administration to enlarge the sphere of democracies, to express concern for human rights in China, and to seek the prosecution of those accused of war crimes in Bosnia. Indeed, some conservative and liberal critics of the Clinton administration also invoke American values, as when, for example, they demand a stronger criticism of China on human rights and take issue with the American president's willingness to be received by his Chinese hosts at Tiananmen Square, the site of the June 1989 killing of democracy protesters. Moreover, these impulses take on greater significance because the United States today stands as the lone superpower and has military might, power projection capability, leadership capacity, economic strength, and cultural influence of unprecedented scope.

Given the uniqueness on both sides, it would be surprising if the interaction between Israel and America did not take on a special character as well. With that consideration in mind, this chapter briefly assesses the development of the special relationship between these two countries, then devotes attention to the domestic American dimension of the relationship, the U.S. role in the Arab-Israeli peace process, and the broader basis upon which this special relationship ultimately rests. In undertaking this assessment, I am seeking to address the more durable and long-term fundamentals of this bilateral interaction and not the flow of daily events or the specific actions and policies of individuals such as Ehud Barak, Yasser Arafat, or individual American policymakers. This inquiry suggests that the overall relationship between the United States and Israel was shaped by the interplay of many factors, but ultimately longer-term concerns have been most important, including strategic considerations, the American national interest, and even religious values, to a greater extent than shorter-term and more narrowly political concerns.

The Early Stages

In contrast to myths commonly held among its neighbors (and by some of its adversaries elsewhere, including in the United States), Israel was far from having been established as an outpost of Western imperialism or an instrument of America. Initially, the European powers remained largely indifferent or even hostile. The animus of Great Britain, in particular, as the retiring colonial power, has been extensively described. Moreover, both Conservative and Labour governments in London pursued such policies. In the years prior to the establishment of Israel, these included a November 1938 British policy statement opposing partition of Palestine; the White Paper of May 1939, limiting Jewish immigration to a total of no more than 75,000 over the subsequent five years, after which it was to be prohibited altogether unless agreed by the Arabs;[2] the antagonistic disposition of the postwar Labour government from 1945 to 1948, and the particular antipathy of Foreign Secretary Ernest Bevin and the Foreign Office, not only in continuing to oppose creation of a Jewish state but in using force to prevent immigration by survivors of the Holocaust and confining those captured in the attempt to detention camps in Cyprus and even Germany.

The Truman administration—in an often told tale—was deeply ambivalent, though ultimately American support was vital. On the one hand, as early as June 1945, President Truman adopted a proposal recommending that 100,000 European Jewish refugees be admitted immediately to Palestine. He communicated it to the British government, which remained unwilling to implement the proposal on the grounds that it would alienate opinion in the Arab world.[3] Ultimately, President Truman's support for partition of Palestine and recognition of Israel came at the very last minute and against the advice and wishes of the Departments of State and Defense. At a bitterly contentious White House meeting on May 12, 1948, Truman's advisor, Clark Clifford, argued strongly for immediate recognition of the Jewish state, but Secretary of State George C. Marshall was strongly opposed and told Truman that if he "were to follow Mr. Clifford's advice and if in the election I was to vote, I would vote against the President."[4] After some confusion and disarray between the White House and the American delegation to the United Nations, the United States did announce de facto recognition only minutes after the announcement of Israel's independence on May 14, 1948. However, the administration did not at first lift an arms embargo, and an Israeli loan request was, as Steven L. Spiegel notes, delayed by the bureaucracy until January 1949.[5]

Only very slowly did the special relationship between Israel and the United States evolve. Over a period of time, it has come to rest on deep-seated factors, including historical memory, Judeo-Christian values, the Holocaust, societal ties, strategic interests, and the tenacity of Israel. But despite these underlying dimensions—many of which were warmly invoked during celebrations of Israel's fiftieth anniversary—the development of the American-Israeli connection was far from a steady progression of close collaboration or patron-client relations. Indeed, at first the relationship was very much at arm's length, and Washington was slow to provide military assistance or economic aid. Crises in the relationship took place in 1953 and especially in 1956–57 over Suez, when the administration of President Dwight Eisenhower and Secretary of State John Foster Dulles applied great pressure on Israel to withdraw from the Sinai

Peninsula, which its troops had captured from Egypt in the October 1956 war.

No additional significant foreign aid was forthcoming until the provision of $86 million in 1952. During the 1950s and early to mid-1960s, aid levels remained low. As late as 1967, the annual aid provided to Israel amounted to just $13 million. However, in the aftermath of the Six-Day War, aid began to increase sharply, with the United States providing $76 million in 1968 and $600 million in 1971.[6]

The Special Relationship

At first, for Israel, the special relationship was more with France than with the United States and was driven largely by the sense of sharing a common enemy, Gamal Abdel Nasser. The French saw the Egyptian president as the key advocate of Arab nationalism and supporter of the Algerian rebels from 1954 onward. For its part, Israel regarded Nasser as the most formidable of its Arab adversaries. Hence France became an important source of arms and of nuclear technology, and ultimately, Israel would win the 1967 war with French more than with American weapons.

Why, then, did the change take place?

Here I draw on a fine piece of scholarship by Abraham Ben-Zvi of Tel Aviv University, in his book, *Decade of Transition: Eisenhower, Kennedy, and the Origins of the American-Israeli Alliance.*[7] Ben-Zvi demonstrates that a subtle but profound shift in American policy toward Israel began not, as is commonly held by historians and analysts, in 1962 with the Kennedy administration's decision to sell Hawk anti-aircraft missiles to Israel, but four years earlier in the second Eisenhower administration. This change in policy occurred not primarily because of domestic American politics but because of strategic factors in the Middle East and a recognition that Israel could be a strategic asset to the United States instead of a burden.

It has long been asserted that the 1962 arms sale decision and change in policy toward Israel was driven by domestic politics. This view holds that Democratic administrations, starting with Truman's and especially Kennedy's and Johnson's, were determined to secure the Jewish vote in certain key states, including New York, New Jersey, Pennsylvania, Illinois, Florida, and California, and that these partisan electoral considerations outweighed more hard-headed and long-standing calculations of America's strategic interests in the Middle East.

Instead, Ben-Zvi demonstrates that the policy shift actually began in the Eisenhower administration, as a gradual recognition of changes in the region and especially after the July 1958 crises in Lebanon, Iraq, and Jordan. During that time, the pro-Western government of Iraq was overthrown. The Hashemite monarchy of King Hussein in Jordan seemed endangered, and the political situation in Lebanon appeared to be so unstable that the Eisenhower administration dispatched U.S. Marines to Beirut for a period of several months.

During this time of serious instability, and particularly in the case of Jordan, Israel showed itself to be the sole staunchly pro-Western power in the region. Ben-Zvi quotes an explicit letter of August 1958 from Secretary of State Dulles to Israeli Prime Minister David Ben-Gurion attesting to this recognition:

> The heart of the matter . . . is the urgent necessity to strengthen the bulwarks of international order and justice against the forces of lawlessness and destruction which currently are at work in the Middle East. We have been glad that Israel shares this purpose, as illustrated by your deeply appreciated acquiescence in the use of Israel's airspace by United States and UK aircraft in their mission in support of Jordan. . . . We believe that Israel should be in a position to deter an attempt at aggression by indigenous forces, and are prepared to examine the military implications of this problem with an open mind. . . . The critical situation in the Middle East today gives Israel manifold opportunities to contribute, from its resources of spiritual strength and determination of purpose, to a stable international order.[8]

It is both sobering and revealing to reflect here that, despite Dulles's uplifting reference to Israel's "spiritual" dimension, the Ten Commandments were not written in 1958. Prior to the crises in Iraq, Jordan, and Lebanon, Israel's claim to a shared religious legacy had not been sufficient by itself to stimulate a more favorable American policy. Instead, it was only after the administration began to recognize the strategic dimension and to appreciate how shaky other pro-Western governments in the region actually were that it started to adopt a more explicitly cooperative policy toward Israel.

In another study, Kenneth Organski reached conclusions consistent with those of Ben-Zvi concerning the basis for American policy toward Israel as ultimately resting more on foreign policy reasons than on domestic politics: "U.S. policy decisions with respect to Israel have, in the main, been made by presidents and presidential foreign policy elites both by themselves and for reasons entirely their own. When the U.S. did not see Israel supporting U.S. interests in stemming the expansion of Soviet influence, it did not help Israel. . . . When U.S. leaders . . . decided that Israel could be an asset in the U.S. struggle with radical Arabs who were perceived as Soviet clients, they helped Israel."[9]

While the shift toward a closer U.S.-Israeli strategic relationship had its origins as far back as 1958, the United States initially took only modest and tentative steps. The relationship expanded slowly and then deepened after the Six-Day War of 1967 and especially after the Yom Kippur War of 1973 and the Egyptian-Israeli Peace Treaty of 1979. As evidence of this, a recent study has shown that while American foreign aid to Israel amounted to $3.2 billion in the years from 1949 to 1973, it grew to a total of $75 billion for the period from 1974 to 1997. Indeed, by the late 1970s, Israel had become the largest single recipient of American foreign aid.[10]

The Domestic Dimension

With the end of the Cold War and the dissolution of the Soviet Union, the sense of foreign threat and thus of the importance of foreign policy has sharply diminished in American public life. After almost six decades of profound external threats to America's most vital national interests and way of life (fascism, World War II, the Cold War), the country no longer confronts such a profound and unambiguous challenge.[11] The United States remains inescapably engaged in foreign affairs, but the priority of the subject has diminished. Domestic politics and budget constraints tend to dominate the presidential agenda and to overshadow foreign policy concerns. This has been evident in the decline in network television coverage of foreign news, as well as in a substantial drop in the importance of foreign policy in presidential and congressional election campaigns.

The Middle East, however, does remain a partial exception to the lessened priority for foreign policy. Security imperatives and threats to American interests do remain more evident in the region than elsewhere. Moreover, when domestic and foreign priorities correspond, the result can be strong public and congressional support for administration policy. This is evident in the Middle East and Persian Gulf, where domestic public and interest group sympathies have been broadly congruent with American national interests. In addition, the Clinton administration's key foreign policy decision makers provide a great deal of continuity, with Secretary of

State Madeleine Albright and National Security Advisor Samuel Berger, as well as their staffs, experienced and closely identified with long-standing administration and American Middle East policies.

Moreover, despite the end of the Cold War, an authoritative quadrennial study of American public and elite opinion on foreign policy provides empirical confirmation of the relative stability of domestic attitudes toward the Middle East. The Chicago Council on Foreign Relations has conducted these studies every four years since 1974. Their 1999 survey found that among the public at large, 69 percent identify an American "vital interest" with Israel, slightly ahead of Great Britain (66 percent) and Germany (60 percent). For their part, "leaders" interviewed for the study responded even more favorably. Over the eight-year period between 1991 and 1999, there was little change in American public opinion toward Israel, with that country continuing to be considered a key ally in the Middle East. Indeed, among elites during the same period, there was actually an identifiable increase (to 86 percent from 78 percent) in the vital interest response.[12]

Despite the controversial prime ministership of Benjamin Netanyahu, which was the subject of substantial criticism not only within the United States but within Israel as well, polling data continue to show strong continued American public support for Israel. For example, an April 1998 poll conducted by the *New York Times* indicated that more than five times as many Americans held a favorable opinion of Israel (57 percent) than of the PLO (11 percent).[13]

Domestic politics do matter, and the role of organized pro-Israel and Jewish groups has been significant. For example, the American-Israel Public Affairs Committee (AIPAC) has increased its stature and effectiveness in conveying its views to Congress and the administration during the past two decades. However, the data given here show that support for close American-Israeli relations extends far beyond the American Jewish community, and pro-Israel Christian-right groups have increased in importance during the same period as well. More broadly, a loose analogy may be found in U.S. policy toward NATO enlargement. On that issue, the Clinton administration's attention to strategic and political factors was reinforced by domestic political support for the admission of Poland, Hungary, and the Czech Republic. Contrary to the arguments of many opponents of NATO enlargement, the ethnic constituencies that favor these policies did not drive the decision, nor was the Polish vote in Cleveland or Chicago the causal factor. But, once the decision was made, this dimension reinforced the original decision and gave it increased weight.[14]

Overall, the American-Israeli relationship is shaped by a combination of factors: historic, moral, ethnic, strategic, political, and institutional. It is also driven by a recognition that the American role in the Middle East peace process requires a close U.S.-Israeli relationship, not "evenhandedness," even though such a policy might at first glance appear to embody a certain logic.

For the United States, a stable Middle East constitutes a vital national interest. In this situation, virtually every step in the Arab-Israeli peace process, from military disengagement agreements after the Yom Kippur War of October 1973, through Camp David and the Egyptian-Israeli Peace Treaty of 1979, the Madrid Conference of 1991, the signing of the Oslo Agreements, the Jordanian Peace Treaty, and even the abortive Israeli-Syrian negotiations, has involved a key American role as catalyst, intermediary, or guarantor. The task for the United States is thus a delicate one. On the one hand, it must not become so involved that Israel's Arab adversaries seek to negotiate with Washington instead of Jerusalem. Indeed, on those occasions when Washington did take on a more overt and interventionist role, the initiatives were unsuccessful (as in the case of the December 1969 Rogers Plan, the 1977 Carter administration initiative to cosponsor multilateral talks in Geneva with the Soviet Union, the September 1982 Reagan Plan, and the October 1989 Five Points of Secretary of State James Baker). On the other hand, the United States cannot distance itself from the process, because in its absence the parties are unlikely to be able to bridge their differences.

The American role stems from several factors: unique American military and economic power, foreign aid to Israel and Egypt, the unwillingness or inability of other powers or international bodies to act, and—less widely appreciated but most important of all—the special relationship between the United States and Israel.

The Arab actors understand that no other country has the intimate link to and credibility with Israel. Of great importance here is the implied role of the United States as ultimate guarantor of Israel's security. Though the Israelis have fought bravely and well and, in response to the bitter lessons of history, have been unwilling to entrust their defense and survival to others, and though, with the single exception of Patriot missile batteries during the 1991 Gulf War, American military personnel have never been committed to Israel's defense, the Arab perception has been that the United States will never allow the military defeat of Israel. This recognition, along with a perception that Israel possesses nuclear weapons, has been of profound importance in motivating Israel's Arab adversaries to negotiate peace. And it is yet another reason why periodic calls for American "evenhandedness" (some well-meaning, others not) are so counterproductive and potentially destabilizing.

Egypt, the PLO, and even Syria did not come to negotiate with Israel because they have become convinced of the wisdom of Theodor Herzl but because their efforts to destroy Israel or to deny its place in the region have led them to a destructive and costly dead end.

Not surprisingly, the United States has become the only viable intermediary in the Arab-Israeli conflict. For Israel, the United States—since at least 1967—has been the one actor consistently sympathetic (and far less vulnerable to Arab pressure). Countries such as Britain, France, Italy, and Japan and international or regional institutions such as the United Nations and the European Union have on occasion been supportive but (with some notable exceptions, as in the case of the Federal Republic of Germany) have shown themselves all too ready to succumb to one or another external consideration: the Arab oil embargo of 1973–74, the lure of markets for arms exports, terrorism, or even (especially in the case of France and Russia) the desire to demonstrate their political distance from the United States.

For Israel, the special relationship with the United States thus has been of fundamental importance. During the height of the Cold War, it worked to counterbalance what could otherwise have been dangerously strong intervention from the Soviet Union. Thus, for example, during the Yom Kippur War of October 1973 the United States played a vital role in military resupply after a week of heavy fighting and serious losses had depleted Israel's reserves of weapons and ammunition. Moreover, on October 24, 1973, when the Soviets threatened to deploy several airborne divisions to aid the surrounded Egyptian Third Army on the east side of the Suez Canal, the administration of President Richard Nixon and Secretary of State Henry Kissinger reacted vigorously. They did so not only in messages to Soviet leaders but in declaring a heightened state of military readiness (DefCon III), alerting the 82nd Airborne Division for possible movement and ordering the aircraft carrier *Franklin Delano Roosevelt* to join another American carrier, the *Independence,* in the eastern Mediterranean.[15] By October 26, the crisis had ended, with the Soviets backing off from their threat and preparations, including dispersing amphibious ships that had been converging toward the Egyptian port of Alexandria.

The intimate ties that the United States has with Israel provide a key security guarantee, but they have not come without a tradeoff in terms of constraints on Israel's freedom of maneuver. In June 1967, at a time when the security connection was less intimate and the United States was heavily involved in Vietnam, Israel took the unilateral decision to preempt militarily after the Johnson administration and the governments of Prime Minister Harold Wilson in Britain and President Charles De Gaulle in France were unable to agree on measures to lift the Egyptian blockade of the Gulf of Aqaba. On this occasion, the Israelis found themselves dangerously exposed to a major military threat but also able ultimately to act on their own against Egypt and Syria after President Nasser had achieved the ouster of the United Nations Emergency Force (UNEF) and deployed large numbers of troops and tanks in the Sinai.[16]

Six years later, however, and more closely connected to the United States, the government of Israeli Prime Minister Golda Meir found itself constrained not to preempt in the hours preceding the Egyptian-Syrian attack on October 6, 1973. Instead, in order to leave no ambiguity on who had started the war, and because of concerns not to jeopardize support from the United States, the Israelis were forced to absorb the costly initial attack before responding.

This pattern of constraints upon Israel's freedom of maneuver was also evident in two subsequent conflicts. In the case of the 1982 war in Lebanon, Israel first obtained a "green light" from Secretary of Defense Alexander Haig before launching its invasion against the forces of Yasser Arafat and the PLO which had come to assert control over southern Lebanon.[17] Avner Yaniv and I have previously hypothesized that the Israeli invasion of Lebanon was compelled not merely by the ambitions of Defense Minister Ariel Sharon but by a strategic logic. As a result, the Israeli government maneuvered vis-à-vis both the Israeli public and the United States, and we argued that the convergence of domestic uproar in Israel along with pressure from the American government caused the Israeli military to besiege Beirut rather than attack it directly in hot pursuit of the PLO.[18]

In turn, the Gulf War of January–February 1991 placed the Israeli government in a difficult position, after Tel Aviv and Haifa became the target of Iraqi Scud missile attacks. Decades of strategic doctrine called for Israel to determine its own course of action and to take firm military measures by means of air or ground attacks against Iraq. Yet because of concern to ensure the anti-Saddam coalition against defection by any of its Arab participants, the Bush administration brought intense pressure to bear in dissuading Israel from acting militarily.

On the other hand, there was a degree of reciprocity in the relationship: accompanying the pressures to discourage Israel from acting on its own, the Americans gave increased emphasis to efforts at destroying Scud missiles by means of air and (along with British Special Forces) covert commando attacks inside Iraq.[19] The United States deployed Patriot missile batteries with American crews in Tel Aviv and Haifa, the first time that Israel had ever relied on forces of another country to come to its defense.[20] Ironically, the impact of the Patriot batteries was ultimately more psychological and political than military: although the results remain disputed, later assessments (and even some initial evaluations during the war) indicated that the Patriots were relatively ineffective against the Scuds.[21]

If the relationship with the United States has thus become one of great intimacy and entanglement, the limits on the capacity of other states to act effectively to influence events in the region and serve as catalysts in the peace process continue to provide a strong contrast. This is evident in the recent experience of French and British leaders visiting the region. In 1997, for example, French President Jacques Chirac found himself and his entourage in a televised shoving match with Israeli security men assigned to protect him during a visit to the Arab Quarter of Jerusalem's Old City. British Foreign Secretary Robin Cook's diplomatically counterproductive spring 1998 visit to Israel serves as another recent illustration. Cook's frustration with the policies of Prime Minister Benjamin Netanyahu led him into a confrontation with the Israeli government. In doing so, he antagonized even the Labor opposition within Israel and many Israelis otherwise quite critical of Netanyahu. As a result, his intervention proved counterproductive, and he was unlikely to be seen as an acceptable intermediary between Israel and its Palestinian and Arab neighbors.

Implications

In sum, the U.S.-Israeli special relationship is the product of a complex mixture of causal factors and incorporates historical memory, religious values, societal ties, considerations of regional stability, and American national interest. Domestic politics within the United States have been a significant contributory factor, and the choices of individual leaders in Washington or Jerusalem can and do impact significantly. Personal relationships do matter, as evident, for example, in the exceptional rapport that developed between President Bill Clinton and the late Prime Minister Yitzhak Rabin, and later between Clinton and Prime Minister Ehud Barak, or the lack of confidence and barely suppressed antagonism between President George Bush and Prime Minister Yitzhak Shamir or President Clinton and Prime Minister Netanyahu. But, at least over the course of the past half century, these longer-term causes ultimately have come to matter most in shaping the relationship and the course of American policy toward Israel.

Notes

1. Richard Rosecrance, ed., *America as an Ordinary Country*.
2. For the text of the White Paper of May 17, 1939, see Walter Laqueur and Barry Rubin, eds., *The Arab-Israeli Reader*, 64–75.
3. Steven L. Spiegel, *The Other Arab-Israeli Conflict*, 21–22.
4. Foreign Relations of the United States Diplomatic Papers (Washington D.C.: U.S. Government Printing Office, 1948), 974–75, quoted in Spiegel, 37.
5. Spiegel, 38.
6. By the late 1970s, Israel had become the largest American foreign aid recipient, and by 1985 the amount of assistance had reached $3 billion per year. See, for example, *New York Times*, April 18, 1998.
7. New York: Columbia University Press, 1998. This discussion of Ben-Zvi's work and its implications is drawn from Robert J. Lieber, "Geopolitics, Local Politics, and America's Role in the Middle East Peace Process," paper prepared for the XVIIth World Congress, International Political Science Association, Seoul, Korea, August 17–21, 1997.
8. Dulles letter of August 1, 1958, quoted in Ben-Zvi, *Decade of Transition*, 59.
9. Kenneth Organski, *The $36 Billion Bargain*, 27.
10. Mitchell G. Bard and Daniel Pipes, "How Special Is the U.S.-Israel Special Relationship?" *Middle East Quarterly* 4, no. 2 (June 1997): 43.
11. For elaboration on the diminished security threat and its wider implications, see Robert J. Lieber, "Eagle without a Cause."
12. John F. Riley, ed., *American Public Opinion and U.S. Foreign Policy*, 13. Fieldwork for the 1998 public survey was conducted between October 15 and November 10, 1998. Elite interviews took place between November 2 and December 21, 1998.
13. Data from *New York Times*, April 26, 1998.
14. For an authoritative account of American decision making on NATO enlargement, see James M. Goldgeier, "NATO Expansion: The Anatomy of a Decision," *Washington Quarterly* (Winter 1998): 85–100.
15. For a detailed account, see Henry A. Kissinger, *Years of Upheaval*, 581–601. See also Raymond L. Garthoff, *Detente and Confrontation*, 376–80. Garthoff describes Brezhnev as making a veiled threat of possible unilateral Soviet action if the United States was unwilling to join in sending Soviet and American troops to impose not only a cease-fire but a comprehensive peace. He also notes that seven Soviet airborne divisions had been placed on alert by October 11–12 (377).
16. For analysis of Israel's preemption in June 1967 and the broader implications concerning the limitations of the United Nations and of the international

system more broadly in dealing with security threats, see Robert J. Lieber, *No Common Power*, 249–52.

17. See Ze'ev Schiff, "Green Light, Lebanon"; Schiff and Ehud Yaari, *Israel's Lebanon War*.

18. Avner Yaniv, *Dilemmas of Security*, especially vii. See also Avner Yaniv and Robert Lieber, "Personal Whim or Strategic Imperative?"

19. See, for example, Michael R. Gordon and Bernard E. Trainor, *The General's War*, 236–47.

20. Lawrence Freedman and Efraim Karsh, *The Gulf Conflict, 1990–1991*, 334–39.

21. Israeli military analysts identified the problem even before the war had ended. See Rick Atkinson, *Crusade*, 277–81. A subsequent, more rigorous analysis is sharply critical of the Patriot missile: "Our first wartime experience with tactical ballistic missile defense resulted in what may have been an almost total failure to intercept quite primitive attacking missiles" (Theodore A. Postel, "Lessons of the Gulf War Experience with Patriot," 124).

3

Israel and the American Jewish Community
Changing Realities Test Traditional Ties

George E. Gruen

It is reported that when French Premier Pierre Mendès-France first visited Israel, he began his conversation with Prime Minister David Ben-Gurion with this declaration: "I want to make it clear that with regard to the components of my personal identity, I consider myself first to be a Frenchman, secondly a socialist, and only thirdly a Jew and Zionist." Ben-Gurion responded, "That's quite all right. Here we read from right to left."

This story highlights the paradox of Israel-Diaspora relations. As Jews we are united with Israelis: Most Jews share a sense of being one family, *Klal Yisrael*. This feeling of solidarity comes to the fore at times of danger, such as during the tense weeks before the Six-Day War, in the aftermath of the Yom Kippur War, or more recently when Israel faced Iraqi Scud missile attacks or a wave of terrorists' suicide bombings. However, as Americans, we are heirs to a distinct history and have grown up in a pluralistic culture that values individual freedom of choice and that has enshrined the separation of church and state in the Constitution.

Although the pioneers who came to Palestine and founded the kibbutzim, moshavim, and cities of the new Yishuv may have shared a common heritage with the Eastern European Jewish immigrants who came to America in the mass migration beginning in the 1880s, their priorities and aspirations were different. These differences found expression in the political and social structures they developed. In the area of state-religion relations, for example, Israelis were influenced not only by their memories of traditional Jewish life back home, against much of which the secularist pioneers rebelled, but also by the institutional arrangements that had been instituted in Palestine by the Ottoman Turks during their four centuries of rule (1517–1917) and that were continued under the British Mandate (1922–48). These arrangements included the *millet* system, under which the religious leaders of each recognized religious community were given broad authority over matters of personal status, such as marriage, divorce, adoption, and inheritance, affecting their coreligionists. There was no provision for civil marriage.

To avoid a major Kulturkampf between the Orthodox and secularist elements of the population, Israel's founding fathers in 1948 decided to defer work on a written constitution and largely adopted the Ottoman/British precedents in the field of state-religion legislation, codified as the "status quo." The Chief Rabbinate in Israel assumed the role of the *Hahambaşi* (chief rabbi in Turkish). It should also be noted that the massive immigration of Jews from the Middle East and North Africa, which began with the *aliyah* (going up) from Iraq and Yemen shortly after Israel's independence and continued with Moroccan, Tunisian, Algerian, and Egyptian Jewry in the 1950s and 1960s, brought large numbers of Jews from traditional Sephardic and Oriental Jewish communities, for whom the American tradition of strict church-state separation was an unfamiliar concept. Moreover, in the Sephardi world, where influences of secularism and European enlightenment came later and where rabbinical scholars were often less rigid and more accommodating to the needs of their constituents in matters of religious interpretation than some of their Ashkenazi counterparts, there did not develop the successful organized challenges to Orthodoxy, such as the Western European Reform and Conservative movements, which today are predominant in the American Jewish community.

Although the American non-Orthodox movements have established a few dozen synagogues and schools in Israel, their congregants are mainly immigrants from the English-speaking world, and they have failed to attract the kind of mass following among native-born Israelis that would make them an effective political pressure group. Since most affiliated American Jews belong either to Conservative, Reform, or Reconstructionist synagogues, they feel increasingly angry, frustrated, and alienated when Israeli political leaders, under pressure from the Orthodox religious parties, appear to support Knesset legislation that would denigrate the status of the non-Orthodox and display indifference to their concerns. Recent key issues have been refusal to recognize conversion to Judaism performed by non-Orthodox rabbis in the United States and refusal to grant permission to Conservative and Reform rabbis in Israel to officiate at marriages or serve on local religious councils. The recent Israeli attempts to tighten the rules on conversion and enshrine in legislation the de facto Orthodox monopoly has resulted in a renewed protest campaign by non-Orthodox American Jewish leaders, with increasingly strident rhetoric between Orthodox and non-Orthodox on both sides of the Atlantic.[1]

Some Orthodox spokesmen have stressed that their insistence on *halacha* (Jewish religious law) as the only acceptable standard for conversion, marriage, and divorce is motivated not by political considerations to maintain their monopoly but out of a profound concern to preserve future Jewish unity, since allowing Reform rabbis—who did not follow *halacha* and had adopted the principle of patrilineal descent—to perform conversions and marriages would result in irrevocably splitting the Jewish community into two categories: one group of Jews whom Orthodox Jews could marry and another group they could not marry because of their—or their parents'—halachically questionable legal status. However, in fact, there is already a large and growing number of persons in Israel of questionable religious status, since many of the 900,000 immigrants from the former Soviet Union either are not halachically Jewish or have brought a spouse who is not Jewish at all. The problem is compounded by the fact that the Israeli legal system does not provide the option of civil marriage. One practical solution, increasingly chosen by those who either do not qualify for rabbinical marriage or who as avowed secularists refuse to go to an Orthodox rabbi, is to travel to Cyprus for a civil marriage, which is then recognized in Israel under the international rules of comity.[2]

Since the lay leaders of the non-Orthodox movements in the United States have generally also been liberal in their political and social views and supportive of the peace process with the Palestinians initiated by late prime minister Yitzhak Rabin, their outrage over the religious issues has sometimes been accompanied by anger and dismay over the timing of certain actions taken by Prime Minister Benjamin Netanyahu, which were certain to provoke the Palestinians and upset the United States. Verbal displeasure among liberal American Jews has been accompanied by threats to reduce or cut off their contributions to the United Jewish Appeal (UJA), the channel for funds to the Jewish Agency for Israel. For example, in March 1997, the San Francisco Jewish Federation decided in a symbolic move to deduct $1 million from its allocation to the UJA "because of Israel's right wing political and religious policies."[3] Instead, it planned to give $500,000 to local Jewish causes and earmarked the other $500,000 directly for Israeli projects that promoted Arab-Jewish understanding and religious pluralism. Federation president Alan Rothenberg commented that "nowhere in the Talmud does it say write a check to the UJA."

Rothenberg rejected a direct appeal by UJA chairman Richard Wexler to rescind this move, on the grounds that elderly Jews in the former Soviet Union would now go hungry because San Francisco had cut its overseas allocation.[4]

This action could no longer be dismissed as a unique and unrepresentative act by a community known for its liberal orientation and idiosyncratic tendencies, for the San Francisco federation already in 1987, during a previous American Jewish confrontation with Israel over tightening the rules for conversion, had shown its independence by diverting $100,000 of its funds to its own Israeli programs, sparking condemnation by the United Israel Appeal, the conduit of UJA funds to Israel. However, as I noted in 1988, "this development, like the growth of the New Israel Fund, presages a more activist and creative role for American Jews in Israel-related philanthropy." The New Israel Fund (NIF), started in 1979 with a modest grant of $100,000 from ten Jewish families in San Francisco, had by mid-1987 obtained annual contributions of $2,574,000 for its programs to subsidize indigenous efforts in Israel to promote Jewish-Arab coexistence, further civil rights and intergroup relations, and deal with social problems that its founders felt had not been adequately dealt with by the Israeli bureaucracy.[5] In November 1997, Gil Kulick, the NIF's communications director, reported that the fund had raised a record $13.5 million in 1996 and enjoyed a further increase of 25 percent in 1997. "We're up by about 50 percent in the last two years," he said, attributing the increase to Jewish fury over the religious pluralism issue.[6]

This was only the most acute manifestation of a broader trend in American Jewish philanthropy. Donors are demanding a greater say in the allocation of their funds and moving away from giving to centralized umbrella groups such as the UJA and local federations to targeted giving to specific institutions with clearly defined objectives. It has been estimated that American Jews have given a total of $700 million annually to individual educational, religious, and charitable organizations in Israel of all kinds, bypassing the bureaucracy of the Jewish Agency.[7]

But increased giving to the New Israel Fund was not the primary worry of the UJA Federation leadership. It was the potential serious erosion of support for their centralized campaign. Following Netanyahu's support for the conversion bill, which passed the first of the required three readings to enact a law by the Knesset on April 1, 1997, the national leaders of both the Conservative and Reform movements in the United States issued a series of unmistakably sharp statements, calling upon "the American

Jewish community to stop at once all contributions to Israeli organizations and bodies—including governmental agencies—which refuse to recognize non-Orthodox forms of Jewish life." The Reconstructionist movement joined the protest and urged American Jews to "restrict their Israel-oriented gifts to organizations actively committed to religious pluralism."[8]

Since many of the lay leaders of the Conservative and Reform movements in the United States have also been prominent financial supporters of the State of Israel, the officials of the UJA and the Jewish Agency have taken notice. Disturbed by reduced giving by Reform Jews in 1996, the fund-raisers prompted many non-Orthodox rabbinical leaders to issue a joint public appeal: "It is important to every Conservative and Reform Jew to support *Klal Yisrael* by making a meaningful gift to the 1997 federation/UJA campaign."

However, at the beginning of March 1997, Chancellor Ismar Schorsch of the Conservative Jewish Theological Seminary proposed that some $100 million to $150 million should be taken "off the top" of the UJA contributions to fund Conservative and Reform institutions in Israel. He said this would compensate for the sums already allocated to Orthodox institutions in Israel. UJA national chairman Richard Wexler, who was also a Conservative lay leader, called Schorsch's idea "reprehensible" since it would take money away from "the needs of our people." The chancellor of the seminary responded that it was precisely such beneficiaries of UJA funds in Israel as recent Russian immigrants, many of whom were denied Orthodox recognition as Jews, who would benefit most from a heightened non-Orthodox religious presence in Israel. The American pressure has already brought some modest results. The UJA and Jewish Agency have agreed to expand their funding for educational and other institutions established by the "various streams" in Jewish life, with some $10 million each going to Reform, Conservative, and modern Orthodox institutions, and they have increased from $15 million to $20 million the sums for educational programs to promote religious diversity, tolerance, and democracy. (The Israelis use the term *zerem* [stream] rather than the American religious "denomination.") Representatives of the Conservative movement have also been successful in lobbying for greater governmental allocations for their network of Talli schools in Israel.

In an effort to defuse the religious crisis, Netanyahu in 1997 appointed the Ne'eman Committee, headed by Finance Minister Ya'akov Ne'eman, to come up with a compromise. Its members, chosen from all denominations, hammered out a proposal to set up a joint Orthodox-Reform-Conservative institute to prepare candidates for conversion, who would then be accepted into Judaism by an Orthodox religious court. A similar procedure had worked for several years in Denver until increasing polarization in the Jewish religious establishment led to its dissolution. But the experiment in Israel immediately ran into trouble when the Chief Rabbinate denounced the non-Orthodox and refused to cooperate with the training institute. Netanyahu told the *Jerusalem Report* that he would impose the Ne'eman Committee report by legislation if the Chief Rabbinate refused to go along but that he hoped he would not have to do so. The proposed compromise was never actually signed by the members of the committee and is currently in limbo. The non-Orthodox representatives pointed out that the Ne'eman proposals rested on cooperation among the various denominations, goodwill, and rabbinate leniency in accepting converts. "A law can't force the rabbinate to convert graduates of the joint institute," said Rabbi Uri Regev, director of the Reform movement's Israel Religious Action Center.[9] The issue came up prominently in mid-November 1998 when the General Assembly (GA) of the soon to be merged Council of Jewish Federations and the United Jewish Appeal convened in Jerusalem. In an interview following his address to the GA calling for "Jewish unity," Finance Minister Ne'eman cited the lack of any pending Knesset legislation on pluralism-related issues as evidence that the controversy had eased and that issues of religious pluralism and the rights of the Reform and Conservative movements in Israel were "no longer at the top of the agenda in the Jewish world." Rabbi Regev responded that, on the contrary, "I hear from Federation workers that the topic is more prominent than ever."[10] The slogan advertising the gathering of the estimated 3,300 U.S. and Canadian leaders of the Jewish philanthropic and communal world was "many people, many roads, one heart." A stated aim was to advance the cause of unity through respect for diversity. In his forty-five-minute opening address to the delegates, Prime Minister Netanyahu also emphasized that the differences between the different religious streams must be resolved "with mutual respect, dialogue, and goodwill."[11]

One major positive step in this direction occurred on November 2, 1998, when Israel's High Court of Justice ordered the Ministry of Religious Affairs to allow Reform and Conservative Jews to sit on the religious councils of Jerusalem, Haifa, Tel Aviv, Arad, and Kiryat Tivon. The decision followed a ruling in 1997 in which the court ordered the ministry to permit Joyce Miller, a Reform Jew, to be seated on the Netanya religious council. Rabbi Regev, who represented the non-Orthodox candidates in court, noted the far-reaching significance of the court's decision and pointed out that it applied to the country's three largest cities and in effect overturned the ground rules for appointing religious council members. "This is a historic milestone that is important in the battle for Israel's identity as a pluralistic state," Rabbi Regev told *Yediot Aharonot*.[12]

The current controversy between American and Israeli Jews about how to handle the conversion issue highlights a crucial difference between the two communities. Israeli Jews constitute a majority in their own sovereign state, in which the Knesset can legislate and enforce laws affecting all aspects of their life as Jews, from Kashrut in state-supported institutions to decreeing Shabbat and Jewish holidays as official days of closing of businesses and public institutions. (Muslims and Christians in Israel have the option of closing their businesses on Friday or Sunday, respectively.)

By way of contrast, American Jews are a vocal and influential but small and diminishing religious minority (approximately 2.5 percent of the population) in a secularized, Christian state, where, despite the formal separation of church and state, Christmas is on the calendar as a recognized national holiday. The decision of American Jews whether or not to affiliate with the organized Jewish community and to what extent to participate in Jewish activities is purely a matter of individual choice. There are no state-supported Jewish religious schools, and there are no state-imposed restrictions on whom individual Jews may marry.

The crucial questions facing those concerned with Israel-Diaspora relations are these: Can the "odd couple" that is American Jewry and Israeli Jewry learn to adjust and create a mutually supportive relationship? Or will the differences grow deeper over time, leading to disenchantment and eventual divorce?

While it is beyond the scope of this chapter to recount in detail the evolution of American Jewish attitudes to the Jewish state, I believe it is important to place the present relationship into historical context. Today when the overwhelming majority of American Jews express at least some support for the Jewish State of Israel, it is easy to forget that at the time of the beginning of the modern Zionist movement at the end of the last century, the great majority of American Jews were not Zionists. Until World War II, most American Jews were at most non-Zionists, for example, the influential American Jewish Committee (founded in 1906 by upper-class Jews of German origin), who supported free immigration to Palestine by those fleeing czarist and later Nazi oppression and helped found the Hebrew University and other cultural and economic endeavors in the Holy Land but did not yet support the idea of an independent Jewish state.

There were also powerful groups in the Jewish community that were vehemently anti-Zionist, including the following:

1. The classical Reform movement, whose members argued that Judaism had been transformed into a universal religion and that Zionism represented a retrograde movement back to an earlier tribal particularism. This view was also stridently propagated by the American Council for Judaism, founded in 1943 to oppose the growing shift within the Reform movement toward support for a Jewish state.

2. The Orthodox religious establishment, which argued that we are in exile as divine punishment for our sins and that political Zionism is a heresy, since it attempts to restore prematurely a sovereign state in the Holy Land by human effort, rather than patiently waiting for the longed-for messianic redemption. The Agudat Yisrael movement became one of the main political vehicles for their views in Israel and the Diaspora. (There were some in the Orthodox community who supported religious Zionism and organized themselves in the Mizrachi movement, which is today represented in the Knesset by the National Religious Party.)

3. Jewish socialists organized in such movements as the Bund, who saw the solution to the Jewish problem in working for a fundamental transformation of the world into a just and peaceful socialist society.

A fourth, less ideological but pragmatic, group of opponents to Zionism were those Jews who were well integrated in Western Europe but who feared that their own status would be jeopardized by overt support for Jewish nationalism. Notable among this group was Sir Edwin Montagu, who as secretary of state for India in the British cabinet in 1917 was concerned that establishment of a Jewish national home in Palestine would be used as an excuse by European anti-Semites to expel the Jews from their midst. It was at his insistence that the Balfour Declaration included an explicit pledge by Britain that "nothing shall be done which may prejudice ... the rights and political status enjoyed by Jews in any other country."[13]

Support for an independent Jewish state in Palestine became a mass movement in the United States during and after World War II, when American Jews learned the full extent of the horrors of the Holocaust and were moved by the plight of the survivors in the displaced persons camps. With most refugees barred from entry into the United States by restrictive immigration policies and precluded from going to Palestine by the British Mandatory Government's White Paper of 1939, support for an independent Jewish state in part of Palestine became the only viable solution. When the leaders of the world Zionist movement accepted the UN proposal to partition Palestine into two independent states, Jewish and Palestinian Arab, the leadership of the American Jewish Committee (AJC) endorsed this practical and democratic solution and helped to lobby for it within the American government.[14] There was a groundswell of public meetings, fund-raising, and even personal volunteering by American Jews on behalf of the fledgling Jewish state.

It should be stressed, however, that American Zionists differed from Eastern European Zionists in one crucial respect. American Zionists, with rare exceptions, had no intention of voting with their feet and actually making aliyah (going up) to Israel. Supreme Court Justice Louis Brandeis, who had headed the Zionist Organization of America during World War I, rebutted charges of dual loyalty by arguing that "being a good Zionist makes one a better American."[15] American Zionism found its expression in economic and political support for the creation and sustaining of a Jewish state in Palestine.

After Israel gained its independence in May 1948, Prime Minister Ben-Gurion would publicly chide the professed American Zionist leaders for not picking up and making aliyah. Once the goal of establishing an independent Jewish state had been achieved, he argued, those Jews who willingly remained in the Diaspora had no right to call themselves Zionists. They were simply "friends of Israel," as indeed, he pointed out, were the majority of the non-Jewish Americans. Ben-Gurion's public appeals for aliyah did not sit well with Jacob Blaustein, a prominent American industrialist, advisor to Washington, and president of the American Jewish Committee. After a series of meetings, the two leaders agreed to an exchange of letters in Jerusalem in 1950 that was intended to spell out the terms of the relations between American Jews and the newly independent State of Israel.

Among the key points in the exchange were these: The prime minister affirmed that "Israel represents and speaks only for its own citizens" and that "American Jews . . . owe no political allegiance to Israel." For his part, Blaustein pledged that American Jews would fully support Israel in its efforts for economic viability and peace and would also press for American and international backing for the new state. But although the committee would encourage individual Jews who might be motivated by religious conviction or pioneering spirit to help build the new state, it would oppose calls for mass aliyah. The American Jewish leader stressed that for the Jews of the United States, "America is home." Both Ben-Gurion and Blaustein pledged noninterference in the internal affairs of the other community. Finally, the prime minister affirmed the economic and political importance to Israel of a strong U.S. Jewish community: "Any weakening of American Jewry, any disruption of its communal life, any lowering of its sense of security, any diminution of its status, is a definite loss to Jews everywhere and to Israel in particular."[16]

When it was revealed that Israelis had recruited Jonathan Jay Pollard, an American Jew working as a U.S. naval intelligence analyst, to obtain and deliver to Israel U.S. data on Arab military capabilities, Jerusalem mayor Teddy Kollek castigated the insensitivity to these principles by the Israelis, who had exposed American Jews to the charge of dual loyalty by selecting an American Jew to spy for them. Kollek, who had been director-general of the prime minister's office in 1950 and had been closely involved in the talks between Blaustein and Ben-Gurion, told a visiting delegation of the Conference of Presidents of Major American Jewish Organizations in Jerusalem in March 1987, "We have to go back to basic principles, and not try to be overly smart."[17]

The Pollard case once again received international attention in October 1998. At virtually the eleventh hour and after all direct Palestinian-Israeli issues had apparently been settled following nine days of intensive negotiations that included the personal involvement of President Clinton, Prime Minister Netanyahu tried to link Israel's acceptance of the Wye Plantation Memorandum on implementing the interim accord with the Palestinians to the release of Pollard from prison with permission to travel to Israel with the Israeli delegation. Pollard had apparently been recruited not by the Mossad, Israel's equivalent of the CIA, but by Lekem, a rival intelligence agency that reported to Rafael Eitan, who had been an associate of General Ariel Sharon. It was therefore speculated that Netanyahu desired to demonstrate to his increasingly disgruntled right-wing supporters, who were unhappy over the territorial concessions he had agreed to in the Wye River Memorandum, that he also shared their concerns by championing the Pollard appeal. Sharon was a key figure in the Likud, serving as foreign minister and minister of national infrastructures. (After Netanyahu's defeat in the 1999 elections, Sharon was chosen to head the Likud.) Although there was considerable support within the American Jewish community for commuting, on humanitarian grounds, Pollard's sentence to time served, Netanyahu's undiplomatic timing made many American Jews uneasy and provoked nearly universal outrage in the

American press. More significantly, George Tenet, the director of the Central Intelligence Agency, reportedly had threatened to resign if Clinton acceded to Netanyahu's request.[18] This was significant, since under the Wye Accord, the CIA was to be given a specific role to monitor and report on compliance by the Palestinians—and the Israelis—with the security-related provisions of the agreement.

At a joint press conference with Netanyahu in Jerusalem on December 13, Clinton was asked about Pollard. The president responded that he had instituted an "unprecedented" review of the case, asking the Justice Department and all other involved governmental agencies and all other interested parties to present their views on the matter by January 1999, after which he promised to review the sentence and "make a decision in a prompt way." A reporter then asked Prime Minister Netanyahu, "Can you explain to the American people why you think Mr. Pollard is worthy of a release at this point?" In a lengthy reply, the prime minister acknowledged that Pollard "did something bad and inexcusable." Noting that "I was the first prime minister" to openly admit that Pollard was collecting information on behalf of Israel, Netanyahu conceded that "he should have served his time, and he did." But he noted that Pollard had been kept virtually in solitary confinement for nearly thirteen years, which was a "very, very heavy sentence." Since Pollard "was sent by us on a mistaken mission, not to work against the United States," but nevertheless broke the laws of the United States, Netanyahu was making this appeal purely on humanitarian grounds. He insisted, "It is not political, it is not to exonerate him, it is merely to end a very, very sorry case that has afflicted him and the people of Israel."[19]

The initial fears in the American Jewish community that the Pollard affair would unleash a wave of anti-Semitism and charges of dual loyalty against American Jews fortunately proved to be exaggerated. It did lead, however, to a tightening of background checks on American Jews working for or seeking employment in the State Department, the Pentagon, and other sensitive security-related positions, and for a time American Jews faced difficulty getting professional assignments to the Middle East. Mathew Dorf reported in December 1997 that many of the Jewish diplomats in the field today "still vividly remember the impact that convicted spy Jonathan Pollard had on their careers. One official said that many are still recovering from the trauma Pollard caused when he was caught spying for Israel in the U.S." Yet this is clearly no longer an insuperable barrier. Indeed, paralleling the full acceptance of American Jews into the mainstream of American political, social, and cultural life (as well as the sharp decline in the relative importance of Arab oil to the U.S. economy), there has been a remarkable change in the personnel of the State Department. In the mid-1940s and through the crucial time of Israel's birth in 1948, the Near East bureau was dominated by "Arabists"—often the sons of American missionaries or oil executives who had served in the Arab world and who were skeptical if not openly antagonistic to the idea of establishing a Jewish state in the heart of a hostile Arab and Muslim world.

Contrast this with the situation today, when Jews are among the key advisers shaping U.S. policy toward the Middle East in general and toward Israel and the peace process in particular. In fact, there are more than a dozen persons in the State Department who are Jewish, and many of them are actively involved in Jewish religious and cultural affairs. Aside from Secretary of State Madeleine Albright, who discovered her own Czech Jewish roots in 1997, avowedly Jewish diplomats with long experience in foreign policy and Middle East affairs include Martin Indyk, the first Jew to be appointed assistant secretary of state for Near East affairs; Ambassador Dennis Ross, the special peace process coordinator; Aaron Miller, Ross's deputy and expert on Palestinian affairs; American ambassador to Egypt Daniel Kurtzer, who has been a key State Department participant in the peace process since the Camp David negotiations with Egypt; as well as presidential adviser Sandy Berger, who heads the National Security Council. Palestinian and Arab diplomats sometimes speak of a "Zionist conspiracy" dominating U.S. Middle East policy, and some of the former Arabists at the State Department lament the ascendance of Jewish Americans. "If any other group had taken over, there would have been a big storm, but with the Jewish-American takeover, nobody has the courage to speak," William Rugh, a former ambassador to Yemen, was quoted as saying in an article titled "Where've the Arabists Gone?" in the October 1997 issue of *Foreign Service,* the professional journal of the American Foreign Service Association.[20]

It is too early to tell whether Netanyahu's raising the Pollard case so publicly will have negative repercussions for American Jews in government service or will influence American public attitudes regarding the loyalty of their Jewish fellow citizens. The prime minister's candid admission that what Israel did was wrong and that Pollard's actions were "bad and inexcusable" may help minimize the damage. On another front, Israeli right-wing opponents of the Oslo Accords have denounced the American Jewish civil servants who are promoting Clinton's peace plan as "court Jews" who do the ruler's bidding to the detriment of the interests of their fellow Jews. Thus the issue of what is the appropriate role for American Jews to play in regard to Israel, in general, and the peace process, in particular, continues to be a matter of debate.

The issue of aliyah also continued to be contentious. Although Ben-Gurion in his letter to Blaustein foreswore public demands for mass aliyah, the first Israeli premier continued to call for voluntary immigration from the United States. In a joint statement with Blaustein in April 1961, Ben-Gurion reaffirmed that the decision "whether they wish to come—permanently or temporarily—rests with the free discretion of each American Jew. It is entirely a matter of his own volition." He appealed to the pioneering spirit of Americans and expressed his belief that *haluzim* (pioneers) would continue to come not only from countries where the Jews are "oppressed and in 'exile' but also from countries where Jews live a life of freedom" and equality. In words that have proven to be prophetic in light of the fact that Israel has become a world leader in high technology, he appealed to American Jews to come and help develop the new state:[21] "We need their technical knowledge, their unrivalled experience, their spirit of enterprise, their 'know-how.' The tasks which face us in this country are eminently such as would appeal to the American genius for technical development and social progress."

It is ironic that many of the technical skills that have rapidly transformed Israel's economy from agriculture and low-tech industry were brought not by American *olim* (those who go up to Israel, i.e., immigrants) but by many of the nearly one million new immigrants from the former Soviet Union. But it might be argued that since the breakup of the Communist Empire and the opening of their doors to free emigration, those olim might also fit Ben-Gurion's category of persons coming voluntarily from relatively free countries.

Although the sharpness of the ideological debate over aliyah has since diminished, American and Israeli Jews continue to disagree on the importance of Diaspora communities. In a joint effort in March 1998, the *Los Angeles Times* and *Yediot Aharonot* commissioned parallel polls of national samples of American and Israeli Jews.[22] Both groups were asked which of these statements came closer to their opinion: "In the long run, I believe it is in the best interest of Judaism to have a significant Jewish population in the United States" or "I believe it would be better for Judaism if as many Jews as possible lived in Israel." Two-thirds of U.S. Jews (66 percent) gave priority to maintaining a significant American Jewish community, while only 15 percent stressed aliyah. The Israelis were more closely divided, with 47 percent wanting as many Jews as possible in Israel but 42 percent acknowledging that it was "in the best interest of Judaism" to have a significant Jewish population remain in the United States. (Figures for the small percentage who said they did not know have been omitted.) These results showed a considerable change from the earlier period when Israelis were indoctrinated with the concept of *shlilat hagola* (negation of the exile). Representative of the older Zionist nationalist view was the comment by former prime minister Yitzhak Shamir, who reiterated the call for massive American aliyah: "But the number of Jews here is insufficient.... And we will not be able to accommodate a few more millions of Jews unless Judea and Samaria remain in our hands.... I want millions more Jews to come here, with the whole country in our possession, including Judea and Samaria." (These are the biblical names for what is generally referred to in the Western press as the West Bank.)[23]

In his address to the General Assembly, Prime Minister Netanyahu also stressed the importance of aliyah. But he placed it in the context of the growing threat to the Jewish people—not from annihilation by enemies as was the case earlier in this century but from the "process of assimilation, loss of identity and intermarriage which threatens, like a powerful centrifugal force, to tear the Jewish people apart." The first solution to that threat, he declared, is "massive aliyah from every country in the Diaspora, including the United States and Canada."[24] American delegates, however, expressed their skepticism that there would be any such massive emigration from the United States "to fill the Negev," as one observer put it, alluding to Ben-Gurion's dream.

When asked about their own personal plans, only 7 percent of American Jews surveyed in the poll said they could ever see themselves moving to Israel, while 16 percent of Israelis said they could see themselves moving to the United States. (The *Los Angeles Times* subdivided the American sample by extent of religious observance. As might be expected, only 3 percent of those with "low" level of observance considered aliyah, but even among those with "high" religious practice only 16 percent had considered aliyah.) These responses correspond to what has in fact happened over the past fifty years. Fewer than 1 percent of American Jews have made aliyah.

There was a dramatic but brief surge in immigration to Israel from the United States and Canada in the years following the Six-Day War of 1967. The Egyptian-provoked crisis in May 1967, when Israel appeared to be in grave and imminent danger of a combined attack by the armed forces of Egypt, Syria, and Jordan, evoked an unprecedented outpouring of political and financial support from American Jews, including many who had been rather distant from Israel in the 1950s and early 1960s. The May 1967 crisis was a time of traumatic revelation for many American Jews who had not been closely identified with Jewish life. They, for the first time, felt, "I, my life, would be diminished if the State of Israel were destroyed!" The crisis also reawakened the nagging awareness among many American Jews that, maybe, they really had not done enough to try to save their European brethren in the period of the Holocaust. The stunning Israeli victory in the June 1967 war also had a positive effect on personal American Jewish involvement with Israel. For many secular Jews, Israel now became a significant element of their personal identity. This was also reflected in an increase in visits and aliyah. Prior to 1967, Jewish immigration to Israel averaged fewer than one thousand per year, and of those who immigrated, roughly half returned to the states after a few years. The total number of American Jews in Israel in 1966 was estimated at between 12,000 and 15,000. However, between 1967 and 1970 that number had more than doubled, the high point being reached in 1970 when 9,200 made aliyah. The reasons have been analyzed in detail elsewhere.[25]

Among the factors drawing more people to Israel at that time were easier access to the Old City of Jerusalem, indications that Israel was proving to be a going concern, the rising standard of living, and the belief that Israel's overwhelming victory had greatly diminished the dangers of traveling to the area. There was also a growing dissatisfaction with the quality of life in the United States at the time. Heightened racial tensions, as manifested for example in the teachers' strike in New York, prompted several hundred Jewish teachers to emigrate. The Vietnam War and concern about an anti-Semitic backlash were other factors.

The Yom Kippur War of October 1973 again traumatized American Jews and evoked financial and political support. In addition, several hundred Americans volunteered to fill the places of mobilized soldiers at kibbutzim and various other institutions. But the war had also revived concern about Israel's vulnerability. Despite progress in the peace process, including formal peace treaties with Egypt and Jordan, there has been no significant surge in American aliyah in recent years. The absence of peace with Syria and Lebanon and the continuing tensions in relations with the Palestinians, including the gruesome televised pictures of the wave of suicide bomb attacks against Israeli civilians, may have been inhibiting factors.

In any case, in 1997 only about 1,800 American Jews moved to Israel.[26] Who were they? Most were highly motivated, idealistic, religious Zionists and ultranationalists. A minority may have been attracted by business opportunities or may have come to join family members who had come earlier. While there are no reliable figures on the number of Israelis living in the United States, primarily in such cities as New York and Los Angeles, estimates of the total range from 200,000 to more than 500,000. Whatever the actual number, it is clearly many times greater than the total number of American Jews in Israel.

Another impact of the Yom Kippur War was the increased questioning within the American Jewish community as to the wisdom of Israeli leaders and their policies. Diaspora Jewish dissent from various Israeli policies increased after the ascent to power of Menachem Begin's Likud bloc in 1977. This bloc presented a Revisionist view that advocated keeping all of the liberated territories of the historic land of Israel, especially Judea and Samaria (the West Bank) and challenged the Labor party's acceptance of the principle of trading land for peace. As American Jewish historian Arthur Herzberg aptly put it, "Begin's victory in 1977 made it inevitable that the question of the 'undivided land of Israel' would, before long, divide the Diaspora."[27]

To be sure, some debate had begun among American Jewry, as it did in Israel, shortly after the Six-Day War, about the possibility of using the captured territories as bargaining chips. However, in view of the Arab League's policy of rejection of any negotiations with Israel, adopted at the Khartoum Summit in August 1967, this debate remained largely theoretical. Another factor inhibiting criticism of Israeli government policies in matters of defense and foreign policy was the standard response of officials, "We have access to secret information that we can not share with you, so trust us, we know what we are doing." However, in the United States, the Vietnam War and the Watergate scandal had eroded public confidence in government, especially among the younger generation. In Israel, the negligence and failures in intelligence assessment that led to the successful surprise Arab attack on Yom Kippur 1973 (*ha-mechdal*, the screw-up) had a similar effect in shattering public confidence in the wisdom and infallibility of the government. Israeli historians are now debating whether the war might have been averted had Israel been more attentive and responsive to Egyptian peace feelers in 1971.

The June 1982 war in Lebanon further deepened the divisions in the American Jewish community. Like most Israelis, American Jews generally supported Israel's initial "Peace for Galilee" operation, when the declared aim was to knock out the bases and infrastructure of the Palestine Liberation Organization within the forty-kilometer range of Israel's northern border and to end the shelling of Kiryat Shmonah and other Israeli towns.

But when the Israeli attack extended to the outskirts of Beirut, with heavy civilian casualties, a painful ambivalence arose within the American Jewish community. "We all cherish Israel," said Rabbi Roland Gittelson, a Reform leader in Boston, but he added that the invasion "threatens to tear us apart. . . . We worry, we agonize, fear, and also doubt." To the feeling of dismay were added shame and even disgust when, in September, pictures appeared of the massacre of Palestinian refugees at Sabra and Shatilla by Israel's Christian Phalangist allies, while Israeli troops stood idly by.[28]

Despite the disturbing news from Lebanon, public opinion polls showed that American Jews still staunchly supported Israel. When Gallup asked (September 22–23, 1982) whether U.S. aid to Israel should be suspended to force an Israeli pullout from Lebanon, 75 percent of American Jews said no, contrasted with only 38 percent of the general public. The same poll asked American Jews what they believed to be the most appropriate role for American Jews concerning Israel. More than one-third (36 percent) advocated that American Jews take an active role in trying to affect Israel's policies; 24 percent said they would support Israel's government regardless of its actions; and another 30 percent thought that the best stance for American Jews would be to maintain neutrality.[29] The outbreak of the *intifada*, the Palestinian uprising which started in Gaza in December 1987 and quickly spread to the West Bank, also found the active and committed American Jewish community deeply polarized and concerned about the direction of events in Israel. A *Los Angeles Times* poll in April 1988 found that 35 percent of the 1,018 Jews surveyed felt that the continued occupation of the West Bank "will erode Israel's democratic and humanitarian character." The evolution of American Jewish attitudes toward the Palestinian issue during the period of the uprising and following the opening of formal Israel-PLO negotiations in September 1993 is examined in detail in two earlier books in this series.[30]

Where do we stand today in the relationship of American Jews to Israel? Nearly three-quarters of American Jews (74 percent) queried in a poll commissioned by the American Jewish Committee in 1998 agreed with the statement "Caring about Israel is a very important part of my being a Jew." Only 23 percent disagreed. The good news for supporters of Israel is that the figure of identification with Israel was almost as great among those under forty (73 percent) as those over sixty (76 percent), and there was little difference based on their political identification in the United States.[31] The disturbing news is that in contrast to the Orthodox, among whom nine out of every ten said Israel was a very important part of their Jewish identity (88 percent), among those who identified themselves as "just Jewish," four in ten did not consider Israel important to their Jewish identity. (It is also possible that some of the 9 percent of the Orthodox who did not consider the State of Israel to be important were members of such anti-Zionist religious groups as the Satmar Chasidim.)

The polling data do not resolve the question of whether "caring" is the same as "closeness." One may care about and be concerned about a sick relative without necessarily feeling that close to him or her. Asked "how close do you feel to Israel?" 80 percent of those over sixty years of age said they felt either very (31 percent) or fairly close (49 percent). In contrast, among those under age forty, fewer than 60 percent felt close, and 41 percent said they felt fairly distant (30 percent) or very distant (11 percent) from Israel. Predictably, 96 percent of the Orthodox but only 59 percent of the Reform and only half of those who defined themselves as "just Jewish" said they felt somewhat close to Israel. The *Los Angeles Times* reported similar results among both American Jews and Israelis. Roughly 60 percent in both samples felt "close," and 40 percent felt "distant" to their counterparts overseas. (They have not given the breakdown by age.)

But beyond verbal support, how close are the actual contacts between American and Israeli Jews? According to the *Los Angeles Times* poll, 41 percent of American Jews said they had visited Israel at least once, and 42 percent said they had friends or relatives there. A survey sponsored by the American Jewish Committee (of a national sample of 1,001 self-identified adult Jewish respondents), conducted in February and March 1998, found a similar percentage of 39 percent who had visited Israel, which was up from only 33 percent in 1993.[32]

Yet if one considers the relative affluence of the American Jewish community, the propensity of American Jews to travel abroad, and the fact that Israel has been an independent state for fifty years, the statistic that only four out of ten adult American Jews have ever gone to Israel, even for a brief visit, should raise questions about the closeness and intensity of their ties to the Jewish state. The AJC poll broke down the results by age. Even among those who were sixty and older in 1998, fewer than half (only 47 percent) had ever visited Israel, while among those under forty it was 39 percent. (When I showed a draft of this chapter in July 1998 to David Clayman, director of the American Jewish Congress office in Jerusalem, he said that I was too pessimistic in my interpretation of the data. He pointed out that according to statistics he had seen, fewer than half of all Americans had ever traveled outside the continental United States. Using this as a benchmark, he said, the percentage of American Jews visiting Israel was quite remarkable.)

As might be expected, among those who identified themselves as Orthodox, nearly seven in ten (69 percent) had visited Israel, and 50 percent had done so more than once. Presumably at least some of the latter had relatives living in the Jewish state. Fewer than one-third of those who identified themselves as Reform Jews (31 percent) or as "just Jewish" (28 percent) had ever visited Israel. Not surprisingly, of those who said they felt "very close" to Israel 69 percent had visited Israel, while among those who said they felt "fairly or very distant" from Israel only 14 percent had ever visited the country.

Is it financial cost that has kept American Jews away? To help remove that obstacle, the Charles Bronfman Foundation has sponsored trips to Israel for teenagers and young adults, and Michael Steinhardt, another prominent philanthropist, recently proclaimed his vision that, *"henceforth and forever, every young Jew born on this planet will be offered, as a birthright, the privilege of a trip to Israel as a gift from the Jewish people"* (emphasis in the original).[33] Bronfman and Steinhardt took the occasion of the General Assembly meeting in Jerusalem on November 16, 1998, to formally launch a $300 million campaign for the first five years of their "Birthright Israel" project. The money is intended to cover airfare and a minimum of ten days in Israel for Jewish youngsters between the ages of fifteen and twenty-six. This initiative was warmly endorsed by Prime Minister Netanyahu in his address to the approximately 3,300 American and Canadian Jewish leaders of the UJA and federations, who were meeting for the first time outside North America in the UJA's sixty-seven years. They were joined by about 2,000 Israeli communal and business leaders.

The audience gave the prime minister a rousing round of applause when he said that they would be shocked: "Yes, Israel is going to give money to the Diaspora to help promote Jewish education.... On the 50th anniversary of the Jewish state, it's time we gave something back." Specifically, he said that Israel would contribute $20 million to the first year of the Birthright program. Netanyahu said that the disturbingly high rates of intermarriage and assimilation in the Diaspora were due in part to lack of solid Jewish education. He pointedly remarked, "The People of the Book are rapidly becoming the people who cannot even read the Book."[34] He praised Charles Bronfman for beginning his address to the GA in Hebrew, and Bronfman himself, who regretted that he had not learned Hebrew as a youngster, told a radio interviewer that he and his wife had attended a six-week intensive language study course the previous summer and planned to continue their Hebrew studies because he realized the importance of Hebrew as a unifying force and as a means to converse with ordinary Israelis.

The Birthright Israel program received mixed reviews. Netanyahu was convinced that such a trip would make an "indelible impression" on the youngsters: "They either stay here or go back forever changed as Jews and they will touch the hearts and minds of other Jews." However, Miami cardiologist Jerome Reich, a delegate to the GA, whose four sons had all visited Israel, agreed that although such projects were crucial in sparking initial interest in Jewish identity, they did not embody the entire Jewish experience. A visit to Israel "is an adrenalin shot but there must be follow up," Reich said.[35]

When the Birthright program decided in 1999 to utilize the nationwide network of campus Hillel centers to recruit college applicants, the program was oversubscribed. A potential long-term benefit was that it enabled Hillel to identify Jewish students for other Jewish activities on campuses.

Delegates at the 1998 GA received copies of a summary of a recent study which found that the youth programs sponsored by the Orthodox National Council of Synagogue Youth (NCSY) had increased the level of Jewish commitment and eagerness to visit Israel even among students who attended public rather than Jewish religious schools. Among alumni of the program, 85 percent had visited Israel or studied in Israel and 6 percent had made aliyah. But obviously a precondition for success was the willingness of their parents to enroll their youth in a program under Orthodox auspices. There is a growing recognition that the organized Jewish community must give a higher priority to funding more intensive Jewish education and fostering family involvement in synagogue and other Jewish communal activities in this country. Among the new initiatives are nationwide outreach programs that provide crash courses in basic Hebrew and synagogue ritual and a more ambitious *Me'ah* (100) program designed by Hebrew College and sponsored by the Combined Jewish Philanthropies of Boston, under which some 500 adults commit themselves to attend two hours a week of high-level lectures plus two hours of homework for a year. The sponsors of these programs realize that such courses will not in themselves solve the problem but are designed to whet the appetite of nonaffiliated adults to become not only more knowledgeable but more involved in Jewish educational and communal life. Such a shift in priorities should increase the likelihood that Jewish teenagers will in fact want to spend time in Israel.[36]

It is an ironic fact that today "more Palestinian Arabs than Jewish Americans speak Hebrew."[37] This has potentially ominous implications for maintaining close Israel-Diaspora ties in the future. Leaders in both the United States and Israel are searching for ways to tackle the problem. In addition to Prime Minister Netanyahu's expressed support for increased funding for Jewish education in the Diaspora, American Jewish philanthropic leaders are also devoting increasing efforts to tackling the problem.

Among the problems that UJA fund-raisers have faced, "apart from the religious pluralism issue in Israel," UJA chairman Wexler noted in an interview with the *New York Times,* was "the perception that Israel's economy is booming and that external threats appear to be disappearing in the wake of [the end of] the cold war." Consequently, he found these to be "the most challenging years we've ever faced." Moreover, younger Jews who are comfortably integrated into American life lack the historical understanding of the precariousness of Jewish existence and the difficult struggle that the Holocaust survivors and the founders of the State of Israel faced. "For my kids the Holocaust is ancient history, and they have no emotional relationship to Israel," Michael Steinhardt confided to *Times* reporter Judith Miller. This has been reflected in the declining proportion of their charitable donations going to Jewish causes. Younger Jews, in fact, are far less likely to give to and through their local Jewish federation. Miller reported studies that showed that only a quarter of Jews aged thirty-two to fifty give, and that only 12 percent of intermarried households, as opposed to 59 percent of all-Jewish households, give to the United Jewish Appeal.[38]

When the AJC-sponsored poll asked, in February–March 1998 about "the current relationship between American Jews and Israeli Jews," roughly half in each group (U.S. Jews 49 percent, Israelis 53 percent) defined it as excellent or good, while 39 percent described it as fair or poor. One reason appears to be the current controversy over conversion and other issues of religion and state. Asked to forecast the state of the relationship in "three to five years," 62 percent of the Americans and 47 percent of the Israelis thought it would remain the same. The Israelis were slightly more optimistic, 25 percent believing the two groups would grow closer (only 17 percent of the Americans did so), while 14 percent thought they would drift apart (12 percent of the Americans).

Asked to compare the current state of the relations between the United States and Israel with the past, 71 percent of American Jews thought they were either better (17 percent) or the same (54 percent). Fewer than one in four (23 percent) thought they were now worse. By contrast, 43 percent of Israelis polled thought they had gotten worse. Only 13 percent thought they had improved.

Israelis were more critical of their own country than American Jews were of the United States. Forty-two percent of Israeli Jews thought their country's policies were "seriously off on the wrong track." More than one-third (36 percent) in both countries thought that Prime Minister Benjamin Netanyahu had caused relations to worsen. (It should be noted that the poll was taken before the intensive American mediating effort, led by President Clinton, that resulted in the Wye River Memorandum, signed at the White House on October 23, 1998, between Netanyahu and PLO leader Yasir Arafat. Clinton reportedly was furious at some of Netanyahu's bargaining tactics.)

Turning to the then-stalled peace process, both the AJC and *Los Angeles Times* polls found the respondents more pessimistic about the prospects for peace than they had been after the Madrid peace talks in 1991 and the Israeli-PLO agreement in September 1993. The *Los Angeles Times* reported that when asked whether they believed Netanyahu was sincere about moving the peace process forward, 60 percent of American Jews said yes, as did 63 percent of the Israeli Jews. There was growing skepticism about Palestinian intentions, and about half of both American and Israeli Jews doubted that Arafat sincerely sought peace.

The American Jewish Committee's 1998 poll found a sharp decline in confidence in Arab peaceful intentions. In a similar poll taken in 1993 shortly after Prime Minister Yitzhak Rabin and Arafat had signed the Oslo Declaration of Principles of mutual recognition on the White House lawn, 50 percent of American Jews said they believed the "goal of the Arabs is the return of occupied territories," while 42 percent felt the Arab goal was still the "destruction of Israel." But by the spring 1998 poll, this had turned around. Now more than two-thirds (68 percent) felt the Arab goal was the destruction of Israel. I wonder to what extent this change is because of the terrorist attacks and the stalemate in the peace process and to what extent it reflects the contrast between the optimistic pronouncements about a new peaceful Middle East issued after Oslo by Prime Ministers Rabin and Peres and the more pessimistic assessments issued by Prime Minister Netanyahu, Ariel Sharon, and other Likud leaders.

American Jews were nearly unanimous (94 percent to 3 percent) in agreeing that the Palestinian Authority had not done enough to curb Hamas and other extremist groups. Yasser Arafat and the PLO continue to have an image problem not only among American Jews but among the American public in general. In their mid-April 1998 poll, the *New York Times* found that two-thirds of Americans (67 percent) believed the PLO had not done enough to prove it was interested in peace. (Only 15 percent thought they had.) Regarding Israel's policies, Americans generally were more closely divided: 43 percent now said Israel had done enough, while 41 percent said it had not—a marked improvement over U.S. public opinion at the height of the *intifada,* when 70 percent of Americans thought Israel was not doing enough to prove it was interested in peace, and only 17 percent thought it had done enough.[39]

Turning to the specifics of the peace process, the *Los Angeles Times* poll found that two-thirds of American Jews (68 percent) approved of there being an "independent Palestinian state in the Middle East." (Possibly some of the U.S. respondents shared the view of Israeli nationalists that there already was a Palestinian state in the Middle East, namely Jordan.) In contrast, 49 percent of Israeli Jews disapproved of an independent Palestinian state, while 44 percent said they approved. The *Los Angeles Times* made this apparent split their headline: "Jews in U.S., Israel differ on Palestinian state, backing is strong here despite skepticism about Mideast peace."

When the *New York Times* in April 1998 asked a more pointed question, "Do you favor a Palestinian homeland in the occupied territories?" the American Jewish respondents were more closely divided: 45 percent were in favor and 42 percent were opposed. (The American public, in general, favored a Palestinian homeland by 38 percent to 28 percent. One-third, or 34 percent, had no opinion.)

The AJC poll also did not support the *Los Angeles Times'* sensational headline of a significant split in Israeli and American Jewish opinion on a Palestinian state. Rather, it confirms the erosion in American Jewish confidence in the Palestinians' peaceful intentions. When asked "Given the current situation, do you favor or oppose establishment of a Palestinian state?" in 1993 shortly after the Oslo Accord, a clear majority of 57 percent said they were in favor, and only 30 percent were opposed. This support has steadily declined: In the 1998 AJC poll, 49 percent said they opposed a Palestinian state "in current circumstances," and only 42 percent still were in favor. (Opinion also seems to have crystallized: While 13 percent of American Jews said they weren't sure in 1993, in 1998 only 9 percent remained undecided.)

There is, however, a widespread and growing feeling that a Palestinian state is inevitable and that the task of the Israeli negotiators (and American mediators) will be to limit its capacity to endanger Israeli security. Indeed, the *Los Angeles Times* reported that two-thirds of both the Israeli and American Jewish respondents believed it likely that a Palestinian state would be established in the future.

American Jews have been critical of some Israeli policies. When the *Los Angeles Times* poll asked whether "things in Israel are generally going in the right direction," only one-fourth (26 percent) of American Jews said yes, while half (49 percent) said they "are seriously off on the wrong track." (Echoing the favorable job performance rating given President Clinton in recent U.S. polls, a significant majority of American Jews, 59 percent, like the American public in general, thought things were going in the right direction in the United States.)

A perennial subject of debate has been what American Jews should do when they disagree with Israeli policies. It is generally agreed that American Jews have the right to express their views on issues of purely Jewish concern, such as conversion, non-Orthodox prayer groups at the Western Wall, or authorization of Conservative and Reform rabbis to officiate or serve on regional religious councils.

American Jews have also occasionally used their power of the purse. As noted above, during the 1997 conversion controversy they again threatened (as some did in 1988) to cut their contributions to the United Jewish Appeal. This prompted the UJA and the Jewish Agency to increase their allocations to non-Orthodox Jewish institutions in Israel and to promise to take other steps to promote pluralism. Interestingly, the *Los Angeles Times* reported that when asked whether Conservative and Reform rabbis should also be allowed to perform marriages and conversions in Israel, 58 percent of the Israeli Jews and an overwhelming majority of 80 percent of American Jews said yes.

In recent years the American Jewish Committee has found a growing readiness among American Jews to criticize *publicly* the policies of the Israeli government. In contrast to 1982, when 43 percent opposed public criticism of Israeli policies by American Jews, in 1998 only one in three (33 percent) still thought it was wrong to do so, while a majority of 64 percent asserted their right to do so.[40] Those who were younger, better educated, more affluent, and more liberal or secular in their religious views were generally more ready to criticize than those who were older, less educated, and religiously Orthodox. (Those over sixty-five were more likely to have personal knowledge of the horrors of the Holocaust, the desperate struggle for Israeli independence in 1948, and the threats to Israel's existence by its numerous Arab neighbors. By way of contrast, for American Jews under age thirty-five, who had grown up after Israel's dramatic victory in 1967, Israel was a Middle East superpower, seemingly invincible, in contrast to the Palestinians who appeared helpless and divided.)

Not surprisingly, the greatest split was in terms of denominational affiliation. Among the Orthodox, a majority of 60 percent thought it wrong to criticize the government's policies (only 35 percent said it was all right to do so), but among the Reform, 72 percent asserted a right to criticize publicly, and only 25 percent thought it wrong. Orthodox Jews in the United States tended to share Netanyahu's views on church-state issues and his tough approach to the Palestinians, while the more liberal Reform Jews were critical on both counts.

However, when it came to matters related to Israel's national security, a significant majority (57 percent) of American Jews agreed with this statement: "Regardless of their individual views on the peace negotiations with the Arabs, American Jews should support the policies of the duly elected government of Israel." Only slightly more than one-third (36 percent) said they disagreed.

Regarding the role of the American government in the peace process, a poll commissioned by the dovish Israel Policy Forum (IPF) in May 1998 may have helped President Clinton decide to take an exceptionally active personal role in trying to bring about the Israeli-Palestinian agreement that was hammered out in nine days of arduous negotiations at Wye River Plantation in October. The IPF poll was conducted following Secretary of State Albright's London meetings with Prime Minister Netanyahu and Chairman Arafat.[41]

Among the poll's key findings were the following. An overwhelming majority of American Jews—80 percent—"support the Clinton Administration's current efforts to revive Israeli-Palestinian negotiations" with only 18 percent opposed. A majority of 54 percent believed that the "current level of American diplomatic pressure on Bibi Netanyahu" was "about right" or "too little." One-third of the respondents (33 percent) said there was "too much" American pressure on Israel. There was also widespread support for an active American role: 83 percent believed it was important "that the United States suggest its own ideas to bridge the gap between the two sides," and a slimmer majority of 63 percent said that "if the current American initiative fails to get the peace process back on track," the administration should speak out about the status of the process. Only one-fourth (26 percent) of the respondents urged the United States "not to speak out."

The Jewish community was more evenly divided when it came to suggestions of unilateral U.S. pressure on the Israeli government. A bare majority of 52 percent supported Secretary Albright's giving Netanyahu "a deadline of [next] Monday to respond to the American proposal," while 44 percent were opposed. However, there was widespread support for what might be regarded as evenhanded pressure for peace rather than just against Israel: 77 percent agreed that "the Administration should pressure Prime Minister Netanyahu and Chairman Arafat to act more constructively and be more forthcoming in negotiations." Only 18 percent disagreed.

American Jews were nearly evenly divided on the security implications for Israel of agreeing to the American proposal for Israel to relinquish an additional 13 percent of West Bank territory. A slim plurality (43 percent) said they agreed with Prime Minister Netanyahu's position at the time that such an extensive withdrawal "will jeopardize Israel's security," while 39 percent said they agreed with "other Israelis [who] say that this will not jeopardize Israel's security because Israel will still hold onto 60 percent of the West Bank and be the overwhelming military power in the area." Nevertheless, there was nearly universal concern for Israel's security, and 97 percent of the American Jews polled believed that "even if Israel signs peace agreements with all of its neighbors, Israel will always need a strong army." Similarly, 98 percent agreed that "beyond the peace process, the U.S. should continue to strengthen its 'special relationship' as Israel's closest ally." The respondents also overwhelmingly supported an American role in ensuring Palestinian compliance with any agreement reached, with 92 percent agreeing that if there were any "security breaches by the Palestinians, then the United States should stand behind the State of Israel."

President Clinton, who was then in the midst of the scandal resulting from his involvement with Monica Lewinsky, a young White House intern, could draw comfort from the continued high level of support in the Jewish community: fully 89 percent believed that "President Clinton has generally been very supportive of the State of Israel," and 80 percent agreed that "President Bill Clinton would not do anything that would harm Israel's security." In terms of his general approval rating, Clinton was viewed "favorably" by 78 percent of the American Jews surveyed, while only 8 percent viewed him "unfavorably." Prime Minister Netanyahu's favorable rating had gone up from 57 percent, in a similar poll taken in September 1997, to 64 percent in May 1998, while 27 percent viewed him unfavorably. PLO Chairman Arafat had also improved his favorable rating to 25 percent, against only 15 percent the previous September, but the Palestinian leader still was viewed "unfavorably" by 70 percent of American Jews. Arafat might draw comfort from the fact that 88 percent of American Jews said they "support the Israeli-Palestinian peace process" and that an overwhelming 96 percent said they believed that "achieving stable peace with the Palestinians" is important "to Israel's security and well-being."

Finally, what do thoughtful Israelis expect of American Jews? In 1988, Jerusalem mayor Ehud Olmert, then a rising young Likud leader (minister of health), told a visiting group of American Jews who had expressed their distress to him concerning Israel's handling of the Palestinian Arab uprising during the early months of *intifada*: "Of course you have a right to express your views and we even welcome your criticisms, because we know they come out of love and a shared concern for our common future." What Israelis could not stand, he said, were those who in response to Israel's rough handling of the Palestinian rioters said, "Well if Israel is that kind of a country, I will have nothing more to do with it." Olmert, who in November 1998 was reelected mayor of Jerusalem, gave this example: "A family discovers that their son has a drug problem, or is charged with a serious crime. If you are really part of a family, you don't walk away and disown the member who is in trouble. You try even harder," he stressed, "to work together to cope with your common problem."

This need to work together was echoed in a special three-page ad placed in the *New York Times* by the UJA Federation on the eve of their historic General Assembly meeting in Israel in mid-November 1998. The ad carried a headline in large type: "Many people, many roads, one heart." The lead paragraph declared: "The people at the 1998 General Assembly share a commitment to *Klal Yisrael*—a world where every Jew is responsible for every other Jew. That commitment is at the heart of a sacred Jewish trust to build, strengthen and care for our community at home, in Israel and in 60 countries around the world. That commitment is at the heart of the UJA Federation Campaign."[42] The GA in Jerusalem concluded with the formal signing by the delegates of a "Covenant between the Jewish People of North America and Israel," in which both sides pledged to "rededicate ourselves to strengthening the links between us to the spiritual and historic centrality of the State of Israel, and to one another. We affirm the values that have sustained us for centuries: belief in one G-d, the special responsibility of Jews to each other's Jewish peoplehood and the love of the people."

Aside from the symbolic value of the covenant, which one reporter termed "window-dressing," the General Assembly did provide a useful firsthand opportunity for Israeli and American Jewish leaders to get to know each other and seriously debate issues of concern. One concern that many American delegates came away with was the question of to what extent the younger generation of Israelis would continue to possess a Jewish identity as Israel increasingly became integrated in the secular global economy and American-dominated mass culture of the twenty-first century. On the Israeli side, as well, there was a maturing of their view of their relationship to the Americans, from recipient and donor to a more equal partnership, to which American Jews, with their unique experience of pluralism, diversity, and political tolerance, had something of value other than money to contribute. Israeli industrialist Dov Lautman, who headed the Israeli delegation to the GA, said that as Israel's own economy developed, the American contribution would be less important in terms of philanthropy than in other realms. "We need to work together to educate [our children] to pluralistic Judaism," he said. This would require developing a system of Jewish education in Israel that would be "not just religious education, but also education toward values" and that would reciprocally "teach American Jewish youth about Israeli society." In addition, he said, it was important that American Jews continued to participate in the local political process by expressing their opinions: "They should not sit there as a silent majority."

It remains to be seen whether the spirit of solidarity and common destiny to which the GA delegates rededicated themselves will in fact be infused into the daily interaction between American Jews and Israelis and within each of the communities. If it is, then the ongoing debates on such divisive issues as the conduct of the peace process and the relationship of Orthodox and non-Orthodox need not lead to a deepening division and eventual rupture but rather to a strengthened sense of peoplehood based on mutual tolerance and understanding for a diversity of views.

Postscript

Since this chapter was completed at the end of 1998, there have been several significant developments in Israel and the Middle East, most notably the suspension by Prime Minister Netanyahu of further implementation of the Wye Agreement after the first phase of withdrawal, ostensibly because of the failure of the Palestinian Authority to fulfill its security-related obligations toward Israel. U.S. and other observers, however, attributed the renewed stalemate in the peace process primarily to the defection of Netanyahu's right-wing supporters and the unraveling of the coalition, resulting in the prime minister's decision to call for early elections in the hope of obtaining a broader mandate for his policies. The Knesset set May 17, 1999, for separate elections for the prime minister and for new members of parliament. A variety of new parties and personalities emerged during the hotly contested campaign, which also witnessed the increasing use of American media consultants and pollsters by the major parties to project their message to voters in television commercials and on billboards.

The election resulted in an unexpectedly decisive first-ballot victory for One Israel (Labor) coalition leader Ehud Barak, who defeated Likud leader Netanyahu by a 56–46 margin in the popular vote. Netanyahu announced his decision to resign from politics within hours of his stunning personal defeat. During the election campaign, One Israel ads dramatized the fact that Barak, a former chief of staff and foreign minister, had led successful antiterrorism campaigns and was Israel's most highly decorated soldier. The ads were effective in countering the Likud charges that a Labor victory would endanger Israel's security. Upon his victory, Barak promised that he would rapidly implement the Wye River Memorandum, enter into permanent status talks with the Palestinians, and vigorously pursue resumption of peace talks with Syria and Lebanon, which had been suspended in February 1996. Barak also managed by early July to put together a broad-based coalition that gave him a comfortable initial majority of 75 in the 120-member Knesset. Barak's victory was also welcomed by most of the Arab world, most notably by President Hafez al-Assad of Syria and young King Abdullah of Jordan, who had succeeded King Hussein after his death from cancer in February and who pledged to continue his father's commitment to peace.

How did American Jews react to these dramatic new developments? To help gauge attitudes within the community, the Israel Policy Forum commissioned a new poll at the end of June 1999 of a representative national sample of 606 American Jews. The IPF had been founded in 1993, at the time when the Oslo Accords had initiated the formal Israeli-PLO talks. IPF's declared objective was to promote support within the American Jewish community and the broader public for the Middle East peace process "in order to strengthen Israeli security and further U.S. foreign policy interests in the region." The IPF had conducted a similar poll after Netanyahu's election in 1996.[43]

The 1999 poll found that American Jews were pleased with the outcome of the May elections: By an overwhelming majority (73 percent to 7 percent), the respondents said they expected Prime Minister Ehud Barak to "do a better job than" his predecessor, Benjamin Netanyahu, in moving the peace process forward" and in "improving Israel's image in the world." Smaller but still clear majorities said they thought Barak would do better in getting the army out of Lebanon, reducing religious-secular tensions in Israel, and improving the country's economy. If they could have voted in the Israeli elections, a majority (58 percent) would have voted for Barak versus only 22 percent for Netanyahu. Nearly half (47 percent) said that U.S.-Israeli relations had gotten worse during Netanyahu's premiership (only 10 percent said they had improved), and a similar 47 percent thought relations would improve under the new premier.

The poll found that American Jews continued strongly to support the Israel-Palestinian peace process (88 percent to 8 percent) but remained skeptical about the Arabs' peaceful intentions and were divided over whether the Palestinian Authority had in fact increased efforts to thwart terrorism. Not surprisingly, an overwhelming 94 percent agreed that "even if Israel signs peace agreements with all of its neighbors, Israel will always need a strong army." Only 24 percent of American Jews had a favorable opinion of Arafat, while 70 percent still viewed the Palestinian Authority chairman unfavorably. The favorable ratings of other leaders about whom the American Jews were queried were, in descending order: Vice President Al Gore, 73 percent; First Lady Hillary Rodham Clinton, 72 percent (apparently not significantly weakened by her support for an eventual Palestinian state); President Clinton, 69 percent; Barak, 63 percent; Netanyahu, 50 percent; Likud party leader Ariel Sharon, 40 percent; Texas governor and Republican presidential candidate George W. Bush, 32 percent favorable (compared to 40 percent unfavorable).

Four-fifths of the respondents wanted President Clinton to make Middle East peace a high priority during his remaining time in office. The responses also reflected somewhat greater flexibility than in previous years. Only half had been aware that President Clinton had postponed moving the U.S. embassy from Tel Aviv to Jerusalem by the May 1999 deadline mandated by a congressional law, citing the need to protect the peace process from disruption. But when asked whether they supported the president's action, 52 percent did so against 30 percent who opposed the postponement. This pragmatic flexibility was reflected even in response to some key issues. When asked "In the framework of a permanent peace with the Palestinians, should Israel be willing to compromise on the status of Jerusalem as a united city under Israeli jurisdiction?" more than one-third (36 percent) now said yes, although a majority (55 percent) still said no. Significantly, 83 percent agreed that it was important that America reassure both sides "that in the end the U.S. will support major goals—for example, for Israel, security and a united Jerusalem, for Palestinians, independent statehood." Similarly a high percentage saw the importance for the peace process of the United States providing tangible benefits, including economic aid, to the Palestinians, and of Washington maintaining close contacts with both sides to facilitate Syrian-Israeli negotiations. By a two-to-one majority (60 percent to 30 percent), the American Jews agreed that if Syria made "real peace" with Israel, the United States should upgrade its diplomatic relations with Damascus and offer economic assistance to Syria. However, on the crucial question of whether the United States should provide troops for a Golan Heights peace monitoring force, if asked to do so by the parties, American Jews were still deeply divided (46 percent said yes, and 44 percent said no).

Shortly before the Israeli elections, the American Jewish Committee released its annual survey of American Jewish opinion that had been based on telephone interviews with 1,000 persons between March 29 and April 18, 1999.[44] Nearly three-quarters of American Jews (74 percent) said they felt close to Israel, and 76 percent agreed with the statement that caring about Israel "is a very important part of my being a Jew." AJC president Bruce M. Ramer commented that "contrary to popular perceptions that American Jews are pulling away from Israel, this survey confirms that indeed there is no erosion in the eternal bond between American Jews and the Jewish state." However, a more detailed breakdown of the respondents found considerable variation in the extent of attachment based on religious affiliation and age: For example, 93 percent of the Orthodox respondents said they felt close to Israel, compared with 83 percent of the Conservative and 69 percent of the Reform. Among respondents sixty years and older, 81 percent said they felt close to Israel, compared with 71 percent of those aged forty to fifty-nine and 67 percent of those under forty.

On questions relating to the peace process, the AJC findings were generally similar to those in the IPF poll. Regarding the stalemate in implementing the Wye River Accord, 88 percent believed the Palestinian Authority was not doing enough to implement the agreement, while 43 percent felt that the Netanyahu government was not doing enough. Asked to give their impression of the three leading candidates for prime minister in Israel, Netanyahu received a favorable rating from 65 percent against 26 percent unfavorable. Barak's rating was 34 percent favorable to 13 percent unfavorable, but 53 percent said they lacked sufficient information to decide. The responses for Yitzhak Mordechai, the third candidate at the time, were similar to those for Barak.

Two-thirds of the respondents agreed with the statement that the goal of the Arabs was "not the return of the occupied territories but rather the destruction of Israel." On the specifics of the peace process, there was considerable division. When asked "Given the current situation do you favor or oppose the establishment of a Palestinian state?" 44 percent favored, and 47 percent opposed. On the issue of Jerusalem, the AJC poll found that some four in ten American Jews (42 percent) agreed with the statement that "in the framework of a permanent peace with the Palestinians," Israel should be willing to "compromise on the status of Jerusalem as a united city under Israeli jurisdiction." A majority of 55 percent still opposed compromise on this fundamental and highly charged issue. However, in response to earlier annual surveys, beginning in 1993, twice as many respondents (60 to 62 percent) had opposed any compromise compared to those willing to consider any negotiated changes in the status quo (30 to 33 percent). On the issue of dismantling Jewish settlements in the West Bank as part of a final agreement with the Palestinians, American Jewish opinion remained divided: While only 5 percent supported the Arab position calling for dismantling all the settlements, a clear majority of 53 percent agreed that "some" should be dismantled, while 40 percent felt that "none" should be removed. American Jews were even more divided regarding the return of the Golan Heights as the price of peace with Syria: 37 percent opposed any return, 32 percent said "only a small part" should be given back, 32 percent said "some of it," while only 4 percent agreed to giving up "most of it," and only 2 percent agreed with the basic Syrian demand that "all of it" be returned to Syrian control. This poll was conducted while Netanyahu's Likud government was still in power and the talks with Syria had been suspended since February 1996.

I would venture to speculate that if Premier Barak, who now enjoys substantial support within the American Jewish community, were to propose a significant Israeli withdrawal from the Golan with adequate security arrangements as part of a final peace agreement with Syria, the American Jewish community would quickly follow the lead of the duly established government of Israel, as it has in the past. During his first visit to the United States as prime minister, in July 1999, Barak placed a high priority on consolidating Jewish support for Israel's peace policies. Barak had been troubled by reports that harsh critics of proposed Israeli concessions to the Palestinians, such as Morton Klein, president of the Zionist Organization of America, had been lobbying Congress to slow down and restrict American aid to the Palestinians and that AIPAC and the Conference of Presidents of Major Jewish Organizations had tended to support the more cautious Likud approach to peace rather than the positions of Labor leaders Rabin and Peres under which the Oslo Accords had been concluded. The fact that the Presidents Conference had recently selected as its chairman Jewish National Fund president Ronald Lauder, who was known as a friend and supporter of Netanyahu, also raised concern among Barak's advisors about a split in American Jewish support for his activist peace policies. Leaders of both AIPAC and the Presidents Conference denied that they had displayed any pro-Likud bias, noting that they had always worked to support the elected government of Israel, irrespective of party. The Presidents Conference also has stressed that its basic objectives are to "strengthen the U.S.-Israel alliance and to protect and enhance the security and dignity of Jews abroad" and that it "speaks and acts on the basis of consensus of its 55 member agencies" whose membership reflected the broad spectrum of American Jewish views on political, religious, and social issues.[45]

In an unmistakable signal that he intended to reward supporters of his activist peace policies within the Jewish community, Prime Minister Barak invited officials of the Israel Policy Forum to join him on July 16 for Friday night dinner at his hotel suite in the Waldorf Astoria. Israeli reporters accompanying the Israeli delegation were also invited. On Sunday, July 18, Barak held back-to-back meetings, first with the IPF and then with the leaders of the Presidents Conference. The *New York Times* noted that Netanyahu had largely ignored the IPF, preferring to invite leaders of the Presidents Conference to his private events. In his meetings with both groups, Barak stressed the need for unity among American Jews. "He said he wanted the American Jewish community to send an unequivocal message in support of the peace process," said Michael W. Sonnenfeldt, who leads the IPF. Barak noted that disputes between American Jewish groups had prevented this unity on the peace process in the past several years.[46]

Prime Minister Barak brought the same message to Washington when he met with leaders of Congress and with AIPAC on July 19. In an unusual, front-page editorial in AIPAC's *Near East Report,* signed by AIPAC's president Lionel Kaplan and executive director Howard A. Kohr, they noted that Barak had told AIPAC that an extraordinary opportunity now existed for Israel to achieve its goal of a comprehensive peace with its Arab neighbors, but that to achieve this goal the diplomatic, strategic, and economic support of the United States would be a "crucial factor." "Therefore, Barak said, he is looking for support from the United States Congress and the American Jewish community more than ever before." The editorial concluded with a pledge: "We told him that AIPAC will spare no effort to support the search for peace, in partnership with the Congress and the administration." Despite the evidence revealed by the recent polls that there were still deep divisions within the Jewish community on some aspects of the peace process, the AIPAC leaders ended their editorial by declaring categorically, "The American Jewish community stands as one with our friends on Capitol Hill and the Executive Branch, to ensure that the steps Israel is taking for peace will result in peace with security for the people of Israel."[47] It remains to be seen whether under Prime Minister Barak's leadership the partnership between Israel and the American Jewish community will be strengthened and revitalized.

Notes

1. For a detailed discussion of the most recent controversy during 1996 and 1997, see Lawrence Grossman, "Jewish Communal Affairs."

2. Hebrew University philosophy professor Yirmiyahu Yovel declared that the Cyprus option was increasingly being chosen by members of the younger generation of Jewish Israelis who refuse to be married by a rabbi because of their "anger and loathing" at what they regard as "oppression" by the Orthodox rabbinate (lecture on "Israel: A Jewish State or the State of the Jews," Columbia University, November 9, 1998). Yovel is also founder of the Jerusalem Spinoza Institute.

3. Stephen Franklin and Storer H. Rowley, "Israel Fears Eroding Support of American Jews," *Chicago Tribune,* April 29, 1997.

4. Grossman, "Jewish Communal Affairs," 148.

5. For an analysis of the earlier crisis, see George E. Gruen, *The Not-So-Silent Partnership.*

6. Judith Miller, "Israel's Controversy over Religion Affects Donations by Jews in U.S.," *New York Times,* November 17, 1997. The story was prominently featured on the front page.

7. Grossman, "Jewish Communal Affairs," 148. See also the comprehensive article on this subject by Jack Wertheimer in the *1997 American Jewish Year Book.*

8. Quoted by David Landau, "The Origins of the Blackmail," *Ha'aretz,* May 1, 1997. For a fuller historical discussion of the splits within the American Jewish community and the impact of the disaffection from Israel on U.S. policy, see

Abraham Ben-Zvi, "Paradigm Lost? The Limits of the American-Israeli Special Relationship," *Israel Affairs* 4, no. 2 (Winter 1997): 1–25.

9. "Premier Talks of Law for Conversion Compromise," *Jerusalem Report*, November 23, 1998, 8.

10. Adam Heilman, "Ne'eman Says Pluralism Is No Longer Tops on Jewish Agenda," *Ha'aretz*, November 18, 1998.

11. Quoted in *Ha'aretz*, November 17, 1998.

12. *Yediot Aharonot*, November 3, 1998; *Jerusalem Post*, November 3, 1998.

13. George E. Gruen, "Nowhere to Go," letter in *New York Times Magazine*, August 11, 1991. Following the expulsion by Kuwait of more than 350,000 Palestinians in the wake of the Gulf War, I cited this precedent and urged international efforts to convince the Arab host states to provide similar assurances to Palestinians living in their own countries as part of the agenda for the forthcoming peace negotiations that might result in creation of an independent Palestinian state in the West Bank and Gaza.

14. For details, see Naomi W. Cohen, *American Jews and the Zionist Idea*. On the evolution of the position of the American Jewish Committee, see *In Vigilant Brotherhood* (New York: AJC, 1964).

15. See, for example, the speech by Brandeis reprinted in Arthur Hertzberg's edited collection, *The Zionist Idea* (1959). For a vivid description of the Zionist–anti-Zionist fights that paralleled the struggle for control between the established German and recent immigrant East European Jews, see chapter 13 of Hertzberg's *The Jews in America* (New York: Simon and Schuster, 1989).

16. For text of the exchange of letters, see *In Vigilant Brotherhood*, 64–69.

17. Cited in Gruen, *The Not-So-Silent Partnership*, 2–3.

18. James Risen and Steven Erlanger, "C.I.A. Chief Vowed to Quit if Clinton Freed Israeli Spy," *New York Times*, November 11, 1998. Not only was this featured as the lead story on the front page of the paper, but Tenet's resignation would have undermined implementation of the Wye River Memorandum.

19. Press conference text issued by Israel Foreign Ministry, Information Division.

20. Quotations cited by Mathew Dorf in "It's Not Your Father's State Department: Jews Flourish in Once-Dead-End Foreign Service," *Jewish Sentinel* (New York), December 5–11, 1997, 2–3.

21. Text in AJC, *In Vigilant Brotherhood*, 65–66.

22. *Los Angeles Times*, April 19, 1998, and "Los Angeles Times Poll Alert" analysis of the results by Susan Pinkus, April 18, 1998, Study 407/408. The Israeli poll was conducted for *Yediot Aharonot* by the Dahaf Research Institute under the direction of Mina Zemach. The size of the American sample was 848, the Israeli 1,011.

23. Interview in the *New York Times*, April 30, 1998.

24. Quoted by Elli Wohlgelernter, "PM: Next 50 years Devoted to Securing Life of Jewish People," *Jerusalem Post*, November 17, 1998.

25. See George E. Gruen, "Aspects and Prospects of the Interaction between American Jews and Israel," reprinted by the American Jewish Committee from *Conference on American Jewish Dilemmas: 1971*, American Federation of Jews from Central Europe, 1971.

26. Serge Schmemann, "Israelis, Proud and Worried, Now Ask, What Is Our State?" *New York Times*, April 20, 1998. Schmemann adds, "a troubling proportion of those who come prove to be extremists."

27. Arthur Herzberg, "Partners," *Present Tense* (January–February 1988), 11.

28. Quoted in George E. Gruen, "The United States and Israel: Impact of the Lebanon War," *American Jewish Year Book: 1984*, 85. For other Jewish comments, see 86–88.

29. See Geraldine Rosenfield, "U.S. Public Opinion Polls and the Lebanon War," *American Jewish Year Book: 1984*, 106–16.

30. See George E. Gruen, "Impact of the Intifada on American Jews and the Reaction of the American Public and Israeli Jews," and George E. Gruen, "American Jewish Attitudes toward Israel." See also Gruen, *The Not-So-Silent Partnership*, 15–19.

31. The American Jewish Committee, *1998 Annual Survey of American Jewish Opinion* (New York, May 1998). The poll was conducted by telephone by Market Facts, Inc., during the period February 19–March 8, 1998, from a national U.S. sample of 1,001 self-identified Jewish respondents. No interviewing took place on the Sabbath.

32. According to Market Facts, Inc., "the respondents are demographically representative of the U.S. Jewish population on a variety of measures." The margin of error was plus or minus three percentage points.

33. Michael Steinhardt, "Universal Birthright Israel: A Rite of Passage for Every Jew," *Contact*, May 1998, published by the Jewish Life Network, sponsored by the Judy and Michael Steinhardt Foundation.

34. Adam Heilman, "Netanyahu to 'pay back' Diaspora Jews," *Ha'aretz*, English edition, November 17, 1998. The project's organizers pledged to raise $100 million from twenty wealthy donors like themselves. They hoped to obtain another $100 million from the Federations and expected the last $100 million to be provided by Israeli sources.

35. AP report from Jerusalem, as posted on the Web by CNN Interactive, November 17, 1998.

36. Author's discussion on December 15, 1998, with Rabbi Pinchas Stolper, senior executive of the Orthodox Union, the sponsor of NCSY. Among other reported findings, 50 percent of NCSY alumni had studied in a yeshiva program in Israel, 58 percent said they were more observant now than when they were raised, 98 percent were married to Jewish spouses, and only 3 percent of marriages had ended in divorce. Fully 92 percent were affiliated with a synagogue, and 69 percent also belonged to another Jewish organization. They were generally highly educated, with 36 percent of men having earned master's degrees and 25 percent

doctorates (the comparable figures for women graduates were 40 percent and 13 percent). The average NCSY alumnus had visited Israel three times. Significantly, the non-Jewish, independent Lilly Endowment funded the study, titled *Faithful Youth: A Study of the National Conference of Synagogue Youth*, by Nathalie Friedman (New York: NCSY, November 1998). Information on the Boston programs is based on discussions in September and November 1998 in Newton, Massachusetts, with Barry Shrage, director of the Combined Jewish Philanthropies of Boston, who stressed that the *Me'ah* project was only one part of a comprehensive plan to build a vibrant, open community of caring, learning, and social justice that will endure for generations to come. The program is detailed in the CJF's *Report of the Strategic Planning Committee: A Culture of Learning, a Vision of Justice, a Community of Caring*, January 1998.

37. Geoffrey Wheatcroft, "A Nation Like No Other," op-ed article, *New York Times*, April 30, 1998.

38. Judith Miller, "Israel's Controversy over Religion Affects Donations by Jews in U.S.," A10.

39. Carey Goldberg with Marjorie Connelly, "For Better or Worse, Israel Is 'Special' in U.S. Eyes," *New York Times*, April 26, 1998. The poll was based on telephone interviews conducted April 15–20 with a nationwide sample of 1,395 adults. Since the subsample of Jewish Americans consisted of 232 persons, the margin of error was 7 percent, against 3 percent for the larger sample.

40. For comparison with the responses from 1981 to 1988, see Steven M. Cohen, *Ties and Tensions*, 44–46. Cohen attributes the decline in willingness to permit public criticism that occurred in 1982 and 1988 to the fact that these were times when Israel was engaged in violent conflict with Palestinians (in Lebanon in 1982 and in the territories in 1988) and was subjected to an unusual amount of criticism in the news media. Cohen noted, "Under such circumstances, the instincts of some Jews were to close ranks behind Israel and to discourage public criticism."

41. The IPF poll was conducted by Penn, Schoen & Berland, who conducted telephone interviews with 500 American Jews on May 6 and 7, 1998. The margin of error was calculated as 4.38 percent at the 95 percent confidence level. Data provided to the author by IPF.

42. *New York Times*, November 9, 1998, A21–23. The ad also featured a valentine-type heart, which was the symbol chosen for "G.A.'98-Israel/November 16–19/UJA Federation of North America."

43. Israel Policy Forum, Executive Summary, July 14, 1999, and detailed poll data provided to the author by IPF. The interviews took place from June 27 to July 1, and the poll was jointly conducted by Ken Goldstein, a consultant to the George W. Bush Presidential Exploratory Committee, and Mark Mellman, "a leading political strategist for the Democratic Party."

44. American Jewish Committee, press release dated May 13, 1999, and detailed unpublished survey results provided to the author by the AJC. The poll was

conducted by Market Facts, Inc., and the margin of error for the sample as a whole is plus or minus 3 percentage points.

45. Quoted from the description provided by the Presidents Conference to the *American Jewish Year Book, 1998* (New York: American Jewish Committee, 1998), 517.

46. Quoted by Jane Perlez, "Barak Pins Hopes for Mideast Peace on Next 15 Months," *New York Times,* July 19, 1999.

47. *Near East Report,* July 26, 1999, 61.

4

Israel and the Arab States

The Long Road to Normalization

Malik Mufti

Israelis have sometimes been heard to express the hope that their country could become a "normal" state like all others. In this chapter I will trace the process of Israel's normalization, at least in its relations with neighboring Arab states. That it has taken fifty years is not surprising. After all, no subsystem can easily accommodate the creation in its midst of an entirely new entity, with all the human displacement and suffering necessarily entailed. Israel and its neighbors fought five wars before they reached such an accommodation. During the first phase of their interaction, until 1967, the Arab states came to learn that they could not achieve their most basic strategic objectives as long as Israel continued to feel insecure. During the second phase, from 1967 to 1994, Israel in turn came to appreciate the necessity of taking into account its neighbors' interests. As a result, only within the last few years has open reciprocity become possible.

Phase I: 1918–1967

The primary concern of the Arab states confronting Israel during this period—even in the wars of 1948, 1956, and 1967—was not the existence or annihilation of Israel. Instead, from their perspective the question of Israel remained throughout subordinate to their inter-Arab ambitions and rivalries. The problem, however, was that the primarily inter-Arab objectives of the claimants to pan-Arab hegemony—first the Hashemites, then Nasser—often came into conflict with Israel's own self-perceived vital security interests. It was this early incompatibility of interests, coupled with a recurrent Arab underestimation of Zionist military capabilities, that explains Arab-Israeli warfare during this period.

1918–1951

The story of the post–World War I conflict in Palestine is primarily the story of two audacious revisionist projects. For the Zionists the goal was the establishment of a new Jewish state; for the Hashemites it was leadership of a unified state comprising the eastern half of the Arab world. For a brief moment, it seemed conceivable that the two projects could be reconciled. Prince Faisal, son of the Hashemite patriarch Sharif Hussein of Mecca, assured the Jewish-American leader Felix Frankfurter in a letter of March 3, 1919, that "we will wish the Jews a most hearty welcome home," adding, "We are working together for a reformed and revived Near East, and our two movements complete one another. The Jewish movement is national and not imperialist. Our movement is national and not imperialist, and there is room in [Greater] Syria for us both. Indeed I think that neither can be a real success without the other."[1]

A shared outlook characterized by pragmatism fostered such contacts. The Zionists had a realistic assessment of what was possible in the aftermath of World War I. As a result, they started out with territorial demands that fell well short of their actual aspirations. For their part, the Hashemites were keenly aware of the capabilities of their interlocutors. As King Hussein of Jordan wrote about his grandfather Abdallah: "He had perceived the Zionist iceberg and its dimensions, while others had seen only its tip. . . . His tactics and strategy were therefore attuned to circumventing and minimizing the possible consequences of a head-on collision."[2] Abdallah's estimation of the balance of power led him to urge Arab acceptance of various proposals to partition Palestine, beginning with the 1937 Peel Commission recommendations, through the British White Paper of 1939, and ending with the 1947 United Nations partition plan. Each time the Palestinian leadership refused, putting nationalist emotion before realistic calculation.

Other Arab leaders could read the handwriting on the wall as well. Egypt's prime minister, Ismail Sidqi, for example, agreed to partition following secret contacts with Zionist emissaries in 1946, although the initiative collapsed with his government shortly thereafter.[3] And Syria's president, Shukri Quwwatli, contacted the Jordanians as hostilities were getting under way in 1948 to warn against military intervention in Palestine.[4] Why then did the Arab states go ahead and attack in 1948, and why did peace prove elusive even after Israel secured its existence on the battlefield?

The answer is that the minimal requirements of the various protagonists remained irreconcilable in 1948. The Zionists sought an independent state in as much of Palestine as possible, including Jerusalem. King Abdallah, eager to press his claim to pan-Arab leadership, felt constrained by public opinion from a formal recognition of Jewish sovereignty. Moreover, he too coveted the holy city. That is why serious fighting between Jordanian and Israeli forces occurred only in the Jerusalem area, on which no agreement could be reached. "Everywhere else," as Avi Shlaim wrote, Abdallah's troops "respected the partition borders and made no attempt to seize Jewish territory."[5] Egypt's King Faruq, for his part, ordered his army to attack against the advice of his top officers precisely in order to prevent Abdallah from expanding his Hashemite domain and thus tilting the Arab balance of power in his favor.[6] A similar consideration motivated the Syrians.

The two main reasons for the interstate aspect of the 1948 war, then, were the inability of the Zionists and the Hashemites to agree either on the extent of sovereignty the new Jewish entity would enjoy or on the precise delineation of their common boundary, particularly around Jerusalem, and the unwillingness of Egypt and Syria to stand aside and watch the Hashemites absorb territories allocated to the Arabs by the UN partition plan. Aborting the Jewish state altogether was not considered a feasible option by Jordanian, Egyptian, and Syrian military planners, and—public rhetoric notwithstanding—does not seem to have figured prominently in their calculations.

As a result of the fighting that ensued, the Zionists were able to capture far more territory than had been allocated to them by the United Nations. Once the outcome on the battlefield became clear, however, why did the warring parties not then conclude a permanent settlement? As our understanding of this period improves—in large part owing to new research by revisionist Israeli scholars—it is becoming clear that the Arab states, at least, did in fact express interest in such a settlement.

Twice before the war even ended, in September and November 1948, King Faruq's envoy Kamal Riad approached the Israelis and offered a separate peace treaty in return for the transfer to Egypt of territories in southern Palestine allocated to the Arabs by the UN partition plan. In August 1949, at the Lausanne conference, the Egyptians came forward with a slightly modified suggestion: putting the entire Negev under independent Palestinian sovereignty as a first step toward peaceful Egyptian-Israeli relations. Israel rejected these proposals, seeing no reason to give up lands it had conquered on the battlefield at considerable human cost.[7]

In Syria, Colonel Husni Zaim, who seized power on March 30, 1949, with CIA assistance after promising the Americans he would "do something constructive" about the Arab-Israeli problem,[8] offered to meet Israeli Prime Minister David Ben-Gurion face to face in order to conclude a full peace treaty. He even offered to settle in Syria fully half of the 600,000 Palestinians who had been made refugees in 1948, asking in return for sovereignty over half of the Sea of Galilee. Again the Israelis refused, and the initiative came to an end with Zaim's overthrow and execution in August 1949.[9]

But it was the Jordanian Hashemites who believed they had the most to gain from pacifying their border with Israel. Beginning in 1921, Abdallah had repeatedly suggested to the Zionists that their mutual interests would be served if the latter were to deploy their local power and international influence on behalf of his efforts to create the unified pan-Arab state promised to his family by Britain during World War I. Having more or less realized his territorial objectives in Palestine after 1948, and resigned to the full independence of the new Jewish state, he now hoped to make peace with Israel both in order to neutralize it as a threat and in order to enlist its backing for his projected pan-Arab drive first northward into Syria, then ultimately southward into the Hijaz.[10]

But having just experienced a bloody encounter with an Arab coalition in which Abdallah's troops proved the most formidable component, Israel's leaders were not inclined to abet his ambitions. After 1948, they consistently opposed Hashemite initiatives such as the Greater Syria Plan, an opposition that arose from (1) a strategic calculation that Arab division was preferable to consolidation under Hashemite (or any other) leadership, since such a consolidation would in itself increase the potential threat to Israel, and (2) wariness about the expansion of British regional power — allied to the Hashemites but perceived as hostile by the Israelis.

Moreover, the Israelis grew reluctant to reach a definitive bilateral settlement with Abdallah even on the narrower question of Palestine.[11] In the course of secret negotiations during 1949 and 1950, Abdallah requested the formal partitioning of Jerusalem as well as a corridor running from Hebron to Gaza's Mediterranean coast. Ben-Gurion not only rejected once again, as he had with Egypt and Syria, any notion of giving up hard-won territory, but he and his colleagues even considered sponsoring an autonomous Palestinian entity in the West Bank in order to thwart Hashemite expansionism.[12] For his part, Abdallah did not feel he had received sufficient concessions or guarantees to enable him to swing his own government and public opinion behind a formal accord with Israel. A limited five-year nonaggression pact, which got as far as being initialed by the two sides in mid-February 1950, therefore never saw the light of day.[13]

As negotiations stalled, Abdallah went ahead and finalized the annexation of the West Bank on April 24, 1950.

By the end of the year, Ben-Gurion and some of his colleagues began questioning the desirability of peace with Jordan altogether: "Various proposals were floated by [Moshe] Dayan for the capture of the Gaza Strip, Mount Hermon, and the West Bank. . . . Dayan wanted Israel to threaten the Arabs and to constantly escalate the level of violence so as to demonstrate her superiority and to create the conditions for territorial expansion."[14] In June 1951, Jordan protested to the United Nations about Israeli efforts to divert Jordan River waters unilaterally, reflecting the deterioration in bilateral relations that marked the last months of Abdallah's rule before his assassination by a Palestinian extremist on July 20, 1951.

This overview suggests that Jordan, Egypt, and Syria each understood the realpolitik imperative of coming to some kind of accommodation with Zionism. Egypt and Syria attacked the new Jewish state not primarily for anti-Zionist reasons but because of their fears of Hashemite expansionism. After the 1948 war—in which, after all, they did not lose any of their own territory—and after their initial approaches to the Israelis were rebuffed, Egypt and Syria saw no need to go beyond the armistice agreements and were satisfied to enter a relationship of "no war, no peace" with their new neighbor. Jordan, by contrast—bound as it was to Israel by their shared involvement in the fate of the Palestinian Arabs and desirous of Israel's help in its other pan-Arab objectives—tried much harder to establish a cooperative relationship. But even Jordan had goals that conflicted with those of the Zionists, particularly on Jerusalem. In the end, all of Israel's neighbors operated in a normative context which obliged them to greet the creation of Israel and the displacement of the Palestinian Arabs with a hostile public response.

Not surprisingly, such an attitude did not encourage Israel to make territorial concessions to Egypt or Syria after the 1948 war. Nor did it induce a willingness to sanction Hashemite expansionism, into either Palestine or Syria. Instead, Israel felt obliged to prepare for a possible "second round" by contemplating further territorial acquisitions. An additional factor promoting Israeli insecurity arose with the proposal made by Western powers in October 1951 to create a "Middle East Defense Command." Because it quickly became apparent that Israel's participation in this alliance was not deemed essential, "Israel's government was relieved to see the proposal collapse as a result of its rejection by Egypt."[15] The prospect of being frozen out of a pro-Western regional military alliance amplified Israel's tendency to view its relationship with the Arab states as a zero-sum game and rendered it even less amenable to concessions.

1952–1967

After King Abdallah's assassination, the focus of Arab interaction with Israel shifted to Egypt, where a military coup in 1952 brought a dynamic new regime to power. Like the Hashemites, Colonel Jamal Abd al-Nasser had revisionist ambitions for hegemony in the Arab world. Unlike the Hashemites, he was able to deploy Egypt's considerable geostrategic resources in order to realize—at least for a time—the objectives of gaining Arab leadership, winning American backing, and neutralizing Israel.

It is noteworthy that Prime Minister Ben-Gurion publicly welcomed the 1952 coup and extended an offer of peace to the new leadership, perhaps calculating that since there were no direct territorial conflicts of interest between the two states, a modus vivendi could be arrived at which would remove Egypt from the array of enemies confronting Israel. For their part, the new Egyptian leaders, who had maintained good contacts with American intelligence officials even before the coup and who were now eager for American support, made conciliatory noises as well. General Naguib, for example, the figurehead of the new regime during its early days, wrote to President Harry Truman to assure him of Egypt's readiness to make peace with Israel.[16] Secret negotiations did in fact ensue, including discussions about Israeli purchases of Egyptian cotton and the possibility of bringing Jewish influence to bear on effecting Britain's withdrawal from its bases in Egypt. Nevertheless, the Egyptians in 1953 made it clear to their Israeli interlocutors that there would be no formal settlement just yet and that Egypt preferred to maintain the status quo of "no war, no peace."

Why? Because Egypt did not believe that it had much to gain from a peace accord—Israel showed no inclination to make territorial concessions, and Nasser felt confident that he could deter any further expansionism on its part—and because it had something to lose: Arab public opinion, an important element in Egypt's regional ambitions. In retrospect, this turned out to be an error of the first order. Israel proved unwilling to tolerate a status quo characterized by no war and no peace in which its main potential protagonist maintained a hostile stance while growing stronger day by day. Nasser's mistake was to underestimate the severity of the divergence between his objectives and those of the Israelis.

Nasser had three primary foreign policy goals: to use radical pan-Arab and anticolonialist ideology in order to seize the mantle of Arab leadership from the Hashemites; thereby to evict Britain from the Middle East and to win the geopolitical and financial backing of the United States; and in the meantime to avoid a military confrontation with Israel—or as the phrase of the day went, to put Israel "in the icebox." Israel, for its part, stung by the casualties it suffered in 1948 and suspicious of the Arabs' unwillingness to conclude peace on its terms after the war, adopted as its fundamental objective the neutralization of all potential threats to its security. That meant preventing the neighboring Arab states from getting too powerful; preventing them from developing too close relations with the United States, the new global and regional hegemon; and contemplating further territorial expansion in pursuit of strategic buffer zones.

It is evident that these two sets of objectives were incompatible. Once Nasser rebuffed Ben-Gurion's early approaches, therefore, the result was a steadily escalating level of tension between 1953 and 1956, driven primarily by Israeli insecurity and further exacerbated by Arab border infiltrations. At first, this tension manifested itself along Israel's other frontiers. An Israeli raid on the Jordanian village of Qibya on October 14, 1953, killed fifty-three civilians in the most serious outbreak of violence along that border since 1948. Five months later, gunmen killed eleven Israeli civilians near Beersheba and provoked another Israeli raid, this time on the town of Nahhalin, that claimed nine lives. Similar incidents began breaking out along the Syrian border, mainly connected with Israel's water diversion efforts. Those efforts were brought to a halt in late October 1953 following a temporary suspension of American aid to Israel. A subsequent announcement in early 1954 that the United States would provide a package of military and economic aid to Iraq in preparation for what would become the Baghdad Pact aroused further concern in Israel about American cooperation with its Arab foes.

By mid-1954, the deepening American relationship with both Egypt and Iraq—and the consequent prospect of a regional military alliance that would exclude Israel—prompted some Israeli leaders to consider more drastic action. In a recent study of this period, Benny Morris wrote that "from some point in 1954, the retaliatory strikes were also designed ... at least as seen by the new IDF [Israel Defense Force] CGS [Chief of the General Staff], Dayan ... to help prod this or that Arab state into a premature war with Israel. Dayan wanted war, ... a war in which Israel could realize such major strategic objectives as the conquest of the West Bank or Sinai, or the destruction of the Egyptian army."[17] Another major Israeli objective was to drive a wedge between the Arabs and the United States. Saboteurs were accordingly dispatched to Egypt to bomb American targets in the hope that Arab nationalists would be blamed, but they were captured and exposed in July 1954. Another fiasco occurred in September when the Israeli ship *Bat-Galim* tried to assert its right to sail through the Suez Canal in order to force Egypt either to acknowledge that right or violate international law. But the Egyptian authorities impounded the ship, and the Western governments rebuked Israel for trying to provoke a crisis. The failure of Israel's wedge strategy became evident on November 6, 1954, when Washington and Cairo signed an economic assistance agreement.

Eventually the Israelis escalated to a more effective tactic, destroying the Egyptian army garrison in Gaza on February 28, 1955. That raid, the first major engagement between the two countries since 1948, had two effects: It induced Egypt to stop trying to suppress infiltrations into Israel from its territory, and it led it to seek new arms supplies abroad. When Washington—anxious to preserve its neutrality—rebuffed his request, Nasser turned to the Soviets and acquired large quantities of tanks and planes in what came to be known as the Czech arms deal of September 1955. On October 23, 1955, Ben-Gurion instructed Moshe Dayan to prepare for war with Egypt.[18] Two additional Israeli raids against Egypt in the fall were followed by a major attack in the Tiberias region that killed fifty-six Syrians on December 11. Morris discounts the argument that those raids were simply retaliation for guerrilla infiltrations: "Ben-Gurion and Dayan had failed to provoke war with Egypt during October-November (Kuntilla and the Sabha); perhaps Egypt could be drawn by an attack on its ally, Syria? This was the thinking behind the [Tiberias] strike.... According to IDF documentation, [the attack] 'had not been preceded by any specific provocation by the Syrians.'"[19]

While all this was going on, both Israel and Egypt, anxious to remain on Washington's good side, maintained the pretense of seeking peace. Two American mediation initiatives launched in May and November 1955, code-named Projects Alpha and Gamma, respectively, generated some contacts through shuttle diplomacy before ultimately foundering on differences over the Negev (Egypt wanted it; Israel refused to give up any land) and Palestinian refugee repatriation (Egypt for, Israel against).[20] In fact neither side was serious. This insincerity is illustrated by the fact that in January 1955, just days after agreeing to meet General Yigael Yadin in Cairo, Nasser aborted the negotiations by sanctioning the execution of two of the captured Israeli saboteurs. For his part, Ben-Gurion invited Nasser to peace talks on November 3, 1955, even as his troops were preparing to wipe out the Egyptian garrison at Sabha the following day.

Still, Nasser kept up the charade as late as 1956, writing in a letter to

President Dwight Eisenhower on February 6 that "in the interest of peace, Egypt recognizes the desirability of seeking to eliminate the tensions between the Arab states and Israel."[21] But the Israelis had had enough. Acting in collusion with Britain and France, they attacked Egypt on October 30, 1956, and occupied the Sinai Peninsula. Although the war was a decisive military victory for Israel, it was an equally decisive political one for Nasser. The United States came out strongly against the tripartite attack and forced Britain and France to withdraw, spelling the end of their colonial presence in the Middle East. On February 20, 1957, Eisenhower announced that he would support UN sanctions against Israel unless it evacuated Sinai as well, and Israel promptly did so. Nasser's prestige in the Arab world soared as a result, leading among other things to the union with Syria in February 1958 and the overthrow of Iraq's Hashemite monarchy five months later.

Israel's retreat from Sinai ushered in a period of quiescence along its frontiers that would last until the early 1960s. Some analysts have interpreted this fact, along with Israel's remarkable inaction in the face of dramatic developments unfolding on the Arab stage, as a reflection of an enhanced sense of security arising from its easy triumph on the battlefield and from intensified American support.[22] It is true that Washington sought to reassure Israel during this period, both verbally and through additional sales of military equipment, including twenty-eight Sikorsky combat helicopters in 1958 and $10 million of radar equipment in 1960. However, a closer look at the 1956–63 period cannot sustain the argument that this was a good time from the perspective of Israel's security interests.

First, far from being checked, Nasser's regional influence rose to unprecedented heights. Not only did Syria's leaders put their country—and armed forces—under his direct rule, his partisans threatened to do the same in Iraq, Jordan, and Lebanon. Second, the strategy of driving a wedge between Egypt and the United States was in shambles, with the two drawing closer than ever in the wake of the 1958 Iraqi coup. Fearful of communist takeovers in both Iraq and Syria, American officials became convinced that the only effective alternative was Nasser's brand of radical pan-Arabism. Third, despite some token gestures, Washington remained unresponsive to Israel's attempts at forging closer bilateral ties. In October 1957, for example, a request from Ben-Gurion for direct and substantial American military aid, as well as a formal security guarantee, fell on deaf ears.[23]

And fourth, Washington explicitly demanded that Israel not interfere in the efforts to counter Arab communism with Arab nationalism. During the 1957 Syrian crisis, for example, as Washington pondered whether Turkish, Hashemite, or Egyptian intervention would prove most effective in thwarting a leftist takeover, the one party barred from playing a role was Israel. Ben-Gurion reluctantly complied, but not without complaining that it was now impossible "to distinguish between Syria and Russia" and asking what the United States government "would do if Israel is attacked by Russia through Syria."[24] Since Washington continued to view Israel as a liability in its anti-Soviet efforts, however, the Israelis were not allowed to intervene in Syria in 1957, just as they were not allowed to intervene when Egypt absorbed that country into the United Arab Republic (UAR) in February 1958, or after the Iraqi coup reshuffled the regional balance of power yet again.

Israel's growing frustration was articulated in another letter from Ben-Gurion to Eisenhower on July 24, 1958, in which he argued that moderate Arab regimes such as those of Jordan, Lebanon, and Saudi Arabia were doomed; that Nasser was now paramount in the Arab world; that behind him stood the Soviet Union; and that the United States should therefore switch its support to a non-Arab alliance comprising Israel, Turkey, Iran, Ethiopia, and Sudan so that it could "stand up steadfastly against Soviet expansion through Nasser."[25] These far-fetched arguments reflected a genuine dilemma: Israel's security imperative of enlisting American support against an increasingly militant Arab world conflicted with the American security imperative of mobilizing Arab allies against communist encroachments.

Washington's attitude toward Israel during this period was summed up in NSC 5820/1, a National Security Council report titled "U.S. Policy toward the Near East," dated November 4, 1958.[26] Its recommendations included continuing to limit arms shipments to Israel, restraining it from exercising its right to use the Suez Canal, and opposing—even to the extent of unilateral military intervention—attempts by any party to initiate an armed conflict. The report concluded, "while U.S. policy embraces the preservation of the State of Israel in its essentials, we believe that Israel's continued existence as a sovereign state depends on its willingness to become a finite and accepted part of the Near East nation-state system."[27] The use of the word *finite* clearly indicates that the recommendation to defend the status quo was directed at least in part against Israeli revisionism.

In short, Israel's low profile during the 1956–63 period was not the outcome of its own security calculations—which mandated a far more activist stance—but was instead imposed upon it by American-Egyptian cooperation against communism in Syria and Iraq. As a result, Israel found itself well and truly in the "icebox."

This situation began to change only in the early 1960s, following a series of developments that led Washington to reassess its relationship with Nasser.[28] First came the breakup of the UAR in 1961, greatly undermining Nasser's pan-Arab power and prestige. Then the emergence of Ba'thist regimes in both Syria and Iraq—radical pan-Arabs who proved even more adept at exterminating communists than Nasser—solved the American dilemma of how to promote anticommunist nationalism without promoting Egyptian revisionism. Finally, Nasser's ill-advised intervention in the Yemeni civil war in 1962 brought him into armed conflict with Saudi Arabia and thereby impinged upon one of Washington's most vital regional interests.

Those events transformed Nasser in American eyes from an indispensable asset into an increasingly dangerous liability. It was time to clip his wings. One way of doing so was to scale back economic assistance. Another was to build up counterweights; on August 19, 1962, accordingly, Israel was informed that President John Kennedy had finally approved its long-standing request to purchase Hawk antiaircraft missiles. Early in the following year, Kennedy told visiting foreign minister Golda Meir that the United States now viewed Israel as an ally.[29]

Nasser responded to the American-Israeli rapprochement by ending his feud with the Soviets and signing a military agreement with them in June 1963. Nevertheless, fully aware that Washington was still the dominant player on both the global and regional arenas, he remained anxious to preserve his prior understanding with it. When a new American ambassador presented his credentials in January 1964, for example, Nasser "expressed the hope that the UAR and the United States could keep the Israeli-Arab question 'in the icebox' while devoting themselves to the development of mutual interests."[30]

But this was no longer an option: Until 1963, the conflicting objectives of Egypt and Israel had failed to break out into open conflict because of a combination of Nasser's ability to make himself useful to the United States and American restraint on Israel. When Nasser's usefulness dwindled so did American restraint, and the contradiction between Israeli and Egyptian interests could no longer be contained. All that remained was for Nasser to give the Israelis an excuse to annihilate him.

Sensing the sea change under way, the Israelis vigorously resumed their wedge strategy and began calling in public and private for an American shift away from Egypt and toward Israel. According to the minutes of a conversation with a visiting American delegation in February 1965: "The Prime Minister [Levi Eshkol], speaking with unusual fervor, said the menace from Nasser was growing from month to month. Egypt was piling up huge stocks of arms. 'I dare to ask the United States to do away with this policy. I declare, and it is a solemn declaration, a guaranteed one, that Israel will not attack anyone.' So, the U.S. should change its arms policy and become a direct supplier to Israel."[31] Sure enough, later that year the United States agreed to sell Israel 210 M-48 tanks worth $34 million. In May 1966, another package involving the sale of tactical aircraft worth $72 million was announced.

Bolstered by this support and further emboldened by its rapidly developing nuclear capability, Israel stepped out of the icebox to pursue its interests actively once again. These interests had not changed since the early 1950s: neutralizing potential threats by isolating neighboring Arab countries from the United States, suppressing their military power, and revising the status quo to Israel's benefit.

Israel began ratcheting up the pressure as early as 1963, when it announced the resumption of unilateral efforts to divert Jordan River waters. And when Egypt, Syria, and Iraq announced their intention to establish a "Tripartite Federation" in April 1963—unleashing another wave of pan-Arab enthusiasm that destabilized Jordan as well—the Israeli response was far more robust than it had been in 1958. According to Uriel Dann, "And so the Israeli general staff devised Plan Granite for the occupation of the West Bank. A military commander there received his contingency appointment as military governor ... and rudiments of an administration began to be thought out. The American government, cognizant of what was going on, tried to calm Israeli fears and, more especially, to dissuade Israel from taking 'sudden action' if Hussein should disappear."[32] In the event, war was averted for the time being when the federation plan fell apart and Nasser and the Ba'thists of Syria and Iraq resumed their feuding.

But the underlying dynamic remained clear. Each Arab state responded to the resurgence of Israeli assertiveness in its own way. Syria—for reasons that remain unclear but may have had to do with domestic instability and the desire of its leaders to gain legitimacy and divert attention away from troubles at home[33]—adopted a hard-line stance, sponsoring Palestinian raids into Israel and clamoring for an all-out military confrontation. Such a stance provoked increasingly violent retaliatory attacks.

Jordan took the opposite tack, seeking to defuse the growing threat by engaging Israel in negotiations and attempting to suppress Syrian-sponsored infiltrations. King Hussein met secretly with Israeli officials for the first time in September 1964, and further contacts followed. Although agreements were reached on limited issues such as water-sharing, these talks did not lead to a more comprehensive understanding.[34] Instead, Israel applied its military retaliation policy to Jordan as well, initiating a series of raids in May 1965 that culminated on November 13, 1966, with the most massive attack on Jordan in a decade. King Hussein became convinced that Israel was now bent on provoking war in order to capture East Jerusalem and the entire West Bank. President Johnson tried to reassure him in a letter which reveals American perceptions of the situation at this critical time:

> Ambassador Burns has informed me of Your Majesty's concern that Israel's policies have changed and that Israel now intends to occupy territory on the West Bank of the Jordan River. While I can understand the reasons for this concern, we have good reason to believe it highly unlikely that the events you fear will in fact occur. In this connection my government's opposition to the use of force to alter armistice lines or borders in the Near East has been made unmistakably clear to all parties concerned. The strong private representations we have made in Israel as well as our forthright public statements make clear that should Israel adopt the policies you fear, it would have the greatest consequences. There is no doubt in my mind that our position is fully understood and appreciated by the Israelis.[35]

Egypt, too, at first sought to continue its policy of avoiding conflict with Israel, initiating a series of Arab summit meetings in 1964 precisely with that purpose in mind. Nasser also proposed the creation of a joint Arab military command under Egyptian leadership, hoping thereby to restrain Syria and prevent it from dragging Egypt into a disastrous war. At least as late as mid-1965, his ambassador in Washington was still urging the United States to keep Israel in the icebox.[36] But within two years this policy changed: Weakened domestically by economic hardship and popular discontent, reeling from pan-Arab setbacks in Yemen and elsewhere, alarmed by the American tilt toward Israel, and taunted by rival Arab leaders for his failure to confront Israel's growing militancy, Nasser tried to reverse his fortunes through a risky gamble. Responding to reports of an imminent Israeli attack on Syria, he marched some troops into Sinai on May 14; two days later, he evicted the UN buffer force that had policed the Egyptian-Israeli border since the end of the Suez war; and on May 22, he closed the Gulf of Tiran to Israeli shipping, thereby providing Israel with a casus belli.

A full explanation of these events lies beyond the scope of this chapter, but it seems that Nasser—with one-third of his army still bogged down in Yemen—was hoping to score a propaganda victory without actually going to war. He apparently calculated that the Americans would restrain Israel as they had in 1956 and that he would thereby emerge as a hero to the Egyptian and Arab masses once again. This interpretation is supported by Yitzhak Rabin, chief-of-staff of the Israeli armed forces at the time, who told *Le Monde* in 1968, "I do not believe that Nasser wanted war. The two divisions he sent into Sinai on May 14 would not have been enough to unleash an offensive against Israel. He knew it, and we knew it." It is also supported by Menachem Begin, who said in a speech in 1982, "In June 1967 we again had a choice. The Egyptian Army concentrations in the Sinai approaches do not prove that Nasser was really about to attack us. We must be honest with ourselves. We decided to attack him."[37]

In any case, on May 30, King Hussein arrived in Cairo and signed a defense agreement that put his armed forces under Egyptian command. Aware that he faced accusations of treachery and a possible uprising at home if he remained aloof, and convinced that Israel would find an excuse to occupy the West Bank anyhow, Hussein calculated that he had no option but to participate in a war he knew perfectly well would end in defeat. By early June, after the creation of a war cabinet in Israel, Nasser too had come to realize the magnitude of the impending disaster. In desperation he called on the United States to mediate, dispatching his vice president to Washington on June 4. But it was too late. The next day Israel launched the campaign that would destroy the armed forces of Egypt, Jordan, and Syria, bring an end to Nasser's ambitions, and lead to the occupation of the Sinai, West Bank, and Golan Heights.

Although I have argued that neither the Hashemite nor the Nasserist revisionist projects necessarily entailed a challenge to Israel's existence, the incompatible objectives of the two sides led relentlessly to conflict. Ultimately, neither Nasser nor the Hashemites were willing to recognize Israel publicly for fear of undermining their bids for pan-Arab leadership. Instead, they were content with a state of "no war, no peace." Israel, for its part, could not accept such an approach so long as the Arabs retained the potential to pose a threat. It felt compelled, therefore, to weaken its neighbors by driving a wedge between them and the United States, by keeping them divided against each other, and by defeating them on the battlefield in order to destroy their military capabilities as well as to gain strategically valuable territories. The consequences were Israeli opposition to both Hashemite and Nasserist pan-Arabism; the failure of American attempts to forge a regional anti-Soviet alliance; and two wars to expand Israel's borders, one unsuccessful (1956) but the other (1967) very much so.

Could it have gone differently? This is a central issue of contention between Israel's revisionist "new" historians and their critics. The more judicious and fair-minded of those critics no longer challenge the major empirical findings of the new historians. Rather, they object to conclusions such as the one that Israel after 1948 "was more intransigent than the Arab states and that she consequently bears a larger share of the responsibility for the political deadlock that followed the formal ending of hostilities."[38] Itamar Rabinovich, for example, essentially recapitulates the historical narrative presented by Avi Shlaim and other new historians while criticizing their "political and moralistic" as well as "emotional" outlooks.[39]

Leaving morality to the ethicists, one is left with the conclusion that Israel's leaders acted in a manner consistent with their interests and capabilities throughout the period under review. The same must be said of the Hashemites: it is hard to see what else either Abdallah (who tried to make peace after 1948) or Hussein (who had to wage war in 1967) could have done given their circumstances. Nasser, however, merits a different assessment. Neither the aggressive fanatic portrayed by his enemies nor the idealistic nationalist imagined by his admirers, he was merely a less adept practitioner of realpolitik. Even if it were granted that popular sentiment would not have allowed him to neutralize Israeli hostility by accepting Ben-Gurion's 1952 peace offer, there is still no excuse for the momentous blunder of 1967. He walked right into the trap set for him and in doing so radically altered the relationship between the Arab states and Israel, ushering in a new era in which the initiative lay squarely with the latter.

Phase II: 1967–1994

Despite their differences, each of the neighboring Arab states before 1967 approached Israel primarily from the perspective of their inter-Arab interests. Israel, for its part, had been anxiously preparing for what it viewed as an inevitable "second round" in order to attain a tolerable level of military, territorial, and diplomatic security. After 1967 the tables were turned. By occupying parts of their territories, Israel forced itself to the top of its neighbors' policy agendas. For Jordan and Egypt—although to a lesser extent for Syria—the recovery of those territories now became an urgent priority. Having finally achieved all of its primary goals, by contrast, Israel felt that it could now afford the luxury of resting on its laurels and letting time pass by. The years between 1967 and 1994 can therefore be understood as a period in which the Arab states pursued various stratagems aimed at inducing Israel to "undo the effects of 1967"—in other words, to return the occupied territories.

1967–1979

Of Israel's three primary Arab protagonists, Syria emerged from the 1967 war with the least sense of urgency. While the loss of the Golan Heights obviously constituted a strategic defeat as well as a political embarrassment, it did not create a new status quo that the Syrian leadership found intolerable. Instead of displaying a willingness to make concessions in pursuit of a settlement with Israel—which it did not believe would be forthcoming anyway—Damascus therefore preferred to rebuild its armed forces while opposing peace initiatives involving the other Arab states.

For Jordan, the consequences of the war were more dire. The loss of the West Bank generated another massive influx of disgruntled refugees; it detached the economically richest part of the country and deprived King Hussein of control over Jerusalem's Muslim holy sites; and more generally it constituted a severe setback to the Hashemite pan-Arab project. His primary objective after 1967 was therefore to regain the West Bank, both for its own sake and in order to satisfy the aspirations of his displaced Palestinian subjects. Since Jordan had no military option, it was clear that a negotiated settlement would have to be pursued; and since each passing year weakened Hussein's hold on the allegiance of the Palestinians under occupation, that settlement needed to come sooner rather than later.

Egypt shared Jordan's sense of urgency but believed it had a wider range of options. The loss of Sinai brought Israeli forces to the edge of Egypt's populated heartland; it deprived Egypt of the revenues generated by the peninsula's oil fields as well as tolls from the Suez Canal, now closed to shipping; it forced Egypt to rebuild its shattered armed forces at a time of economic difficulty; and it dealt a crushing blow to the regime's prestige at home and abroad. Nasser's overriding objective therefore became to recover Sinai. Convinced that Israel's demand for unconditional peace talks was a ploy to humiliate him and that it had no intention of giving him a deal that would salvage his reputation, he rejected negotiations until he had a stronger hand to play. Unlike the Syrians, he felt a keen sense of urgency about reversing the outcome of the 1967 war; unlike the Jordanians, he still hoped to augment his diplomacy with military force.

On the other side, Israelis emerged from the war virtually unanimous in the conviction that there would be no return to pre-1967 borders: Jerusalem would be retained in its entirety, and there would need to be additional border adjustments to take into account security concerns. When the American secretary of state, Dean Rusk, reminded Israel's foreign minister, Abba Eban, that Israel had always denied such territorial ambitions, Eban replied, "We have changed our minds."[40] But there was no such consensus about what to do with the rest of the occupied land and its Arab population. Some advocated a joint condominium over the West Bank in which the Israelis would control security while the Jordanians would oversee local administration and police the populace; others suggested creating an autonomous Palestinian entity; and still others called for outright annexation. Since King Hussein found even the first of these options unacceptable, and since Nasser as yet showed no inclination to yield, Israel chose to avoid a divisive internal debate by putting off indefinitely any decision on the ultimate disposition of the occupied territories.

It was in this context that Nasser launched his "war of attrition" in March 1969, hoping that a campaign of artillery bombardments and commando raids would produce a steady trickle of Israeli casualties, thereby eroding Israel's triumphalist mood and forcing it into a more accommodating stance. Not only did this strategy fail to produce the desired outcome, Nasser's increasing reliance on Soviet support against devastating counterattacks drove Washington to intensify its backing for Israel and thus further strengthened the latter's resolve. Defeated once again, Nasser called off his war of attrition on August 8, 1970, by accepting both an American-brokered cease-fire and the principle of negotiation with Israel on the basis of UN Resolution 242. He never recovered from this final humiliation, dying literally of a broken heart less than two months later.

King Hussein took advantage of the cover provided by Nasser and immediately accepted Resolution 242 as well, ushering in a period of improved relations with Israel. He also removed a major source of tension by cracking down in September 1970 on the Palestinian Liberation Organization (PLO), which had provoked Israeli retaliatory strikes with its cross-border infiltrations during the previous two years. Fearing that Nasser's and Hussein's acceptance of Resolution 242 heralded separate peace agreements, Syria invaded Jordan in an attempt to bolster the PLO. American and Israeli troop deployments, however, forced the Syrians to retreat after suffering considerable losses at Jordanian hands. Within a year, King Hussein had uprooted the PLO from his country entirely.

Despite such cooperation, the gap between King Hussein's minimal requirements and what Israel was prepared to concede remained unbridgeable. Israel's best offer—one articulation of which has come to be known as the Allon Plan—involved the annexation of parts of the West Bank (mostly around Jerusalem), control of a security belt along the Jordan River valley, and Jordanian administration over the remaining densely populated areas. King Hussein's counteroffer—summarized in his "United Arab Kingdom" plan of March 15, 1972—was for Israel to withdraw from all of the West Bank including East Jerusalem and for the two banks then to be united in a federation ruled by himself. Neither side could accept the other's proposal, and a stalemate ensued. The situation was tolerable for Israel but not for Jordan, which saw its hopes of regaining the West Bank slip away as the Israelis built up their settlements and the Palestinians grew increasingly radicalized.

In Egypt, meanwhile, Nasser's successor, Anwar Sadat, pursued his own diplomatic campaign aimed at undoing the effects of 1967. On February 15, 1971, he told UN mediator Gunnar Jarring that Egypt would sign a binding and final peace agreement with Israel if it withdrew from Sinai. Israel rebuffed this overture. On April 2, Sadat tried again, offering to reopen the Suez Canal in return for a partial Israeli withdrawal from Sinai as a first step toward a total withdrawal. Despite the fact that Defense Minister Moshe Dayan himself had made this proposal five months earlier, Israel again killed the initiative by insisting that the issue of a total withdrawal not be raised at that point.

In frustration, Sadat three months later declared 1971 a "year of decision" that would end either in real peace or in war. Concluding that he meant to resume the war of attrition, Israel responded with another military buildup. On November 22, 1971, the same day that the U.S. State Department announced the end of its mediation efforts, the Senate—citing Egyptian violations of the August 1970 cease-fire—voted to allocate $500 million in military aid to Israel. The year ended humiliatingly for Sadat: On December 31, his deadline was marked by news reports of an agreement by President Richard Nixon to provide Israel with a major shipment of Phantom jets and Skyhawk fighter-bombers. Violent student riots erupted in Cairo.

In July 1972, Sadat expelled all his Soviet military advisers in another effort to enlist Washington's mediation. Instead, the Americans reached the opposite conclusion: that only total support for Israel would force the

Arabs to turn away from Moscow and accept whatever settlement Israel offered. In February 1973, Sadat reached out to the Americans yet again, sending his national security adviser to Washington for talks. Secretary of State Henry Kissinger told him that the American government saw no point in another diplomatic initiative; if Egypt wanted peace, it would have to negotiate with the Israelis directly.

Backed by such strong support, the Israeli position hardened further. Dayan, declaring that there would be no peace settlement during the next fifteen years, advocated moves to incorporate parts of the occupied territories—not just around Jerusalem but also in Sinai. According to Nadav Safran, the idea was that if such an approach frightened the Arabs into negotiating on Israel's terms, that would be fine; if they continued to resist, then that would justify the creeping annexation of more land.[41]

Sadat's decision to wage war in 1973, then, was a desperate act aimed at accomplishing what his diplomatic campaign of the previous two years had failed to do—to force Israel and the United States to the negotiating table by jolting them out of their complacency. His war plan reflected this limited objective: crossing the Suez Canal and overwhelming Israel's fortifications; penetrating at most five or six miles into Sinai; then digging in and resisting counterattacks until—he hoped—the superpowers worked out a cease-fire. A critical element of the plan was for Syria to open a second front in the north and thereby divert part of Israel's forces. Since President Hafez Assad would not have gone along with Sadat's true objective—it would be achieved too quickly for Syria to make equivalent gains in the Golan Heights—the Egyptians deceived their allies by promising a far more ambitious attack forty miles into Sinai.[42] Once again, however, there is no adequate account of Syrian calculations. King Hussein, seeing no conceivable benefit in such an enterprise, remained aloof altogether.

In any case, Sadat's gamble paid off. Partly due to effective planning and partly to Israeli overconfidence, the Egyptians and Syrians scored impressive initial gains following their surprise attack on October 6, 1973. Alarmed by the scale of the fighting, as well as the level of Soviet military support for the Arabs, and concerned also by the international economic repercussions of the Organization of Petroleum Exporting Countries (OPEC) oil embargo, Henry Kissinger and other American officials responded in the manner Sadat had hoped for: preventing the Israelis from turning their successful counterattacks into a complete rout of the Egyptians and Syrians by pushing through UN cease-fire Resolution 338 on October 22.

Sadat's success in demonstrating the bankruptcy of the 1967–73 status quo led to Israeli and American reassessments. Since it was now clear that ignoring Egypt altogether was not a cost-free policy, the Israelis—particularly after the ascension of Yitzhak Rabin to the prime ministership in April 1974—reverted to their earlier strategy of trying to reach a separate peace with it. The Egyptians, for their part, understood that the realization of their primary objectives (the recovery of Sinai and the neutralization of the Israeli military threat) required a detachment from the more intractable Syrian-Israeli, Jordanian-Israeli, and Palestinian-Israeli disputes.

Ironically, therefore, Washington's resumption of its efforts to seek a comprehensive settlement brought it into conflict with both Israel and Egypt—hence their lukewarm response to Kissinger's desire to proceed simultaneously with negotiations on all fronts. In any case, Syria's own continuing reluctance to take any steps beyond a disengagement agreement with Israel in May 1974 shut down that track almost immediately. And although Jordan remained as eager as ever to recover the West Bank, Israel was unwilling to go beyond its Allon Plan offer, and King Hussein continued to find it unacceptable. As a result, Rabin rebuffed Kissinger's mediation efforts, telling him that there was no rush since "Hussein won't run away."[43] Sadat then put the nail in the coffin by going along, despite his assurances to Kissinger to the contrary, with the Arab summit meeting decision in October 1974 to recognize the PLO as the sole legitimate representative of the Palestinian people.

In this way Israel and Egypt cleared the path to their separate peace, which—after several ups and downs, including the election of Menachem Begin's more hard-line Likud government in May 1977, Sadat's trip to Jerusalem in November 1977, and the Camp David talks of September 1978—reached its conclusion with the signing of the Egyptian-Israeli peace treaty in Washington on March 26, 1979. It was the culmination of a process that began in 1952 with Nasser's rejection of Ben-Gurion's attempt to remove Egypt from the Arab-Israeli equation. That rejection initiated a hostile dynamic which did not end until the maximalist ambitions of both sides reached a dead end—Egypt's in 1967 and Israel's in 1973. Now, twenty-seven years later, the two states were back where they began, with one important difference: a formal treaty to minimize the danger that their inevitable regional rivalries would again explode into war.

1979–1994

Israel made peace with Egypt in order to strengthen its hand against its other Arab protagonists: "Rabin believed Syria to be fundamentally opposed to peace, by stages or otherwise, and therefore wanted to drive a wedge between it and Egypt and place himself in a favorable position to deal with it forcefully."[44] And Menachem Begin agreed to return Sinai only because he thought Egypt's neutralization would allow him to hold on to the rest of the lands conquered in 1967. He accordingly reaffirmed the annexation of East Jerusalem in August 1980 and effectively annexed the Golan Heights as well by extending Israeli law over it in December 1981.

There remained, however, the question of what to do with the bulk of the Palestinian territories. Were they to be annexed in toto as Israel's right wing suggested, or should the more densely populated areas be granted some form of autonomy, perhaps in association with Jordan, as most Labor party leaders seemed to prefer? Israel's indecision on this question rendered King Hussein's dilemma all the more acute: In order to realize his long-standing objectives—recovering the West Bank and neutralizing the threat posed to his country by the Arab-Israeli conflict—not only did he need to elicit from the Israelis a more forthcoming settlement than even the Labor party was willing to consider, now after Rabat he also had to maneuver around the PLO and its rival claim to Palestinian leadership.

Jordan's inability to break through this logjam and Egypt's Arab isolation left Syria as Israel's main protagonist during the half-decade following 1979. Assad understood the dangers confronting him. Sadat's defection deprived him of his main military ally and opened the door to peace settlements by Jordan and the PLO as well, threatening to leave Syria face-to-face with an increasingly daunting Israel. His fundamental objections therefore became (1) to avoid premature peace talks until Syria gained as strong a negotiating hand as possible; (2) to make sure that Jordan and the PLO did not defect as well in the meantime; and (3) to avoid a direct military confrontation with Israel. In pursuit of those objectives, Assad embarked on his twin policies of "strategic parity" (a major Soviet-sponsored arms build-up to provide a measure of deterrence against Israel) and the "eastern front" (alliances with Iraq, Jordan, Lebanon, and the PLO to balance Israel's enhanced power and to lock them into Syria's own diplomatic timetable).

Assad's worst fears were realized on June 6, 1982, with Israel's invasion of Lebanon. The outbreak of civil war there in 1975 had prompted both Syria and Israel to intervene almost immediately in order to prevent each other from dominating that strategically located country. By decade's end, however, Israel switched to a more offensive posture. Defense Minister Ariel Sharon conceived an ambitious plan aimed at (1) placing a friendly Maronite regime in power in Beirut, thereby (2) outflanking and further isolating Syria, and in the process (3) liquidating the PLO as a political rallying point for the Palestinians of the occupied territories[45] and (4) scuttling the new American comprehensive peace initiative launched by Secretary of State Alexander Haig on May 26, 1982. Israel's 1982 invasion therefore reflected the predominance of those Israelis who viewed Egypt's neutralization as an opportunity to halt the peace process vis-à-vis all its other Arab protagonists.

At first the offensive went well. Israeli troops entered Beirut on August 4, 1982, forcing the PLO forces to evacuate by month's end and inducing the Lebanese government to sign a peace treaty on May 4, 1983. But Assad refused to acknowledge defeat in Lebanon, spearheading a counteroffensive that entailed the assassination of Israel's satrap Bashir Gemayel on September 14, 1982; the U.S. Beirut embassy explosion that killed 63 people on April 18, 1983; military exchanges with American forces trying to prop up the Lebanese government, including the shooting down of two U.S. warplanes; the explosion that killed 241 U.S. Marines on October 23, 1983; and a series of suicide bombings against Israeli forces, the largest of which claimed 40 lives in Tyre on November 4, 1983. Assad's successful campaign forced the Americans to leave Lebanon in February 1984, the Lebanese government to annul its peace treaty with Israel in March 1984, and the Israelis to complete their withdrawal from Lebanon (except for a narrow border strip) in June 1985. Lebanon became a Syrian protectorate.

Israel's Lebanese adventure thus failed in its primary objectives at the cost of some 600 soldiers killed, tensions with the United States, worldwide condemnation because of the civilian casualties involved, and serious fissures within the Israeli body politic itself. Begin and Sharon could take some comfort from the easing of pressure for further negotiations with the Arabs: President Ronald Reagan's peace plan of September 1, 1982—which called for a freeze on Israeli settlement and Palestinian "self-government" in association with Jordan—gave way after the debacle in Beirut to an embittered, hands-off attitude. Without American backing, King Hussein's efforts to enlist the PLO in a joint peace initiative during the mid-1980s foundered as well. Despite the Likud's success in thwarting the peace process, however, the primary effect of the action in Lebanon was to highlight for many Israelis the limits of military power as a means of achieving external security.

A corollary effect—demonstrating the limits of a hard line for internal security—came in December 1987 with the outbreak of the *intifada*. This spontaneous outpouring of Palestinian anger convinced a growing number of Israelis that the post-1967 status quo was no longer viable and that negotiations with credible Arab interlocutors on the future of the occupied territories were now necessary. But it also led King Hussein to remove himself from that role on July 31, 1988, by severing Jordan's administrative ties to the West Bank. Since passions had finally boiled over, he sought to get out of the storm's path and to leave the responsibility of addressing popular aspirations to the PLO. If the PLO met Israel's conditions, Hussein hoped that Jordan would still have an important role to play in the ensuing settlement. If it did not, then the occupation would continue and the PLO's bankruptcy would become apparent to Palestinians everywhere.

In fact the PLO leadership responded almost immediately by voting on November 14, 1988, to accept UN Resolution 242. Yasser Arafat subsequently proclaimed his recognition of Israel "as a state in the region" and renounced terrorism. By year's end, an open dialogue between American and PLO officials was under way. Still, it would take one last shock to bring Israel and the PLO to the negotiating table, and Iraq's invasion of Kuwait in August 1990 provided it. It did so in three ways. First, it made the oil-rich Gulf states more dependent than ever on American protection and therefore induced them to lend their energetic backing to American-sponsored peace initiatives for the first time. Second, it led them to punish Arafat's support for Saddam Hussein by cutting funding to the PLO—a development that brought the organization to the brink of collapse. The PLO commander in Lebanon complained in August 1993 that the financial crisis had reduced his fighters to "beggars" and called on Arafat to resign, while Faisal Husseini told a crowd in Hebron, "We are facing a total national collapse of all our institutions."[46] Arafat was clearly going under by the end of 1993.

And third, the Kuwait War forced Israel to reassess its geopolitical situation. Iraq's defeat had neutralized a major threat and weakened the PLO, but it also shattered the crucial premise of Israel's indispensability to the United States. Israel's leaders had long argued—and since 1967 successfully—that Washington should rely on them to secure its interests in this oil-rich region. Now that those interests finally came under serious challenge, however, Israel proved a liability rather than an asset and was pushed reluctantly to the sidelines by an American administration anxious to preserve its Arab coalition. The sight of American and Arab troops fighting together evoked the long-feared prospect of exclusion from a U.S.-led regional alliance. This was a major factor in inducing Yitzhak Rabin and others to push forward with the process begun in 1979 of "normalizing" Israel's role in the Middle East.

After Labor won the elections of June 1992, accordingly, Rabin and his foreign minister, Shimon Peres, moved to exploit Arafat's desperate plight. Secret negotiations in Oslo led to a "Declaration of Principles" signed on the White House lawn on September 13, 1993, according to which the PLO would abandon armed struggle and Israel would begin withdrawing from Arab-inhabited areas in the West Bank and Gaza. Noting that key issues such as the ultimate extent of Israel's withdrawal, settlements, and East Jerusalem were left unresolved, many observers pointed out the magnitude of Arafat's capitulation. Thomas Friedman, for example, described Arafat's first public letter to Rabin as "a letter of surrender, a typewritten white flag, in which the PLO chairman renounces every political position on Israel that he held since the PLO's founding in 1964."[47] Abd al-Wahab Badrkhan agreed, calling Arafat "a leader with nothing left but his weakness to offer in return for being allowed to survive."[48] In the fall of 1993, Arafat was indeed a drowning man grasping at the straw Rabin offered him. And what a straw it was: In terms of the amount of land remaining under Arab control, the deal Arafat accepted was worse than all the previous ones rejected by Palestinian leaders from the 1937 Peel partition plan, through King Hussein's 1972 United Arab Kingdom proposal, and down to the 1979 Camp David framework.

The Declaration of Principles effectively brought the Palestinian-Israeli conflict to an end. All that remains is to determine what percentage of the occupied territories Israel will keep. It also finalized Israel's normalization in the region, allowing Jordan, for example, to conclude a peace treaty of its own on October 26, 1994. Syria remains aloof, but its long-dreaded isolation vis-à-vis Israel suggests that a negotiated settlement along that front as well is simply a matter of time.

It took Egypt twelve years and Jordan twenty-seven years to elicit peace agreements from the country that defeated them in 1967. If the magnitude of that defeat forced the Arab states to come to terms with Israel, Israel was gradually induced to reciprocate by four consecutive shocks between 1967 and 1994: Sadat's 1973 surprise attack, the 1982–85 Lebanon fiasco, the outbreak of the intifada in 1987, and the 1990–91 Kuwait war. Egypt's was the easiest path, involving a straightforward exchange of land for peace that restored the status quo ante. Jordan, however, failed to regain the West Bank because what Israel was prepared to offer King Hussein could not accept. The ensuing delay on the one hand radicalized the Palestinians and consolidated the PLO's position as their representative, and on the other allowed Jewish settlements to proliferate in the occupied territories to such an extent that a return to pre-1967 lines is no longer conceivable.

It was a stroke of luck for the Israelis that circumstances created in Arafat an interlocutor willing to solve their intifada problem by accepting an updated version of the Allon Plan and willing to end their regional isolation by legitimizing them as peace partners. As a result, Jordan was able to sign a treaty that assured Israeli respect for its sovereignty, preserved the Hashemites' special status in Jerusalem, left open the possibility of an expanded Jordanian role in the Arab-controlled segments of the West Bank should the PLO yet falter, and enabled King Hussein and his successors to cooperate openly with Israel in their other regional endeavors.

Phase III: 1995–

By 1995 the Arab-Israeli relationship had in several respects come full circle. Egypt and Jordan, if not yet Syria, no longer have territorial disputes with Israel and so can resume the pursuit—interrupted in 1967—of their broader regional interests. Just as the "struggle for Syria" dominated the Arab agenda during the 1950s, for example, a similar "struggle for Iraq" appears to be unfolding today. Once again Arab interests diverge, with Jordan's efforts to shape the post-Saddam order—perhaps through a Hashemite restoration—running into Syrian and Egyptian opposition. And once again, those divergent Arab interests impinge on Israel in different ways, with Jordan as usual eager to enlist its support and Egypt equally characteristically trying to push it back into the icebox.

In other respects, however, there are important differences between the 1918–67 and post-1994 periods. First and foremost, Israel today feels strategically secure and territorially satisfied. This feeling allows it to view its relations with its Arab neighbors from a perspective other than a zero-sum game, so that it no longer automatically feels threatened if one of them gains in strength or if another draws closer to the United States. Joint interests and therefore joint endeavors have become possible.

Second, the PLO's recognition of Israel has legitimized peaceful interaction with it. Egypt will continue to compete with Israel for regional influence—in the process no doubt bringing back into play old cards such as Palestinian aspirations, water, and nuclear proliferation—but it will do so within the framework of its peace treaty, careful never to repeat Nasser's suicidal 1967 blunder. Syria, whether it concludes a formal peace with Israel or not, will always view it as a competitor and look to Egypt and others for support. While another war on this front cannot be ruled out altogether—particularly if Assad's successors prove a less capable lot—so long as Syria's rulers base their actions on a careful calculation of power balances, such an escalation seems unlikely. And Jordan, finally, has used its peace treaty to transform its relationship with Israel into a veritable alliance.[49] As bilateral security and economic cooperation proceed apace, it remains to be seen how far Israel will now be willing to support the Hashemites' inter-Arab aspirations. In light of Israel's much enhanced strategic position, certainly, most of the reasons for its earlier wariness about Hashemite pan-Arabism no longer hold.

Israel's normalization, then, formalizes the reality of its existence fifty years after the fact. It does not usher in an era of amity and integration, as some idealists seem to hope. Instead, as the Middle East prepares to split into yet another set of hostile axes, the only novelty is that Israel will increasingly become simply one player among others—no more and no less likely to provoke enmities or alliances than, say, the Arab states are vis-à-vis each other. To that extent, the Israeli yearning for normality is coming true.

Notes

1. Quoted in Walter Laqueur, ed., *The Israel-Arab Reader*, 21.
2. Hussein, "Introduction," in King Abdallah, *My Memoirs Completed: "Al-Takmilah,"* trans. Harold Glidden (London: Longman, 1978), xvi.
3. Avi Shlaim, *Collusion across the Jordan*, 76.
4. Abdallah, *My Memoirs Completed*, 21.
5. Shlaim, *Collusion*, 239.
6. See Michael Scott Doran, *The Politics of Pan-Arabism: Egyptian Foreign Policy, 1945–1948* (New York: Oxford University Press, forthcoming).
7. Ibid., 317, 346–47, 486–88.
8. Miles Copeland, *The Game of Nations*, 42.
9. Shlaim, *Collusion*, 428. See also the memoirs of Zaim's foreign minister, Amir Adil Arslan, *Mudhakkirat al-Amir Adil Arslan: al-Juz' al-Thani, 1946–1950*, 839–47.
10. See Yoav Gelber, *Jewish-Transjordanian Relations, 1921–48*, 16, 175–76, 219; Shlaim, *Collusion*, 81–82, 423–24; and Itamar Rabinovich, *The Road Not Taken*, 105, 118. For similar approaches by other Hashemite leaders, see Gelber, 13, and Shlaim, 90–91.
11. So much so that in the words of Avi Shlaim (*Collusion*, 453), in 1949 "all the pressure to move swiftly forwards towards comprehensive peace came from Jordan; it was Israel that was holding back."

12. Ibid., 509–10, 532; Rabinovich, *The Road Not Taken*, 60.

13. Shlaim, *Collusion*, 575.

14. Ibid., 590–91. See also 571 for Ben-Gurion's second thoughts on peace with Jordan.

15. Nadav Safran, *Israel: The Embattled Ally*, 343–44.

16. January 16, 1953, letter from President Truman to the chairman of the House Committee on Foreign Affairs. *United States Declassified Documents* (henceforth *USDD*) 1986 (Washington, D.C.: Carrollton Press, later Research Publications International, 1975), microfiche: 003506.

17. Benny Morris, *Israel's Border Wars, 1949–1956: Arab Infiltration, Israeli Retaliation, and the Countdown to the Suez War*, Oxford: Clarendon Press, 1993, 178–79.

18. Ibid., 279.

19. Ibid., 364–65.

20. Ibid. 286–88.

21. *USDD-1981*: 192C.

22. For example, Safran, *Israel: The Embattled Ally*, 368.

23. Douglas Little, "The Making of a Special Relationship," *International Journal of Middle East Studies* 25 (1993): 565.

24. August 1957 telegram from the U.S. embassy in Tel Aviv to the State Department. *USDD-1987*: 002092.

25. *USDD-1989*: 000518.

26. *USDD-1980*: 386B.

27. Ibid., 9.

28. For a more detailed look at American-Egyptian relations during this period, see Malik Mufti, "The United States and Nasserist Pan-Arabism."

29. Safran, *Israel: The Embattled Ally*, 374.

30. January 3, 1964, letter from Ambassador John S. Badeau in Cairo to President Lyndon Johnson. *USDD-1976*: 274C.

31. Memorandum of conversation between an American delegation led by W. Averell Harriman and top Israeli officials dated February 25, 1965. *USDD-1978*: 204C.

32. Uriel Dann, *King Hussein and the Challenge of Arab Radicalism*, 133.

33. For one such explanation, see Yaacov Bar-Siman-Tov, *Linkage Politics in the Middle East*.

34. Moshe Zak, "The Jordan-Israel Peace Treaty: Thirty Years of Clandestine Meetings," *Middle East Quarterly* 2, no. 1 (March 1995): 53–59.

35. November 23, 1966, letter from President Lyndon Johnson to King Hussein. *USDD-1984*: 001844.

36. Memorandum of conversation between Secretary of State McGeorge Bundy and Ambassador Mostafa Kamel dated July 15, 1965. *USDD-1984*: 000956.

37. Both quotes appear in Deborah J. Gerner, *One Land, Two Peoples*, 71.

38. Avi Shlaim, "The Debate about 1948," *International Journal of Middle East Studies* 27, no. 3 (August 1995): 300.

39. Rabinovich, *The Road Not Taken*, 219.

40. Quoted in Little, "The Making of a Special Relationship," 578.

41. Safran, *Israel: The Embattled Ally*, 474.

42. See the account by the mastermind of Egypt's 1973 campaign, General Saad el-Shazly, *The Crossing of the Suez*, 37, where he writes, "I was sickened by the duplicity."

43. Quoted in Safran, *Israel: The Embattled Ally*, 538.

44. Ibid., 540.

45. As one senior Israeli official put it before the invasion: "It's not that the PLO is a real military threat to Israel. Their forces in Lebanon are nothing really. But if we wipe them out militarily they will lose all their political power. That is what we are really aiming at." Quoted in the *Sunday Times*, London, May 2, 1982.

46. *International Herald Tribune*, August 25, 1993.

47. *New York Times*, September 10, 1993.

48. *Al-Hayat*, September 14, 1993.

49. See Robert B. Satloff, "The Jordan-Israel Peace Treaty."

5

Israeli Thinking about the Palestinians
A Historical Survey

Mark Tessler

The Pre-State Period

An early slogan of the Zionist movement was "A Land without People for a People without Land." This was an exaggeration, of course, for Zionists knew from the beginning that Palestine, the territorial focus of their aspirations, was indeed inhabited. Nevertheless, the slogan does indicate the failure of many early Zionists to recognize that the Muslim and Christian Arabs living in Palestine had legitimate rights and aspirations, and to consider whether and how an accommodation might be worked out between these rights and those of the Jews.

At the beginning of the nineteenth century, the population of Palestine was approximately 250,000–300,000, of which only about 5,000 were Jews. Moreover, not only was the Jewish population tiny in both relative and absolute terms, it was also limited with respect to dispersion. There were concentrations only in Jerusalem and three other cities of special spiritual significance, Hebron, Tiberias, and Safad. Jerusalem contained nearly 50 percent of the total. Yet as late as 1833, there were only 3,000 Jews in the city. Finally, the pious Jews of Palestine neither constituted a self-sufficient political community nor viewed themselves as the vanguard of a movement dedicated to returning Jews to the Promised Land. Many devoted themselves principally to prayer and Torah study and were dependent on donations from abroad.

The first organized migrations of the modern Zionist movement began in 1882, and in the two decades that followed the Zionist Organization and a series of associated international institutions came into existence.

Among these was the Jewish National Fund, established in 1901 for the purpose of raising money for land purchases and community development in Palestine. Between 1882 and the turn of the century, the size of Palestine's Jewish population more than doubled, growing to approximately 50,000, and a foundation was laid for its development into a modern political community.

Although conflict between the Yishuv, as the new Zionist colony was called, and the indigenous Arab population of Palestine was not intense during the last years of the nineteenth century, anger and resentment among Palestinians became increasingly visible during the years leading up to World War I. The extent of anti-Zionist sentiments should not be overstated: There were instances of cooperation and even friendship between Arabs and Jews. Nor was the growing Zionist presence the only concern of Palestinian notables and the country's narrow class of urban intellectuals. Issues of development and relations with Ottoman Turkey, which controlled Palestine at this time, were also important. Nevertheless, the Palestinian elite became increasingly politically conscious, and in some cases politically militant, and anti-Zionist themes were expressed by many of the new political associations and newspapers that appeared in the years before the war. As stated elsewhere, following a more thorough review of developments during this period, "Anti-Zionism was limited, though by no means absent, among the Arabs of Palestine prior to 1908; but it increased rapidly after the Young Turk Revolution and had reached serious proportions by the eve of World War I, even though its locus and intensity continued during this period to be at least somewhat constrained by a variety of social and political considerations."[1]

Two considerations contributed to growing political consciousness among the Palestinians. One, of course, was the expanding Zionist presence. By 1914, the number of Jews in Palestine was about 85,000, compared to an Arab population of about 604,000. Palestinians feared that the Zionists would change the character of the country and, eventually, come to dominate it economically and politically. It is in this connection, as part of the diplomatic maneuvering that followed the war, that six Palestinian patriotic and religious societies and more than one hundred prominent individuals addressed a petition in November 1918 to the British military authorities occupying the country. The petition denounced the Balfour Declaration and stated, in part, while "we have always sympathized profoundly with the persecuted Jews and their misfortunes in other countries . . . there is a wide difference between this sympathy and the acceptance of such a [Jewish] nation . . . ruling over us and disposing of our affairs."[2] Similar sentiments were voiced at a meeting called by the Jerusalem and Jaffa Muslim-Christian societies and held in Jerusalem in February 1919. Sometimes described as the First Palestinian National Congress, the meeting brought together about thirty politically active men from all parts of the country.

Palestinian political consciousness was fostered in equal or even greater measure by developments in neighboring Arab countries, particularly Syria and Egypt. In these countries, as elsewhere in the Arab world, nascent nationalist movements were expressing anti-imperialist sentiments and calling for political independence, and the political forces fueling these developments had an impact in Palestine as well. There was not always agreement on the shape of the polity in whose name independence was demanded. In Palestine, some called for the creation of an independent Palestinian state, but this did not become the position of the majority until the late 1920s. In the immediate postwar period, most Palestinian intellectuals sought to realize their national aspirations within the framework of "Greater Syria." They sent representatives to meetings in Damascus and joined others in calling for the independence of a Syrian state that would embrace not only present-day Syria but also Palestine, Transjordan, and Lebanon. This is sometimes described as the "Southern Syria" tendency in Palestinian politics.

While some Zionist supporters assert that the Southern Syria trend demonstrates that Palestinians never considered themselves a national political community, it is a spurious argument so far as Palestinians are concerned. On the one hand, the late development of territorially defined nationalism was common in the Arab world and in many other parts of the Third World as well. As a consequence, the right to self-determination proclaimed by Palestinians was, and is, no less valid than that put forward by the inhabitants of many other territorial units. Indeed, in some Arab countries, among them Libya, Jordan, Saudi Arabia, and Algeria, citizens define themselves in terms of a political identity that took shape even more recently than that of the Palestinians. On the other hand, and perhaps more important, Palestinians insist that the legitimacy of their right to self-determination did not, and does not, depend on whether their first calls for independence were issued in the name of Palestine or Greater Syria. Either way, they contend, they have an inalienable right to reside in and rule over their ancestral homeland, managing their own affairs in accordance with the evolving will and political consciousness of the majority of their country's citizens.

It is against this background, in light of the emergence of Palestinian nationalism and opposition to the Zionist project, that the inadequacy of early Zionist policy may be seen. A failure to deal meaningfully with the Palestinians was particularly characteristic of Zionist leaders in Europe, which remained the headquarters of the Zionist movement during this period. The attitudes and policies of Jews in the Yishuv were more complex, although here as well there were important shortcomings.

The view that Zionists in Europe did not give adequate attention to relations with the Arabs of Palestine, at least at the outset, is expressed by one scholar in the following terms: "Zionist leadership, centered in Europe, was sufficiently removed from the scene to allow it to vacillate and procrastinate insofar as efficacious steps in the field of relations with the Arabs were concerned," a situation which "prevented the Zionist Head Office and executive from appreciating the real issues at stake and therefore from making, or even accepting, concrete suggestions as to the way in which to achieve the sought after friendship with the Arabs of Palestine."[3] Thus, as late as the Tenth and Eleventh Zionist Congresses, held respectively in Basel in 1911 and in Vienna in 1913, many delegates asserted that antagonism toward the Jews did not reflect the opinion of most Palestinians and should not be exaggerated. Also suggesting that low priority was attached to improving Arab-Jewish relations is the failure of the Zionist Organization to place an official representative in Palestine until 1908, when it opened the Palestine Office in Jaffa.

Still another indication is the focus of post–World War I Zionist diplomacy, particularly that of Chaim Weizmann, who became president of the Zionist Organization in 1920. The attention of Weizmann and most other Jewish leaders outside Palestine was directed not toward Palestinian leaders but rather toward Faisal, the third son of Husayn, the *sherif* of Mecca. Weizmann and others regarded Faisal as the leader of an authentic national movement, parallel to their own. Alternatively, Weizmann sought no more than proper economic relations with the Arabs of Palestine and in fact was openly critical of the liberal attitude toward local Palestinian aspirations held by some Jews in the Yishuv. In contrast to his genuine regard for Faisal, Weizmann held the Arab political class in Palestine in low esteem. On one occasion he described its members as "dishonest, uneducated, greedy, and unpatriotic."[4]

Some scholars point out, persuasively, that considerations other than ignorance and disinterest contributed to the inadequacy of Zionist policy toward the Palestinians. According to Yosef Gorny, for example, institutional weakness and poverty, Arab perceptions of Zionist strength notwithstanding, prevented the movement from addressing the issue of Jewish-Arab relations in a more coherent fashion. Political motivations were also important, especially a desire to deny legitimacy to the contention that Palestinians feared and opposed the growing Jewish presence in the country.

Even more important, perhaps, were the normative assumptions held by many and perhaps most of the Zionist leaders in Europe, assumptions that led them to regard the Palestinian Arab problem as transient and thus of secondary importance. A few, such as Ahad Ha'am, warned of a confrontation with the Arabs and urged action to prevent its emergence. Others, however, including such prominent figures as Theodor Herzl, Max Nordau, and Dov Ber Borochov, as well as Weizmann, were convinced that Palestinian Arabs would benefit from the Zionist enterprise and that their opposition would therefore dissipate. These Zionist leaders believed in universal progress and the superiority of Western culture, which led them to assume that the institutions and values brought to Palestine by Zionism would eventually give rise to a "great, strong and open Jewish society [that] would absorb the Arabs into its midst in one way or another."[5] Beliefs of this nature, as well as weakness and political calculations, led many European Zionists to deny that there was an Arab-Jewish conflict in Palestine requiring more of their attention.

Whatever the relative weight of these contributing factors, it is clear that Zionist leaders based in Europe did not give adequate attention to the Arabs of Palestine. These men may not have been wholly ignorant of the situation in Palestine, but they nonetheless failed to appreciate the intensity of Palestinian nationalism and the need to seek an accommodation with it. As stated in the report of a symposium in Jerusalem, "there is no doubt that all the Zionist executives and almost all the currents in the Zionist movement underestimated the strength of [Palestinian] Arab nationalism and the weight of its opposition to Zionist aspirations."[6]

In contrast to Zionists based in Europe, Jews in the Yishuv were heavily exposed to Arab sentiments and buffeted directly by Arab discontent, and in this environment there were some who dedicated themselves to fostering greater cooperation between Palestine's Jewish and Arab inhabitants. As early as the 1890s, there was a small group of Jews in Palestine, men such as David Yellin and Israel Belkind, who studied and translated Arabic literature and discussed what they believed to be the common, pre-Islamic, cultural origins of the Jewish and Arab peoples.[7] This positive orientation toward the Arabs was articulated in the years that followed by men such as Yitzhak Epstein, Yosef Luria, and Nissim Malul, among others. All were ardent Zionists, fully committed to Zionist immigration and a Jewish renaissance in Palestine. It was also their belief, however, that the success of the Zionist project depended, more than anything else, on good Jewish-Arab relations and on the adoption by Zionism of a positive attitude toward the Arabs. As expressed by Epstein, these issues "outweigh all others" and are the questions "on the correct solution of which depends the realization of our national aspirations."[8]

Gorny's important study of Zionism and the Arabs identifies three additional schools of thought within the Yishuv during this period. One is a "separatist outlook," which stands in direct ideological opposition to the "integrative perspective" of men such as Epstein, Luria, and Malul. Those who championed a separatist orientation spoke of the dangers of friendship with the Arabs, arguing that this would threaten both Zionist political aspirations and the Jews' high standard of morality and civilization. Moshe Smilansky, for example, a prominent Yishuv leader, wrote in 1907 that separation was a prerequisite for the attainment of a Jewish majority in Palestine. In addition, he urged Jews to "keep their distance from the fellahin and their base attitudes . . . lest our children adopt their ways and learn from their ugly deeds."[9] Beyond this, many advocates of separation asserted that intercommunal conflict in Palestine was unavoidable, and for this reason they opposed giving assistance to the Arabs. Such assistance would not produce acceptance of Zionism, they argued; it would only make the Arabs stronger and, thereby, undermine the security of the Yishuv. Finally, many separatists denied the legitimacy of Palestinian political ambitions, asserting, for example, as did Smilansky, that the nationalism of the Arabs had no validity in Palestine and that in fact the Arabs themselves were not even a nation, being nothing more than a collection of warring factions and tribes.

Sadly, support for this separatist outlook increased with the deterioration of Arab-Jewish relations during the years immediately before and then after World War I. Its advocates insisted that mounting tension in Palestine demonstrated the folly of those naive and childish dreamers who called for friendship and cooperation with the Palestinians. In fact, however, the presence of such attitudes among some members of the Yishuv was probably a cause as well as a consequence of the poor relations between Jews and Palestinian Arabs.

In between the extremes of integration and separation was a school of thought that Gorny describes as "liberal." Prominent among those associated with this orientation was Arthur Ruppin, head of the Zionist Organization's Palestine Office. These liberals, whose motives were at once self-interested and sincere, argued that good relations with the Arabs should be a central goal of Zionist policy. Although they did not favor integration, they stressed the importance of knowing more about the Arabs and their culture. Thus, for example, Ruppin once responded to an inquiry from Russian Zionists by writing that unpleasant incidents kept occurring in the Yishuv "simply because the Jew understands neither the language nor the customs of the Arab."[10] These pragmatists also called for Zionist action to redress legitimate Arab grievances, including land purchases that resulted in the eviction of peasants. In addition, according to Gorny, the views of Ruppin and other liberals implied a belief that the Arabs should have a say in Palestine's future, although this did not mean they considered the Palestinians' claim equal to that of the Jews.[11]

The final school of thought identified by Gorny, which he characterizes as a "constructive socialist outlook," fits less easily on an ideological continuum ranging from integration to separation. It is important, however, precisely because it came to occupy the center of gravity in Yishuv politics. Associated with Labor Zionism and reflected in the writings of Yitzhak Ben-Zvi, David Ben-Gurion, and other leaders of the second *aliya*, this perspective addressed a contradiction between the requirements of Zionist development on the one hand and socialist solidarity on the other. Applied to Palestine, this concern initially expressed itself in debates about both the ethical and the practical implications of struggling for Jewish employment at the expense of Arab workers, instead of permitting or even encouraging Jewish employers to hire Arab laborers and promoting the formation of a labor movement in which Jewish and Arab workers would make common cause. With time, however, there emerged a consensus among mainstream Labor Zionists that the national cause of the Jewish people must be given priority over considerations of social class with the potential to unite Jewish and Arab workers. At the same time, even as they placed nationalism above socialism, some Labor Zionists acknowledged that Arabs, as well as Jews, had historical rights in Palestine. Many also expressed a belief that their programs, though perhaps exacerbating tension in the short run, would eventually form a basis for peaceful coexistence between Palestine's Jewish and Arab inhabitants. Ben-Zvi, for example, reasoned that policies favorable to Jewish labor would promote the development of the Yishuv, and that this in turn would make the needs of the Jewish working class less pressing and create resources with which to promote the well-being of Arab as well as Jewish laborers.[12]

In the years that followed, Zionists and Palestinians increasingly came into conflict. There were regular and intense episodes of intercommunal violence, beginning in the early 1920s and especially from 1929 onward.

Fueling Arab grievances was the steady growth of the Yishuv, particularly as reflected in continuing Jewish immigration and land purchases. Thus, as noted by a British commission of inquiry following the disturbances of 1929, "the immediate causes" provoking violence on the part of the Palestinians were "the Arab feelings of animosity and hostility to the Jews consequent upon the *disappointment of their political and national aspirations* and fear for their economic future" (italics added). The commission noted that Arab sentiments were also the result of the "landless and discontented" class being created by the expansion of the Yishuv, and it accordingly recommended that limitations be placed on Jewish immigration and land purchases.[13]

Zionists disputed these conclusions, claiming that most Palestinians recognized and appreciated the benefits brought to them by Zionist development and that the Arabs were thus being stirred up by agitators, radicals, and criminals. A similar argument was advanced by some Zionists, including Weizmann and the Revisionist leader Vladimir Jabotinsky, in response to the sustained Palestinian violence between 1936 and 1939, which is frequently known as the Arab Revolt or the Arab Rebellion. Disputing the legitimacy of Palestinian aspirations and fears, Jabotinsky, for example, told the commission of inquiry investigating these disturbances that "the economic position of the Palestinian Arabs, under the Jewish colonization and owing to the Jewish colonization, has become the object of envy in all the surrounding Arab countries, so that the Arabs from those countries show a clear tendency to immigrate to Palestine."[14]

In fact, however, independent observers, as well as objective Israeli scholars, have shown that the 1936–39 rebellion reflected both widespread Arab opposition to Zionism and genuine Palestinian patriotism. The revolt also had authentic grassroots leadership and broad popular support, thus being the creation neither of self-appointed and unrepresentative ideologues nor of rabble-rousers and criminal elements. As described by a British observer, it was rather "a peasant revolt, drawing its enthusiasm, its heroism, its organization and its persistence from sources within itself."[15] Accordingly, the British commission investigating these disturbances, the Peel Commission, concluded that the violence initiated in 1936 had been caused by "the desire of the Arabs for national independence" and by "their hatred and fear of the establishment of the Jewish National Home." The report added that these were "the same underlying causes as those which brought about the 'disturbances' of 1920, 1921, 1929 and 1933" and also that they were the only underlying causes, all other factors being "complimentary or subsidiary."[16]

The 1947–48 war, which resulted in Israel's independence, was fought against this background. In response to the escalating violence, the Peel Commission and subsequently the United Nations recommended the partition of Palestine, proposing to give both the Zionists and the Palestinians a portion of the country for the establishment of their respective states. The Arabs rejected partition, however, initiating a war in which the Zionists emerged victorious, with the result that Israel declared its independence on May 14, 1948, and shortly thereafter was recognized by the international community.

The war was a disaster for the Palestinians. First, the territory that the United Nations had proposed for a Palestinian state was swallowed up by others. About one-third was taken by Israel, which immediately incorporated the captured lands into the borders of the new Jewish state. The rest was taken by Israel's neighbors, by Jordan in the case of the West Bank and by Egypt in the case of the Gaza Strip. Second, the war resulted in the flight of approximately 750,000 Palestinians from their homes in the territory encompassed by Israel. These Palestinians took refuge in the West Bank, Gaza, Jordan (the East Bank), Lebanon, and elsewhere. Taken together, these developments effectively ended, at least for the time being, any possibility for the creation of an Arab as well as a Jewish state in Palestine.

While supporters of Israel quite properly point out that none of this would have occurred had Palestinians and other Arabs accepted the compromise offered by the United Nations, Israel nonetheless bears a considerable responsibility for the Palestinian disaster. This is a controversial subject, and there are differing interpretations of events during this period. Still, there is no doubt that Palestinian complaints have substantial validity.

Many of the actions and policies about which Palestinians complain were associated with *Tochnit Dalet,* or Plan D, which was formulated by Israeli military leaders in March 1948 as a program for the defense of the new Jewish state. In the judgment of critics, however, Plan D had a political as well as a military objective, and some accordingly describe it as a blueprint for preventing the emergence of a Palestinian state and expelling the Palestinian population. They point out, as does one prominent Israeli critic, that Plan D provided for the capture by Jewish forces of areas in the Galilee and the Tel Aviv–Jerusalem corridor that had been allocated to the Palestinian state by the United Nations, and that it also dealt in detail with "the expulsion over the borders of the local Arab population in the event of opposition to our attacks." Therefore, this Israeli analyst continues, "the aim of the plan was annexation—the destruction of Arab villages was to be followed by the establishment of Jewish villages in their place."[17] Plan D was not put into effect officially until Israel declared its independence on May 14, although some writers report that it guided Zionist military activity from the time it was formulated two months earlier.

Moreover, by the summer of 1948 Israeli leaders had become more conscious of the benefits that would result from the departure of the Palestinians. Decisions and actions by mainstream Zionist institutions and leaders, sometimes at the highest level, were therefore taken with the explicit intent of driving Palestinians from their towns and villages. The July campaign to expel the Arabs of Lydda and Ramleh illustrates this particularly clearly. By the concluding stages of the conflict, in the fall of 1948, there appears to have been an even more widespread and explicit effort to "facilitate" the Arabs' departure. Military operations in the south of the country, conducted in October and November, left almost no Palestinian communities in place behind the advancing Israeli lines.[18]

The Post-Independence Period

As in the early years of modern political Zionism, most leaders of present-day Israel have until very recently been unable or unwilling to recognize and address seriously the national rights of the Palestinians. After the 1947–48 war, the conflict was viewed by most observers as a struggle between Israel and the Arab states, rather than between Israel and the Palestinians. Nor was this unreasonable, given the loss of the territorial base that the United Nations had proposed for an Arab state in Palestine and the attendant flight of the country's Arab population. Dispersed, disorganized, and for the most part leaderless, without a territorial base and under the control of others, the Palestinians ceased to be active participants in either the diplomatic or the military arena. Furthermore, Israel fought wars with neighboring Arab states in 1956 and 1967, and diplomatic initiatives at this time were addressed almost exclusively to securing peace between these states and Israel.

After the 1967 war, however, the Palestinian dimension reemerged and gradually reclaimed its central place in the now eighty-five-year-old Middle East conflict. The Arab state dimension faded during the 1970s, although it did not disappear altogether. By contrast, the Palestinians steadily became more involved in political and military confrontations with Israel and a more prominent player on the stage of international diplomacy.

Two developments are responsible for this change. First, Israel captured the West Bank (including East Jerusalem) and Gaza Strip during the June 1967 War, thus taking control of all of historic Palestine. Further, approximately one million Palestinians now lived in the territories occupied and administered by the Jewish state. In the years that followed, Palestinian political life in the West Bank and Gaza expanded in both intensity and scope, partly in response to the harshness of occupation and partly in response to opportunities created by Israel. There were elections in the West Bank in 1972 and 1976, for example, making it easier for new Palestinian leaders to come to the fore and give voice to nationalist sentiments. There was also considerable institutional development. For example, new or expanded universities not only emerged as important centers of opposition to the Israeli occupation, they brought together politically conscious young men and women who found many opportunities to demand recognition of the Palestinians' right to self-determination.

Second, the Palestine Liberation Organization established itself as an influential and authentically Palestinian political institution. The PLO had been created in 1964 as a puppet of Nasser and other Arab leaders. In 1968, however, the organization put in place new, independent, and legitimate Palestinian leadership, with Yasser Arafat at its head. The organization also adopted a new National Charter which affirmed the national rights of the Palestinian people and insisted that Palestinians' statelessness was the core problem of the Arab-Israeli conflict. International recognition of the PLO, and of the Palestinian cause more generally, increased steadily during the 1970s, coming first from Arab governments but thereafter from socialist and other European countries. In November 1974, Arafat was invited to address the General Assembly of the United Nations. The decision to invite the PLO was taken by a vote of 105 to 4, with 20 abstentions.

The Israeli response to these developments was, and remained until recently, a vigorous denial that the Palestinians were a people possessing legitimate national rights. Israeli spokesmen argued that Palestinian Arabs had never conceived of themselves as a separate nation, as had the Egyptians and the Syrians, for example, and that, consequently, there was no such thing as Palestinian nationalism. It is in this context that Golda Meir, at the time Israel's prime minister, issued her much-publicized June 1969 declaration that the Palestinians do not exist, asserting that the recent and artificial national claims advanced by the PLO were in no way comparable to the ancient and historically legitimated national rights of the Jewish people.

Meir's remarks may be understood, in part, as a response to the 1968

PLO Charter and related Palestinian declarations. Palestinians called for the "de-Zionization" of Israel. They asserted that the Jews were a religious group, not a nation; argued that the Jews therefore did not themselves possess national rights; and accordingly proposed that the Jewish state of Israel be replaced by a nonsectarian, democratic, and secular state that would serve all of its citizens, Jewish, Muslim, and Christian, on an equal basis. For example, a January 1969 meeting of the Central Committee of Fatah, the largest and most powerful faction in the PLO, adopted a seven-point declaration which proclaimed that "the final objective of its [Fatah's] struggle is the restoration of the independent, democratic State of Palestine, all of whose citizens will enjoy equal rights regardless of their religion."[19]

But while Meir's remarks may to some extent be understood as propaganda designed to counter that of the PLO, this is not an adequate explanation. As in the early years of Zionism, Israeli leaders, and Israelis in general, have been disinclined to come to terms with, or even to recognize, the national aspirations and rights of the Palestinian people. At the heart of Meir's statement was an inability to see the Palestinians as Israelis and Zionists demand, quite rightly, that they themselves be seen, as a national community with the right to self-determination and, if they so chose, a collective national existence in the form of an independent state. This characterization does not apply to all Israelis, but it does describe what was until very recently the orientation of all but a small segment of the country's Jewish population.

This attitude toward Palestinian nationalism was clearly visible in the years after 1967 in the platform of the Labor Alignment and in statements by the party's leaders.[20] Labor had always been the dominant faction in Israeli politics, and this remained the case until the first government led by another party, Likud, was formed in 1977. Ben-Gurion and Ben-Zvi were Laborites, as were Golda Meir, Moshe Dayan, Abba Eban, and many other of Israel's most prominent politicians. All of these individuals denied that Palestinians constituted a people with national political rights. Labor not only refused to recognize the PLO, they insisted that should Israel withdraw from any part of the West Bank and Gaza as part of a peace settlement, the surrendered territory would be given to the Arab country that controlled it between 1948 and 1967, not to the Palestinians as a foundation for their state.

Palestinians and other Arabs sometimes claimed that Labor would not agree to a withdrawal from these territories under any conditions, and they pointed to the construction of paramilitary Jewish settlements in the

Jordan Valley to support their contention. They also observed, correctly, that some prominent Labor politicians opposed anything more than minor modifications of the post–1967 war territorial status quo. A different view was put forward by Israel's right-wing parties, however. In the 1969 election campaign, for example, Gahal, the precursor of Likud, criticized the Labor-led government both for a failure to deepen Israel's presence in the occupied territories and for putting obstacles in the way of private groups prepared to organize their own settlement initiatives. Gahal's platform described the territories as "liberated Jewish patrimony" that should remain entirely under permanent Israeli sovereignty and to which Israeli law should be extended.[21] But while Labor rejected such calls and won the election decisively, they refused to consider surrendering any territory to the Palestinians or even to negotiate with the PLO about the possibility of compromise. Indeed, Labor, like Gahal and later Likud, rejected the contention, increasingly recognized in international diplomatic circles, that the PLO was the sole legitimate representative of the Palestinian people.

Labor's position remained constant even after candidates identified with the PLO won about 75 percent of the seats in the West Bank municipal elections of April 1976. Israel was to some degree surprised by the results of the balloting. Possibly reflecting Zionism's historical blind spot regarding Palestinian nationalism, the Jerusalem government had underestimated the strength of nationalist sentiments and PLO legitimacy among Palestinians in the West Bank. Otherwise, Israeli authorities might not have permitted the election to take place or, at the very least, they would have made it much more difficult for pro-PLO candidates to campaign. Interestingly, the negligence of the Labor-led government was criticized not only by right-wing Israelis but also by traditional, pro-Jordanian West Bank notables. Some of the latter went so far as to allege that Israel actually welcomed the victory of PLO supporters, presumably because it enabled Jerusalem to claim that "radicals" had come to power and "there is no one to talk to" about the future of the occupied territories.[22]

Labor's policy toward the West Bank was frequently described as the Jordanian option, meaning that any part of the territory relinquished by Israel would be given to Jordan and that it would then be up to King Hussein to determine whether, and to what degree, there would be a territorial expression of Palestinian national aspirations. This policy was made more concrete in what became known as the Allon Plan, put forward by Yigal Allon, a Labor party leader who served as minister of labor in the government of Golda Meir. The essence of the unofficial but influential Allon Plan was that Israel should establish a permanent defensive perimeter along the eastern border of the West Bank but should not settle the heavily populated heartland of the territory, which would be returned to Jordan in the context of a peace settlement. But even Allon, who was believed to have gone too far by Labor's more conservative wing, had no inclination to deal with the PLO. On one occasion in 1975, by which time he had become foreign minister, Allon referred in a UN General Assembly speech to the "absurd pretensions of the so-called Palestine Liberation Organization," which he went on to describe as "a congeries of feuding terrorist gangs whose principal victims are the Arabs of Palestine themselves."[23]

Likud came to power in 1977, and its rejection of Palestinian national rights was even more unequivocal than that of Labor. Likud was committed to Israel's retention of the West Bank and Gaza, referring to the former territory by the biblical designations of Judea and Samaria and insisting that these are part of the indivisible "Land of Israel." Although Likud and its precursors were composed of several different factions, there had almost always been agreement on the platform of the party's dominant Herut wing, on *Shlemut Hamoledet*, "the right of the Jewish people to Eretz Yisrael [the Land of Israel] in its historical entirety, an eternal and incontestable right." As noted earlier, this was the position of Gahal, formed by a merger of Herut and the Liberal party in time for the 1969 elections. It remained the platform of Likud, into which Gahal evolved prior to the 1973 elections. In the 1977 elections, which brought Likud to power, the party again campaigned on the traditional Herut position: "The right of the Jewish people to the Land of Israel . . . Judea and Samaria will never be turned over to any foreign rule; between the sea and the Jordan there will be only Israeli sovereignty. Any plan that involves surrender [of this territory] militates against our right to the Land, will inevitably lead to a Palestinian state . . . and defeats all prospects for peace."[24]

Once in power, Likud adopted a three-part strategy toward the Palestinians and the occupied territories. First, it mounted a vigorous settlement campaign. This included the construction of new Jewish settlements in the West Bank and Gaza, financial incentives for Israelis to move into these new communities, and spending on roads and other infrastructure investments designed to make living in these settlements more appealing. There had been settlement activity under previous Labor-led governments, of course, primarily in the Jordan Valley but on a limited scale in other areas as well, most notably in the Etzion Bloc south of Jerusalem. By the time Likud came to power in 1977, the West Bank, excluding East Jerusalem, contained about 4,000 Jews living in thirty-four communities, four in areas which, under the Allon Plan, Labor had indicated a willingness to relinquish.[25] By the end of 1977, however, there were more than 5,000 Jewish settlers in the West Bank, and the numbers rose to 7,500, 10,000, and 12,500 respectively during the following three years, with the actual number of settlements more than doubling by the end of 1980. Likud retained control of the government in the elections of 1981, and by the end of that year the number of Jewish settlers in the West Bank exceeded 16,000, almost 30 percent more than a year earlier. By the end of 1982, the number stood at 21,000, another 30 percent increase. At this time there were 104 Jewish settlements in the West Bank, 70 of which had been built since Likud came to power in 1977.[26]

Second, the Likud-led government undertook to suppress all expressions of Palestinian nationalism or support for the PLO in the West Bank and Gaza. Universities in general, and Birzeit University near Ramallah in particular, were prominent targets. In November 1981, Israeli authorities charged Birzeit students with engaging in political activities and ordered the university closed. This followed several days of student protests commemorating the anniversary of the Balfour Declaration, but Palestinians, and even some Israelis, described the closure of Birzeit as a political act unrelated to genuine security considerations. It was also judged to be a form of "collective punishment," designed to intimidate Palestinians and penalizing students and faculty who had not even taken part in the protest demonstrations. There was interference in the affairs of other West Bank universities during this period as well. The censorship of Palestinian newspapers published in East Jerusalem and the banning of newspapers and books from entry into the West Bank and Gaza were yet another part of Israel's campaign against Palestinian nationalism. For example, *al-Fajr*, considered to be nationalist in orientation, was closed for nine days in November 1981 and then later in the month for another thirty days. Beginning in April 1982, distribution of *al-Fajr* and *as-Sha'ab* was prohibited in the West Bank and Gaza and, so far as books are concerned, there was a significant increase in the number of titles that were banned from sale or distribution in the territories.[27]

Finally, and perhaps most indicative of Israel's attitude toward Palestinian political aspirations, the Likud-led government sought to foster the emergence of alternative leaders and political institutions in the West Bank and Gaza. By mid-1982, the government had dissolved nine Palestinian municipal councils, arguing that this action was taken not in response to unrest in the territories but to correct the fundamental error made by previous Labor governments in permitting these bodies to be elected in the first place. To replace these officials, Israel had for almost two years been working to establish a network of Palestinian "Village Leagues," an alternative leadership structure headed by traditional notables and others opposed to the PLO. A key contributor to the Village League policy was Menachem Milson, a professor of Arabic literature at the Hebrew University of Jerusalem who became civilian administrator of the West Bank at this time. Milson argued in a 1981 article in *Commentary* magazine that most Palestinians in the occupied territories would be willing to deal with Israel were they not prevented from doing so by PLO threats and intimidation. Entitled "How to Make Peace with the Palestinians," the article recommended that Israel limit the activities of West Bank and Gaza leaders tied to the PLO and foster the emergence of an alternative leadership class, which, Milson asserted, would be not only more compliant but also more representative of the Palestinian masses.[28]

In fact, however, despite offering the leagues funds and administrative authority, Israeli officials were unable in many districts to persuade Palestinian notables to take part in the plan, and in most other districts authorities succeeded only in winning the cooperation of marginal figures. The leagues were thus unable to strike roots; aside from gaining the support of some members of their leaders' immediate families and clans, the leagues could not claim any substantial constituency. Indeed, they tended to attract elements from the social and political margins of Palestinian society, individuals who were not only viewed as collaborators and quislings by most other Palestinians but who, in at least some cases, were deemed to be social misfits, thus adding further to the artificial nature of the Israeli-sponsored institutions. One Israeli commentator described league members as "questionable types... unsavory characters who are ready to work for anyone."[29]

Israeli officials were eventually forced to recognize the flaws and contradictions in their policy, based, as it was, on the assumption that the PLO did not represent the Palestinian people and that there was an alternative, authentic, leadership waiting to step forward. In the spring of 1984, the Defense Ministry's coordinator for the occupied territories, General Benyamin Ben Eliezer, described the leaders of the leagues as "quislings," and soon thereafter the Federation of Village Leagues was officially disbanded.

Reasons and Prospects

While there are some important exceptions to this picture, the overall conclusion is clear. From the beginning, most mainstream Zionists were unwilling or unable to view the Palestinians as a political community with legitimate national aspirations and rights, in precisely the same way, in other words, that Zionists demanded that the world view the Jewish people.

Exceptions to this pattern were present during the early period, as well as later. This was reflected in the integrationist orientation of some Yishuv leaders, in some of the work of the Palestine Office under Arthur Ruppin, and in the program of Brit Shalom, an organization seeking Arab-Jewish reconciliation in Palestine. Ruppin, for example, who was also a member of Brit Shalom, wrote in 1922 about the need for a "general understanding between Jews and Arabs with the aim in view of bringing about a flowering of the whole East through common cultural endeavor."[30]

The anti-Palestinian sentiments expressed by mainstream Zionists have not only been the result of ignorance, insensitivity, and/or outright hostility. They have also been, at least in part, an understandable response to hostility on the part of the Palestinians. Palestinian Arabs have been opposed to the Zionist enterprise from the beginning, and some Palestinians and other Arabs later sought to portray the Jews as a *religious* community without legitimate *national* rights, sentiments that were later codified in the 1975 UN "Zionism Is Racism" resolution. Against this background, it is perhaps understandable that Zionists would not be predisposed to look favorably on the Palestinians' own political agenda and might feel compelled to respond in kind to what they considered propaganda based on prejudice and stereotype. Whether a different pattern might have emerged had either side displayed greater understanding of the other is a question that cannot be answered. But even if this is an unrealistic proposition, this dynamic of hostility deserves to be counted among the reasons that Zionists and Israelis have had difficulty coming to terms with Palestinian nationalism.

On the other hand, this is not an adequate explanation. Palestinians themselves frequently emphasize guilt and denial as the most important factors shaping Zionist attitudes. Their argument is that asking a people to surrender a large portion of its ancestral homeland to foreigners, or to a people that has not lived there for two millennia, cannot be justified, and that Zionists know this, however much they may pretend otherwise. Rather than face up to the immorality of imposing themselves by force on Palestine's indigenous population, however, Zionists and their supporters simply deny the existence, or at least the legitimacy, of a competing claim to the land they seek to inhabit.

Although this Palestinian analysis may be self-serving, it is not necessarily without some degree of merit. Moreover, objective and pro-Israeli analysts have offered assessments that are at least somewhat similar. In an important new study, Alan Dowty, a prominent political scientist who has spent many years in Israel, argues that the Jews' understanding of their history may have predisposed them to deny the objective basis for Palestinian and Arab concerns. "The Jewish world view is . . . the product of twenty centuries of religious and ethnic persecution," he writes, "the Holocaust is merely the latest and most brutal chapter in a long history." As a result, he suggests, "Wars with Arab states were not seen as events in international politics rooted in a territorial dispute, but as acts of primordial hostility that evoked images of the Holocaust and other historical attempts simply to kill Jews. Acts of terrorism were not seen as political actions designed (however brutally) to achieve Palestinian national aims but as plain and simple acts of antisemitism." Furthermore, according to Dowty, historically derived blinders colored the Jews' view of Arab moderation as well as Arab hostility: "Demonstrations of Arab moderation were regarded with suspicion, as they were likely to be tactical maneuvers rather than abandonment of the basic design of destroying Israel. This primordial 'us-them' view of the conflict clings to the assumption of unyielding hostility as an explanation that makes sense of a threatening world and reinforces the Jewish self-image as the perpetual victim of unreasoning hatred, rather than as simply the party of a conflict."[31]

Regardless of the relative explanatory power of these and other hypotheses, Zionists and Israelis have historically been unwilling to accept a symmetry between their own national aspirations and those of the Palestinians. Significantly, however, an important transformation of Israeli attitudes has taken place during the last decade. This is of course reflected in the 1993 Declaration of Principles (DOP) signed by Israel and the PLO. The declaration's preamble states, in part, that it is time for Israelis and Palestinians "to put an end to decades of confrontation and conflict, recognize their mutual legitimate and political rights, and strive to live in peaceful coexistence and mutual dignity and security to achieve a just, lasting and comprehensive peace settlement and historic reconciliation."

Even before the DOP was signed, however, this transformation was well under way. For example, in the 1992 Israeli election campaign, Labor turned away from its historical insistence on a Jordanian solution to the occupied territories and called for dealing with the Palestinians and the PLO. Moreover, Labor won the elections, and the party formed a governing coalition with Meretz, a political party whose platform calls for the establishment of a Palestinian state alongside Israel and which emerged from the balloting as the third largest party in the country, after Labor and Likud.

In fact, there was evidence of a significant shift in Israeli public opinion by the late 1980s, with opinion polls conducted at this time documenting a growing willingness to consider talks with the PLO. For example, 58 percent of the respondents in a March 1989 *New York Times* survey said Israel should negotiate with the PLO, and 59 percent said the same thing in a *Yediot Aharonot* poll conducted a month later.[32] It is also significant that 59 percent of those surveyed for the *New York Times* poll disagreed with the proposition that Palestinians want "a Palestinian state plus all of Israel in the long run," meaning that much of the Israeli public believed there to be a basis for negotiating with the PLO. Still another survey, conducted in May 1990, sought to assess attitude change and reported that the Israeli public, taken as a whole, had moved to the left in its thinking about the Palestinian problem, the PLO, and other aspects of the Arab-Israeli conflict.[33] Finally, it is significant that while support for negotiations with the PLO was most pronounced among Israelis who identified with Labor or parties further to the left, the March 1989 *New York Times* poll reported that this was also the position of 49 percent of the respondents expressing a preference for Likud.

Helping to bring about this dramatic change in Israeli thinking was a peace initiative launched by the PLO in the summer and fall of 1988. This included statements by PLO and other Palestinian leaders calling for a "two-state solution," thereby offering recognition of the Jewish state in return for the establishment of a Palestinian state alongside Israel. This breakthrough was made official at a meeting of the Palestine National Council convened in Algiers in mid-November, and the final communiqué also called for an international peace conference to be convened on the basis of UN Resolutions 242 and 338, for Israeli withdrawal from all Palestinian and Arab territories occupied in 1967, for settlement of the question of Palestinian refugees in accordance with relevant UN resolutions, and for UN guarantees for security and peace between all states in the region, including the Palestinian state.[34]

Even more important than this peace initiative, however, was the Palestinian uprising, or *intifada*, that began in December 1987. The uprising convinced a growing number of Israelis that Palestinians would not acquiesce in their country's occupation of the West Bank and Gaza, as Likud and others had claimed they would, and that right-wing Israelis who insisted occupation would be cost-free were thus either fools or liars. Indeed, many, including many of Israel's leading military experts, came to the conclusion that a failure to deal seriously with the Palestinians was proving to be quite costly. Ze'ev Schiff, the highly respected military affairs editor of *Ha'aretz*, offered the following account of the Israeli thinking that gained currency at this time, and of the role of the intifada in fostering these attitudes: "As a result [of the intifada], for the first time since 1967, many Israeli strategists have reoriented their approach to West Bank and Gaza security concerns. Israel has learned that the strategic importance of the area is not only a function of territorial depth, but also of the activities of the populace. The uprising has taught Israel that ruling the West Bank and Gaza does not automatically provide greater security to the rulers. What was once considered a security belt may now be a security burden. Israel has learned that one nation, particularly a small one, cannot rule another nation for long; that 3.5 million Israelis cannot keep 1.5 million Palestinians under perpetual curfew."[35]

Significantly, sentiments of this sort were also expressed by Yitzhak Rabin, defense minister and architect of Israel's campaign to suppress the intifada during its early years. Rabin, who went on to lead the Labor party to victory in the 1992 election and signed the Declaration of Principles with Yasser Arafat the following year, stated early in 1988 that "You cannot saddle the IDF with a mission that is outside its proper function. The unrest in the areas reflects a problem that can only have a political solution." Similarly, speaking almost a year later, the defense minister stated that the riots in the West Bank and Gaza "express a sense of frustration that no one in the Arab world, in the international community or in Israel had created any expectation of a political settlement." And still later in 1989, Rabin declared that whereas he had formerly believed "the best path for Israel was to keep the conflict and the solution within the framework of Israel's relations with the Arab states . . . the reality today is that the only partner with whom Israel can, perhaps, enter into a political process is the Palestinians . . . and whoever does not see this is not reading the map correctly."[36]

The evolution of Rabin's thinking about the Palestinians and peace parallels were experienced by substantial segments of the Israeli public.[37] Indeed, even a few leaders of Likud revised their thinking. The most prominent Likud politician to call for a dialogue with the PLO at this time was Shlomo Lahat, the mayor of Tel Aviv. Lahat told an interviewer in 1988, even before the PLO had presented its peace plan, "I believe a Palestinian state is inevitable. I believe, unfortunately, that the PLO represents the Palestinian people. I know that the price of peace and real security is withdrawal [from the occupied territories]."[38]

On the strength of this political transformation, and following the 1993 Israel-PLO accord, there developed a peace process that at the time appeared to open a dramatic new chapter, and perhaps the final chapter, in the Israeli-Palestinian conflict. Within months of the accord, Israel was holding meetings and negotiating ambitious joint ventures with businessmen, entrepreneurs, and diplomats from many Arab countries. The rapid pace of change, as well as the potential for expanded cooperation in the future, were described in the following terms in a May 1994 article in the *International Herald Tribune:*

> Israel's transition from pariah to potential partner is most evident in the overtures to Israelis by Arab governments and businessmen seeking potentially lucrative deals. Since September [1993], Israeli officials have received VIP treatment in Qatar, Oman, Tunisia and Morocco. Qatar is studying how to supply Israel with natural gas. Egypt has launched discussions on a joint oil refinery, and officials talk of eventually linking Arab and Israeli electricity grids. . . . Millionaire businessmen from Saudi Arabia, Kuwait, Qatar and Bahrain are jetting off to London, Paris and Cairo to meet Israelis, while Jordanians, Egyptians and Lebanese are rushing to Jerusalem for similar contacts.[39]

The peace process was something of a roller coaster through spring 1996, in the run up to the Israeli elections. There were setbacks and disappointments, of course, but there were also significant achievements, as indicated by the *International Herald Tribune* article. Indeed, it was in response to the progress being made that both Israeli and Palestinian extremists carried out tragic acts of violence in an effort, unfortunately successful, to derail the peace process by increasing distrust among Israelis and Palestinians. Yet it remains an important lesson of the period between 1993 and 1996 that most Arab countries do not have any independent grievances against Israel. They may agree that a historic injustice was done to the Palestinian people, but if an accommodation acceptable to the Palestinians can be obtained, they are ready, indeed eager, to put the past behind them and to cooperate with the Jewish state in developing the Middle East for their mutual benefit.[40]

The mood changed dramatically when Benjamin Netanyahu became Israel's prime minister in June 1996. Relations between Israel and Palestinians in the West Bank and Gaza deteriorated steadily, and the peace process itself came to a virtual standstill. There remained a basis for hope, however. A substantial majority of Palestinians continued to support the principle of a historic compromise with the Jewish state, although it should be added that most also expressed doubt about the intentions of the Israeli government.[41] Similarly, on the Israeli side, more than half of the country's Jewish population continued to support a two-state solution to the Israeli-Palestinian conflict.[42] Thus, with Ehud Barak's sweeping victory in the elections of May 1999, advocates of peace on both sides of the historic Israeli-Palestinian divide looked forward to recapturing the momentum of the immediate post-Oslo period.

In his inaugural address, Barak included a message to Israel's neighbors and told Palestinians that he recognized their suffering. Echoing Yasser Arafat's frequent calls for "a peace of the brave," he also stated that both sides must look to the future and stop focusing on the "account settling of historic wrongs." Finally, distinguishing his approach from that of his predecessor, and articulating what appeared to be the view of most of his countrymen, the new prime minister did not describe Israel as weak and surrounded by dangerous enemies but rather as looking ahead with strength and confidence.

The speed and extent of progress toward peace remains to be seen, of course. While both Israeli and Palestinian authorities are committed to serious and constructive negotiations, the final status issues on the agenda of these negotiations will be resolved only if both sides are prepared to make difficult decisions and accept painful compromises. Israeli hardliners, like their Palestinian counterparts, will be arguing in this context that their own side is being asked to give up too much and, in any event, that the other side cannot be trusted to honor the agreements it signs. Further, after years of rejection and denial, the proportion of Israelis who find such arguments persuasive may well be significant. A similar political dynamic is operating among Palestinians, and so progress toward genuine and lasting peace is by no means assured.

Yet the final word should be one of cautious optimism. Public opinion polls, as well as the 1999 elections, demonstrate that most Israelis are ready for peace based on territorial compromise and an accommodation with Palestinian nationalism. The polls also show that most Israelis expect, and apparently accept, that the peace process will result in the establishment of a Palestinian state alongside Israel. Against the background of this ongoing transformation of mainstream Israeli attitudes toward the Palestinians, and with a government committed to peace emerging from the 1999 Israeli elections, there is reason to hope that the peace process will not be derailed by the difficult issues that remain to be resolved and that the years ahead will indeed bring meaningful progress toward ending more than a century of Israeli-Palestinian conflict. Should this occur, the result for both Palestinians and Israelis will be the fulfillment of historic and legitimate aspirations: self-determination and statehood for the Palestinians and security and acceptance by its neighbors for Israel.

Notes

1. Mark Tessler, *A History of the Israeli-Palestinian Conflict*, 133. Other sections of this chapter also draw heavily on this volume, which may be consulted for additional detail.
2. Ann Mosely Lesch, *Arab Politics in Palestine, 1917–1939*, 85–96.
3. Yaacov Ro'i, "The Zionist Attitude to the Arabs, 1908–1914," in *Palestine and Israel in the Nineteenth and Twentieth Centuries*, ed. Elie Kedourie and Sylvia G. Haim (London: Frank Cass, 1982), 35, 38.
4. Jon Kimche, *Palestine or Israel*, 146.
5. Yosef Gorny, *Zionism and the Arabs, 1882–1948*, 38.
6. Gershon Shafir, *Land, Labor, and the Origins of the Israeli-Palestinian Conflict, 1882–1914* (Cambridge: Cambridge University Press, 1989), 204. The symposium was held at the Zalman Shazar Center in Jerusalem.
7. Emile Marmonstein, "European Jews in Muslim Palestine," in Kedourie and Haim, *Palestine and Israel*, 9.
8. Gorny, *Zionism and the Arabs*, 43.
9. Ibid., 50.
10. Ro'i, "The Zionist Attitude," 39.
11. Gorny, *Zionism and the Arabs*, 66.
12. Ibid., 73.
13. Formed in September 1929, the commission was headed by Sir Walter Shaw and is often called the Shaw Commission. For additional discussion, see Tessler, *A History*, 236.
14. February 11, 1937; quoted in Laqueur and Rubin, eds., *The Arab-Israeli Reader*, 59.
15. John Marlowe, *The Seat of Pilate* (London: Cresset Press, 1959), 137–38. For additional evidence in support of these conclusions, based on a careful and comprehensive study by an Israeli research group, see Yehoshua Porath, *The Palestine Arab National Movement*, 260 ff.
16. The Peel Commission Report, 110–11. For a useful summary, see Neil Caplan, *Futile Diplomacy, Volume II*, 58 ff.
17. Simcha Flapan, *The Birth of Israel*, 42.
18. Tessler, *A History*, 291–307. This work summarizes many studies and different points of view about the Palestinian exodus.
19. Laqueur and Rubin, eds., *The Arab-Israeli Reader*, 372–73.
20. The Alignment, or Labor Alignment, refers to a union composed of various political parties associated with Labor Zionism.
21. Real Jean Isaac, *Party and Politics in Israel*, 148.
22. Rafik Halabi, *The West Bank Story*, 118.
23. Tessler, *A History*, 486.
24. Isaac, *Party and Politics*, 156.
25. Shaul Mishal, *The PLO under Arafat*, 130–31.
26. Meron Benvenisti, *The West Bank Data Project, 1987 Report: Demo-*

graphic, Economic, Legal, Social, and Political Developments in the West Bank (Jerusalem: Jerusalem Post, 1987), 55.

27. Benny Morris, "The IDF Tells How—and Why—Books Are Banned," *Jerusalem Post,* April 6, 1982.

28. Menachem Milson, "How to Make Peace with the Palestinians." See also Menachem Milson, "The Palestinians in the Peace Process," *Forum* 42–43 (1981).

29. Zvi Barel, in *Ha'aretz.* May 5, 1982.

30. Susan Hattis, *The Bi-National Idea in Palestine during Mandatory Times,* 39–40.

31. Alan Dowty, *The Jewish State,* 87, 89.

32. Tessler, *A History,* 724–25. For additional discussion, see Mark Tessler, "The Impact of the Intifada on Political Thinking in Israel," in *Echoes of the Intifada,* ed. Rex Brynen.

33. Giora Goldberg, Gad Barzilai, and Efraim Inbar, "The Impact of Intercommunal Conflict: The Intifada and Israeli Public Opinion."

34. For details, see Don Peretz, *Intifada,* 211–14.

35. Ze'ev Schiff, *Security for Peace,* 15.

36. *Davar,* September 29, 1989.

37. For an extended discussion of this point, see Tessler, "The Impact of the Intifada."

38. *Jerusalem Post,* September 14, 1988.

39. Caryle Murphy and Nora Boustany, "When Former Enemies Turn Business Partners," *International Herald Tribune,* May 24, 1994.

40. Mark Tessler, "Israel at Peace with the Arab World." For an additional discussion of Arab attitudes toward peace with Israel, see Mark Tessler and Jamal Sanad, "Will the Arab Public Accept Peace with Israel: Evidence from Surveys in Three Arab Societies," in *Israel at the Crossroads,* ed. Gregory Mahler and Efraim Karsh (London: I. B. Tauris, 1994).

41. Information about the attitudes of Palestinians in the West Bank and Gaza is provided by regular opinion polls conducted by the Center for Palestine Studies and Research (CPSR). The results of these polls are frequently reported in the *Journal of Palestine Studies.* Another Palestinian polling organization, the Jerusalem Media and Communications Centre, also conducts regular surveys, and its findings are usually similar to those reported by CPSR.

42. For example, several polls taken in 1997 reported that about 50 percent of the Jewish Israeli public would support the creation of a Palestinian state, provided this was accompanied by appropriate security arrangements. See, for example, *Jerusalem Report,* May 1, 1997.

6

Labor during Fifty Years of Israeli Politics
Myron J. Aronoff

The Labor movement, the constituent parties of which have evolved through several incarnations over the past century, deserves considerable credit for its major role in the founding of the State of Israel and for contributions to Israel's many remarkable accomplishments. It is also justifiably criticized for many failures during the lengthy period it dominated the political system and even for failures in the opposition. Such a comprehensive evaluation of Labor's record, however, is well beyond the scope of this chapter. My more modest goal is to evaluate the most important legacy of the Labor party on the political system—its dominance and loss of dominance—which contributed both to its successes and to its failures.

First, I evaluate the importance of its attainment of a position of dominance in the creation of a dominant party system for determining a pattern of attitudes and behavior which carried over after it lost its dominant position. Second, I review my earlier explanation of the reasons for Labor's loss of both power and dominance in 1977 and clarify my position, which has been significantly misrepresented in a recent study of the party. Third, I demonstrate how Labor's defeat in 1977 resulted in the emergence of a competitive party system which was not initially apparent to many, if not most, political actors and observers. I evaluate polarization of the Israeli polity as a result of this failure to perceive structural change and in terms of the shifting power of social groups—the relative political marginalization of a former elite and the entry of formerly marginal groups to the centers of power. Fourth, I examine Labor's return to power in 1992 and its very narrow loss in 1996. Fifth, I discuss the behavior of Labor following its defeat in 1996 and the dilemma it faced in bringing down the Netanyahu government in midterm at the risk of significantly delaying the peace process. Finally, I briefly evaluate the significance of the results of the 1999 election as an indication of yet another major transformation of the party system.

Dominance Established in the Yishuv

There is a scholarly consensus that Labor achieved a dominant position in the nascent political system by 1935 which lasted until 1977.[1] There is disagreement (addressed below), as to whether Labor then ceased to be a dominant party. Labor's leaders projected a vision of pioneering Zionism that captured the imagination of many who did not even adhere to it. Mapai established the ideological preeminence of Labor's interpretation of Zionism by simultaneously marginalizing the parties to its left and to its right and by marginalizing to the point of virtually silencing the non- and anti-Zionist Arabs and Haredi Jews.[2] The accomplishment of these tasks was facilitated by both the shaping of collective memory through the creation of national myths and through building the institutional bases from which Labor attained political dominance.[3]

Although Yosef Gorni emphasizes the importance of ideology and Yonathan Shapiro stresses the primacy of institution building, it is essential to understand that these processes were mutually reinforcing and that their combination was critical for achieving Mapai's dominant position in the Yishuv.[4] My contribution to this particular debate has been to stress the significance of the fact that ideological preeminence preceded and paved the way for political dominance and to document how Labor first lost its ideological dominance well before its electoral defeat in 1977. This is most important in establishing whether Labor continued to be a dominant party while in the opposition. At the height of its power, Labor dominated all of the key institutions of the state and its version of Zionist discourse was established as a hegemonic political culture. Following Maurice Duverger, I have argued that this type of dominant party system is a relatively rare phenomenon characterized by the identification of the dominant party with a historical epoch.[5] Such dominance involves belief. It occurs when the party's ideological interpretation of reality captures the public imagination and becomes internalized by broad sectors of the public.[6]

The burden of integrating the mass immigration in the early years of the state, the remnant of European Jewry as well as the bulk of North African Jewry who arrived as impoverished refugees, strained the capacity of the new state born in mortal conflict with all of its neighbors. National survival and security were preserved, the homeless *olim* were housed and fed, and many (but by no means all) found some kind of employment. Their children were socialized in state schools that provided a national Zionist education. However, the well-founded perception of paternalism on the part of many of the European veterans of Mapai toward the newcomers from North Africa and the Middle East, coupled with differential rates of social, economic, and political mobility, was to prove costly in the long run when their sons and daughters deserted Mapai for the more nationalist and religious appeal of Menachem Begin's rhetoric. They were able to claim centrality in Israeli society and politics through an affirmation of patriotism without having to transform themselves into new Hebrews modeled on the Ashkenazi Sabra prototype.[7]

Dominance Lost

Prolonged possession of power breeds arrogance. The elite of a dominant party long in power become a self-perpetuating oligarchy who take their positions for granted and who come to assume that they have a natural right to rule. When this happens, the elite is no longer responsive to the party rank and file, much less to the public at large. They are unresponsive to social, economic, cultural, and political changes. This is particularly costly in a society as dynamic as Israel. This, in very general outline, is what happened to Labor.[8] I trace the continuity of several major characteristics of Achdut Ha' avodah that emerged in the formative period of the Yishuv (1919–30) analyzed by Shapiro, and I suggest that they loaded the dice in establishing a pattern of behavior which influenced perceptions and behavior during the period of Labor dominance and even thereafter.[9]

My introduction to *Power and Ritual in the Israel Labor Party: A Study in Political Anthropology* presents a cultural approach to the study of politics. Chapter 4, which compares the suppression of two highly controversial issues (religion and the state and Histadrut issues) from the agenda of the national party conference, analyzes the political culture of the party. It examines the pervasive sense of political inefficacy at all levels of party leadership below the elite and evaluates the impact of the taboos preventing criticism of the elite and their policies and the suppression of open debate in party forums. Chapter 5 is devoted to an analysis of ritualization of politics in one of the party's most important forums. It documents how this pervasive political culture constrained the party from changing leadership or policy immediately after the 1973 war, which further eroded public confidence in it.[10]

Demographic change (especially the changing composition of the electorate), the role of age, class, and ethnicity, and the secular-religious divide also played a role in Labor's decline. For example, my analysis (in chapter 6) of continuity and change in representation in party institutions revealed the systematic underrepresentation of the very sectors of the population that were growing in size and importance among the electorate—for example, poorer and less well educated Israelis living in development towns and urban slums, most of whom were Jews of Middle Eastern background; younger Israeli-born Jews; and Arabs—which I argued helped to explain their growing disenchantment with Labor.[11] Similarly, my analysis of party center and local branch relationships (chapter 7) documented the widespread sense of political inefficacy of local activists in the party branches—particularly in the outlying development towns populated primarily by Jews of Middle Eastern background.

The divisiveness caused by the conquest of territories during the Six-Day War is a central theme in my analysis of internal party divisions that threatened party unity (particularly in chapter 8).[12] I also devote an entire chapter (11) exclusively to an analysis of the impact of the *intifada*. This subject plays an even more important role in my analysis of the polarization of Israeli politics after the defeat of Labor during the Likud era.[13] The importance of the religious-secular division is analyzed in the suppression of issues dealing with the subject (chapter 4).[14]

Cultural and Political Polarization

Menachem Begin mobilized a successful electoral coalition of the formerly marginalized—the nationalist right, Jews of Middle Eastern background, national religious, and ultra-Orthodox Jews. The leaders of both Labor and the Likud initially failed to grasp the significance of the fact that the political system had undergone significant transformation into a competitive party system. This is a central theme of my *Israeli Visions and Divisions* (1989). In the preface to the revised and expanded 1993 edition of *Power and Ritual in the Israel Labor Party,* I state, "The transition from a dominant party to a competitive party was as difficult for the Likud, the leaders of which in certain respects continued to act as if they were still in the opposition, as it was for Labor, whose leaders continued to act as if they were entitled to govern the nation" (xi).[15]

Yossi Beilin makes a similar point. Yet, he also suggests (mistakenly, in my estimation) that Labor may have actually retained its dominant position "even within the framework of the opposition" through its identification with the values of the society, the penetration of broad social strata, and continued control over many areas of life.[16] Whereas I reject this conclusion, Lochery makes it a central theme of his book: "Israeli society, even those who had supported the Likud, continued to view the Labour

Party as the dominant party or the establishment.... Moreover, the Likud in its first period of government did not try to challenge the view of the Labour Party as the establishment."[17] He fails to distinguish between a "dominant party" and an "establishment." The former requires a position of ideological hegemony and dominant political power—both of which Labor lacked. The Likud fostered the image of Labor as an "establishment," or elite, as a term of disparagement which played on ethnic and class resentments against Labor. I return to this point below.[18]

Whereas the struggle between Labor and the Likud between 1977 and 1981 appeared as "a struggle for dominance"[19] from the perspective of their leaders, my evaluation at the time—that the era of Labor's dominance ended with its political defeat in 1977—seems vindicated by historical developments.[20] It is essential to differentiate between the perceptions of the political actors and an objective evaluation of political realities. My research documented Labor's loss of ideological hegemony before its electoral defeat in 1977. It lost control of the overwhelming bulk of its resources when it lost control of the government's budget.[21]

By 1981 the leaders of Labor began to comprehend that their defeat in 1977 was not merely a fluke, and the leaders of the Likud had gained self-confidence in their ability to lead the nation. Although Menachem Begin realized he was the leader of the government rather than the opposition, he never seemed to fully comprehend the major change in the nature of the political system. Consequently his attempts to achieve the kind of dominance for the Likud that had been held by Labor in the earlier era contributed to the polarization of the polity. He attempted to rewrite history by elevating his mentor Vladimir Jabotinsky to the pantheon of Zionist heroes and by rehabilitating the reputation of the dissident Irgun underground which he commanded as well as the more extreme Lehi. In partnership with Gush Emunim, which became the ideological vanguard of the settlement movement, he partially succeeded in erasing the Green Line 1949 armistice borders from the map and the imagination of significant numbers of Israelis.[22]

However, at least half of the Israeli population, led by a significant proportion of the nation's intellectuals, creative artists, and leading media political commentators, continued to adhere to the more liberal and humanistic interpretation of Zionism associated with Labor. Therefore, Begin (and his successors Shamir and Netanyahu) failed to establish the political dominance of the Likud or the ideological hegemony of the more militantly nationalistic version of Zionism which he articulated. Ofira Seliktar, Lilly Weisbrod, Charles Liebman, and Eliezer Don-Yehiya (among others) mistakenly thought he had succeeded at the time. I criticized their conclusions and argued that, "Begin's newly reformulated reinterpretation of revisionist Zionism was neither a New Zionism nor a new civil religion, but a new ideological variation on an old familiar Zionist tune designed to mobilize a broader electoral constituency. . . . It is questionable whether the particular combination of folk religion and nationalism is sufficiently institutionalized (reified) to survive the demise of Begin as leader of the Likud."[23] Yet, Begin did succeed in legitimating his more nationalistic ideology, policies, and rhetoric, and in shifting the center of Israeli politics more to the right for nearly two decades.[24]

During this period the leaders of the Labor party were still in a state of shock and failed to undertake a serious soul searching to determine the reasons for their defeat. Rather, they traded mutual recriminations and excuses and engaged in a lengthy fratricidal competition between Yitzhak Rabin and Shimon Peres for leadership of the party. However, over the years they did manage to reform and democratize the selection of party leaders and candidates for the Knesset by establishing a system of primary elections. These reforms produced party lists with many younger candidates who were far more representative of the membership and the electorate than the lists selected by the previous oligarchic nominations committees, with the notable exception of the representation of women. The primaries also produced more independent Knesset members, which weakened party discipline.[25]

Electoral parity between the two major parties and deadlock in efforts to form a coalition with smaller parties resulted in an unprecedented agreement between Labor and the Likud to share power and rotate the premiership with Peres and Shamir alternating as prime minister and foreign minister between 1984 and 1988. This government accomplished two important goals. It succeeded in withdrawing Zahal (the Israeli army) from most of Lebanon and dramatically reduced the highest inflation in Israeli history. A slight electoral edge to the Likud in the 1988 election produced a National Unity government but without rotation and with the Likud in control. The sharp divisions between Labor and the Likud on how to resolve the Palestinian popular uprising (intifada) brought their cooperation to an end in 1990 with Labor resigning and the Likud heading the caretaker government until the election in 1992.

Labor Returns to Lead the Government: 1992–1996

The direct primary election of the party's candidate for prime minister by members of the Labor party gave Yitzhak Rabin the edge over his perennial rival Peres. Even close allies of Peres supported Rabin in the belief that he had greater electoral appeal. This assessment proved correct as Labor formed a narrow coalition with the newly formed Meretz alliance and Shas in 1992. Ironically, by appointing Meretz leader Shulamit Aloni as minister of education and culture and insisting on retaining the defense portfolio for himself, Rabin failed to form the broad consensual coalition he wanted.[26] Yet, this failure made it possible for him to achieve his primary goal of pursuing peace with the Palestinians and his Arab neighbors.[27]

When Rabin introduced his government to the Knesset for its approval, he boldly declared, "We must overcome the sense of isolation that has held us in thrall for almost half a century. We have to *stop thinking the whole world is against us*" (emphasis added).[28] He thereby signaled a fundamental ideological reorientation away from the emphasis on the Holocaust and Israel's isolation in the world, which had been the motifs of the Likud governments. It was precisely this reorientation that led the hard-line Rabin to think the unthinkable and, when it became justifiable in terms of Israel's long-term security interests, to shake the hand of Arafat.

Tragically, given his personality and lack of oratorical skills, Rabin was unable to effectively use the bully pulpit of his office to educate his countrymen and to convince the doubters of the correctness of this decision. Although trusted by the public, Rabin failed to convince enough of them of the wisdom of the course he had chosen. Rabin's life-long rival and successor as prime minister, Shimon Peres, was unfortunately perceived by many Israelis as being untrustworthy. Although he articulated a grand vision of a new Middle East, Israelis and Arabs alike (for different reasons and equally unjustly) questioned his motives. Ron Pundak, who along with Yair Hirschfeld first negotiated with PLO representatives in Oslo, observed that the accords "needed an aggressive marketing campaign. Rabin was never interested, and Peres was already galloping towards his New Middle East. To this day people don't understand the process. . . . Rabin, Peres and company were always on the defensive, instead of explaining Oslo to Israelis as a Zionist act, par excellence."[29]

Pundak and Hirschfeld were sent again by Yossi Beilin (then deputy foreign minister) to Stockholm, where they negotiated a document with

Abu Mazen (representing the PLO) that linked the interim process with a declaration of principles on the final status agreement. Pundak claims that the document "had been tailor-made for Rabin" with strong security dimensions built in. Negotiations were completed on October 31, five days before Rabin was assassinated. He never saw the document. According to Pundak, Peres was concerned about the evacuation of settlements from the Jordan Rift. He claims that "as soon as Rabin was assassinated, it was over. We knew Peres would shelve it, and that is what he did."[30]

The Declaration of Principles with the PLO, the Interim Agreement with the Palestinian Authority, and the peace treaty with Jordan would not likely have been concluded with a broader coalition. Yet the narrow coalition which was dependent upon the parliamentary support of the two Arab parties, coupled with the controversial nature of the agreements with the Palestinians, intensified the political polarization. Not just the militant right but even Likud leaders questioned the legitimacy of agreements the support of which depended on the parliamentary support of Arab parties. Boundaries of civil discourse were breached to the extreme of posters depicting Rabin in a kaffiyeh with the caption "traitor" and Rabin depicted in a Nazi storm trooper uniform appearing in opposition rallies. Verbal violence escalated into physical violence and culminated in the assassination of Rabin on November 4, 1995, by a militant religious law student who claimed religious justification for his deed.[31]

Peres, as Rabin's successor, also failed to convince a majority of Israelis to follow his lead. In fairness, it should be noted that he lost his substantial lead in the polls primarily because of several dramatic suicide bombings (carried out by Hamas and Islamic Jihad) in succession shortly before the election. This is a vivid example of how political extremism and terrorism can pay. The assassination of Rabin and the suicide bombings aimed to undermine support for Labor and thereby put a stop to the peace process. The militant Jews and Islamicists worked to achieve the same end. Peres lost to Netanyahu in 1996 by less than 30,000 votes (less than 1 percent) for the first direct election in Israeli history of an Israeli prime minister. Ironically, since Labor received the most Knesset mandates, Peres would have been invited to try to form a coalition government under the old electoral laws. I discuss further consequences of the electoral changes and recent efforts to change the system again below.

In the middle of Labor's term at the head of government, it suffered the biggest political defeat since the 1977 Knesset election. In May 1994, Labor renegade Chaim Ramon led his RAM coalition of former Laborites, Ratz, Shas, and the Arab Jewish list to victory in the Histadrut election.

"For the first time in the seventy-five-year history of the Histadrut it is not dominated by Labor. The inclusion of both the haredim and Israeli Arabs in the executive breaks the gentlemen's agreement that has excluded such ostensibly non-Zionist groups from top positions of power in key Zionist institutions."[32] Ramon and most of his followers who were originally members returned to Labor after Rabin's assassination, and Ramon served as minister of interior in the reconstituted government led by Peres. At the time of writing he is deputy party leader under Ehud Barak and a member of his government.

Labor's Return to the Opposition: 1996–1999

Since Peres had repeatedly failed to lead Labor to victory, the party turned to a younger leader. Ehud Barak, former chief of staff of the Israel Defense Forces, was brought into the cabinet by Yitzhak Rabin, his mentor and patron. When Peres reconstituted the coalition government after the assassination of Rabin, he made Barak foreign minister. Peres, who wanted to control Defense himself, sought to appease Rabin's supporters and assure the public with the appointment of Barak (long identified with Israel's security) to the top foreign policy post. However, this appointment undercut his own loyal protégé, Yossi Beilin. Beilin, as deputy foreign minister under Peres, had been largely responsible for initiating the Oslo process and had risked his political career in doing so. Barak, who failed to vote in favor of the Interim Agreement with the Palestine Authority in the cabinet, later defeated Beilin in the competition for the leadership of Labor.

Barak's first initiatives were disappointing as several ended in blunders. For example, he made a much needed initiative to win back voters of Middle Eastern background (Mizrachim) by holding the first Labor convention since he was elected party leader in Netivot, a development town in the northwestern Negev near Gaza. In this town of 20,000 populated primarily by working-class Mizrachim, in the spirit of penitence in the week before Yom Kippur, Barak received the endorsement by the conference of a public apology for the past treatment of Middle Eastern Jews by the party in the early decades of statehood. "In identification with the pain and suffering, in my name and in the name of the Labor Party, I ask forgiveness from those who were caused this suffering."[33] Whereas some saw this as a gimmick, others reserved judgment to see if Barak and the party would demonstrate their change of heart through deeds. They did not have to wait long.

Barak's political lieutenant, a former general and ranking Labor

Knesset member, Ori Orr, gave an interview to Moroccan-born journalist Daniel Ben-Simon that undid whatever good had been done by the party's endorsement of Barak's apology. Orr said of party colleagues of Middle Eastern background: "I can't speak to them as I do to others who are *more Israeli.*"[34] He went on to make disparaging remarks about "problematic" Moroccans. Barak, rather than reacting immediately, vacillated a full day and a half before demanding his old army buddy resign from his party positions, but he did not demand that he resign from the Knesset.

Another blunder was over the party's candidate for mayor of Jerusalem. After Barak failed to persuade the party's strongest potential candidate (Uzi Baram) to run, he turned to Shimon Shetreet. Realizing that Shetreet didn't have a chance against Olmert, the Jerusalem party functionaries made a deal with Olmert (ultimately endorsed by Shimon Peres and Jewish Agency head Avraham Burg). Changing his mind, Baram announced his candidacy, which he was forced to withdraw when Shetreet refused to step aside. Barak dismissed the renegades from their party positions in Jerusalem. Olmert (a primary candidate for leadership of the Likud following Netanyahu's resignation) won a big victory in Jerusalem. Hirsch Goodman concludes, "Barak seems sorely lacking in political skills. Apparently he has yet to learn that, unlike generals, politicians can't order people to vote for them. He also can't seem to get the party to rally behind him, obviously can't enforce discipline, has had trouble retaining senior staff who disagree with him and, most critically, has totally failed to articulate a clear and resounding alternate message to Netanyahu's policies."[35] Fortunately, Barak appears to have learned from his mistakes.

Shimon Peres posed a serious dilemma for Barak, who had trouble deciding whether to go all out to attempt to neutralize his influence or to embrace him and form a genuine partnership as Rabin had at the end of their tumultuous relationship. Peres resents having been forced to yield the party leadership to the much younger and less experienced Barak, who refused to create a special post of party president for him.[36] Peres floated the idea of Labor joining a National Unity government if Netanyahu would commit to the peace process, yet he reportedly turned down Netanyahu's offer of the foreign ministry when David Levy resigned the post in January 1998 because the government was destroying the peace process. Barak received conflicting advice on how to deal with Peres. Avraham Shochat and Benjamin Ben-Eliezer, loyal members of Rabin's former inner circle, advised him to fight Peres. Others argued for cooperation since Peres was needed to return Labor to power.[37]

Barak's reaction to a proposal by Peres and other Labor MKs to give

Netanyahu a political safety net in order to enable him to make concessions to the Palestinians was crudely emphatic: "The Labor party is turning itself into a political and public joke. It needs political Viagra to get itself up."[38] Peres was criticized for "undermining Barak's future challenge of Netanyahu."[39] Yossi Beilin articulated the political dilemma Labor faced after the Wye Agreements: "How far are we going to go to support this government because we don't want it to be toppled against the background of the Washington agreement? We can't give him a blank check."[40] In fact, bringing down the government derailed progress in the peace process for several months as Netanyahu froze the implementation of the Wye Agreements after Labor forced new elections.

There was realistic concern that further delay could deteriorate into a new form of intifada which would strengthen the opponents of peace on both sides. Scenes reminiscent of the intifada occurred in December as Palestinians rioted demanding the release of security prisoners from Israeli prisons. Military commentator Ehud Ya'ari calls this the "prisoners' Intifada."[41] An intelligence assessment given in testimony to the Knesset Foreign Affairs and Defense Committee predicted the possibility of a new intifada if the peace process fails.[42]

The dilemma seriously divided Labor along different lines than the traditional factions and patron-client relationships. Peres and Chaim Ramon (deputy leader of the party) favored a National Unity government, which Barak and Peres protégé Yossi Beilin strongly opposed. Barak rebuffed offers to join the government sent by Netanyahu. Beilin claimed, "We don't trust Netanyahu. It would be very artificial to enter government and serve as ministers under him. From the outside we can exert pressure if he tries to do something like expropriate Palestinian land. But once we're inside, we've lost the lever."[43]

Netanyahu used a parliamentary maneuver and the visit of President Clinton to Israel to postpone a vote of no confidence in his government for two weeks. He failed in his attempt to bring former foreign minister David Levy and his Gesher faction back into the coalition when Shas vetoed making him finance minister, and the Likud refused to give Gesher several hundred seats in the Likud's central committee. After having also failed to woo back the right and to bring Labor into a unity government, Netanyahu had no choice but to accept a deal with Labor to withdraw a scheduled vote of no confidence in the government (which would have meant a new election within sixty days). Instead, on December 22 Labor presented a motion to dissolve the government, which passed by a huge majority of eighty-one to thirty.

The 1999 Elections: The Race for Prime Minister

In the election of the prime minister held on May 17, 1999, Ehud Barak won an impressive personal victory over Benjamin Netanyahu. In many ways the election focused on the character of the two contenders (three other candidates withdrew late in the race), and Netanyahu was found wanting by a solid majority of voters.[44] Netanyahu succeeded in alienating those who worked most closely with him including Likud occupants of the most important cabinet posts, many of whom defected from both the government and the party. Benny Begin led the new ultranationalist National Unity, while former foreign minister David Levy joined Barak's One Israel. The new Center party was formed by Yitzhak Moredechai (whom Netanyahu fired as defense minister), former finance minister Dan Meridor, and former mayor of Tel Aviv Roni Milo. They were joined by the unaffiliated newly retired chief of staff of the Israel Defense Forces, Amnon Lipkin-Shahak.

Barak had banked on attracting Lipkin-Shahak to his side at Labor's helm after he ended his service in July, 1998.[45] However, Shahak was unwilling to align himself with Labor because he considers the party tired and disconnected from the voters.[46] Barak was following the Labor tradition (emulated by other parties) of parachuting former chiefs of staff (and other high-ranking officers) into top party posts. This is how Rabin was recruited and how he brought Barak into the party. This election was unique, however, because for the first time the generals entered politics directly to change the political leadership and the security policy.[47]

Barak, emulating British prime minister Tony Blair's success, renamed his party New Labor and then formed an electoral alignment (One Israel) with David Levy's Gesher and the liberal Orthodox Meimad. Emulating President Bill Clinton, he hired American political strategists James Carville, Stanley Greenberg, and Robert Shrum.[48] Depending upon professionals and a close network of former army buddies, Barak emphasized his own candidacy for premier and minimized the role of the party in the campaign. Such tactics helped Barak to defeat Netanyahu but failed to prevent the erosion of Labor's parliamentary representation and did little to restore public confidence in the party. As a hybrid between parliamentary and presidential systems, electoral reform in Israel appears to have produced the worst of both systems.

The Fifteenth Knesset: Transformation of the Party System

The most significant result of the parliamentary election is that both major parties continued their steady decline in representation in the Fifteenth Knesset elected the same day that Barak was elected as premier. Labor (which was then in the alignment with Mapam) went from a peak of 56 Knesset mandates in 1969 to 26 in 1999 (including Gesher and Meimad), more than halving the representation in thirty years. The Likud declined even more dramatically from 48 seats in 1981 to 19 mandates in 1999. The two parties collectively declined from 95 seats in 1981 to 45 seats in 1999. This may constitute the end of the dominance of the two-party bloc and yet another transformation of the party system. Although the trend began before the direct election of the prime minister, this "reform" encouraged and resulted in widespread split-ticket voting, which worked to the detriment of the two major parties and to the advantage of those appealing to religion and/or ethnicity/nationality, with the greatest success being enjoyed by Shas, which combined both.

Even though the new law for direct election of the prime minister seriously weakened Labor and the Likud, Netanyahu and Barak both resisted changing it for narrow personal and short-range political reasons. Each thought the law would work to his advantage and feared antagonizing smaller parties whose support they anticipated they might need for a coalition. In the meantime, Yossi Beilin and the Likud's Uzi Landau sponsored a bill to restore the old electoral system, which passed the first reading of the Knesset in a 50 to 45 vote in May 1998. Knesset members of both major parties were shaken by polls indicating that Shas might double its size in the 1999 election under the current system and that Labor and the Likud would together get barely 50 seats.[49] In fact, Shas dramatically increased its representation in the Fifteenth Knesset from 10 to 17 mandates, and Labor (26) and the Likud (19) collectively declined from 66 to merely 45 seats.

Barak was sufficiently concerned even before the election to appoint a top-level committee (composed of two former ministers of justice and Barak's two top rivals for party leadership) to examine Labor's position. Committee members Yossi Beilin and Haim Zadok support a return to the old system, and Chaim Ramon and David Liba'i favor amending the present system. Barak may be swayed by the committee's final report to change his position and support the change. Despite Netanyahu's firm commitment to the present system, a majority of Likud Knesset members voted for the Beilin-Landau bill. Netanyahu's weakened leadership within the Likud prevented the enforcement of strict party discipline on a second vote on this issue on December 21, 1998, when the Knesset again voted to overturn the direct election law. The bill failed, however, to become law in time for the 1999 elections.[50] Given the parliamentary growth of "special interest" parties, this may have been the last chance to reverse the diminution of the power of the major blocs and the resulting realignment of the party system.[51]

On one hand the increased representation of formerly marginalized sectors such as the ultra-Orthodox Jews, Mizrachim, new immigrants (particularly from the former Soviet Union), and Arabs represents a net gain for the democratic representation of diverse interests. On the other hand, particularly given the deep political and cultural conflicts between the interests and aspirations of these groups (including contradictory models of Israeli nationhood), it complicates the formation of stable coalition governments. This is a classic democratic dilemma: how to balance the tension between the needs for representativeness and governability.[52]

Conclusions

Those who worked for reconciliation with the Palestinians, peace with Jordan, and the normalization of Israel's role in the region have helped create a sense of the inevitability of the continuation of the process among increasing numbers of Israelis. More and more Israelis who would never have dreamed of recognizing the PLO a few years ago are becoming reconciled to the idea of living alongside a Palestinian state.[53] Recent polls indicate that 55 percent of surveyed Israelis say the Palestinians deserve their own state while 69 percent say they believe Palestinian statehood is inevitable.[54] The signing of the Wye Accords, backed by 75 percent of the Israeli public, signals the first broad consensus on security policy since the political polarization produced by the results of the 1967 war.

Given the logic of security dilemmas, changes in state security (decrements or increments) are likely to lead to political violence, particularly when tied to identity politics.[55] Whereas the peace treaties with Egypt and Jordan and the possibility of successfully completing an agreement with the Palestinians and Syria are perceived by the majority to increase Israel's security, a militant minority believes the opposite. Therefore, particularly as a final status agreement with the Palestinians would require further Israeli territorial concessions, there is a serious possibility of violent resistance from among the most militant settlers and their supporters.[56] The majority, who perceive increasing security from external threat, are more likely to focus on highly divisive internal issues of identity politics, the role of religion in the state, and competing visions of collective identity.

Barak needs to clearly articulate a vision of the future that is less grand and abstract than Peres's New Middle East. This vision must convince the majority of Israelis that it is in their interest to take the necessary risks for peace. Labor can play its historical role in setting the national agenda only by offering a realistic alternative vision to the religiously inspired, exclusive ethno-nationalism that has been the legacy of the Begin era. It would set the tone for defining Israeli identity inclusively following a liberal civic model of nationalism exemplified in Israel's declaration of independence. Like his mentor, Yitzhak Rabin, Barak announced the goal of forming a broad consensual government and concluding peace with Israel's neighbors. For Rabin, the goals were mutually exclusive, and his failure in the first goal made possible progress toward the second one. Conditions have changed. If Barak plays his cards well, demonstrates genuine leadership, and succeeds in educating the Israeli public and bringing it along with his government's policies, he can build a fairly broad and representative coalition that can make progress toward a just and lasting peace with the Palestinians and with Syria.

The even more challenging goal, however, will be to create a government and implement policies that will foster greater tolerance and which will achieve a balance between allowing the competing visions of Israeli nationhood while fostering a sense of unity, common purpose, and destiny among its diverse and contentious populous. No single individual, no matter how gifted, can accomplish these daunting goals alone. Barak will need to utilize his party to a much greater extent than he did during the election campaign to accomplish these goals. While the more open democratic processes of nominating candidates for the Knesset and party leader have produced some negative results, such as erosion of party discipline in the Knesset and a proliferation of private members' bills, they have also advanced some gifted leaders. If Barak learns to listen to the advice of his closest peers in the party (like Beilin and Ramon) who have far more party and political experience than he, his chances of mobilizing the great potential of a revitalized party will bode well for him and for the future of Labor. However, if he chooses to further marginalize the party's role and act like a president, he is less likely to succeed in his goals and will contribute to the further erosion of Labor and the development of an even more fragmented party system. His first test will be the nature of the government he forms and the program it presents to the Knesset and the nation. High on the domestic agenda should be a serious proposal for electoral reform.

Notes

1. Peter Medding is the only expert of whom I am aware who disagrees. Ever since I reviewed his classic book *Mapai in Israel,* we have carried on a stimulating professional debate on this and many other points, especially over our conflicting evaluations as to the extent to which the party was democratic. For example, Medding argues that his analysis provides impressive evidence against Michels' iron rule of oligarchy (303). In *Power and Ritual in the Israel Labor Party,* I conclude that "the Israel Labor Party would have to be placed between the two ideal-type paradigms of Michels and Medding, but is much closer to Michels' than Medding seems willing to admit" (239). In *The Israeli Labour Party,* Neill Lochery briefly summarizes Medding's skepticism about the application of the concept of dominant party to Mapai (Reading, U.K.: Ithaca Press, Garnet Publishing, 1997), 24–25.

2. Myron J. Aronoff, "Myths, Symbols, and Rituals of the Emerging State"; Myron J. Aronoff, "The Origins of Israeli Political Culture"; and Dan Horowitz and Moshe Lissak, *Origins of the Israeli Polity.*

3. Nurit Gertz, *Captive of a Dream: National Myths in Israeli Culture [Shevuyah b' halumah]* (Tel Aviv: Am Oved, Ofakim Series, 1988); Yael Zerubavel, *Recovered Roots: Collective Memory and the Making of Israeli National Tradition* (Chicago: University of Chicago Press, 1995); Nachman Ben-Yehuda, *The Masada Myth;* and Zeev Sternhell, *The Founding Myths of Israel.*

4. Yosef Gorni, *Achdut Ha'avoda 1919–1939;* Yonathan Shapiro, *The Formative Years of the Israeli Labour Party.*

5. Maurice Duverger, *Political Parties.*

6. Myron J. Aronoff, "Israel under Labor and the Likud: The Role of Dominance Considered," in *Uncommon Democracies,* ed. T. J. Pempel (Ithaca: Cornell University Press, 1990).

7. Arnold Lewis, "Ethnic Politics and the Foreign Policy Debate in Israel," and Joel Migdal, "Changing Boundaries and Social Crisis: Israel and the 1967 War," in *War as a Source of State and Social Transformation in the Middle East,* ed. Steven Heydemann (Berkeley: University of California Press, 2000).

8. Neill Lochery (*Israeli Labour Party,* 44–45) summarizes scholarly explanations for the decline of Labor, categorizing them in four frameworks—political dynamics, political culture, the influence of the Arab-Israeli conflict in domestic politics, and political economy. In his summary, he fails to do justice to several scholars' work, including mine. He ignores my analysis of the complex cumulative long-term factors and the more immediate causes for Labor's defeat—mentioning only two factors in the first category. In fact my analysis encompasses the first three of the four approaches. See my review of Lochery's book in *Middle East Journal* 53, no. 2 (Spring 1999): 300–301.

9. Lochery terms these "conditioning effects" (*Israeli Labour Party,* xvii–xviii).

He fails to cite my original formulation of the point, although I don't use this particular term. See, for example, Aronoff, *Power and Ritual in the Israel Labor Party*, 165–66. My discussion of the notion of "loading the dice" first appears on p. 3.

10. It is difficult to imagine how a serious reading of this book (much less my other publications listed in Lochery's bibliography) could have resulted in ignoring the centrality of political culture in my analysis of Labor and explanation for its decline.

11. In fact, women were the only group in the population dramatically underrepresented in party institutions and leadership that did not desert the party in significant proportions.

12. See, for example, my analysis of the Galili Statement in Aronoff, *Power and Ritual in the Israel Labor Party*, 30, 31, 145, and the debate over it on pp. 146–51. For a systematic analysis of Labor party positions on national security, see Efraim Inbar, *War and Peace in Israeli Politics*.

13. Aronoff, *Israeli Visions and Divisions*.

14. Although I analyze the suppression of political and economic issues related to the Histadrut, I do not engage in a political economy analysis of the decline of Labor. For that the reader must turn to the work of others. Michael Shalev, "The Political Economy of the Labor Party in Israel: Dominance and Decline in Israel," in Pempel, ed., *Uncommon Democracies*; and Michael Shalev, *Labor and the Political Economy in Israel* (London: Oxford University Press, 1993).

15. In support of the point, for example, I quote Moshe Carmel's speech in the Labor national party convention in November 1991 and Galia Golan, who was a member of the Central Committee at the time, both of whom noted Labor's failure to comprehend its role in the opposition (Aronoff, *Power and Ritual in the Israel Labor Party*, xi, xiv). This is another theme adopted by Lochery (*Israeli Labour Party*, 63) without crediting my previously published formulation of the point.

16. Yossi Beilin, "Dominant Party in Opposition."

17. Lochery, *Israeli Labour Party*, 65.

18. At least eleven of the Fourteenth Knesset members were children of Knesset members. Yael Dayan, a third-generation Knesset member is also the niece of President Weizman. Many of the Likud "princes," such as Benny Begin (who resigned from the Knesset after the poor showing of the National Unity party, which he led in the 1999 election), are among them. Benjamin Netanyahu is the nephew of a former Supreme Court justice. See Gershom Gorenberg, "Good Old Boys," *Jerusalem Report*, August 31, 1998, 54. Dalia Rabin-Pelosoff, daughter of the late prime minister Yitzhak Rabin, was elected to the Fifteenth Knesset on the new Center party list. The fact that Netanyahu and other leading members of the Likud are also a part of the establishment did not prevent them using the label to stigmatize Labor.

19. Beilin, "Dominant Party in Opposition," 41.

20. Myron J. Aronoff, "Political Polarization."

21. Lochery's (*Israeli Labour Party*, 107) summary of the development of the party during the period 1948–88 indicates a lack of comprehension of this point. The period 1948–77 is redundantly characterized as "Dominant Party with Power." His term for the period 1977–81, "Dominant Party without Power," is an oxymoron. He calls the period 1981–84 "Non-Dominant Party without Power," which is meaningless.

22. Ian S. Lustick, *For the Land and the Lord*.

23. Myron J. Aronoff, *Israeli Visions and Divisions*, 129. My critique of the proponents of this position is in chap. 6 (126–29). See also Charles Liebman and Eliezer Don-Yehiya, *Civil Religion in Israel*; Ofira Seliktar, *New Zionism and the Foreign Policy System of Israel*; Lilly Weisbrod, "From Labour Zionism to New Zionism."

24. Aronoff (*Israeli Visions and Divisions*); Dan Horowitz and Moshe Lissak, *Trouble in Utopia*; and Jonathan Shapiro, *The Road to Power*.

25. Myron J. Aronoff, "Better Late Than Never."

26. Myron J. Aronoff, "Labor in the Second Rabin Era."

27. Myron J. Aronoff and Yael S. Aronoff, "Explaining Domestic Influences on Current Israeli Foreign Policy," and Myron J. Aronoff and Yael S. Aronoff, "Domestic Determinants of Israeli Foreign Policy."

28. Aronoff and Aronoff, "Explaining Domestic Influences on Current Israeli Foreign Policy," 86.

29. Ron Pundak interviewed by Leslie Susser, "Unhappy Birthday," *Jerusalem Report*, September 28, 1998, 24.

30. Ibid., 25.

31. Ehud Sprinzak, *Brother against Brother*.

32. Myron J. Aronoff and Pierre Atlas, "The Peace Process and Competing Challenges to the Dominant Zionist Discourse," 54.

33. Joel Greenberg, "In Spirit of Atonement, an Apology to Sephardim," *New York Times International*, September 30, 1997, A4.

34. Gershom Gorenberg, "Good Old Boys" (emphasis added).

35. Hirsh Goodman, "Labor Pains," *Jerusalem Report*, October 26, 1998, 56.

36. He founded the Peres Peace Center, which coordinates investment in the peace process and has become a major fund-raiser for Palestinian projects. Leslie Susser characterizes the view of Peres in the Labor party as "respect tempered by irritation at the crochety dad who won't let go of the family business." Leslie Susser, "He Just Keeps Rollin' Along," *Jerusalem Report*, April 2, 1998, 12.

37. Ibid., 13.

38. "The Reporter," *Jerusalem Report*, August 17, 1998, 11.

39. Ehud Ya'ari, "Persistent," *Jerusalem Report*, August 17, 1998, 29.

40. Deborah Sontag, "Peace Accord Leaves Israeli Labor Party in a Tough Spot over Whether to Topple Netanyahu," *New York Times*, October 29, 1998, A6.

41. Ehud Ya'ari, "Terminal Oslo," *Jerusalem Report*, January 4, 1999, 28.

42. Hirsh Goodman, "The Price of Survival," *Jerusalem Report,* January 4, 1999, 56.

43. Ibid.

44. Netanyahu's record as prime minister was a major liability. The *Economist,* October 11–17, 1997, 17, featured his photograph on the cover under the heading "Israel's serial bungler." The editorial called Netanyahu's election "a calamity." It cited his undermining of the peace process and the bungled attempt by the Mossad to assassinate Hamas official Khaled Meshal in Amman, Jordan, on September 25, 1997. Netanyahu alienated his right-wing support by his compromise with the Palestinians at the Wye peace talks and then alienated the moderates by failing to implement the agreements.

45. Barak was so desperate to recruit Shahak, he told a closed party forum that he reserved the right to name eight top places on the party's next Knesset list. He wanted to assure that people "like Amnon Shahak and Shimon Peres won't have to run around seeking votes in the primaries." Leslie Susser, "Barak confident that Shahak will join him," *Jerusalem Report,* August 3, 1998, 4, 6.

46. Deborah Sontag, "Israeli Blocs: Humpty-Dumptys Right and Left," *New York Times International,* December 23, 1998, A3.

47. Yoram Peri, "The 'Democratic Putsch' of the 1999 General Elections," a paper presented at the Fifteenth Annual Meeting of the Association for Israel Studies, May 23–25, 1999.

48. Adam Nagourney, "Have Attack Ad, Will Travel," *New York Times Magazine,* April 28, 1999, 42–48, 61, 70; Dan Caspi, "When Americanization Fails? From Democracy to Demedemocracy in Israel," *Israel Studies Bulletin* 15, no. 1 (Fall 1999): 1–4.

49. Leslie Susser, "Perhaps the Old System Wasn't So Bad After All . . . ," *Jerusalem Report,* July 6, 1998, 14.

50. Bills must pass three readings in the Knesset to become law. A change in the election system requires a majority of sixty-one votes.

51. Hirsh Goodman uses the lesson of the local elections to call on Netanyahu and Barak to "lead and take joint responsibility for mutually acceptable change that restores the mandate to the majority. . . . It needs immediate cooperation by the two to restore sanity to our political system. If they fail, they will be nurturing a monster that ultimately will consume them and all they stand for." Hirsh Goodman, "Voting Disaster," *Jerusalem Report,* December 7, 1998, 56.

52. Myron J. Aronoff, "The Americanization of Israeli Politics: Political and Cultural Change," *Israel Studies* 5, no. 2 (2000): 92–107.

53. Ehud Ya'ari reports: "In Washington, Ariel Sharon displayed readiness for a Palestinian state that would be limited to zones A and B, constituting some 42 percent of the West Bank, as well as in most of the Gaza Strip" ("Terminal Oslo," 28).

54. "14 Days: Peace Index," *Jerusalem Report,* April 26, 1999, 8.

55. Manus I. Midlarsky and Myron J. Aronoff, "Security Dilemmas: Changes

in State Security and the Onset of Political Violence," a paper presented at the Fortieth Annual Convention of the International Studies Association, Washington, D.C., February 16–20, 1999.

56. Myron J. Aronoff, "The Prospects of Jewish Terrorism in Light of the Likely Progress in the Peace Process," lecture delivered at a symposium on Sources of Religious Terrorism in South Asia and the Middle East sponsored by the Council on Foreign Relations and the Office of Counter-terrorism Coordinator, U.S. Department of State, Brookings Institution, Washington, D.C., June 16, 1999. See also Myron J. Aronoff, "Political Violence and Extremism—A Review of Ehud Sprinzak's Brother Against Brother," *Israel Studies* 4, no. 2 (Fall 1999): 237–46.

7

The Right in Israeli Politics
The Nationalist Ethos in the Jewish Democracy

Ilan Peleg

Modern political Zionism has been characterized from its very first days by conflictual notions of the essence of the Zionist project and ways for implementing it. The common denominator of all factions within the Zionist movement was the call on the Jews to return to Zion, to immigrate to Eretz Israel, and to build there an autonomous Jewish society. Yet, beyond this fundamental common goal, diversity of views dominated the Zionist camp.

Thus, although some prominent early Zionists, including Theodor Herzl, were committed to the secular, progressive ideals of the Enlightenment, envisioning a liberal democratic polity, other Zionists, notably Ahad Ha'am and Eliezer Ben-Yehuda, focused mainly on the promotion of Jewish culture. Labor Zionists supported the establishment of a society based on equality, self-reliance, physical work, and social justice. While religious circles sought to combine halachic Judaism and national independence, Vladimir Jabotinsky and the Revisionists introduced a model of military power, national pride, grandeur, conquest, and domination.[1]

Dan Horowitz and Moshe Lissak, in their authoritative volume *Trouble in Utopia: The Overburdened Polity of Israel*, thought that there were inherent contradictions within the infrastructure of the Zionist ideology. The clearest contradiction was between Jewish particularistic values, reflected in the desire to establish a nation-state, and universalistic-humanistic values.[2]

These contradictions did not disappear with the establishment of Israel in 1948. On the contrary, they became more pronounced, especially following the expansion of Israel's territorial control into the Arab-inhabited areas of the West Bank and the Gaza Strip, as well as the Sinai Peninsula and the Golan Heights.[3] In fact, the domestic conflict within Israel's Jewish community developed into a full-fledged Kulturkampf, a deep, multifaceted struggle among Israeli Zionists over the essence of the State of Israel.[4]

This cultural war between various Zionist camps is at the center of the analysis offered in this chapter. The fiftieth anniversary of Israel is an appropriate occasion for a broadly conceived, historical assessment of one of the camps, the right, involved in this political battle.

The Israeli Right: Conceptualization

This chapter is about the role of the Israeli right in the politics of the country between 1948 and 1999. Its purpose is to offer a conceptual framework for the understanding of the right; to identify the right as a political camp marked by a number of typical characteristics; to offer a brief developmental, dynamic picture of the Israeli right by focusing on its role in five distinct periods between 1948 and 1999; and finally, to begin a discussion of the impact of the elections of 1999 on the future of the Israeli right.

Conceptually, employing the right-left continuum for the analysis of any political system is merely "a useful shorthand . . . to understand and order the political scene."[5] Like any other "shorthand," the notions of "right" and "left" are of some, but necessarily limited, utility. I see the usefulness of the notion of "right" and "left" and the employment of the right-left continuum as twofold:

> (1) the use of this conceptualization might help the analyst to locate certain organizations (for example, political parties), persons (for example, political leaders), and ideas (for example, election platforms) in their *relationships* to other organizations, persons, or ideas, thus placing them in a context—this is the *relativistic* use of the notions of "right" and "left";
> (2) the use of the right-left continuum might assist the analyst in determining the content (or substance) of the position taken by a certain individual or group—this is the *absolutist* use of the notions of "right" and "left" in political analysis.

In this chapter, I intend to use the concept of the political right in a dual capacity, relativistic and absolutist. In the first capacity, an analysis would be offered which attempts to assess the position of those who are identified as part of the Israeli right in relation to the position of those who are ordinarily located at the center of the political map or at its left wing. To the extent to which certain individuals or organizations show a consistent and stable tendency to stake a position at the same place on this analytical continuum, this conceptual tool has some explanatory and predictive usefulness.

As an absolutist conceptual instrument, the right-left continuum is more complicated and problematical. Nevertheless, it is useful insofar as it tends to focus attention on the role of political ideology, a factor of great importance in many political systems, including Israel's. A political ideology is a normative belief system that presents a set of goals and identifies means for achieving them. If one can draw systematic and consistent differences between the political ideologies of different political actors—individuals and groups alike—one can use such a differentiation for explaining their respective political behaviors within a broad philosophical context.

In regard to Israel, a few commonly made arguments reflect the importance of the left-right language: (1) the argument that the Israeli public is evenly divided between left and right indicates that analysts believe that one can intelligently place Israelis along a right-left continuum, and (2) the argument that Israel has "drifted" to the right since 1967 indicates that analysts believe that they are capable of showing the ideological direction toward which the country has moved. Asher Arian believes that the data bears out *both* arguments, and his position strengthens the belief that the employment of a left-right concept is indeed useful.[6]

In this chapter, I will often refer to the relative position of parties on the right (for example, Herut, Gahal, and Likud) and leaders on the right (for example, Begin, Shamir, and Netanyahu). I will compare them to the positions taken by other Israeli parties and leaders. My hypothesis would be that right-wing parties and leaders have indeed exhibited—ideologically and behaviorally—a relatively nationalist position, although their position has not been by any means entirely fixed. Secondly, in the next section I will attempt to offer an overall ideological characterization of the right, arguing, in effect, that the content of the right's belief system remains fundamentally unchanged despite changes in the conditions of the state, the region, and, indeed, the world. Thus, while the *relativistic* analysis that will be made of the right tends to focus on the dynamics of change and especially on the ways in which parties and leaders adjust their positions to the positions of others in the political system, the *absolutist* analysis of the right tends to highlight the *fixed* nature of the right's ideology. The two types of analysis do not contradict but complement each other.

Defining the Right: An Ideological Approach

A broad, historical perspective of the Israeli right since the establishment of the State of Israel in 1948, and in many ways since the early 1920s (the birth of Revisionism), indicates that this political camp has followed, quite consistently, a more or less coherent political ideology. This political ideology included a few central elements: (1) *normative goals* (that is, objectives based on values); (2) *means* for achieving these goals; and (3) a set of *myths, symbols, and taboos* designed to mobilize supporters for the ideological goals and justify the means for their achievement.

At the center of the normative world of the Israeli right there has always been, exclusively, the Jewish nation: the *nationalist ethos* could be viewed as the heart and soul of right-wing politics from the early 1920s to the late 1990s. Vladimir (Ze'ev) Jabotinsky (1880–1940), the Founding Father and intellectual light of almost all Israel's right-wingers, is the man who offered the myth of the *power of the nation* as the fundamental normative goal for Zionists to achieve. While labor Zionists spoke the language of creating a model society, an egalitarian community based on socialist values, agricultural work, self-sufficiency, and participatory democracy, Jabotinsky's Revisionism called for the establishment of *Malchut Israel*—the Kingdom of Israel—on both sides of the Jordan River, rejected any and all plans for compromise with the Arabs, and developed a set of values to fit its overall ideological position. These values included an emphasis on military power, discipline, organization, and physical courage, but, above all, the establishment of Jewish statehood within large territorial boundaries.

As an ideology, the Israeli right has consistently maintained a series of typical characteristics:

(1) emphasizing the *power of the nation* as a measure of all things, a meta-value to the exclusion of all other values (for example, peace and compromise with other national groups, social justice, egalitarian society);

(2) presenting the *outside, non-Jewish world* as not only attitudinally hostile but actively involved in efforts to destroy Israel and the Jewish people;

(3) demonstrating a pronounced emphasis on power, particularly in its military form, as a sole instrument in the relations between nations—a *militaristic approach* to international relations has characterized the right more than any other Israeli political camp;

(4) dehumanizing all opponents of Israel, particularly the Palestinians and other Arabs, often by using such powerful historical references as the Holocaust and biblical taboos such as "Amalek";

(5) emphasizing *maximal territorial expansion*—based on claimed nationalistic rights—as a value clearly distinguishing the right from centrist and leftist forces in Israeli politics;

(6) identifying internal (that is, Jewish) *opponents* as "enemies of the people," non-patriotic traitors, enemy sympathizers, and otherwise undesirables—and fighting against such opponents not only through verbal assaults but, in certain cases, through *violence*.[7]

These "Six Pillars" of the Zionist right-wing ideology, as we may want to call them, have been present in virtually all forms of right-wing Zionism since the 1920s, although the expression of these ideas may have varied from era to era, and although different brands of right-wing ideology may have had different emphases, angles, and language usages to express these fundamentals.

Even the most general comparisons reveal that different spokesmen of the Zionist right have not changed their message dramatically, although some variation on the right-wing nationalist theme does emerge from an examination of Jabotinsky's Revisionism, Begin's Neo-Revisionism, and Netanyahu's ideas and policies.

National Power

The Israeli right was born about a quarter of a century prior to the birth of Israel itself. The man responsible for that birth, Jabotinsky, the intellectual father of the Zionist right, rejected in 1922 an early British compromise proposal to the evolving Arab-Jewish conflict, arguing that the future of the Jewish nation required territorial control of Eretz Israel in its entirety, on both banks of the Jordan.

Yet, Jabotinsky (and then Begin, Shamir, and Netanyahu) was not merely a "territorialist"—he emphasized repeatedly the centrality of national power above any other value. For the Zionist right, during the Mandate (1922–48) and since the establishment of the State of Israel (1948), the goal was not merely national existence and survival but also national power and grandeur for the Jewish state; the approach of the right has clearly been overcompensatory.[8] This approach is evident not only in Jabotinsky's writings (with their clear Machiavellian tone) and in Begin's speeches (with their emphasis on Jewish power in the post-Holocaust era) but also in the more analytical, updated version of Netanyahu.

In his 1993 book, *A Place among the Nations: Israel and the World,* the future Israeli premier clearly returns to the traditional theme of nationalistic power: Greater Israel is to encompass all of the occupied territories, its survival will be based on overwhelming strength and on deterrence posture, and so on.[9] It is clear that for Netanyahu, as for previous nationalist leaders, the choice has always been between a status of a regional superpower—domineering, expansive, armed to the teeth, and in control of other peoples—and survival itself. A smaller Israel, at peace with its neighbors and integrated into the Middle East, has simply not been a preferred choice for Likud's leaders.

The Outside (Non-Jewish) World

Interestingly, this particular dimension has seen some significant changes in the position of the Israeli right. Jabotinsky believed that the Zionists could greatly benefit from the support of non-Jews; he was particularly a great admirer of the British, and his general approach to the world was liberal and cosmopolitan. Begin and Shamir, on the other hand, saw the world as fundamentally anti-Jewish, a hostile place in which Israel can rely, ultimately, only on itself and its Jewish brethren. Their position reflected the thinking of the post-Holocaust Israeli right. Netanyahu was somewhat in the middle in terms of his attitude to the outside world. He argued, self-righteously, that the world applies stricter standards of behavior to Israel than to other countries when it criticizes the Jewish state for human rights violations in the territories.[10] He maintained that there is a "psychological bedrock underneath" the negative attitude of the world toward Israel and an inability to come to terms with Jewish power.[11]

Militarism

Jabotinsky was an unabashed militarist, fully reflecting the colonialism of his time and his own Machiavellian thinking. Begin, who became the commander of the Etzel (National Military Organization, IZL, or Irgun) when he was merely thirty, was a military enthusiast during the Mandatory era (when his organization carried on a military campaign against both Arabs and British despite the Yishuv's policy of restraint). His overall militaristic approach was also reflected in his policies—and the means adopted for achieving them—when he served as Israel's prime minister, culminating in the ill-fated war in Lebanon in 1982. The Netanyahu approach to international politics was reminiscent of Jabotinsky's and Begin's attitudes. For Netanyahu, peace was not a function of mutual recognition and acceptance but a function of strength, deterrence, and domination. Chapter 7 of his 1993 book is entitled "The Wall," an allusion to Jabotinsky's call to the Jews to build an iron wall that would force the Arabs to accept them. The message is straightforward: to survive, Israel must establish a military "wall" by controlling the Samarian and Judean mountains.

Dehumanization of Opponents

The Arab-Jewish conflict in Palestine is more than one hundred years old. It is the type of conflict that invites the dehumanization of the opponent, perceiving it as an inalterably hostile creature who must be defeated. Although most Zionists adopted a negative position toward the Arabs, especially after 1920, the right has been considerably more hostile than other brands of Zionism. Nevertheless, the position of the right has not been fixed but has evolved from one era to the next. Jabotinsky perceived the Arabs as a backward people who would, nevertheless, fight against Zionism. They must be defeated by force, he advised.[12] For Begin and his brand of post-Holocaust Neo-Revisionism, the Arabs were the latter-day bearers of the anti-Semitic germ, not merely an indigenous population resisting European settlers. The transformation is reflected in the frequently used reference to the Arabs as "Amalek," the biblical nation who fought the Hebrews and whom God commanded the Israelites to annihilate. Such powerful cultural symbols legitimize the idea of an unlimited war against the Arabs and dehumanize them.

Netanyahu's position toward the Arabs was more complex than either the Revisionist (Jabotinsky) or the Neo-Revisionist (Begin). His overall approach was close to the traditional right-wing position; he refused to recognize "the force, authenticity, let alone legitimacy of Arab nationalism,"[13] viewed Arab-Jewish relations as inalterably hostile, and saw only power solutions to the dispute. Netanyahu also expressed the view that the Palestinian problem is an artificial dilemma—he compared the Palestinians to the Sudeten Germans (!)—and insisted that the Palestinians have no justified claim in any part of Eretz Israel.[14] In regard to the PLO, Netanyahu dismissed all of its moderate pronouncements, and he described autonomy for the Arabs as a permanent solution for the West Bank, with Israel maintaining full sovereignty.[15] The policy of the Netanyahu government toward the Israeli-Palestinian peace process was quite compatible with these ideological positions.

Territorial Expansion

Although in regard to some issues the right's position has not been entirely consistent, on the central issue of demanding maximal territorial expansion, the Zionist right wing has demonstrated a remarkable degree of consistency. The Founding Father, Jabotinsky, demanded that every new member of his Revisionist party take a formal vow supporting the principle of *Shlemut Hamoledet* (Greater Israel), the right of the Jewish people to Eretz Israel in its entirety (that is, on both sides of the Jordan River). Begin continued to insist on the implementation of this idea, although the establishment of the Hashemite Kingdom of Jordan and the drawing of the armistice lines between it and the State of Israel (1949) effectively killed the idea. When Israel conquered the West Bank and the Gaza Strip, Begin's parties (first Gahal and then Likud) were among the strongest supporters of Greater Israel, now applied only to Western Palestine. Like Begin, Netanyahu was, above all, a territorialist: He demanded as much as possible under ever-changing political conditions. Territorialism does not stand for a fixed position but for a generalized approach toward keeping as much land as possible regardless of other values. The territorial imperative was as important for Netanyahu as it had been for Jabotinsky, Begin, and Shamir. Again, those fundamental attitudes were reflected in his negotiating position, at least until October 1998.

Internal Opponents

Nationalist, right-wing ideology is based, invariably, on the idea that the source of all good and virtue is the nation. The ideology calls upon all those who belong to the nation to support the goals set by the nationalist elite and the means adopted to fulfill them. Resistance or opposition to the nationalist program usually leads to the identification of the person as a disloyal traitor who sympathizes with the enemy rather than with his own people. Since the nationalist program is considered to be of supreme value, whenever such opposition is of measurable effectiveness, the deviant is likely to be the target of not only criticism but actual sanctions, and even violence.

The Israeli Right: A Developmental Approach

In the second section of this chapter, I attempted to identify the ideological foundations of the Israeli (and pre-Israeli) right. In a general way, most of these ideological principles have not changed significantly since the appearance of a distinct right-wing camp among Zionist Jews in Mandatory Palestine in the early 1920s. In this section, I will add a dynamic dimension to my previous analysis, assessing the development of the Israeli right between 1948 and 1999, against the background of the emergence of

Jewish independence in Eretz Israel in 1948 and Israeli territorial expansion following the 1967 war.

In general, one may distinguish five periods in terms of the status of the Israeli right in the political life of the country: (1) marginality and the lean years (1948–66); (2) rehabilitation (1967–76); (3) golden age and decline (1977–91); (4) temporary retreat (1992–95); (5) resurrection and heightened sophistication (1996–99).

The establishment of the State of Israel in May 1948 found the Zionist right in disarray. The new Israeli government was led by David Ben-Gurion of Mapai (the Labor party). Menachem Begin, the leader of the IZL, an underground organization with pronounced right-wing leanings, decided to establish a political party that would compete with Mapai in the forthcoming elections for the Knesset (1949). Prior to the dissolution of the IZL, Begin, in a departing shot, issued a declaration calling for the liberation of the entire homeland, including the Gilad, east of the Jordan River.

The new right-wing party headed by Begin, Herut (Freedom), continued to promote a policy based on territorial expansion, despite the fact that the 1949 armistice lines quickly became the accepted de facto borders of the State of Israel. By promoting the territorial imperative, Herut condemned itself to a position of marginality within Israel's body politic.

In most other matters, Herut similarly promoted, between 1948 and 1965 (when it joined the liberals in Gahal), the fundamentals of right-wing ideology. Its approach to foreign policy was clearly militaristic: it was supportive of frequent and extensive use of force as an instrument for dealing with Israel's neighbors. Within Mapai, the ruling party, two opposing approaches, dovish and hawkish, emerged.[16] Herut's policy remained monolithically hawkish.[17] When Israel's Reprisal Policy was initiated, in the early 1950s, it found in Herut a consistent supporter. In fact, Herut demanded even larger reprisals and hoped that the escalation along the armistice lines would eventually lead to a total war, giving Israel an opportunity to "liberate" the remainder of the occupied homeland.

Herut's hostility toward the Arabs and its radicalism on other foreign policy matters helped its great rival, David Ben-Gurion, to marginalize the opposition party, despite (or maybe because of) the increasing similarity between his position and theirs. When the issue of reparations from Germany came up in 1952, Herut led not only a strong verbal assault on the proposed agreement but also a physical attack on the Knesset. A number of years later, Herut led the attack on Mapai's leadership in connection with the Kastner trial, a trial leading eventually to the assassination of Dr.

Kastner. This behavior made it easy for Ben-Gurion and his associates to paint Herut as an irresponsible, radical party that could not be allowed to lead the country or even be a member of the ruling coalition.

In a general way, beyond all specific issues, Herut's position invariably reflected the essence of the right wing—a strong sense of nationalism, even beyond rational calculations of national interest. The reparations from Germany brought out this trait rather dramatically. Despite the fact that Israel had significant economic and political reasons to receive the German reparations, Herut vocally and violently opposed the government's efforts to obtain them. The reason cited was national honor and pride. Begin called the mere negotiations with the Germans *chilul hashem* (the defamation of God's name), "the ultimate abomination, the likes of which we have not known since we became a nation."[18] The right's opponents were depicted as people who brought shame on the nation.

The radicalism of Herut perpetuated its marginality. The party remained a small and insignificant opposition group. Its vocal attacks on the government were dysfunctional in terms of its own interests. In the mid-1960s, however, Herut began to rehabilitate itself, a process that, along with the results of the 1967 war, eventually led it to power. At the first stage of this rehabilitation process, Herut was successful in forming with the liberals a new party alignment called Gahal (Bloc of Herut and Liberals). This move gave Herut the respectability it craved, without forcing it to openly give up its radical stands on foreign policy matters.

The second step toward rehabilitation came as a result of the 1967 war. As it became clearer in Israel during late May 1967 that war with a large Arab coalition was inevitable, pressure mounted on the Israeli premier and defense minister, Levi Eshkol, to give up the defense portfolio and form a government of national unity. Eshkol finally agreed to transfer the defense ministry to General Moshe Dayan and to appoint Menachem Begin as a member of his government. Thus, Arab radicalism and threats gave Begin a golden opportunity not only to gain popularity among his supporters but to prove to other Israelis that his exclusion from politics was unwarranted and unjustified. Begin, a consummate political and charismatic leader, made the most of his opportunity. As a member of the Eshkol and Meir governments, he treated these Labor prime ministers with the utmost respect while, at the same time, forming with others (notably Moshe Dayan) a right-wing coalition against any diplomatic moderation. In 1970, when the Meir government accepted an American proposal to a cease-fire with the Egyptians (designed to end the War of

Attrition with Egypt), Begin quickly resigned from the Meir government, reminding the public that he was still the old nationalist (but now a respectable one).

The rehabilitation process of Menachem Begin was further strengthened with the establishment of Likud, a broad-based right-wing coalition which included not only the traditional hawkish Herut and its liberal allies (that is Gahal) but also new supporters of Greater Israel, including many old Laborites. In March 1977 this coalition of nationalists won the Israeli election, thus commencing the Golden Age of the Israeli right.

The cornerstone of Likud's foreign policy during the Golden Age (1977–82) and following it (1983–91) was the effort to maintain Israel's control over the territories occupied during the 1967 war in the face of international pressure to withdraw, internal dissent, and a bad demographic situation. Recognizing that immediate annexation of the West Bank and Gaza was beyond Israel's power, Begin chose to focus a considerable amount of his resources on neutralizing Egypt (a policy resulting eventually in the Camp David Accords and the Egyptian-Israeli Peace Treaty) and on containing the pressure from Lebanon and Syria (resulting in the Lebanese wars of 1978 and 1982). Begin's "southern strategy" and "northern strategy" were, however, intimately and directly linked with the central goal of annexation, an integral goal of the Revisionist plan since the early 1920s.

During Begin's premiership, one can distinguish between two eras, a periodization that makes sense only if one ties it to the overall strategy and the political ideology of the Israeli right. In the first period, lasting between Begin's rise to power in 1977 and the signing of the Egyptian-Israeli Peace Treaty in 1979, Begin's government pursued a policy designed to neutralize Egypt as a member of the anti-Israel Arab coalition. This seemingly moderate policy—mistakenly described as an overall "peace" policy by Begin and others—was implemented by such men as Foreign Minister Moshe Dayan and Defense Minister Ezer Weizman.

Both of these leaders resigned their posts in frustration when the period of radicalization (1980–83) was inaugurated. They were replaced by a cast of characters much closer to Begin's traditional right-wing thinking: Foreign Minister Yitzhak Shamir, Defense Minister Ariel (Arik) Sharon, IDF Chief of Staff Rafael Eitan, and so forth. The new policy elite carried out an extensive settlement program in the West Bank, Gaza, and the Golan Heights (which it then, de facto, annexed) and led Israel to the ill-fated Lebanon War (June 1982). It is essential to realize, however, that the "moderate" policies of 1977–79 and the "radical" ones of 1980–83 were designed to achieve the same goal: Israeli annexation of the West Bank and Gaza.

The Lebanon War, the jewel in the crown of the radicalization period, was truly reflective of Herut's traditional foreign policy goals, style of operation, and even fundamental values. The primary and most immediate objective of the war was to achieve Herut's long-held ideological goal: the annexation of the West Bank and Gaza. By destroying the PLO in its center, Lebanon, Likud leaders hoped to force the inhabitants of the West Bank to accept the autonomy plan offered to them by Begin. Chief of Staff Eitan said, candidly, that the war in Lebanon was a continuation of "the battle for Eretz Israel."[19] The second, more general, objective of the Lebanon War was to regain Israel's overwhelming military superiority in the Middle East, a position challenged by the course and the results of the 1973 war; this goal was directly linked to the militaristic tradition of the Israeli right. The third objective of the 1982 war was the establishment of Israeli hegemony in the entire Middle East, a new balance of power in which Israel would be completely dominant.[20] In order to create the new Middle Eastern order, the Likud government converted Israeli foreign policy from deterrence and prevention (which characterized Labor's security policy) to a policy of control and compellence. The new Likud policy utilized warfare for purely political objectives, and its final goal was to establish Israel as a Middle Eastern regional superpower.[21]

Begin's ambitious policy eventually collapsed under its own weight, as did its main promoter, Israel's premier. The sudden retirement of Menachem Begin from politics and the complete failure of the Lebanese operation led to the decline of Likud's foreign policy. Lebanon marked the limits of Israel's power and set limits on the right's territorial and political ambitions. The elections of 1984 ended in a draw, leading to the establishment of a national unity government with the Likud as one, but only one, of the senior partners. Thus ended the Golden Age of Likud's rule.

In 1988, however, the Likud returned to power as the leading partner in the coalition. Under the leadership of Yitzhak Shamir, the Likud pursued an aggressive settlement policy in the occupied territories, antagonizing Israel's strongest international supporter, the United States. In fact, the personal relationship between President George Bush and Prime Minister Shamir deteriorated because of the latter's refusal to slow down the settlement push.

During the last years of Shamir's prime ministership, the polarization among Israeli voters reached new extremes. While Laborites' inclination toward dovish solutions to the Israeli-Palestinian dilemma grew, many Lukudniks remained committed to the status quo and to hawkish solutions. Thus, in a series of personal interviews with Israeli Knesset members in 1990, it was found that while 46 percent of Likud MKs supported the establishment of Palestinian autonomy under Israeli sovereignty, no Labor MK adopted this position. At the same time, 44 percent of Labor leaders supported a Jordanian-Palestinian state (with the West Bank as part of it), but none of Likud leaders did.[22]

The Shamir government, leading the right by adopting its traditional ideological line, antagonized large segments of the Israeli public by giving significant economic priority to the settlements. The public had a strong sense, particularly toward the crucial 1992 elections, that the government's commitment to the settlements was at the expense of immigration absorption and Israel's poor development towns. This linkage was strengthened when the U.S. government refused to extend a $10 billion loan guarantee to Israel for the purpose of absorbing Soviet immigrants unless the Shamir government committed itself to halt construction in the occupied territories, an idea that Prime Minister Shamir rejected out of hand. The U.S. demand "touched a raw nerve of the Likud's ideology,"[23] and Likud failed to "adjust to the new international climate"[24] that the U.S. demand reflected.

Yitzhak Shamir, who led Likud during its period of decline, exhibited throughout the election campaign of 1992 an inflexible and overly doctrinal position, a stand that proved highly dysfunctional in terms of his own party's political interests. Thus, toward election day, when it became clear that Labor and Likud were running neck and neck, one of Likud's leaders (Roni Milo) tried to persuade Shamir to declare Likud's support for Israeli withdrawal from Gaza, a highly popular move in all quarters of the Israeli population. Shamir, representing the old Revisionist line on *Shlemut Hamoledet* (Greater Israel), angrily refused.[25] One political commentator, writing under the title "Pragmatic Labor, Ideological Likud," noted that while Labor was projecting itself as a centrist party committed to "security," Likud retained an image of an old-style ideological party that had managed to miss the opportunity for peace and undermined U.S.-Israeli relationships.[26] Clyde Haberman wrote in the *New York Times* that "the real winner [in the Israeli election] was pragmatism and the big loser uncompromising ideology."[27]

Shamir's political ineptness led, in June 1992, to Likud's loss of power and the return of Labor to power. Yet it is essential to recognize that, even in decline, Likud maintained the integrity of its ideology intact. Likud went into opposition, a period of temporary retreat (1992–96), without bowing to the "new international climate" or even the post-*intifada* trend among the Israeli people. As I commented in a previous article, "It is in this context that Shamir's political legacy must be assessed not as a legacy proven invalid, but as one that, for its supporters, went into a mere temporary decline. The objective of electing Netanyahu as Likud's leader was to revive the Revisionist legacy, not to bury it."[28]

Benjamin Ze'ev Begin vowed after the 1992 electoral defeat that Likud would bounce back *without compromising its basic message:* Keep Israel strong, expand Jewish settlements in the territories, and hold on to the entire land, which he called "our sacred Jewish soil." The entire leadership of Likud, now under Benjamin Netanyahu, was committed to this ideological line.

While leader of the opposition for more than three years (1993–96), Netanyahu consistently stuck to the traditional ideology of the Israeli right, as originally outlined by Jabotinsky, later developed by Begin, and eventually applied by Shamir. A short time after his election as Likud leader, Netanyahu published a 467-page book, *A Place among the Nations: Israel and the World,* which could be accurately described as "Revisionism for the 1990s."

Although one might find some variation on the Revisionist themes in Netanyahu's book, its essence is the adaptation of all of Revisionism's "fundamentals" to Israel's current challenges: Netanyahu recommends the eventual annexation to Israel of all of the occupied territories,[29] negates any political rights for Palestinians in the land, blames the "world" for being too harsh in its criticism of Israel,[30] adopts a militaristic position, and presents a picture of nationalistic grandeur in Eretz Israel.

About six months after Netanyahu's election as chairman of the Likud (March 1993), and simultaneously with the publication of *A Place among the Nations,* the major breakthrough in Israel-PLO relations occurred with the signing of the Declaration of Principles, establishing autonomy in the occupied territories and a framework for negotiating a permanent solution for the Palestinian problem. The so-called Oslo Accord (signed in Washington on September 13, 1993) was a massive blow to Netanyahu's position that "there will not be any additional territorial concessions."[31] Moreover, it undermined and negated every one of the long-held ideological positions of the Israeli right: It recognized the Palestinians as a party to the conflict, it gave the Palestinians direct control over parts of Gaza and the West Bank (while implicitly promising them other parts), and it even implied—albeit not directly—the establishment of an independent Palestinian state, alongside the State of Israel.

Oslo triggered, as expected, a most powerful and negative reaction on the part of the Israeli right. In an op-ed piece in the *New York Times* entitled "Peace in Our Time?"—typically unable to avoid the right's habitual Holocaust fixation—Netanyahu argued that Israel required the Judean and Samarian mountains as a defensive wall (a reference to Jabotinsky's famous metaphor), a wall without which there will be a "mortal danger" to her survival.[32] Netanyahu's right-wing allies competed with each other in painting the first meaningful peace overture between Israelis and Palestinians in the darkest possible colors. Yitzhak Shamir described the Labor government as "people who destroy the state," Tsomet leader Rafael Eitan talked about Oslo as "the destruction of the Third Temple,"[33] and Menachem Begin's friend Israel Eldad mourned about "our settlements, children and grandchildren in Judea and Samaria ... [that] are now being thrown away, becoming a desert in Eretz Israel and given to savages thirsty for the blood of our children."[34]

Although Netanyahu's response to the Israeli-PLO agreement could be interpreted politically—he could not have survived as leader of Likud without the most fanatical opposition to Oslo—it can equally be read ideologically and psychologically. Oslo represented a total betrayal of every one of the right's principles, and Netanyahu, now the right's recognized leader, could not but reject it in the strongest possible language. Rather than admitting that the prophecy of Greater Israel failed,[35] Netanyahu and his colleagues displayed the operation of a closed mind: dealing with the world not as it is but as their ideological prism wanted it to be.[36]

Following the endorsement of Oslo by the Israeli Knesset, the right under Netanyahu continued its vehement opposition to the agreement. Some individuals and groups on the far right adopted, in addition, violent tactics toward the government, often with the tacit encouragement of the more moderate elements within Likud, including Netanyahu himself. He and his colleagues "refused to put any significant distance between themselves and those who took to the streets to demonize Peres and Rabin."[37]

The assassination of Yitzhak Rabin on November 4, 1995, generated a few immediate benefits from the perspective of the Israeli right. The removal of Rabin placed at the leadership of Labor a person (Peres) with significantly less credibility in the eyes of the public than that of the slain prime minister. The killing resulted in early elections and led, eventually, to the return of the right to power in the summer of 1996. Benjamin

Netanyahu, who became Israel's premier in June 1996, I would argue, was committed to two principles: carrying out the right's ideological program in spite of the new and increasingly difficult circumstances; and doing so in a softer, more sophisticated manner than his predecessors, Begin and Shamir. For at least the first two years of his administration, he was remarkably successful in achieving both tasks simultaneously.

The most significant questions in regard to the Netanyahu leadership of the Israeli government after June 1996 are the following: Was Netanyahu guided by the traditional ideology of the right or did he adopt, as some observers predicted he would, a pragmatic and nonideological policy?[38]

It is clear that, at least insofar as the pre-October 1998 period is concerned, the former hypothesis is correct:

(1) Netanyahu was, on the whole, consistently loyal to the ideology which has characterized the right since the early 1920s and to the policies of the right since the late 1960s—one would be hard pressed to identify serious deviations from the nationalist ethos on all of its components (see above). To call the 1996 election "post-ideological" is a misnomer;[39] all indications are that Netanyahu was playing for time in hope of easing the pressures around him.

(2) To the extent to which Netanyahu deviated from the right's ideology—as in his agreement to withdraw from Hebron or meet with Arafat—these deviations were merely tactical retreats designed to maintain the right's ideology and policy and not to undermine them (while Rabin's acceptance of Oslo, for example, seemed to have reflected a genuine, long-term change).

The results of the 1996 election made it possible for Netanyahu to move in a variety of directions. In general, the Israeli public has been evenly split on the issue of the peace process and the eventual disposition of the territories, thus giving elected political leaders "enormous leverage" in terms of their ability to pursue different policies.[40] On a number of occasions—Begin in 1977–79, Rabin in 1993–95—Israeli leaders have used this leverage to adopt new, bold initiatives that have changed the course of history forever. By and large, they were supported by the Israeli public.

Had Netanyahu been committed to Oslo or even an improved Oslo from the beginning of his administration in 1996, as he said he was, he could have pushed the peace process forward and gained significant benefits for Israel. Politically, the center and the left had to support a peace policy of a right-wing government, as they did in 1977–79. The legally binding obligations taken by the Rabin government could have easily been used by the Likud government in its efforts to sustain the peace process that Oslo generated.

Moreover, the continuation of the peace process could have been facilitated since it rested on a number of central values held by Israel's Jewish majority: (1) strengthening Israel as a Jewish state rather than as a binational Arab-Jewish state (which an annexation would imply); (2) achieving a final settlement of the Arab-Jewish conflict through a negotiated agreement; (3) enhancing the quality of Israel's democracy, which suffered significantly from the perpetuation of the occupation and the resulting human rights violations.[41] The same aspirations and values that sustained Rabin's peace policy could have sustained a Netanyahu peace policy, even if such a policy would be somewhat different in tone and in content than the Rabin-Peres strategy of 1992–96.

All indications are, however, that Netanyahu decided, from the beginning of his tenure as Israel's prime minister, to slow down the peace process significantly. "Netanyahu's first 100 days undermined the accumulated benefits of [Israeli-Palestinian] partnership built up since summer 1993," noted one observer;[42] "his government *demanded* more of Arafat . . . and it gave in return not *little,* but nothing."[43] Although Netanyahu announced during the 1996 electoral campaign that he was committed to Oslo, a position which he adopted only after Rabin's assassination, his behavior from 1996 to 1999 indicated a mere formal commitment. Netanyahu's refusal to meet Arafat for months after his election, his approval of a number of controversial projects (for example, the Jerusalem tunnel, Har Homa, and the expansion of settlements), and his humiliating proposals to the Palestinians (often accompanied by unrealistic demands) indicate a systematic strategy to prevent the Oslo train from reaching its destination: a comprehensive, Israeli-Palestinian negotiated settlement.

In fact, in regard to the central Palestinian issue, "there is complete continuity of policy . . . between [Netanyahu's] administration and all previous Likud governments. This continuity includes the mode of implementing the policy as well as its core principles."[44]

In terms of competing values within the Israeli public, it is clear that for Netanyahu, the nationalist values of Greater Israel were more important than the alternative values of strengthening Israel's Jewishness (by withdrawal from all Arab-inhabited territories), promoting democracy and human rights, and making peace a reality. Thus, Netanyahu opted to sustain the value system offered by the Zionist right since the early 1920s.

During his tenure as prime minister, Netanyahu was severely criticized in Israel and the world as being incompetent, irresponsible, a careless adventurist, and so forth.[45] Such interpretations of Netanyahu's behavior are, in my opinion, wrong. Decisions described as indicating incompetence—for example, the opening of the Jerusalem tunnel or the approval of the Har Homa project—were entirely consistent with his overall political strategy. Although Netanyahu could not have come out openly against the peace process—as his predecessor Shamir did after his defeat in 1992— his actions spoke for themselves.

Moreover, in view of the overwhelming support for Oslo in the world, in the region, and in Israel itself—support that forced Netanyahu to formally accept Oslo—he had to adopt a cautious, sophisticated policy: A direct attack on Oslo could have led to severe domestic and, worse, international consequences. Netanyahu's strategy was to avoid confrontation with the United States, often by cultivating the religious and political right wing in America; to keep together his coalition of diverse ethnic, religious, and political forces; and to use his considerable powers as Israel's "Great Communicator."

Netanyahu's ideological and political rivals routinely accused him of being inconsistent, deceitful, mercurial, shifty, and so forth. Although such accusations might have had validity on the tactical level, they were baseless on the strategic level. Although Netanyahu shifted his position on specific issues (for example, from vocal opposition to Oslo to guarded acceptance of Oslo), frequently removed his closest advisers from office (for example, Dore Gold, Avigdor Lieberman), and adopted new styles of operation (for example, at the end of his rule he tended to consult with his ministers more than at the beginning)—he remained remarkably consistent in his overall strategy on Oslo. While he accepted it formally, he did all he could to slow it down and minimize what he saw as its damage.

Despite the fact that in the heat of the 1996 campaign, Netanyahu had to accept Oslo,[46] there is little reason to believe that he ever intended to voluntarily carry out a set of obligations directly negating his long-term ideological convictions. His policies following the 1996 elections were entirely consistent with his opposition to Oslo.[47] Those policies resulted in the long freeze in the peace process after the summer of 1996.

Netanyahu's line proved highly costly for Israel's national interests:

(1) As one observer noted, the peace process has been on the verge of dying as a result of Netanyahu's policies: "the election of the Likud government under Benjamin Netanyahu threatens to stalemate the overall peace process and lead to an escalation of violence, perhaps even war."[48]

(2) Israel's "intimate strategic coordination" with the United States, which peaked under Rabin, was gone during the Netanyahu era, while American support for the PLO increased,[49] a development that could seriously affect Israeli interests if and when the final status negotiations get under way.

(3) Israel's special relationships with Jordan deteriorated. King Hussein wanted Netanyahu to win in May 1996, being worried about the closeness of the Peres-Arafat relations, but he quickly lost faith in the new prime minister. The king feared that the collapse of the peace process would radicalize the Palestinians. Following the assassination attempt of Khaled Mashal in Amman, Hussein reportedly said to Netanyahu: "You've destroyed everything that we've built among us!"

(4) A similar, if less drastic, process evolved in the relations with Egypt. Following the 1996 elections, Mubarak warned his Arab brethren to be patient and give Netanyahu a chance, but when Israeli-Palestinian relations deteriorated, he changed his tune. He refused to attend the Washington summit (between Clinton, Netanyahu, Arafat, and Hussein) following the Jerusalem tunnel crisis and made it known that he saw Netanyahu as a person who deceived him.

In some ways, U.S. diplomacy in the region enabled Netanyahu to ignore Israel's obligations, especially in terms of additional withdrawals from the occupied territories. The American ambivalence was reflected as early as the fall of 1996 in an article by Richard N. Haass of the Brookings Institution. Haass advised U.S. policymakers to lower their expectations: "Netanyahu may go to China, but he is unlikely to go to Syria."[50]

Haass's approach was, of course, exactly what Netanyahu wanted—a way out of the Oslo Agreements without directly repudiating them. More importantly, however, Haass's analysis was dangerous because it was based on the wrong historical assumptions: "At a minimum, history shows that thanks to deterrence, it is possible to maintain 'no war, no peace' for extended periods."[51] In reality, however, a "no war, no peace" condition has always led to wars in the Middle East. In pressuring Netanyahu to come to the Wye Plantation in October 1998, the Clinton team repudiated Haass's advice.

From the perspective of domestic Israeli politics, Netanyahu's policy of endless negotiations without results proved highly successful. The prime minister relied on a conservative alliance comprised of three major forces:

Israel's nationalist right (mainly the Likud), its radical right (for example, parties such as the NRP or Tsomet), and what Ehud Sprinzak has called "the soft right, an odd melange of ultra-Orthodox Jews and secular immigrants from the former Soviet Union."[52] Netanyahu skillfully played on the animosity of the soft right toward the Arabs and the Israeli left, using the soft right as a safety belt against attacks by other right-wingers.

As in the case of Netanyahu's "no war, no peace" diplomacy toward the Arabs, his domestic game was extremely volatile. As in the case of foreign policy, Netanyahu went from one domestic crisis to the next, ending in his own downfall in May 1999.

The Elections of 1999

By any measure, the elections of May 17, 1999, were an unmitigated disaster for the ideological right in Israel. A camp that came to power exactly twenty-two years before, on May 17, 1977, when Menachem Begin triumphed over Labor's coalition after thirty years in opposition, was soundly defeated. Its leader, Benjamin Netanyahu, who predicted reelection, lost to his rival, Ehud Barak, by an unprecedented margin. Worse yet, Likud, the leading party on the right, gained only nineteen seats in the new Knesset, merely two more than the Haredi-Sephardi Shas.

At the time of writing (July 1999), it is impossible to predict with authority and certainty the precise political consequences of Likud's debacle. Yet, it is clear, at least in the short term, that the future of Likud's political ideology is rather bleak.

The first item on the political agenda of Israel in its postelection era was the establishment of a governing coalition under the new prime minister, Ehud Barak. Although for several weeks following the 1999 elections it was rumored that Likud might be invited to join Barak's government, eventually this was not the course chosen by Israel's new leader.

There is no doubt that Barak's governmental coalition will be dominated by political forces that support territorial compromise in the West Bank, the Gaza Strip, and the Golan Heights, a policy which Likud's leaders (including Prime Minister Netanyahu) have rejected but were forced to grudgingly implement.

The Barak government includes One Israel (old Labor, plus David Levy's Gesher and the moderate-religious Meimad), and the liberal and dovish Meretz. While the hawkish, nationalist, and religious Mafdal is included in the government, with only five mandates it has been substantially weakened and it might be marginalized within the new governing coalition. The other religious parties in the coalition could go along with any territorial compromise negotiated by Barak, although this is by no means certain.

From the perspective of coalition politics, Likud's future is altogether unpromising. Moreover, in the next elections, Likud could be seriously challenged for primacy among more conservative, nationalist, and traditional voters by the emerging Shas. It could very well decline as Israel's leading force on the right.

The second major dilemma for Likud is that of its future leadership. Bibi Netanyahu, Likud's leader since 1993, has left behind a party which is divided, conflictual, and ambivalent about its future political path. Several individuals within Likud have emerged as potential leaders, declaring their intention to compete for the position of Likud chairman. The elections for the chairmanship are planned for September 1999 and it is likely that the winner will lead Likud in the next general elections for the Knesset and will stand as a candidate for prime minister.

The three announced candidates for the Likud leadership are Jerusalem mayor Ehud Olmert and former ministers Ariel Sharon and Meir Shitreet. A victory for Shitreet, an unlikely result, will signal, clearly and unmistakenly, that Likud has moderated its foreign policy position since the previous treasury minister abstained in the Knesset vote on the Oslo Accords (while the rest of the Likud members opposed Oslo vocally). Olmert and Sharon will represent a more nationalist line, although both have demonstrated capacity to compromise.

The emergence of Sharon as Likud's top leader will be highly problematical. The charismatic, energetic Sharon had been a divisive figure in Israel for decades. Many Israelis view him as personally responsible for the Lebanon War of 1982, including the Sabra and Shatila massacres (leading to the banning of the ex-general as defense minister by an Israeli judicial commission).

Ehud Olmert will probably prove a serious contender for Likud leadership. He is a sophisticated politician, a gifted fund-raiser, and a man with a substantial political base (Jerusalem city hall). There is evidence that Olmert has prepared himself for this battle for quite some time, moderating his political positions in an effort to conquer the center.

In the final analysis, anyone elected to lead Likud (Sharon was to win the election in September 1999) will have to decide whether he will maintain the party's ideological purity (and, therefore, oppose the inevitable move toward an Israeli-Palestinian territorial compromise) or carry the traditional right toward a more centrist, moderate position.

Notes

1. Ilan Peleg, *Begin's Foreign Policy, 1977–1983.*
2. Dan Horowitz and Moshe Lissak, *Trouble in Utopia,* 157.
3. Peter Medding, *The Founding of Israeli Democracy, 1949–1967.*
4. Ilan Peleg, *The Middle East Peace Process,* especially the Epilogue.
5. Asher Arian, *The Second Republic;* Asher Arian and Michal Shamir, "The Primarily Political Functions of the Left-Right Continuum."
6. Arian, *The Second Republic,* 356, 358.
7. The Rabin assassination (November 4, 1995) was, thus, only one act of violence taken by the right. See, for example, Ehud Sprinzak, *Brother against Brother.*
8. Jay Gonen, *A Psychohistory of Zionism* (New York: Mason/Charter, 1975).
9. Benjamin Netanyahu, *A Place among the Nations,* 250–53.
10. Ibid., 170, 177, 397.
11. Ibid., 397–98.
12. Israel Kolatt, "The Zionist Movement and the Arabs," 138.
13. Shlomo Avineri, *The Making of Modern Zionism,* 179.
14. Netanyahu, *A Place among the Nations,* chap. 3.
15. Ibid., 351.
16. Uri Bialer, "David Ben-Gurion & Moshe Sharett."
17. Yehoshafat Harkabi, *Arab Strategies and Israel's Response,* 127–51.
18. Howard M. Sachar, *A History of Israel: From the Rise of Zionism to Our Time* (New York: Knopf, 1979).
19. *Ha'aretz,* July 9, 1982.
20. Yoram Peri, "From Coexistence to Hegemony," *Davar,* October 1, 1982.
21. Zvi Lanir, "The Political and Military Objectives in Israel's Wars," in *War by Choice* (Tel Aviv: Kibbutz Meuhad, 1985), 117–56.
22. Gad Barzilai and Ilan Peleg, "Israel and Future Borders," 68.
23. Jonathan Mendilow, "The 1992 Israeli Electoral Campaign: Valence and Position Dimensions," in *The Elections in Israel,* ed. Asher Arian and Michal Shamir (Albany: SUNY Press, 1995).
24. Gideon Doron, "Labor's Return to Power in Israel," 27.
25. Arie Avnery, *The Defeat,* 22.
26. Ruvik Rosenthal, "Crucial Choice," *New Outlook* 35, no. 3 (May–June 1992).
27. June 28, 1992.
28. Ilan Peleg, "The Likud under Rabin II."
29. Netanyahu, *A Place among the Nations,* 349.
30. Ibid., 397–98.
31. *Yediot Ahronot,* May 21, 1993.
32. September 15, 1993.
33. *Yediot Ahronot,* September 15, 1993.

34. *Yediot Ahronot,* September 24, 1994.

35. Leon Festinger et al., *When Prophecy Fails.*

36. Milton Rokeach, *The Open and the Closed Mind* (New York: Basic Books, 1960); Charles G. Lord et al., "Biased Assimilation and Attitude Polarization: The Effect of Prior Theories on Subsequently Considered Evidence," *Journal of Personality and Social Psychology* 37, no. 1 (1979): 2098–2109.

37. Joel Marcus, "Shlumiel in the Head," *Ha'aretz,* October 7, 1997.

38. Richard N. Haass, "The Middle East," 57; Shalom Lappin, "Netanyahu and the Palestinians: Pragmatism or Ideology?" *Jewish Quarterly* 43, no. 4 (Winter 1996–97): 33–36, esp. 33.

39. David Makovsky, "The Country's First Post-Ideological Election," *Jerusalem Post,* May 23, 1996, 9.

40. Asher Arian, *The Second Republic,* 360.

41. Peleg, *Human Rights in the West Bank and Gaza: Legacy and Politics* (Syracuse: Syracuse University Press, 1995).

42. Adam Garfinkle, "Israel and Palestine," 9.

43. Ibid., 7.

44. Lappin, "Netanyahu and the Palestinians," 33.

45. Marcus, "Shlumiel in the Head."

46. Yossi Klein Halevi, "His Father's Son," *Jerusalem Report,* February 5, 1998, 12–16, esp. 12. For a sophisticated scholarly analysis of Netanyahu's electoral strategy, see Jonathan Mendilow, "The Likud 1996 Campaign: Between the Devil and the Deep Blue Sea," in *The Elections in Israel, 1996,* ed. Asher Arian (Albany: SUNY Press, 1999).

47. Gideon Samet, "Tricks Instead of a Settlement," *Ha'aretz,* March 2, 1998.

48. Jerome Slater, "Netanyahu, a Palestinian State, and Israeli Security Reassessed," 677.

49. Ze'ev Schiff, "Doubtful Victory," *Ha'aretz,* January 30, 1998.

50. Haass, "The Middle East," 57.

51. Ibid., 58.

52. Ehud Sprinzak, "Netanyahu's Safety Belt," 18–19.

8

Religio-Politics and Social Unity in Israel
Israel's Religious Parties

Chaim I. Waxman

Most students of Israeli society agree that although Israel is not as secular as are most modern societies, it is not a theocracy. And yet religion plays a much greater role within the Israeli polity than it does, for example, within the American polity. Israel was established as a Jewish state, and the vast majority of Israel's Jews—secular as well as religious—agree that Judaism is a basic and necessary component of being Jewish and, therefore, of Israeli society and its political culture. As a consequence, the nature of religious conflict in Israel is much different than it is in other modern societies.[1] It is not simply a conflict between religious and secular Jews. Indeed, the division of Israel into these two camps is a major oversimplification. The ideologically secular are actually a relatively small minority in Israel, though they are a vocal minority and are prominent in academia and the media. The largest sector is the traditionalist sector, that is, those who are religiously traditional but not observant according to Orthodox standards. The Orthodox Jews themselves may be subdivided into *Haredi,* or ultra-Orthodox, and modern Orthodox. The different religious perspectives of these groups has long served as a source of tension, even in the pre-state era. It is not unique to Israel and is characteristic of many Jewish communities in the modern era. The basic conflict in Israel is over the limits of religion within the political sphere, and the basic tensions are those which emerge from the power struggles between religious and secular parties. But the impact and consequences of these conflicts are not then limited to specific Israeli political parties. They have had a major impact on relations between Israel and the Diaspora at various times in recent years.

The Israeli elections of 1996 resulted in significant gains for the religious parties. For the first time, the religious parties garnered more than twenty Knesset seats. These gains are not, as might be assumed, owing to the higher birth rate among religious Jews than among secular Jews. Nor are the gains the product of a massive *ba'al teshuva*, or "religious return" movement, or the result of a mass exodus of the secular from Israel or its political system. Rather, the gains appear to be the product of the religious parties' pursuit of ideological and ethnic politics. As Eliezer Don-Yehiya has indicated, although the political relevance of class divisions in Israel declined after the Six-Day War, ideological and ethnic divisions did not. Since the 1980s, two of the largest religious parties have responded to the ideological and ethnic rifts, with Shas playing the ethnic card and attracting traditional, nonreligious, Sephardim, and the National Religious Party (NRP) playing the ideological card.[2] Moreover, with Labor's victory in 1992 and the prominence of Meretz in the Labor coalition, many of the Sephardim and the religious felt that they had no alternative but to return to the religious parties. From 1977 to 1992, many felt that the Jewish character of Israel and the interests of the religious communities were in good hands under the Likud. With Labor's victory in 1992 and especially with its partnership with Meretz, which projected an antireligious stance, many among the religious returned to the religious parties. There is no question that the rift is very deep. However, the rhetoric of protagonists on both sides should be avoided. The fact is that the religious-secular rift is not new in Israel. Indeed, it preceded the establishment of the State of Israel by decades. There were clashes at the early Zionist congresses, and they were not limited to verbal assaults; the antagonists came to physical blows on more than one occasion.[3] Despite the rhetoric by extremists on both sides, the empirical evidence indicates the persistence of a basic unity among Israeli Jews that is much stronger than any differences between them with respect to the issue of religion in Israeli society.[4] This is not to suggest that the issue is not a serious one. On the contrary, it is one of the most serious domestic issues in Israel. However, at the present time, it does not threaten the very fiber of the society, as some have suggested. This chapter raises the question of whether the recent patterns of Israeli religio-politics will further exacerbate and even threaten that underlying social unity.

The religious parties in Israel cannot be analyzed, particularly by a sociologist, without considering how Israelis perceive those parties and the impact they have on "the religious situation" there. Three religious parties in the 1996 elections won sufficient votes for seating in the

Knesset: Shas, the National Religious Party (NRP), and United Torah Judaism (UTJ). Those elections presented them with the greatest electoral gain in Israel's political history. Together, they won almost 20 percent of the votes and gained twenty-three Knesset seats. The previous high was eighteen seats, and, perhaps even more significant, the religious parties suffered an aggregate decline in 1992 from eighteen to sixteen seats. In other words, their 1996 feat was an increase of 50 percent in their number of seats. (See table 1.)

The 1996 electoral gains were actually experienced by only two of the three religious parties, Shas and the NRP. UTJ succeeded solely in retaining the four seats it had previously held. Shas, by contrast, increased its parliamentary power from six to ten seats, and the NRP increased from six to nine seats. How one views these gains depends on the background against which they are measured. On the obvious level, the gains of Shas were the greatest. Shas, an acronym for Hebrew of Sephardi Torah Guardians, was founded in 1984 when its leaders seceded from Agudat Israel, which is headed by Ashkenazim. But Shas's origins go back even further and are, in part, an ironic consequence of an action by the NRP in the previous year.

In 1983, a rift between the NRP and the Ashkenazi chief rabbi, Shlomo Goren, led to the NRP's pushing through legislation which limited the tenure of the chief rabbis to ten years, with the consequence that Goren and his Sephardi counterpart, Rabbi Ovadia Yosef, would soon be forced to leave office. Simultaneously, Yosef and his colleagues felt that Agudat Israel had been oblivious to the needs of Sephardim both within the party itself and within the world of higher *yeshivot,* academies of Torah learning. Local elections in Israel's cities were taking place that year, and Rabbi Yosef and his colleagues decided to run their own slates in Jerusalem and Bnai Brak, very probably as a trial balloon for subsequent national elections. The party was originally to be called Sach, an acronym for Sephardi Haredim, but that name was rejected by the electoral council. The name Shas was chosen instead.[5] The party, although officially Haredi, made its focus the ethnic rather than the religious issue, and it appealed to all Sephardim, regardless of the affiliate's religious conduct. It also differed from the Ashkenazi Haredi Agudat Israel in that it did not demur from Zionism. Rather, it referred to itself as a Haredi, rather than secular, Zionist party.[6]

Shas's achievements in the local elections in Jerusalem and Bnai Brak took everyone by surprise, and it decided to run a slate in the 1984 national elections. For that campaign, Shas attained the support of Rabbi

Table 1. Number of Knesset seats of religious parties, 1949–1999

	1949	1951	1955	1959	1961	1965	1969	1973	1977	1981[a]	1984[b]	1988	1992	1996	1999
Aguda group[c]		5	6	6	6	6	6	5	5	4	4	7	4	4	5
NRP[d]	16	10	11	12	12	11	12	10	12	6	4	5	6	9	5
Shas											4	6	6	10	17
Total	16	15	17	18	18	17	18	15	17	10	12	18	16	23	27

a. These figures do not include Tami, a Sephardi party which was not explicitly a religious one although, in effect, it was. It received three seats in 1981 and one in 1984.
b. In 1984, Poalei Aguda joined with Matzad to form the Morasha list, which won two seats. The figure for the Aguda Group includes the two seats won by Agudat Israel and the two of Morasha.
c. Includes Poalei Agudat Israel and/or Degel Hatorah.
d. In 1949, there were four religious parties, Aguda, Poalei Aguda, Mizrachi, and Poalei Mizrachi, and they ran on a joint religious list. Mizrachi and Hapoel Hamizrachi were separate parties until 1956, when they merged into the NRP.

Eliezer Shach of Bnai Brak, the spiritual leader of the Lithuanian sector of the *haredim*, who had long feuded with Rabbi Simcha Bunim Alter, the spiritual leader of Gur hasidim and the head of Agudat Israel. In its initial election, Shas achieved four Knesset seats. Its record, thus, is one of growth from an initial four, to six in 1988, to ten in 1996, and to seventeen in 1999.

The impressive success which Shas has had in such a brief time may be attributed to its appeal to the large Sephardi population, many of whom felt alienated from and neglected by the traditional parties which are Ashkenazi-dominated. In addition, because of different historical circumstances than those of the Ashkenazim, Sephardim do not have the kind of religious-secular polarization that is present in Ashkenazi communities, and Shas, especially through its dynamic political leader, Arye Deri, was able to appeal to and attract traditional, though not Haredi nor even religiously observant, Sephardim. The traditional Sephardi masses are willing to have rabbinic leaders, such as Rabbi Yosef, and do not find this troublesome. On the contrary, they readily accept it. Thus, despite Deri's conviction, in March 1999, on numerous counts of fraud and obstruction of justice, he remained the political leader of Shas and had the backing of both Rabbi Yosef and the masses of Shas voters who viewed his years-long trial as an Ashkenazi campaign against Sephardi political leaders. Indeed, Deri produced and widely distributed a sophisticated videocassette and CD-ROM entitled *"Ani Ma-ashim"* ("I Accuse"), in which he presented his case for an Ashkenazi-elitist conspiracy not only against him but against Sephardim as a group. In one segment, after relating the prosecution charges of his affluent lifestyle, Deri showed his own modest apartment in the Har Nof section of Jerusalem and contrasted it with the luxurious private homes of the very judges who found him guilty.

Despite the predictions of some that his conviction would harm Shas in the election, Deri's campaign was actually highly successful. The fact that Meretz and, especially, Shinui ran vitriolic anti-Haredi campaigns probably also contributed some votes to Shas, in reaction to what was viewed by some traditional Israeli Jews as unjustified and unprecedented hostility toward religion in general. Be that as it may, Shas's Knesset representation grew from ten to seventeen seats, a much greater growth than that of any other party, and it became the third largest party, in terms of Knesset representation. Deri himself, however, was forced to resign from the party's leadership when Ehud Barak made it clear that he would not enter into any coalition negotiations with Shas as long as Deri, a convicted criminal, remained at its helm.

As for the NRP, it has had a much more erratic experience in recent years. The history of the NRP goes back to the early days of the World Zionist Organization (WZO). When the Fifth Zionist Congress in 1901 resolved to enter the educational sphere, many religious members of the WZO, who believed that secular nationalism was antithetical to Judaism, refused to acquiesce to a program of secular Zionist education. Under the leadership of Rabbi Isaac Jacob Reines, the Mizrachi movement was founded in Vilna in 1902 as the religious Zionist organization within the WZO. It was the first recognized separate federation within the World Zionist Organization. The name is an acronym for *mercaz ruhani* (spiritual center), and its banner was, "The Land of Israel for the people of Israel according to the Torah of Israel." In 1904, a world conference of Mizrachi was convened in Bratislava, Czechoslovakia (then Pressburg, Hungary), and the Mizrachi World Organization was founded with the objective of educating and promoting religious Zionism in all religious Jewish circles. The first convention of the American Mizrachi Organization was convened in 1914, under the influence of Rabbi Meir Bar-Ilan (Berlin), who was then general secretary of the world Mizrachi organization, in Hamburg (Altona), and who had toured the United States extensively during the previous months.

After World War I, a group that, in addition to being sympathetic to the goals of Mizrachi, believed in settlement and labor, formed the Hapoel Hamizrachi (Mizrachi Labor) Organization, which went on to found a series of religious kibbutz and moshav settlements. Although Hapoel Hamizrachi worked very closely with Mizrachi, the two were separate, autonomous organizations and initially remained so when they were transformed into political parties in the Knesset. They merged in 1956 and became the National Religious Party (NRP). From 1951 to 1977, they jointly occupied ten to twelve seats in the Knesset.

After the Six-Day War, as Don-Yehiya has elucidated,[7] activist messianism in the religious Zionist community emerged and spread as a result of developments within Yeshivat Mercaz Harav, the yeshiva founded by Rabbi Abraham Isaac Kook and then headed by his son, Rabbi Zvi Yehuda Kook. Under the latter's influence, the yeshiva became the spiritual center of activist messianism, and it produced the core leaders and activists of Gush Emunim. This activist and radical group incorporated notions which legitimated "any means necessary" (to borrow a phrase from American black nationalists of the 1960s) in the pursuit of its goals. This meant that not only the interests of other countries but also those within Israel, even if instituted by the government of Israel, could be blatantly ignored if they hindered the realization of the messianic goals. Mercaz Harav also took on a central role in the educational system of religious Zionism, especially in the systems of yeshiva high schools and nationalist, "*hesder,*" yeshivas which developed during the late-1950s and 1960s, largely in reaction to a growing secularism within the public religious educational network. As a result, the ideology of radical religious Zionism was propounded as religious dogma in the increasing number of schools to which religious Zionist parents sent their children, and it increasingly gained adherents within the religious Zionist community.[8]

During the early 1970s, a bitter dispute between the radicals and moderates erupted within the national religious ranks, and the victory of the territorial maximalists abruptly ended the tradition of a separation between religion and politics in the religious Zionist community. Since then, despite the forebodings of senior members of the party, the NRP has changed from a democratic party led by a religiously conscious and politically astute laity to a party in which the religio-political rulings of rabbis determine policies and action.

Although the NRP gained three seats in 1996, that increase was the first that the party had experienced in a decade and a half. In 1981, the party had lost half of its twelve seats, and it declined from its representation of two-thirds of the combined religious parties to less than half. It had lost even further in 1984 and 1988 and declined to less than a third of the combined religious parties' votes. The 1992 elections gave the NRP a modest gain of one seat, but that only brought it back to what its number of seats had been in 1981. The increase to nine seats and about 40 percent of the combined religious parties' votes in 1996 appeared to suggest a major change in the party's electoral fortunes.

However, NRP suffered a major setback in 1999, with the loss of four Knesset seats as the result of a combination of factors. Most significantly, the formation of the "National Unity" (*ihud hale-umi*) coalition, consisting of Rehavam Zeevi's Moledet, Benny Begin's Herut, and Hanan Porat's Tekuma parties, drew significant numbers of highly nationalistic religious Zionists from NRP because, prior to his defection, Porat had long been an activist within NRP and, ironically, he had sworn his allegiance to NRP when he returned to the fold after the collapse of his earlier attempt at establishing a strong joint religious-secular nationalist party.

In addition, NRP was not able to attract more moderate religious nationalists because of its maneuverings, which placed a number of strongly nationalistic candidates at the top of the list despite the wishes of the party's membership, as manifested in its primary elections, for a more moderate list. In addition, in the 1999 election campaign, the Haredi party, UTJ, projected itself as a nationalist party. Deputy Housing Minister Meir Porush, son of Aguda leader Menachem Porush, claimed to have delivered more Jewish housing to the territories than any of his predecessors, and the slogan for the party was, "We will go on believing and building." The significantly increased presence of haredim in the territories is due less to their ideological commitments to Judea and Samaria than to their high birth rate and relatively low economic status, which makes housing within the "Green Line" less affordable for them. That new presence as well as the increasingly strident nationalism of UTJ drew those in the national religious camp who viewed NRP as too weak either in its religious or national commitments.[9]

Probably related to NRP's dramatic decline, 1981 also marked a significant change in the nature of the relationship between the Zionist NRP and the non-Zionist Haredi parties, the most significant of which, Agudat Israel and Degel Hatorah, combined to form UTJ in 1992. In contrast to the acrimony which traditionally marked their relationship, they now functioned as partners in a coalition, the factions of which had similar goals and values. This change was a product of three basic developments. There were religious changes in the national religious camp, as mentioned previously, with the emergence of rabbis as determiners of political positions. There were also political changes within the Haredi camp. If, as I have argued elsewhere, there has been a "haredization" of American Orthodox Judaism,[10] it seems appropriate to characterize the developments in Israel as "the *hardalization* of Israeli Orthodoxy," "*hardal*" being a play on the Hebrew term for mustard and an acronym for "*Haredi-leumi,*" or "Ultra-Orthodox-nationalist." The nationalism of the haredi sector should actually not be all that surprising. The masses were probably always highly nationalistic. Indeed, it appears that there is, in many countries, a correlation between political conservatism and religious conservatism. The Haredi leadership has, until recently,[11] officially been non-nationalistic because of the opposition to secular Zionism, but that did not prevent the masses from being nationalistic. Their increasing nationalism appears to be rooted in their greater sense of security within Israeli society. By security, I do not mean security from external challenges but, rather, from internal ones. In the pre-state and early-state periods, the Haredi sector felt threatened from the secular majority and was, thus, somewhat ambivalent on the entire notion of Israeli sovereignty. In recent decades, however, almost the entire Orthodox sector of Israel, Haredi and modern Orthodox,[12] has grown and developed a sense of self-confidence.

Haredim, in particular, not only do not feel threatened by the secular, they are confident to the point of triumphalism and, if anything, believe that the days of secularism in Israel are numbered. They are also reacting to challenges to the "status quo" by non-Orthodox segments of Israeli society by aligning themselves with the more nationalistic parties that have typically been more open to religious traditionalism, as will be discussed below.

The term *status quo* in this context dates back to a letter, signed by David Ben-Gurion, Rabbi Judah Leib Fishman (Maimon), and Yizhak Gruenbaum, in the name of the Jewish Agency, which was sent to leaders of Agudat Israel in June 1947, wherein it was agreed that in the State of Israel, the religious situation would continue as it had previously been, with freedom of religion in the private sphere and with traditional Judaism in the public sphere. As outlined in the letter, the Jewish Sabbath, Saturday, would be a national day of rest; all kitchens in government-run buildings would adhere to the kosher dietary laws; marriage and divorce would remain in the realm of the rabbinic courts; and the various educational streams—religious, secular, and independent—would be institutionalized within the state.[13]

Almost since the beginning, the Orthodox and the secular have each alleged that the other side has abrogated the "status quo agreement."[14] For example, throughout the years, one of the most persistent issues of strife has been that of Sabbath observance, which has become both a national issue and a local one. On the national level, the NRP has consistently sought to have the government enact and enforce a Sabbath Law, under which all nonessential public facilities, and especially buses, trains, and El Al, Israel's national airline, would cease operation from sundown Friday to sunset Saturday. Some of the parties, especially Mapam, were opposed to any such restrictions. A compromise was worked out to the effect that the Sabbath was accepted as an official day of rest, but the specifics of the law, what was and what was not forbidden, were left to the local municipalities. The result was that, except in Haifa and several other areas, public buses did not run on the Sabbath. To the Orthodox Jew, the observance of the Sabbath is one of the most basic precepts of Judaism; it is the fulfillment of a Commandment, and it serves as testimony to the very act of Creation. To many non-Orthodox, even if the Sabbath does have some religious significance, the Sabbath Law is a great inconvenience, if for no other reason than the fact that Saturday is the only day which one might spend shopping or at leisure with family and friends. The unavailability of public transportation, especially if one cannot afford a car or a private taxi, may be viewed as an unjustifiable restriction of a basic freedom.

Even more serious is the open conflict which has persistently erupted on the local level, most notably in a growing number of sections of Jerusalem which have amassed large numbers of Haredim. In these neighborhoods, many of the residents attempt to bar all traffic on the Sabbath on the grounds that it disturbs the Sabbath peace. The Haredim and their secular counterparts hold frequent demonstrations and counterdemonstrations, which frequently become violent confrontations between the demonstrators and the police, with neither side being noted for its restraint. Although the modern Orthodox have tended to eschew such demonstrations, many of them are sympathetic to the overall attempt to maintain the religious significance of the Sabbath. Indeed, it was over the issue of an alleged violation of the Sabbath by the state that the NRP legitimated its secession from the ruling coalition, which led to the fall of the first Rabin government in 1977.[15]

The other major issue has been that of "Who is a Jew?" This issue is, on the one hand, much more basic than that of the Sabbath but, until recently, except for a few cases, it was viewed as a somewhat esoteric question. The question derives from the founding of the state as the "Jewish state" and the variety of interpretations given to the significance and raison d'être of that state, with the answers ranging from those who conceived of it in completely secular terms to those who perceived it from a specifically religious perspective. The issue burst forth as a real question in 1958, with the immigration of Jews from countries behind the Iron Curtain, where there had been considerable intermarriage and many of the new immigrants had non-Jewish wives. The question arose as to whether these wives and their children could be registered as Jewish on their identity cards. To the Orthodox, this was not merely a particular problem insofar as these wives and children were concerned; it was a much broader problem because when these children grew up and married, they might involve many others (their spouses) in the problem of intermarriage. After a bitter debate and the resignation of Mizrachi from the government, Prime Minister Ben-Gurion took the unique step of writing to forty-five "Sages of Israel" throughout the world, asking them to give their opinion on the question of Jewish identity and how to register Israelis of mixed marriages. The majority responded in accordance with the Orthodox view.[16] The issue abated with the decision of the government to leave registration to the Ministry of the Interior, which in 1960 returned to NRP control.

In 1962, the question of "Who is a Jew?" erupted once again, but this time on a much more isolated level, with the case of "Brother Daniel," a Jewish-born Catholic monk who applied for Israeli citizenship under the Law of Return, which grants the right to automatic citizenship to any Jew upon immigration. Brother Daniel (Oswald Rufeisen) requested citizenship and Jewish nationality on the grounds that he was born Jewish and that he still regarded himself as ethnically Jewish. The case came to the Supreme Court, which ruled (not unanimously) that by being an apostate, he had broken his historic link with Judaism and thus was not eligible to enter under the Law of Return. As to his nationality, that space on his identity card was left blank.

The issue arose once more as a national question with the arrival of a large group of Bene Israel, Jews from India who had, for centuries, been isolated from world Jewry, and among whom, it was suspected, intermarriage was commonplace. With its sweeping ruling, which in effect gave all of the Bene Israel full legitimate status as Jews, the Chief Rabbinate itself became embroiled in a bitter conflict with many other rabbis, especially those of Agudat Israel, which has never accepted the authority of the Chief Rabbinate. The latter began to hedge and apply qualifying conditions to its original liberal decision. These qualifications, in turn, incurred the wrath of the non-Orthodox community. Even with these qualifications, there were some rabbis who refused to abide with the decision of the Chief Rabbinate, which resulted in the Knesset's demanding that legal charges be brought against all resisting rabbis. A not atypical ad hoc arrangement between the Ministry of Religious Affairs and the rabbis quieted the situation temporarily, to the dissatisfaction of many of the Bene Israel. In mid-1964, the Knesset (including the NRP) strongly condemned the Chief Rabbinate and ordered it to satisfactorily resolve the plight of the Bene Israel immediately. In the end, the Chief Rabbinate accepted a compromise and rescinded the decrees which singled out the Bene Israel, substituting a general order to investigate all cases which involved questions about the legitimacy of the parents.

Again, the issue quieted down for a while, but not without far-reaching consequences. First of all, the Chief Rabbinate had now come to be perceived as an insensitive and heartless obstacle to the ingathering of downtrodden Jews from the Diaspora, even in the eyes of many who had previously given tacit support to its functioning. Moreover, the stature and authority of the Chief Rabbinate were significantly diminished as a result of the disparaging and defamatory character of the public arguments and debates between many rabbis of differing opinions.

The next major episode in the "Who is a Jew?" issue involved the Shalit and Helen Seidman cases. The former involved the non-Jewish wife of an Israeli Navy lieutenant who wanted to have her children registered as Jewish nationals; the Seidman case involved a woman who had been converted by a Reform rabbi (and who had subsequently married a Kohen, a member of the priestly tribe who, according to traditional Judaism, are forbidden to marry converts), a conversion which is not legitimate according to Jewish law.[17] To these cases were then added the issue of intermarriage among the recent arrivals from countries behind the Iron Curtain. A number of rabbis raised serious questions about the validity of a number of conversions performed in those countries, and the rabbi of the Lubavitch *hasidim,* Rabbi Menachem Mendel Schneerson, alleged that Israeli officials were counseling Soviet-Jewish émigrés with non-Jewish spouses to claim Jewish parentage for their spouses upon their arrival in Israel, so as to avoid any problems. The fear among some of those in the non-Orthodox community was that if Russian-Jewish émigrés encountered difficulties upon their arrival in Israel, those Jews still in Russia might be discouraged from attempting to emigrate. On the other hand, the Orthodox, while cognizant and sympathetic to the plight of Russian Jewry, opposed risking what it viewed as the future of Judaism through evasive detours of this dilemma.

With the emergence of Shas as a significant component of the ruling coalition, the entire issue of "Who is a Jew?" has become much more politicized because it has sought to enact legislation which would recognize only conversions performed according to the mandates of *Halakha,* Jewish religious law, as defined by the Orthodox rabbinic elite. This would, in effect, delegitimate conversions by Reform and Conservative rabbis in Israel and abroad, and it has thus become a major matter affecting relations between Israel and Western Jewish communities, especially the American Jewish community.

Although the "status quo agreement" has endured for more than half a century, it appears that both the religious and the secular are increasingly unhappy with it, and its endurance is highly questionable. As Aviezer Ravitzky points out, both sides perceive that conditions now are radically different from when the agreement was reached. One secular argument, for example, is that in the past there were relatively few haredim who were exempted from military service but that today the numbers are much too high to justify the religious exemption. One religious argument is that private transportation on the Sabbath was exempted from the law prohibiting the operation of buses because there were very few private cars. Today, however, the proliferation of private cars traveling on the Sabbath makes a mockery of the law establishing the Jewish Sabbath as an official day of rest.[18]

Above and beyond these changes, there have developed a number of basic "culture shifts" in Israel,[19] among both the secular and religious nationalists, with the result that there is today, particularly among the secular, much less emphasis on the corporate character of Israel and a much greater emphasis on the individual. The importance of the state is increasingly perceived in terms of the extent to which it guarantees individual rights. By contrast, among the religious nationalists, there has been a dramatic increase in the significance of the philosophy of Rabbi A. I. Kook, which focuses on the inherent corporate character of the Jewish people and the inevitable expansion of holiness among the people and within the Holy Land, Eretz Israel. Thus, both the secularists and the religious nationalists are increasingly unhappy with the "status quo agreement," which was a pragmatic compromise.[20]

That the pattern of "antagonistic cooperation"[21] which has prevailed for the past half-century may no longer be tenable is further suggested by the fact that both the haredi and modern Orthodox sectors have a greater sense of self-confidence, and they now feel much less threatened by each other and increasingly view themselves as having a common antagonist, secularism. They are, thus, less concerned with challenging each other and are more ready to cooperate with each other. The cooperation is still limited and only de facto at times, but it is no longer inconceivable to envision explicit mutual cooperation between their respective rabbinic leaders.

Some religious Zionists viewed the post-1967 developments, including what they perceive to be a growth of religious fundamentalism within mainstream religious Zionism, as antithetical to Jewish tradition and the historic principles of religious Zionism. Accordingly, in 1975, they founded Oz Veshalom and Netivot Shalom, two religious Zionist peace movements which ultimately merged.

Meimad is another reaction to Mizrachi's moves to the nationalist and religious right. Broader in scope than Oz Veshalom–Netivot Shalom, it initially formed as a political party with a more moderate approach to the territories than that of the NRP. However, when it failed to gain sufficient votes for a Knesset seat in the 1988 elections, it reorganized as a public action movement which deals with a range of important social and political issues in Israel from a religious-ethical perspective. Primary among its objectives have been the prevention of a Kulturkampf, or culture war, in Israel and a bridging of the growing gap between the religious and secular communities. Its spiritual leader is Rabbi Yehuda Amital, who is also the cofounder and co-head of Yeshivat Har Etzion, a higher yeshiva in the Gush Etzion region which incorporates army service in its program. After the assassination of Yitzhak Rabin, his successor, Shimon Peres, appointed Amital a minister in his cabinet. Amital's main efforts were devoted to fostering moderate religious Zionism and bridging the gap between the religious and secular communities. If subsequent developments are any indication, his efforts did not bear much fruit.

Meimad returned to active politics in the 1999 campaign and joined with Labor and others to form the One Israel slate, headed by Ehud Barak. Although Barak won decisively, it is an open question whether Meimad helped attract a significant number of One Israel votes. It may well be that Meimad lost in stature because it changed from a social movement to a political organization.

The involvement of the Haredi sector in the Israeli political system has increased since the ascension of the Likud to political leadership in 1977. The initial and, perhaps, clearest manifestation was their joining the government. In 1988, there were numerous rifts in Agudat Israel, and Habad *hasidim* promised that the widely revered Lubavitcher Rebbe, Rabbi Menachem Mendel Schneerson, would give a blessing to all those who voted for Aguda. Two years later, in 1990, the Rebbe devoted much of his energy to an all-out effort to prevent Shimon Peres from forming a coalition. By 1996, Haredi political activity was not limited to Habad and a handful of others. Then, many haredim played very active roles in the Netanyahu campaign. The fact that he was also the clear choice of the NRP fostered an alliance between the haredi parties and the religious Zionist ones and resulted in Netanyahu's winning of approximately 90 percent of the votes of Orthodox voters.[22]

As was mentioned previously, the Haredi masses are today among the most nationalistic in Israeli society, and they appear to be even more nationalistic that the religious Zionist sector which was previously viewed as a stronghold of the political right.[23] Surveys consistently reveal that the overwhelming majority of Haredi respondents hold strong nationalistic views. Contrary to the widely circulated notion that the Sephardim of Shas and the Ashkenazi haredim represented by the Degel Hatorah party are, in principle, amenable to territorial compromise on the basis of *pikuah nefesh*, that is the primacy of life and saving life,[24] the evidence indicates otherwise. Although the respective leaders of Shas and Degel Hatorah, Rabbi Ovadia Yosef and Rabbi Eliezer Schach, might consider territorial compromise on that basis, their followers staunchly oppose such compromise. It is, therefore, no surprise that a very small percentage of haredim supported the Oslo peace accords. One survey found that "only 9 percent of the Haredi respondents were in favor of the peace process, as opposed to 24 percent among the national-religious and 56 percent among the secular."[25] Indeed, already in 1994, only 4 percent of the haredim supported the Oslo negotiations, whereas among religious Zionists four times as many, 16 percent, supported them.[26] And, in 1998, when Netanyahu signed the Wye Accords, Habad cut all ties with him and indicated that he was no better than Ehud Barak.

Given the widespread perception that the Haredim do not serve in the army, there was resentment in some quarters over their right-wing politics because their votes may move the country to a war in which they will not fight. Indeed, the issue of military service was among the most divisive in the religious-secular rift, possibly even more so than that of religious coercion.

In all probability, however, this issue will wane in the foreseeable future, as a result of several factors. In the 1999 coalition agreements, an agreement was reached according to which the Haredi parties agreed to the notion of military service for its males after a deferment of five years for those engaged in study in a yeshiva. Also, there has been an increase in the number of Haredim who present themselves for military service. Much more important than both of these is the fact that the Israeli army is becoming increasingly professional and is less dependent on mass conscription. Indeed, top army officials have conceded that they would not know what to do with the Haredim if, indeed, they did present themselves for service in significant numbers. There are indications that there will be radical changes in the role of the military in Israeli society. Among these changes will be an end to universal service as it exists today and, thus, an end to the military service issue in the religious-secular rift.

The increasing participation of Haredim in the political process is strikingly apparent in their rates of voting. Some estimates suggest that their rate of voter participation in elections for the prime minister and Knesset significantly exceeds that of any other segment of the Israeli population, and that it does so in municipal elections by as much as 20 to 50 percent. To some extent, the high rate of Haredi voter participation stems from some of the same sociological characteristics that have resulted in the growth of that community. As I have discussed elsewhere,[27] as contrasted with the modern Orthodox, the Haredi community is characterized by a clear sense of authority. This is so because the notion of submission to the authority of the tradition as espoused by the experts of the tradition is one of the most basic characteristics of all religious orthodoxies. Authority and tradition are prerequisites for religious orthodoxy. Within an orthodoxy the individual is expected to internalize tradition so as to perceive himself as not having any choice but to conform to all of its dictates. The notion that the individual has the ability to choose is heretical, as Peter Berger elucidates. As he points out, "the English word 'heresy' comes from the Greek verb *hairein,* which means to choose. A *hairesis* originally meant, quite simply, the taking of choice."[28] From the perspective of religious orthodoxy, one has no choice,[29] and from the perspective of traditional Jewish Orthodoxy, the absence of choice included the inevitable submission to the ultimate authority of the rabbinic-scholarly elite.

The submission of the Haredi masses to the authority of the rabbinic elite renders the potential for organization and mobilization much greater within that community. This is especially so since the realm of the authority of the rabbinic elite is much broader than that of religious leaders in more modern communities. Within the framework of haredism, the authority of the rabbinic leadership is not limited to that which in modern society is defined as the strictly religious realm. To the Haredi, there is no distinction, because every aspect of life is within the purview of *Halakha,* Jewish religious law, and therefore every decision of the rabbinic leader is *Halakhic,* Jewishly religious, and as binding as his decisions on matters such as what is kosher.

There is also, within the haredi community, a great concern with acceptance, that is, with being accepted as part of the community and behaving according to the standards set down by the community's leadership. This makes for a high degree of conformity in such matters as dress and general patterns of behavior.

In addition, communication within the Orthodox community is greatly facilitated by the fact that members, Haredi and modern Orthodox, can be found in synagogues and yeshivot, schools of Jewish religious education. They are, therefore, highly "reachable." The relative ease of communication enhances the potential for organization within that community.

As a result of the greater potential for communication and organization, as well as the submission to central authority figures, the Haredi leadership are able to get out the vote when they decide to. Their sense of affinity for the political parties of the right and their partnership with those parties have resulted in their having an increasingly vested interest in maintaining and extending those ties. They therefore are much more likely to call upon their followers to support those parties. As a result, the Haredi masses typically follow their leaders' calls and deliver their votes in large numbers to the Likud and their allies. Even in the 1999 elections, when there were no unambiguous calls from Haredi leaders to support a specific candidate, haredim and, indeed, most Orthodox voters overwhelmingly voted for the parties of the right.

In contrast to the increasing voter participation of the haredim, the secular sector appears to be experiencing a pattern not dissimilar from that found in the United States, namely, a decrease in the rate of voter participation. Thus, while the rate of voting in religious Bnai Brak increased from 79 percent in 1973 to 84 percent, as compared to the national rate of about 78 percent, it decreased in the largely secular area of Givatayim, from 89 percent in 1973 to about 82 percent in 1996.[30]

The recent challenges to Orthodox control of the rabbinate and, concomitantly, the Personal Status Law, which governs such matters as marriage and divorce, have strengthened the Orthodox determination to maintain its control over these areas by increasing their alignment with those parties prepared to cede that control to them. This was a major factor in a massive Haredi demonstration against Israel's Supreme Court in February 1999, because the Haredim believed the court was insensitive to its perspective and what it has viewed as the agreed-upon status quo, ever since the government of Ben-Gurion. Invariably, it has been the political right which the Haredim view as their ally in this battle, and that relationship will probably continue, despite the fact that all of the religious parties joined the Barak coalition. They joined the coalition for pragmatic reasons even as they are ideologically and emotionally closer to Likud and other parties on the right. The question that remains is whether the increased power of the Haredi parties will lead to their greater acceptance as a legitimate and integral part of Israeli society or whether those religio-politics will, in turn, lead to a real Kulturkampf in the Holy Land.

Notes

Author's note: This is a revised and updated version of a paper presented at the conference "Israel at Fifty: Visions and Challenges," Baltimore Hebrew University, May 3, 1998. I wish to express gratitude to my dear friend Eliezer Don-Yehiya, for his most helpful critical comments on a draft of this chapter.

1. Charles S. Liebman and Eliezer Don-Yehiya, *Civil Religion in Israel*, and Charles S. Liebman and Elihu Katz, eds., *The Jewishness of Israelis*.
2. Eliezer Don-Yehiya, "Religion, Ethnicity and Electoral Reform."
3. Ehud Luz, *Parallels Meet*.
4. Katz and Liebman, *The Jewishness of Israelis*.
5. Moshe Horowitz, *Rabbi Schach* [Hebrew], 131–43.
6. Arye Dayan, *The Story of Shas* [Hebrew], 7.
7. Eliezer Don-Yehiya, "Does the Place Make a Difference?: Jewish Orthodoxy in Israel and the Diaspora," in *Israel as a Religious Reality*, ed. Chaim I. Waxman (Northvale: Jason Aronson, 1994), 60.

8. Cf. Ehud Sprinzak, *The Ascendance of Israel's Radical Right*, 107–66.

9. Cf. Herb Keinon, "A Most Uncommon Marriage," *Jerusalem Post*, April 30, 1999, B1.

10. Chaim I. Waxman, "The Haredization of American Orthodox Jewry."

11. At least until the 1999 election campaign, when UTJ projected itself as a nationalist party. See above and note 9.

12. Charles S. Liebman, "Modern Orthodoxy in Israel," *Judaism* 47, no. 4 (Fall 1998): 405–10.

13. Zerah Warhaftig, *Hukah le-israel: Dat umedina* [Hebrew] (Jerusalem: Mesilot, 1988), 34–36.

14. Eliezer Don-Yehiya, "The 'Status-Quo Agreement' as a Solution to Problems of Religion and State in Israel," in *Religion and Politics in Israel*, ed. Charles S. Liebman and Eliezer Don-Yehiya (Bloomington: Indiana University Press, 1984), 31–40.

15. The case involved an Israeli plane which landed after the onset of the Sabbath. At any rate, it seems certain that the NRP would have left Labor and allied itself with the Likud.

16. Baruch Litvin and Sidney B. Hoenig, eds., *Jewish Identity: Modern Response and Opinions* (New York: Feldheim, 1965).

17. Charles S. Liebman, "Who Is Jewish in Israel?" *American Zionist* December 1970, 27–31.

18. Aviezer Ravitzky, *Freedom Inscribed: Diverse Voices of the Jewish Religious Thought* [Hebrew] (Tel Aviv: Am Oved, 1999), 267–69.

19. The term *culture shifts* is from the work of Ronald Inglehart: *Culture Shift in Advanced Industrial Society* (Princeton: Princeton University Press 1990), and *Modernization and Postmodernization: Cultural, Economic, and Political Change in 43 Societies* (Princeton: Princeton University Press, 1997).

20. Ravitzky, *Freedom Inscribed*, 269–70.

21. The term is adapted from William Graham Sumner, *What the Social Classes Owe to Each Other* (Caldwell, Idaho: Caxton, 1954).

22. Don-Yehiya, "Religion, Ethnicity and Electoral Reform."

23. Ehud Sprinzak, "Netanyahu's Safety Belt."

24. Kopelowitz and Diamond, for example, argue that, in contrast to the "messianic ideology" of the NRP, which weakens democracy, Shas's religious approach strengthens democracy, including making it more amenable to territorial compromise. Ezra Kopelowitz and Matthew Diamond, "Religion That Strengthens Democracy: An Analysis of Religious Political Strategies in Israel," *Theory and Society* 27, 1998, 671–708.

25. Shahar Ilan, "They Believe in the Booth," *Haaretz*, March 31, 1998.

26. Ibid.

27. Waxman, "The Haredization of American Orthodoxy."

28. Peter L. Berger, *The Heretical Imperative*, 27.

29. This is one interpretation of the verse, "Lo tukhal lehit'alem" ("You *will not be able to* avoid it") (Deuteronomy 22:3).

30. Ilan, "They Believe in the Booth."

9

The Arab Parties

Elie Rekhess

The 1948 War of Independence created a unique situation—an Arab minority amidst the Jewish State of Israel. The nearly 150,000 Arabs who chose to stay in their homes and become Israeli citizens remained, at the same time, emotionally, nationally, culturally, and religiously bound to the outside Arab world. This necessarily resulted in a serious crisis of loyalty and identity.

Today the Arab and Druze population in the pre–1967 war borders of Israel numbers more than one million, constituting approximately 18 percent of the total population. In fact, one can say that every sixth Israeli is a non-Jew. The non-Jewish population in Israel is heterogeneous. It is composed of Muslim Arabs (76 percent), Christian Arabs (15 percent), and Druze (9 percent). There is also a small Circassian minority. Of the Muslim community, a large segment are Bedouins (nearly 150,000, constituting some 15 percent of the total non-Jewish population and 20 percent of the Muslims). The formerly nomad Bedouin community is presently concentrated in the southern part of Israel (the Negev), where it undergoes a process of resettlement. The Druze, originally an offshoot sect of Islam, is a recognized religious community with autonomous religious institutions. The majority of the Christian Arabs are Greek Catholics (37 percent). The rest are Greek Orthodox (30 percent), Catholics (23 percent), Maronites (5 percent), and others (5 percent).

As Israel celebrates its fiftieth anniversary, the question of Jewish-Arab relations inside Israel is becoming increasingly critical. This chapter seeks to examine the present situation of the Arabs in Israel, both from a historical perspective and in light of recent developments related to the ramifications of the political process between Israel and the Palestinians.

Before 1948, little thought had been given to the possibility that the future State of Israel might harbor an Arab minority. The Zionist movement hardly dealt with the matter. Equality of rights was mentioned in broad terms, but there was no in-depth discussion of its ideological significance or practical implications. However, once the State of Israel was established and the existence of a sizable Arab minority became an indisputable reality, Israel was compelled to formulate a policy.

The first broad policy guidelines adopted by the government were included in Israel's Declaration of Independence. The declaration represents an effort to synthesize the traditional Jewish worldview with the national aspirations of Zionism and the Western concept of a liberal democracy. Thus, the declaration, on the one hand, proclaimed "the establishment of the Jewish state in Palestine, to be called Israel," yet, on the other hand, it simultaneously emphasized the democratic-liberal norms of the nascent Jewish state. Addressing the Arab population directly it said, "In the midst of wanton aggression, we yet call upon the Arab inhabitants of the State of Israel to return to the ways of peace and play their part in the development of the state with full and equal citizenship and representation in all its bodies and institutions, provisional or permanent."

The principles of equality and justice were clearly established in the declaration: "The State of Israel . . . will promote the development of the country for the benefit of all its inhabitants; will be based on the precepts of liberty, justice and peace taught by the Hebrew prophets; will uphold the full social and political equality of all its citizens, without distinction of race, creed or sex; will guarantee full freedom of conscience, worship, education and culture; will safeguard the sanctity and inviolability of the shrines and Holy Places of all religions."

The same principle, in a somewhat more detailed formulation, underlay the relevant sections of Israel's first government program presented to the Knesset in March 1949: "In the law which will stabilize the democratic and republican regime in the State of Israel, total equality of rights and obligations will be assured to all citizens, irrespective of religion, race and nationality, [and] freedom of religion, conscience, language, education and culture will be guaranteed."

In practical terms, Israel adopted a dual policy toward the Arab minority, underlined by two contradictory considerations: one that was security-oriented and viewed the Arabs as a potentially "enemy-affiliated minority," and another, drawing upon liberal and democratic principles, that argued for integration of the Arab minority into Israeli life. Under the immediate impact of the battles of 1948 and hardened by the memories of thirty years of violent confrontation preceding the war, the security-oriented perspective was based on the assumption that the Arabs presented a danger to the very existence of the state. The policy manifested itself in the institution of military government in areas densely populated by Arabs. The military government was abolished in 1966. There was no clear-cut division between advocates of a security-oriented approach and supporters of the more liberal views. Rather than divide into two camps, many public figures labored to live with both views at one and the same time.

Consequently, along with strict security procedures, Israel applied an integrationist policy. This process came to be known in the professional literature as "Israelization." All Arabs remaining in the country were granted full Israeli citizenship including the right to vote and be elected. Arabic was virtually granted the status of an official language, although Hebrew was the state language. Coins, postage stamps, and banknotes had Arabic as well as Hebrew inscriptions. Arabic remained the language of instruction in all state-maintained Arab schools. Government ministries gradually began to implement development plans for the Arab population, attempting to bridge the sizable socioeconomic gaps existing between the two communities. Immediate efforts were made to rehabilitate the economy of the Arab villages, develop health services, and promote the educational system. The integrative process was, nevertheless, extremely slow during Israel's first two decades. It was seriously impeded by years of military rule, widespread expropriation of Arab lands, discrimination, and inequality. Since the mid-1960s, Israel's policy toward the Arab minority has undergone a major transformation. Those Israeli Jews who had dreamt that one day they would miraculously wake up to a reality of an Israeli state with no Arab citizens were disillusioned. So were the Israeli Arabs who had dreamt the opposite.

The conditions that prevailed until the Six-Day War allowed the vast majority of the Arab minority to maintain a delicate balance between the Israeli and the Arab components of their identity. They were physically detached and isolated from the rest of the Arab world. The 1967 war, however, changed the scene dramatically, launching a return to their Palestinian roots. The war resulted in the reunification of the Israeli Arabs with their Palestinian brethren in the territories. As contacts deepened, a strengthening of the Palestinian consciousness of the Israeli Arabs became increasingly evident. This process, which came to be known as "Palestinization," accelerated following the 1973 war and the emergence of the PLO. Yasser Arafat's speech to the U.N. General Assembly in 1974 and the PLO's achievements in the United Nations enhanced its image in the eyes of Israel's Arab minority. Increasingly, Israeli Arabs expressed support for the PLO and Palestinian self-determination. The PLO, for its part, responded favorably and encouraged these changes.

The strengthening of the Israeli Arabs' national awareness did not stand in necessary contradiction to their continued integration in Israeli society. The model that evolved did not reflect a zero-sum game. Palestinization was not a mutually exclusive process, in the sense that it categorically outweighed Israelization. On the contrary, parallel to the reformulation of national identities and political affiliations, the Arab minority underwent an intensive process of socioeconomic change, modernization, and Westernization. The economic progress of the Israeli Arabs led to a substantial rise in living standards, accompanied by a parallel rise in the level of expectations, especially among the younger generation brought up and educated in Israel. The Arab sector's almost exclusive model for evaluating its situation was the level of development of the neighboring Jewish populations. Comparisons revealed sizable gaps in almost every socioeconomic sphere: industrialization, housing, land, education, local infrastructure, employment, and so forth. The socioeconomic discrepancies between Jews and Arabs became even more accentuated because of the rapid demographic growth of the Arab population. By the mid-1990s the Arab sector had grown to nearly one million. This substantial increase led to a dramatic growth in material needs, which the government was only partly able to satisfy.

The continuing government neglect, the widening socioeconomic discrepancies, and the mounting expectations all resulted in the 1970s in an accumulating sense of frustration and deprivation. The increasing socioeconomic stress and the process of Palestinization profoundly modified the Israeli Arabs' political behavior. Political activism replaced a more passive, "quietist" approach. The new strategy was based on a firm decision to struggle for the achievement of full civil equality, a demand based on the commitment of the Israeli government in 1948 to grant full equality to the Arab citizens of the state. Since the 1970s, we have been witnessing a much more militant approach which has manifested itself in the organization of full-scale mass protests, rallies, demonstrations and strikes, campaigning against the government, the establishment of countrywide action-oriented organizations such as the Arab Mayors' Forum, and the occasional blurring of the line separating the struggle for civil equality from a struggle for national rights.

The Oslo process and the Israel-PLO accords of September 1993 marked the beginning of a new era in Jewish-Arab relations inside Israel.[1] On the one hand, it weakened the external Palestinian ties of the Israeli Arabs and lessened the intensity of Palestinization. Large segments of the Arab minority felt relieved by the fact that, at long last, Israel acknowledged the

PLO and the legitimate rights of the Palestinians. The former Labor-led government and, to a large extent, the present one have, in fact, accomplished the goal for which the Arabs themselves had been striving for so many years. Those objectives included the demand (1) to recognize the PLO, (2) to withdraw from the Gaza Strip and the West Bank, and (3) to call for the establishment of a Palestinian state. While the latter goal is still far from being realized, the political process initiated between Israel and the Palestinians was conceived by the local Arabs as a first step toward its fulfillment. After these breakthroughs had been made, many Israeli Arabs felt that they had done their share in the general effort to resolve the Israeli-Palestinian conflict, in the sense that they had waged a political campaign in Israel in the 1970s, the 1980s, and the 1990s, thus paying their debt to the external Palestinian cause.

This viewpoint did not imply losing total interest in the PLO or the Palestinian Authority (PA). The Israeli Arabs continued to identify with the PA, expressed solidarity with the Palestinian stand in the negotiating process, and even showed a readiness to be mobilized whenever riots erupted in the territories such as in the case of the Hebron Massacre (1994) and the disturbances and clashes over the opening of the Jerusalem Tunnel in 1996. But other than political protest and identification, mostly on the declarative level, the Israeli Arabs began to gradually detach themselves from the external Palestinian cause. The fact that a PA had been established led Israeli Arabs to be less involved in the struggle for the PLO. One interesting parameter which may help us examine the extent of this change is the degree of willingness or eagerness on the part of Israeli Arabs to move and resettle in a future Palestinian state. Polls conducted in the 1980s showed that between 15 and 20 percent expressed such interest. Recent polls indicate that the percentage has dropped to nearly zero.

It seems that the Israeli Arabs are reluctant to exchange the democracy practiced in Israel for the problematic legal system in the PA. The existence of a malfunctioning, corrupt, and security-oriented administration in the territories discouraged many of the local Arabs from the idea of moving to the territories, on the one hand, and provided them with an unexpected new yardstick to evaluate and reassess—positively—their lot inside Israel. When such comparisons were made, the ultimate outcome was growing appreciation of their status as Israeli citizens. Indeed, the other facet of the decrease in the intensity of the external Palestinian context expressed itself in the strengthening of the "Israeli context." The peace process prompted many of the Arabs in Israel to internalize their Israeliness to an even greater degree. Many felt that due to the fact that Rabin, and later Benjamin Netanyahu himself, acknowledged Arafat and met with him in person, Palestinian national existence had been legitimized. In other words, no longer did the Palestinian identity of the Arabs in Israel, from their own perspective, automatically imply disloyalty to or non-identification with the State of Israel.

In the 1950s, a prominent leader of the Arab community in Israel, 'Abd al-'Aziz Zuebi, encapsulated the dilemma of the Arab authority, saying: "My state is at war with my people." In the mid-1990s, the statement was rephrased: "My state is in a peace process with my people." Also, the fact that the PLO, or at least large segments of the PLO, accepted Israeli legitimacy encouraged many of the local Arabs to accept the reality of an Israeli state as well as their status in it as a national minority. This accommodative, or integrationist, trend expressed itself clearly in a poll conducted by the Adenauer Foundation-sponsored program on Arab politics in Israel, at Tel Aviv University. The poll, carried out in October and November 1997, included a representative sample of 600 Arabs and Druze interviewees. One of the questions related to military service, from which the Arabs are exempted. The respondents were asked to consider an alternative option of national service. "What's your position regarding imposing National [community-oriented] Service on the Arab population in Israel, side-by-side, with the promise of full equality?" they were asked. Seventeen percent said they were "very favorably disposed" toward the idea, and 16 percent said they were "favorable" (33 percent jointly). They were further asked for their position on "military service." The results were surprising: 11 percent were "very favorable" and 12 percent "favorable" (23 percent jointly).[2] It is doubtful whether similar responses would have been given in the late 1980s. The question on national/military service had stipulated the promise of full equality. Indeed, the quest for equal status with the Jews in Israel began to preoccupy the Arab public in Israel increasingly after the peace process had begun. The level of expectations of the Arab population for the fulfillment of equality had risen considerably since 1993.

This trend was strongly influenced by the Rabin government established in 1992. Rabin admitted that the government had neglected the Arab sector and promised to do everything possible to close the substantial gaps between the Jewish and Arab communities. The government began to vigorously implement its promised commitment to the Arab sector by significantly increasing development budgets. By 1996, it had achieved considerable progress in the fields of transportation, tourism, health, labor, and welfare. Of special significance was the Knesset decision in 1993 to equalize the child allowances paid by the National Insurance Institute. Until then, Israeli Arab families were denied the extra child payments accorded to Jewish families whose members served in the army.[3] While these actions were welcomed by the Arab public, they were insufficient to substantively close the gap between the Jewish and Arab sectors of Israel's population. Pressing issues of primary importance, such as education [classrooms, curriculum, rate of dropouts], the resettlement of Bedouin, unrecognized Arab villages, housing, municipal budgets, and economic development remained problematic.

In many respects the situation further deteriorated under the Likud government established in 1996. Prime Minister Benjamin Netanyahu, in the immediate period after his election, pointedly raised the expectations of the Arab sector, making a number of goodwill gestures toward them. Thus, for example, a day after the elections, he visited the Arab town of Taibe in central Israel and pledged to put the issue of the social imbalance between Jews and Arabs high on his agenda.[4] The promises, however, remained on the declarative level only. In contrast to the Labor government, which, despite its disappointing parliamentary behavior toward the Arab MKs, had demonstrated openness to the Arab cause and adopted an unprecedented liberal policy toward the Arab sector, Netanyahu's government did not prioritize the Arab cause. Moreover, unlike the Rabin government, which needed the Arab Knesset members in order to secure a blocking majority in the Knesset, Netanyahu was not dependent on Arab parliamentary support and could therefore virtually ignore the Arab issue.

The question of the Israeli Arabs had indeed been mentioned in the Likud's election campaign and in the new government's policy guidelines, but only marginally and in a context reminiscent of the patronizing policies of Israeli governments in the 1950s and 1960s. Only three short paragraphs were devoted to the Arab population in the new government's guidelines, compared to ten in the former government's platform. A commitment was made to promote the full integration of the minorities in Israel, but emphasis was laid on special efforts to advance minorities who have joined their fate with the Jewish people and the State of Israel and those who serve in the state's security forces, that is, the Druze and Bedouin, who are traditionally conscripted into the Israel Defense Forces, but not the large body of Arabs, who are not. The guidelines also included a promise to increase budgets for municipal councils and absorb a larger number of academicians in government ministries.[5] No mention was made of the goal of equality, however, or of the issues of housing, welfare, education, and other pending issues.

The Arab leadership responded critically to the government's guidelines, rebuffing the "minorities" approach as reflecting a colonial spirit of "divide and rule" that sought to depict their society as fragmented, factionalized, weak, and divided between varied ethnic and religious groups—Arab, Druze, Circassian, Muslim, Christian, and Bedouin. Instead, the Arab Supreme Follow-up Committee, in a memorandum presented to the prime minister in early August 1996, demanded the implementation of full equality in all avenues of life and a recognition of the Arabs' "national right" to be considered a "national minority [as well as] citizens of the State of Israel."[6] Somewhat belatedly, four months after the elections, the prime minister's office appointed a senior official, Rami Simsolo, to deal with the needs of the Arab population. The appointee, an army reserve colonel, was named advisor on Arab affairs, signifying the revival by the new government of a concept and a position that had been abolished in 1985 in a move toward a genuine attempt at the time to integrate the Arab citizens of Israel without relying on Jewish intermediaries.

Subsequently, in October 1996, Netanyahu gave Tourism Minister Moshe Katsav an additional ministerial responsibility, that of minister in charge of Arab affairs, a decision reportedly made by the prime minister in light of complaints that he was out of touch with the Arab community. The prime minister's office announced that the appointment was part of Netanyahu's policy "to narrow gaps between Arabs and Jews in Israel."[7] This move, too, was controversial, as the position of minister of Arab affairs, introduced in 1984, had been abolished by Rabin in 1992 in the conviction that a separate ministry for Israel's Arab citizens hindered rather than helped their full integration. Minister Katsav said that his appointment should be welcomed because it was aimed at helping the Arab sector. He acknowledged that the Arab sector had not been sufficiently developed over the years, but he anticipated the provision of jobs, housing, industrial start-ups, town planning, and other services for Arab citizens.[8]

The continuous neglect of socioeconomic issues led to an intensification of the struggle for equalization, greater awareness of the socioeconomic gap that divided Jews and Arabs, and greater preparedness to wage a struggle in order to eliminate deprivation and discrimination. Especially frustrating was the financial situation of the Arab local councils which had worsened significantly as a result of rising costs—without compensatory budgetary adjustments as had been received by Jewish municipalities. In late 1996, the heads of the debt-ridden Arab councils decided on a series of large-scale protest measures to pressure the government to bail them out of their financial plight, opening their campaign with a heated demonstration outside the offices of the treasury and the interior ministry. Following this up, the heads of the Arab local councils pitched a protest tent opposite the prime minister's office in Jerusalem for nearly forty days.[9]

One party that seemed to gain from this state of neglect was the Islamic fundamentalist movement in Israel. Muslim fundamentalism has steadily gained power among Israeli Arabs since the late 1970s. The process was nourished by the post-1967 exposure to the intensive religious life of the West Bank and Gaza, access to the Muslim holy sites of Jerusalem and Hebron, the permission given in 1978 to perform the pilgrimage to Mecca, and the Iranian revolution. The mainstream fundamentalist group to emerge, the Islamic movement, was founded by Sheikh Abdallah Darwish. It followed a nonmilitant path, advocating the classical Muslim Brotherhood strategy of evolutionary religious-political change. The Islamic movement deepened the Islamic roots of the local population by education and persuasion and in a short time changed the character of rural society. Mosque attendance in the villages increased rapidly. Young men grew beards, covered their heads, and wore the traditional long gown. Western music, the symbol of corrupt alien morals, according to Islamic fundamentalists, was banned, and campaigns were launched to eradicate drinking. The movement's greatest success was to mobilize Israel's Muslims to carry out Islamic-oriented work in their own neighborhoods. Volunteers built village roads, put up bus stop shelters with separate waiting spaces for men and women, and opened kindergartens, libraries, and clinics. The Islamic movement provided practical solutions to pressing daily hardships. Its community work filled a vacuum created by years of government neglect. While secular activists led campaigns of verbal protest, the Islamists showed that people could do things for themselves rather than clamor for the authorities to help. They achieved a convincing balance between two basic aspects of Islam: faith as a personal and emotional experience, and religion as a social-political framework. This view proved to be a prescription for political success in the 1989 and 1993 municipal elections, when the Islamic movement made substantial gains.[10]

More complex than the struggle for equality on the material level is the question of equality on the political-national level. Here the trends have been characterized by contradictory orientations. On the one hand, the integration of the Arab community into Israeli politics had been significantly enhanced since the early 1990s. The Arab population has been actively participating in the political process. The 1996 elections to the fourteenth Knesset marked a steep rise in Arab turnout: from 69 percent in 1992 to 77 percent in 1996. This rate was the highest since 1973 (80 percent) and for the first time since then nearly paralleled the general rate of electoral participation, which was 79.3 percent.[11]

Furthermore, Arab and Druze representation in the Knesset in 1996 reached an unprecedented record of twelve members (five representing Hadash—the Democratic Front of Peace and Equality; four representing the Arab United List; two representing Labor; and one, Meretz). It was also noticeable that the vast majority of the Arab community sought greater involvement in the decision-making process. In the aforementioned poll, 80 percent of the respondents said they supported the appointment of an Arab to the government being responsible for the government's policies (the questionnaire did not indicate whether this was a Labor or Likud government).[12]

The Arab population seems to have opted clearly and unequivocally for the Knesset as the main vehicle for political activity. In the 1997 Tel Aviv University poll, interviewees were asked: "What, in your opinion, is the most effective method for the Arabs and Druze to achieve equality?" Forty-four percent said: "Parliamentary activity by members of the Knesset"; 25 percent said: "activity by such bodies as the Committee of Heads of Arab Councils"; 18 percent chose "legal acts of protest" (strikes, for example); and only 1 percent chose illegal demonstrations.[13] As a result of the significant demographic growth of the Arabs in Israel (3 percent per year), their political weight has increased proportionately. Today they represent 12 percent of the general Israeli electorate. Their physical growth has, however, not been matched by a parallel growth in their political influence.

Traditionally, Arab parties and individual Arab MKs were excluded from any significant share of decision-making responsibilities. This state of marginality began to change following the 1992 elections when Arab representatives were able to play a more crucial role in the formation of Rabin's government. Had it not been for the Arab Democratic Party (ADP) and Hadash support, Rabin would not have been able to bring together a "blocking majority" of sixty-one members, as against the fifty-nine-member opposition bloc composed of right-wing and religious parties. Arab parties failed, nevertheless, to be fully incorporated into mainstream Israeli politics.

In the 1996 Knesset elections, Israel introduced a new electoral reform based on the system of a split vote with direct elections for the office of prime minister and a separate vote for parliamentary parties. Of the total valid Arab votes, 94.8 percent were cast for Shimon Peres, a monumental rate of support, especially in comparison with the results in the Jewish sector, where Peres obtained about 44 percent, losing the premiership. By comparison, only 5.2 percent of the total Arab vote supported Netanyahu, emanating primarily from small traditional groups of Arab, Druze, and Bedouin supporters of the Likud. As was the case in the Jewish sector, the electoral reform allowed the Arabs to split their vote between support for the prime minister they favored and the list for the Knesset that directly represented their communal interests. As a result, the elections spawned multiple Arab parties and the establishment of new Arab political movements. In addition to the two veteran parties, the Arab Democratic Party and Hadash, two new organizations made it to the Knesset.

The first was the National Democratic Alliance (NDA), an amalgamation of several small leftist factions, headed by Dr. Azmi Bishara, of Nazareth, a former community activist and a lecturer in philosophy at Bir Zeit University. The party's platform advocated a change in the definition of the State of Israel from a "Jewish state" to a "state of all of its citizens" and the granting of a special recognized status of "national minority" to the Arab population of Israel, which would be expressed by Arab cultural autonomy. NDA leaders openly criticized the nature of the Israeli-Palestinian agreements as insufficient for securing the Palestinian national interest. The NDA joined forces with Hadash, running for the Knesset on a joint list.[14]

The second was the Islamic movement in Israel. In late March 1996, it reversed its long-held position of staying out of Israeli parliamentary elections when its General Congress endorsed the participation of the movement in the Knesset elections within the framework of a unified Arab party list headed by an Islamic movement candidate. The initiative to reverse the previous decision came from the group of Islamic leaders associated with Sheikh Abdallah Darwish, leader of the Islamic movement's pragmatic faction. According to a statement published by the movement's ideological body, the *Shura* (Consultative) Council, the motivation for this effort was the desire to unite the fragmented Arab vote, put an end to the state of factionalization in the Arab community in Israel, and prevent a situation in which, as a result of increased factionalism, Arab representation in the Knesset would be weakened or even eliminated. Darwish had been making strenuous efforts to consolidate the Arab vote and to become the unifying force behind the scenes since the late 1980s but had failed because of internal opposition in the Islamic movement and the absence of the right political conditions for redrawing the Arab political map.[15]

The reversal by the General Congress of its previous position caused an immediate crisis within the movement. In a surprise move, two of the more radical leaders, Sheikh Kamal Khatib and the Mayor of Umm al-Fahm, Ra'id Salah, announced that they did not view themselves as bound by the Islamic movement resolution to participate in the Knesset elections, a move which actually caused a split.

The pragmatists, however, chose to disregard the radicals' views. They negotiated the establishment of the Arab United List (AUL) based on an alliance between the Islamic movement and MK 'Abd al-Wahhab Darawsha's ADP. An Islamist, 'Abd al-Malik Dahamsha of Kafr Kana, a lawyer and a former security prisoner, was named head of the new list. Darawsha and his ADP colleague MK Talib al-Sana were given second and third place, respectively, while the fourth place was reserved for another representative of the Islamic movement, Tawfiq Khatib of Jaljuliyya.

The electoral reform of the Israeli system and the introduction of the split vote significantly strengthened parties that represented communal interests, such as Hadash and the AUL. Hadash, which ran on a joint list with the new NDA, attained 37 percent of the total Arab vote, as compared to 23.2 percent in the previous elections, increasing its strength in the Knesset from three to five seats. Although the NDA had a small electorate, the fact of amalgamation itself drew voters who would not have supported either of the movements had they run separately. In addition, Hadash gleaned several thousand Jewish votes, amounting to an estimated half-mandate.[16] Similarly, the AUL won 25.4 percent of the Arab vote, as compared to the ADP which obtained 15.2 percent when it ran alone in 1992. This gave the AUL four seats in the fourteenth Knesset, as compared to two held by Darawsha's party in the previous Knesset. The primary reason for the increase in the list's strength was the co-option of part of the Islamic movement.

The rise in strength of Hadash and the AUL came largely at the expense of the parliamentary vote for the Labor party — 16.6 percent as compared to 20.3 percent in the previous elections, as well as the nearly total disappearance of the vote for the Jewish right — 5.2 percent the Likud, the NRP and Shas together, as compared to 19.3 percent in the previous elections. The sharp drop in the latter case was attributable to the fact that those parties were no longer in the government, as well as to their opposition to the peace process. Meretz, by contrast, increased its strength in the Arab sector slightly, from 9.7 percent in 1992 to 10.5 percent in 1996, because of both its pro-peace stand and its ministers' record during the previous four years—especially that of the minister of education—in improving the level of public services in Arab localities and in co-opting more Arabs into government service. Conceivably, Labor neglected its party campaign in the Arab localities in favor of efforts to bring out the vote for Peres in the campaign for prime minister.[17]

Nevertheless, despite the growth in Arab representation in the Knesset in 1996 and the profound strengthening of the Arab parties, the outcome of the 1996 elections was that the Arab political system maintained its traditional state of marginality. As part of the opposition, the Arab Knesset members remained powerless and unable to practically influence the course of events, either domestically or in the Israeli-Palestinian sphere. Furthermore, under the Likud, the tendency to delegitimize the Arab vote became more popular. As crucial decisions regarding the future of the West Bank, the Golan Heights, and Jerusalem became more imminent after the peace process began, spokesmen for the right argued that Arabs should be excluded from critical Knesset votes. The call to disqualify the Arab vote was based on the assumption that the Arabs' loyalty in such votes would be automatically given to the Palestinians. In other words, the demand to delegitimize the Arab vote stemmed from the claim that no Jewish majority existed in the Knesset in favor of implementing the Oslo Accords.[18]

The underscored state of political marginality, combined with its increased alienation by the Jewish right wing and the growing sense of its potential electoral power, encouraged the Arab political system to seek alternative channels to materialize its influence and thus put an end to the chronic state of political paralysis. One such idea raised by Arab political quarters in the beginning of 1997 was the presentation of an Arab candidate for the forthcoming elections to the office of prime minister. The idea was warmly received by the Arab public. The aforementioned survey conducted by Tel Aviv University in November 1997 found that 75 percent of the respondents either strongly supported or moderately supported having an Arab candidate for prime minister. Those surveyed were asked who they would vote for if the candidates were Prime Minister Netanyahu and Labor party chairman Ehud Barak. More than half, 52.3 percent, said they would cast their ballot for Barak (compared to nearly 95 percent for Shimon Peres in the 1996 elections), while only 3.2 percent said they would opt for Netanyahu. The remainder were either undecided, would not vote, or cast a blank ballot.[19] When an unnamed Arab candidate was added to the mix, the results changed dramatically. The figure of support for Netanyahu remained the same but that for Barak dropped considerably to 30 percent. Moreover, the Arab candidate received 45 percent of the vote. Those who would cast blank ballots, not vote, or remained undecided dropped to approximately 18 percent.[20]

The signal to Barak from these findings was that the Arab vote was not automatically "in his pocket," thus refuting a widespread belief that whatever the circumstances were, the Arabs would be compelled to vote for a Labor party candidate and categorically reject a candidate of the right wing. Barak, however, the study showed, had not won the trust of the Arabs who disliked his military past and viewed him as another version of Netanyahu. Furthermore, the findings illustrated that the Arab public was seriously considering "punishing" Barak by imposing a second round in the race for premiership. If an Arab candidate ran as well, it would necessitate a second ballot, unless Netanyahu were to receive more than 50 percent as required for a clear majority in the first round. In case of a second round, the Arabs believed, Barak would become more dependent on the Arab vote and, as a result, more likely to negotiate their political demands.[21] In the end, however, with the help of Arab votes, Barak was to win the first round of elections in May 1999, while the Arab parties won a record ten seats (Hadash 3, UAL 5, and the new Balad party 2).

Arab intellectuals and politicians have highlighted in recent years what they have regarded as the incompatibility between the two features of Israel—being a state of the Jewish people on the one hand and a democracy espousing equality for all its citizens on the other. Arab elites claim that from an Arab perspective, a non-Jewish citizen (an Arab or a Druze for this purpose), cannot be fully equal to his Jewish counterpart, since certain laws in the country pertain to Jews only. The most popular example of such legal discrimination, raised by Arab spokesmen, is the Law of Return. Furthermore, the argument goes, how can the Arabs feel equal and truly identify with a state, the symbols of which are all so profoundly Jewish: the Star of David blue-white flag, the "Menorah" emblem, the anthem which speaks about Jewish aspiration of return to Zion?[22]

Arab intellectuals are seriously discussing different solutions for what they see as an inherent contradiction in the Israeli reality. Others speak of the need to change Israel's character so that it becomes "a state of its citizens" in which the collective rights of the Arabs will be recognized. It is important to emphasize that the calls for "a state of its citizens" or autonomy, threatening as they may sound to Jewish ears, are being made *within* the Israeli context and not as an expression of a separatist or secessionist orientation. Furthermore, it is reasonable to believe that the calls to strip Israel of its Jewish/Zionist symbols do not reflect a realistic belief on the part of the Arabs that the minority can enforce such a major transition on the Jewish majority. Rather, the demand may be seen as a tactical move, designed to shake up the Jewish leadership and as a reflection of disappointment in the inability of Israeli Arabs to attain civil rights.

Yet, concurrently, these new orientations also profoundly express the effects of the twin process of Palestinization and the growing national awareness of the Israeli Arabs. While the Palestine-Israeli peace negotiations are hopefully destined to make it easier for the Arab citizens of Israel to reconcile their Palestinian national identity with their more pronounced Israeli sense of belonging, in some respects the agreement has had a diametrically opposite effect. The Israeli recognition of the national rights of the Palestinian Arabs undoubtedly strengthened the national consciousness of the Arabs in Israel. Furthermore, it imparted legitimization to the claim of the Arabs in Israel for a more particularistic status, even though not a separatist one.

As was mentioned earlier in this chapter, one of the outcomes of the peace process was a lesser degree of interest, on the part of the Israeli Arabs, in the *external* dimension of the Palestinian issue. However, their Palestinian national awareness acquires new direction as they now focus on their collective status as a national minority *inside* Israel. In other words, what we witness is a *localization* of the national process within the Israeli context. This trend expresses itself in the aforementioned discussion of the desirable nature of the state and a heightened interest in issues pertaining to the national identity of the Arabs in Israel such as the national content of the Arab schools' curricula and, more importantly, the question of Arab lands: a campaign to allow Arabs in Israel who had been dislocated from their ruined villages inside Israel in 1948 and were resettled in neighboring Arab villages to return to the historical sites of their original villages, a demand to allow the Muslim community to administer its *waqf* (religious endowment) property, a campaign to grant municipal status to dozens of Arab settlements which the government refused to recognize, and so forth.

Nonetheless, by 1999 it was clear that Israel's Arab community had begun to score at least symbolic victories in its fight for equality. In March 1999, for the first time in Israel's history, an Israeli Arab man, Abdel Rahman Zuabi, was selected to serve on Israel's Supreme Court, and an

Israeli Arab woman, Rana Raslan, won the 1999 Miss Israel beauty pageant and represented Israel in the Miss World pageant.

In many ways, the Arab citizens of Israel have come a very long way since 1948. Their standard of living has greatly improved, although it does not yet match that of their Jewish fellow citizens. In addition, from being affiliates of Israeli Jewish parties such as Labor, the Israeli Arabs have created political parties of their own that secured a record nine seats in the 1996 Israeli elections and rose to ten in the 1999 elections. The Israeli Arabs have also moved from a status of distrusted alien minority to one of active participant in Israeli political life, a process greatly aided by the Oslo Accords of 1993, which, while recognizing the national rights of the Palestinian Arabs, enabled the Israeli Arabs to concentrate on securing equality within Israel. Nonetheless, their continuing lack of equality within Israeli society, the growing influence of Islam, and a possible collapse of the peace process could start Israel's Arab community down the path of asserting its rights to national separatism.

Notes

1. Elie Rekhess, "Israel's Arab Citizens and the Peace Process," 200.
2. "Political Positions of the Arab and Druze Populations in Israel—Results of a Public Opinion Survey," program on Arab politics in Israel, Tel Aviv University, December 1997 (mimeographed).
3. Rekhess, "Israel's Arab Citizens," 191–96.
4. "The Arabs in Israel," in *Middle East Contemporary Survey,* ed. Bruce Maddy-Weitzman, vol. 20, 1996.
5. *Ha'aretz,* July 16, 1996.
6. Kol Hatsafon (Acre), August 2, 1996.
7. *Ha'retz,* October 18, 1996.
8. *Jerusalem Post,* October 23, 1996.
9. *Ha'aretz,* October 16, 18, December 1, 1996; *Jerusalem Post,* November 15, 24, December 9, 1996.
10. Elie Rekhess, "Resurgent Islam in Israel."
11. Sarah Ozacky-Lazar and As'ad Ghanem, "The Arab Vote in the Elections to the 14th Knesset, May 29, 1996."
12. "Political Positions."
13. Ibid.
14. See platform published in *Kull al-Arab* (Nazareth), April 12, 26, 1996, and discussion in Lazar and Ghanem, "The Arab Vote in the Elections to the 14th Knesset."

15. Elie Rekhess, "The Islamic Movement in Israel."

16. Lazar and Ghanem, "The Arab Vote in the Elections to the 14th Knesset."

17. Ibid. See also Binyamin Neuberger, "The Elections to the Knesset within the Arab and the Druze Public," *Data and Analysis,* no. 3 (Tel Aviv Program on Arab Relations in Israel, Tel Aviv University, 1996).

18. Rekhess, "Israel's Arab Citizens," 195.

19. "Political Positions."

20. Ibid.

21. *Jerusalem Post,* December 4, 1997; *Al-Sinara* (Nazareth), December 5, 1997; *Al-Ittihad* (Haifa), December 5, 1997.

22. Rekhess, "Israel's Arab Citizens," 199, 201.

10

The Changing Political Economy of Israel
From Agricultural Pioneers to the "Silicon Valley" of the Middle East

Ofira Seliktar

Israel's uniqueness among immigrant nations is well known. Its founders were East European immigrants who were influenced by a socialist-nationalist ideology that called for the "normalization" and "social redemption" of the Jewish people. To this end, they glorified agricultural endeavor and tried to change the occupational structure of the arriving immigrants. Together with the advanced egalitarian ethos that was at the core of this Socialist-Zionist ideology, these principles structured the economic thinking of the Yishuv period.

Many economic activities were undertaken to further national and social causes rather than because they followed a clear economic rationale. The expectation was that the central organs of the Yishuv would play a major role in the economy and that the economic activities would eschew the profit motive that threatened the voluntaristic and egalitarian spirit of the community. Economic laws of profitability and efficiency were either ignored or thought to be irrelevant to the larger communal goals. As one observer put it, the Socialist-Zionist dreams "were assumed to be achievable by the sheer will power of the pioneer."[1]

The creation of a sovereign state in 1948 and the twin burdens of security and the absorption of a mass immigration tested some of the most cherished tenets of Socialist-Zionism. Reluctant to give up the founding ideology, the leadership of the new state was forced to adjust its policies to domestic and international economic realities. In spite of a gradual recognition that market forces might provide a better foundation for a viable Israeli economy and polity, there has been a great reluctance by both the Labor party and its Likud rival to make a full transition to an internationally competitive market economy. Still, the domestic and international imperatives have made such a transition all but inevitable in the long run.

Creating a New Economy: 1948–1973

The economic challenges facing the new state were formidable. Unlike the transition in other colonies where the transfer of power was orderly, the British cut off financial ties and disrupted the supply of food and gasoline to the Jewish State. The Arab boycott and a de facto blockade made the task of the nascent government even harder. The general mobilization of the population and the need to finance the war effort, coupled with the arrival of a mass immigration, seemed to bring the economy to the breaking point. Between 1948 and 1951, 687,000 immigrants arrived, more than doubling the population to some 1,400,000. Although the rate of immigration subsequently slowed, all in all, between 1948 and 1965 Israel absorbed some 1.2 million immigrants. Of the new arrivals, 55 percent came from Asia and Africa, and most lacked education and capital.

A series of emergency measures, including an extensive system of rationing, price controls, and temporary shelter construction, solved some of the initial problems. The exodus or removal of some 700,000 Arabs also helped in the absorption effort. The abandoned Arab property was estimated to be worth as little as $500,000 and as much as $4.2 million. Most of the 58,000 housing units, stores, and farms were turned over to Jews, alleviating the acute housing shortage.[2]

However, the long-term decisions about Israel's economic future revealed a number of clashing imperatives. At the most normative level, the Labor leadership was concerned that the new immigrants, as well as many of the veteran Israelis, would reject the communal and egalitarian ethos of the Yishuv. To ensure a more equitable distribution of scarce resources and limit economic self-interest, the ruling Mapai party had created a state-supervised economy that would "limit the liberty of the individual to work for his selfish objectives."[3] The network of government interventions was very extensive and included control of capital markets, price and wage controls, foreign exchange controls, and micromanagement of agriculture, industry, and the service sector of the economy. All in all, Israel had created the most advanced socialist economy outside the Soviet bloc.

The government used its control to shape the economic structure of Israel. Agriculture, the preferred occupation of the Socialist-Zionists, was considered the most important endeavor in the new state. In addition to their ideological appeal, agricultural settlements had served to disperse the population around the sparsely occupied borders and as a means of achieving food self-sufficiency. The latter policy, also known as food security, was thought to create independence from international pressure and a hedge against a possible future blockade, as Levy Eshkol, one of the economic architects of Israel, pointed out.[4] In 1953, the Ministry of Agriculture and the Jewish Agency jointly adopted a seven-year plan aimed at creating a level of output that would make Israel self-sufficient in food by 1960.

Accordingly, the cultivated area grew from 1,650,000 *dunam* in 1949 to about 4,500,000 dunam in 1959 (about 1,125,000 acres), including half a million dunams farmed by Arabs. In 1961, the number of those employed in agriculture reached a high of 127,000. Gross investments in agriculture reflected this trend; the average investment in agriculture as a percentage of all investment in the 1947–57 period stood at some 12 percent.[5] Agriculture was highly centralized; the government and the Jewish Agency owned 91 percent of the land. In addition to the kibbutzim, a large number of moshavim (cooperative settlements which shared machinery and marketing boards) were created for the new immigrants, who were reluctant to join the kibbutzim. The number of kibbutzim went up from 177 in 1948 to 270 in 1960, the number of moshavim rose from 104 to 366 in the same period.[6]

To sustain this large expansion, the government decided to institute a network of subsidies to the agricultural sector. In addition to generous capital subsidies, the farmers enjoyed subsidized rent and water, reflecting the then belief that adequate profitability can be achieved only if the farmers are protected from market mechanisms. However, in spite of nominal growth, the agricultural sector had shown considerable inefficiencies. One reason stemmed from the mixed farming method that was prevalent since the Yishuv period; the average moshav unit included a small area of mixed crops and a dairy. To remedy the situation, the Jewish Agency tried to push a plan for more efficient industrial crops. Making matters worse, by 1952 the urban market for high value-added products such as vegetables and dairy goods was saturated and export opportunities were limited.

Levy Eshkol, who was appointed finance minister, joined the so-called war against the cow. He managed to implement his reforms against considerable ideological opposition from those who feared that the "industrialization" of farming would dilute its pioneering ethos. Still, the agricultural sector remained inefficient because the low value-added crops such as wheat, barley, and cotton could be grown economically only on the large land tracts that the moshavim lacked. However, the transition to industrial crops which Eshkol advocated increased considerably the cost factor in agriculture and highlighted the problems of the water economy of the new state.

During the Yishuv period the amount of Israel's water potential had been hotly disputed. In 1944, the Mekorot Water Company arrived at an annual estimate (adjusted to the 1948 territory of Israel) of 3,450 million cubic meters (MCM). Later reports spoke of some 2,700 MCM, but a series of confidential surveys carried out by the Ministry of Agriculture in the late 1950s showed the water potential to be an alarmingly low 1,800–1,700 MCM. Out of this number some 400 MCM were estimated for urban and industrial use, leaving the farmers with an annual potential of some 1,300 MCM. Since many of the industrial crops like cotton and sugar beets were water intensive, the subsidies distorted the profitability factor and threatened to deplete the water resources of Israel. When the surveys were published, they created a political firestorm, and there was considerable pressure to abort the final stage of the National Water Carrier project that was scheduled to carry water from the Sea of Galilee to the Negev. Some experts, including the government's own economists, described the project as an "absurd economic proposition," but arguments about population dispersion and the military security of the Negev carried the day.[7]

The government was also unwilling to change its allocation and pricing methods for water. Water was allocated according to a historically based quota rather than actual use structure, which benefited the veteran settlements, most of whom were kibbutzim. The water subsidies, whereby the price was nationally "averaged," eliminated the need to pursue market rationality in crop production. For instance, cotton and sugar beets, two water intensive crops, were cultivated in semiarid regions. Efforts to change the price of water to reflect the cost of capital, depreciation rates, energy, and irrigation were met with fierce resistance from the powerful farmers' lobby. Because of the failure to eliminate water subsidies, the productivity of the agricultural sector was quite low compared to industry. According to one estimate, the value added per investment of $1 in industry was 2.5 times as productive as in agriculture.[8]

In a partial recognition of these economic and hydrological realities, the government quietly abandoned the autarchic seven-year plan, but commitment to an agricultural way of life remained high. Even before the limitations on agriculture became obvious, the Labor leadership was forced to consider an urban-based manufacturing alternative. The manufacturing base of the Yishuv was limited to light industry, phosphates and potash from the Dead Sea, and diamond polishing. The influx of immigrants in the postindependence period and Israel's needs for sources of foreign exchange prompted the government to initiate an industrial drive.

Both imperatives were highly urgent. The labor force grew by almost 65 percent from 1950 to 1958, a figure that could not be absorbed by the agricultural sector. The average unemployment rate in the first decade was around 7 percent, a relatively low number despite the fact that construction and light industry offered only limited opportunities. The government "make-work" projects and an expanding public sector provided a large share of the new jobs. Critics contended that the unusually high percentage of Israel's labor force in the government sector represented a form of hidden unemployment.[9]

The balance of trade presented an equally pressing challenge. From the very beginning there was a realization that Israel was unique among nations in its high level of imports over exports. The ratio of imports to GNP in the 1950s was 30–40 percent and the annual trade deficit hovered around $300–$400 million. Indeed, according to one study, the ratio of import surplus to GNP stood at 24, twice as much as the second highest country. The comparable average rate for developed countries in this period was 2 and for the underdeveloped ones was 7.[10] Expanding the manufacturing base was aimed at decreasing Israel's dependency on foreign capital. This so-called economic independence was to be achieved through the twin policy of import substitutes known as *tozeret haaretz* (products of the land) and vigorous exports.

In order to expand the industrial production capacity, investment in industry was accelerated. Starting in 1958, gross investment in industry increased by 28 percent followed by an average increase of some 20 percent in the next five years. According to the orthodox (market) model of industrialization, Israel's underemployed labor force should have been employed in export industries set up by foreign investors and driven by a profit motive. However, ideological imperatives, the population dispersion policy, and other national goals hampered market rationality. Initially, the mandate for collective action led to a strong preference for the government and Histadrut sector. Direct government ownership was most prevalent in the larger industries such as Israel Chemicals and later the Israel Aviation Industry. The Histadrut (Israel's combination Labor union and industrial conglomerate) managed to enlarge its manufacturing base through its holding company Koor: among others, the ambitious Steel City near Acre and chemical plants were built.

Even when private investment was sought, it had to follow the socialist ethos and contend with a host of restrictions and limitations imposed by the government. For instance, in the early 1950s, hundreds of Jewish entrepreneurs came to Israel to offer their investments. They were warmly received but were discouraged by the restrictive 1950 Law for the Encouragement of Capital.[11] In any case, the government, which was determined to control the economic process, settled on the concept of directly underwriting would-be entrepreneurs, who were selected for the so-called approved investment roster. Much of this private enterprise was directed to development towns that supplemented the moshavim as a vehicle for population dispersion. The system produced huge inefficiencies and outright abuse. Part of the capital invested was allocated suboptimally, and some of the enterprises specialized in products that Israel had no competitive advantage in. With few exceptions, the textile industry that was the mainstay of the development towns was not profitable; it had to be repeatedly bailed out because of the government's fear of raising unemployment in this politically volatile sector.

Other industrial ventures fared even less well, creating what one economist described as "prominent failures"; highly inefficient projects that consumed capital, distorted the local markets, and produced substandard goods or services.[12] One notorious example was the repeated efforts to establish an Israeli car industry. In spite of heavy and continuous subsidies and protective barriers, the Illin and Autocars cars and buses were so inferior and overpriced that the scandal finally prompted the Knesset to intervene. The Timna Copper Mines and the Somerfin shipping venture added to the list of fiascos.

Israel's centralized economy facilitated such failures. Levy Eshkol and Pinhas Sapir, the all-powerful minister of trade and industry, who was dubbed "the Sun King," knew very little about industry and technology and were easily manipulated by would-be-entrepreneurs. Under the prevailing system, the Manufactures Association, which represented all private companies, quickly realized that political pressure was the most effective way for maximizing profits. Over the years, in addition to favorable terms on capital, the association obtained favorable exchange rates for the dollar, protective import barriers, and, most important, monopolies.[13]

Under normal circumstances, such radical violations of market rationality would have led to a ballooning trade deficit and a crushing national debt. What protected Israel were the large injections of funds from abroad, especially the unilateral transfers in the form of German reparations, American grants, and the contributions of world Jewry. The German reparations agreement, signed on September 10, 1952, was worth

$850 million, in addition to personal restitution and pensions. Between 1950 and 1965, unilateral transfers amounted to $4,355.8 million as opposed to long-term loans that reached $2,134.4 million.[14] Economists have argued that these unilateral transfers kept the Israeli government afloat in spite of economic mismanagement. As one observer put it, the government "was secure in the knowledge that aid is forthcoming," and, as a result, "it could embark on economic ventures without having to bear the political consequences of making the tax payer foot the bill."[15] The Israeli leadership seemed to be well aware of this fact. When farmers once complained to Levy Eshkol about the drought, he commented that "the most important thing is that there is no drought in America."[16] Of course, there were negative sides to the unilateral transfers. Israel had to shelve its goal of attaining economic independence and, what is worse, had few incentives to increase productivity. In the view of one economist, "having learnt how to get funds from abroad, the Israelis may have made less effort to produce."[17]

The unilateral transfers and long-term loans helped to raise Israeli standards of living beyond the productive capacity of the country. During the initial period, the government decided to institute an austerity program (*tzena*), a severe form of price and wage controls and goods rationing. Carried out by the finance minister, Dov Yosef, the 1949–51 tzena regime was aimed at assuring basic equality in distribution of scarce resources and a redistribution of wealth from the upper strata of the society to the poorest sectors. The policy backfired on Mapai when the hardship produced a temporary dip in immigration and an increase in emigration. Worse, the General Zionists, a party that promoted a market economy, increased its Knesset representation from seven to twenty seats in the 1951 elections. In spite of their dedication to pioneering and egalitarianism, the Socialist-Zionist leaders learned two important lessons from the austerity episode. First, in order to retain political power, Mapai had to guarantee the population a Western-style standard of living. Such an imperative was also pressed by the Histadrut, whose wage goals were often higher than those of comparable sectors in European countries. Second, the chief criterion by which the Israeli economy must be judged is the success in integrating immigrants and preventing emigration. Emigration threatened the Zionist goal of ingathering exiles and underscored the physical fragility of the new state. Reluctant to give up its socialist ethos and fearful of the political and social fallout of economic hardship, the government resorted to deficit spending to support a vast array of subsidies and welfare services.

The inflationary pressures of such deficit financing were quick to follow. Although the government managed to reduce the two-digit inflation of the 1950–52 period to below 5 percent in the following few years, the threat of inflation and the attendant dependence on an import surplus was widely recognized. For instance, the foreign trade deficit rose from $220 million in 1949 to $342 million in 1960. In 1959, the World Bank and senior Israeli economists published studies that urged the government to liberalize the economy in order to reduce deficit spending and increase competitiveness. Such measures were also warranted because Israel had begun its negotiations with the European Common Market on a trade agreement. The public debate that followed these publications focused on resource misallocation and the high cost of protectionism and other forms of government intervention in the economy. Free market advocates argued that the economy had reached a stage in its development at which the government could no longer act as the sole arbiter. They also complained that, instead of building a proper infrastructure of roads and telecommunication services, the government squandered precious foreign capital on such ill-fated ventures as the car industry and the steel mill.[18]

Although Eshkol and Sapir at first rejected such criticism, the government adopted the New Economic Policy (NEP) in 1962. The NEP package, whose main objective was to lessen Israel's dependence on foreign aid, called for a reduction in imports and a corresponding increase in exports. Domestic consumption and public investment were curtailed, the multiple exchange rate system was abolished, and the Israeli lira was devalued. In spite of a temporary improvement in the balance of payments, the NEP did not work. Since the government could not keep spending down, the economy became overheated and the inflation rate rose to 8 percent in 1966.[19] To cool off the economy, the government decreased sharply the investment rate, triggering a recession. The unemployment rate went up from 4 percent in 1965 to 10 percent in 1966 and 12 percent in 1967, and there was a corresponding increase in emigration. The 1967 war put a stop to these restrictive policies, but there was no cure for the underlying structural problems. On the contrary, the rapid increase in government outlays in the military and civilian sectors revived the inflationary spiral. The period between 1966 and 1972 was characterized by rapid economic growth fueled by large investments in defense-related industries.

The frequent Cost of Living Adjustments (COLA) had shielded the population from the worst consequences of inflation by adjusting the nominal wages to increases in the consumer price index (CPI). COLA was first used during the Yishuv period as a temporary measure, but it was formalized in a July 1957 agreement. Economists have regarded wage-indexation as the transmitter or even generator of inflationary pressures, both on the cost and on the demand side. Indeed, the deficit spending, fueled by COLA, pushed the inflation rate from a low of 6.1 percent in 1971 to 20 percent in 1973. It was at this juncture that the Israeli economy and, indeed, the entire political and social system were rocked by the Yom Kippur War.

From Socialism to Populism: 1973–1985

The Yom Kippur War has often been described as a watershed in the Israeli economy; it wrought havoc on the GNP and gave rise to the twin problems of stagnation and high and chronic inflation. Before 1973, the economy, in spite of its numerous problems, had registered high rates of growth. In the 1950s the GNP grew at an average annual rate of 11.1 percent, and in the 1960s the rate was 9 percent. Since 1973 and throughout most of the 1980s, economic growth had virtually stopped: in 1982, the growth rate was zero. The inflation phenomenon was equally dramatic; in the first year after the October war, the inflation rate stood at 39.7 percent, declining slightly to 34.6 in 1977.

There has been no shortage of explanations for the turn for the worse that the Israeli economy took after the war. One popular theory focused on the dramatic increase in defense spending after 1973. Israel had always spent a high percentage of its GNP on defense; between 1955 and 1961 that number stood at 8.3 percent and then it went up to 16 percent between 1962 and 1972. However, between 1974 and 1980 the rate increased to the unprecedented level of 27.8 percent, followed by a slight reduction to about 23.2 percent for the 1981–85 period.[20] The theory holds that, by diverting so much of its budget to defense, Israel could not maintain the high level of investment needed for growth. These huge public payouts, without a corresponding increase in the productive sector, had also fueled inflation.

The "explosion" of commodity prices at the end of 1973 and especially the steep rise of the cost of oil undoubtedly fueled this inflationary trend. Worse still, the prices of imports soared, creating a large increase in Israel's negative balance of trade: In 1975, the trade deficit rose to $4,016 million as compared to $1,283 million five years earlier. The Bank of Israel declared that the balance-of-payments problems had reached "unsustainable proportions," and the government pledged to put the issue at the top of its agenda.[21]

While acknowledging these trends, many economists have pointed out that there were deeper structural problems that caused the post-1973 stagflation. They have explained that the relatively high rates of growth in the previous decades were fueled by immigration and foreign capital transfers. Most of this growth stemmed from providing immigrants with basic needs and the related construction infrastructure. Because such early stage investments are growth producing, they have masked the substantial inefficiencies in the Israeli economy. For instance, construction and infrastructure industry accounted for the bulk of the growth and also nourished allied sectors such as cement and glass.

Early industrial investments in most countries are relatively straightforward and normally include textile, steel, and chemicals. Opportunities in these fields are easy to identify, and even a cumbersome centralized planned economy can manage them. Yakir Plessner, one of the major proponents of this theory, noted that though the "economy grew [it] does not mean it performed efficiently," adding that even the communist economies had grown very fast during their initial stages.[22] Other economists agree that the economy had "run out of steam" when it failed to switch from growth based on immigration to alternative strategies.[23] In a more complex and diverse environment, growth opportunities are less obvious, and the economy must rely on private entrepreneurs, rather than on cumbersome government bureaucracies, to identify competitive niches. Although this problem was already evident in the 1960s, the Labor government was either unable or unwilling to adjust the economic institutions.[24]

Indeed, the Likud party during the 1977 election campaign made much the same argument. When Likud won the election, it was dubbed the *maapach,* a terms that conveys a radical switch, not the least because the winners promised to radically reform the economic system of Israel. This was hardly surprising, since the Liberal faction, the heirs to the General Zionists who were in charge of the economic platform of Likud, were dedicated to a free market and a reduction of government's intervention in the economy. Simcha Erlich, the head of the Liberal faction and the finance minister in the new government, promised to turn Israel into the "Switzerland of the Middle East."

More specifically, the Liberals promised to dismantle the extensive regulatory system that had been in place since the Yishuv period, privatize the public sector, liberalize the foreign exchange market, and abolish subsidies on staples, transportation, and gasoline. Milton Friedman, the well-known champion of a market economy, helped develop the reform plan, which attempted to make Israel competitive in the global markets through an increase in exports. There was hope that, ultimately, a cut in the trade deficit would lead to an increase in economic independence, a stand that the nationalist Likud had championed since its inception.[25]

Under the leadership of Erlich, the government devalued the Israeli currency by 48 percent, the second largest devaluation in the country's history, and instituted a free-floating exchange rate tied to a basket of currencies. The size of the devaluation and the float were dictated by the desire to get rid of the exchange rate subsidies for exports and give the Israeli currency a "real" market value. Import duties were lowered and some restrictions on foreign exchange transactions were removed, especially on short-term capital movements in and out of Israel; Israeli citizens were also allowed to hold foreign exchange indexed bank accounts known as *patam*. In accordance with orthodox theory, these steps were expected to stimulate exports and improve Israel's balance-of-payments problem.

However, the devaluation was not accompanied by reductions in domestic expenditures. During the 1977–79 period, the government actually increased its expenditure by 1 percent, reversing the 22 percent decline that had been achieved by Labor in the preceding year. There was also a 15 percent increase in investment, compared to a fall of 18.6 percent in the previous year. The cost of relocating the military infrastructure from the Sinai Peninsula, following the Israeli-Egyptian peace treaty of 1979, added to the ballooning government expenditures.[26] The domestic deficit as a percentage of GNP stood at 15.1 percent in 1978 and 16.0 percent in 1979, financed by foreign borrowing and, increasingly, the printing of money. The inflationary pressures that emerged from high domestic demand, coupled with the liberalized foreign exchange policies, were immediate and dramatic. The annual inflation rate rose to 50.6 percent in 1978 and 78.3 percent in 1979, abetted by the devaluation that made imports more expensive. Israel's balance of payments also took a dramatic turn for the worse. Because of high domestic demand, exports rose only by 8 percent in 1978–79, compared with 29 percent in 1976–78. At the same time, imports increased by 14 percent, leading to a trade deficit of $3.9 billion in 1979.

Likud's inability to control spending constituted a major reason for the failure of the market reform. An initial move to remove subsidies on staples was quickly squashed, and the government was also anxious to shield its citizens from the impact of inflation. Tax brackets were fully indexed and the interest rates on government-controlled credits were not adjusted to keep up with inflation. According to some estimates, the public came to benefit from a capital subsidy of IL 25 billion, a figure that exceeded 10 percent of the GNP.[27] There was also no effort to tackle the structural problems of the economy. Labor relations remained problematic, the private sector was as dependent as ever on the government, and the top-heavy public sector continued to grow. If anything, the quality of management of the public companies deteriorated; with few qualified managers, the Likud filled the board of directors with political appointees of varying degrees of competence.

Even the most perfunctory analysis of the Likud structure illustrates why the government failed to push ahead with market reforms. The Liberals, who advocated market economy, were a small faction beholden to the larger populist Herut, whose main base of support were the underprivileged Oriental Jews. These voters were most likely to suffer from cuts in subsidies and welfare programs, and the privatization of the inefficient industrial base in the development towns would have created intolerable levels of unemployment. As one observer put it, many of Herut's "constituents are addicted to government protection and subsidies—and do not have any real interest in the operation of an unfettered market economy."[28] Moreover, the hard-line Herut had its own version of a nationalist agenda that took precedent over economic rationality. The expansion of Jewish settlements in the West Bank and Gaza mandated large government expenditures; Ariel Sharon, the minister of agriculture and a leader of the settlement drive, was able to triple the Jewish population in the territories in spite of budgetary constraints. Large payments to the religious parties in the Likud coalition further strained the budget.

Failing to arrest the economic free-fall, Simcha Erlich was forced to resign; he was replaced, in November 1979, with Yigal Horovitz, the head of a small faction in the Likud. Horovitz tried to introduce a series of deflationary measures in order to improve the balance-of-payments situation and rein in inflation. Horovitz, who urged the public to reduce spending and adopt an austerity policy, was hampered by the failure of individual ministries to stay within their reduced budgetary allocations, a development that necessitated the passage of second and third budgets in the 1980–81 fiscal year. Inflation increased to 133 percent in 1980, and Horovitz was forced to resign in January 1981, after the government failed to back him up in wage negotiations.

With the national elections set for spring, the Likud appointed Yoram Aridor, a Herut faction man, to head the Ministry of Finance. The populist Aridor abandoned all efforts to cut the government deficit and tried to deal with the inflationary process by reducing duties on imported consumer goods and cutting taxes. The rate of the devaluation of the shekel was also slowed, and the effective rate of subsidies on consumer goods was increased. There was a considerable public outcry over the new policies; the academic establishment described them as "voodoo economics," and the press accused Likud of bribing the electorate. However, the new strategy, which increased the public's purchasing power, apparently helped the Likud to win the election. Commenting on the outcome, one economist wrote that the "change of finance ministers represented the triumph of populism over liberalism and austerity."[29] Even with power assured for another four years, Aridor was reluctant to modify his policy, which was ingeniously labeled *kalkala nehona* (the proper economy). During the second half of 1981, subsidies were slightly reduced, but wages in the private and public sector, now fully indexed, kept pushing up inflation. The war in Lebanon, which broke out in June 1982, added pressure to deficit spending and both the balance-of-payments problem and inflation began to spiral out of control. The net foreign debt (after assets abroad were deducted) grew from $11.6 billion in 1980 to $18.3 billion in 1983, and the inflation rate rose from 120.3 percent in 1982 to 145.7 percent in 1983.

Adding to the atmosphere of malaise was the banking share scandal. Ever since the 1970s, banks had bought up their own stocks to prop up their value, making bank shares extremely attractive to the public. On average, the rates of return on these shares were much higher than on nonbanking stocks, and they were also far more liquid. By the early 1980s, illegal manipulations had increased the value of the banks' stocks more than seven times the value of the banks' accounting equity. To make matters worse, banks borrowed dollars abroad in order to buy their shares at home, making themselves vulnerable to a large devaluation of the Israeli currency. The Ponzi-like scheme blew up in October 1983 when the public tried to redeem their stocks. The banks could not pay, and the government was forced to guarantee these shares, effectively assuming some $7 billion in stock obligations and nationalizing the largest Israeli banks. After Yoram Aridor resigned in October 1983, Yigal Cohen-Orgad, the fourth Likud finance minister, was appointed with a mandate to implement a deflationary program, decrease subsidies, and devalue the shekel. However, a general election was scheduled for the summer of 1984 and the program was quickly abandoned.

The 1984 elections, which resulted in a deadlock between the two major parties, led to a National Unity Government in September. Shimon Peres, the Labor party leader, became the prime minister, and Yitzhak Modai, a free-market advocate from the Liberal faction of Likud, was appointed finance minister. The new government faced a dire economic situation; inflation had accelerated from a rate of 311 percent in the first quarter of the year to 536 percent in the third quarter, and foreign reserves had dwindled to a very low level, at one point reaching $1.6 billion. The government attempted to reduce the rate of inflation by imposing short-term wage and prize freezes, but the underlying problem of high-level government expenditures, financed by printing money and other inflationary measures, was not tackled. There was also no improvement in the terms of trade, and even the generous unilateral transfers, which had actually increased since 1973, ceased to help. The problem of short-term and long-term debt servicing became so acute that it threatened to add to insolvency. By June 1985, it became clear that only drastic reform could save the Israeli economy. Implicit in this view was a realization that both the socialist formula of Labor and the populist formula of Likud had become bankrupt.

Toward a Market Economy: 1985–1998

Well before the economy spiraled out of control, there was a growing chorus of voices that preached the virtues of a market economy. Ezra Sohar, medical doctor turned economic critic, had for years derided the socialist ethos of the country.[30] He and other detractors have pointed out that the distortions stifle private initiative and create pathologies such as the black market, estimated at some 7–15 percent of the GNP. Academic experts and some members of the business community had advocated radical changes in order to increase the global competitiveness of the Israeli economy. What is more, the American administration had also become concerned with the poor performance of its erstwhile ally.[31] When Israel asked for an emergency aid package of $1.5 billion and deferment on debt payment, the pro-market Reagan administration urged the government to adopt a comprehensive reform program. High-ranking American economic advisers and a team of Israeli economists formed the Joint Economic Development Group (JEDG) to fashion a new approach.

The Stabilization Program launched in July 1985 had two parts. Under the first part, the shekel was devalued by 18.8 percent and COLA payments were temporarily suspended. As a result, real wages were slashed to their 1978 level, and when the COLA was reinstated, it was not fully indexed to inflation rates. The second part committed the government to reducing an array of government programs, including subsidies for exports and for basic goods and services. In addition, there was a price freeze, and the shekel, which had been introduced in 1980, was converted to a new shekel at a rate of one thousand old shekels to one new shekel (NS). The Stabilization Plan was successful in slashing the rate of inflation and improving the balance of payments, but the recovery was short-lived. By the second half of 1987, a recession set in and an inflation rate of 20–30 percent had surfaced. Critics have pointed out that the 1985 reform did not touch upon the core problems of the Israeli economy, namely public ownership of most economic enterprises. Since such enterprises do not operate according to criteria of profitability, their productivity has been low, and the government has to engage in costly and frequent rescues.

As if to underscore this theme, in the late 1980s, the government was forced into two large bailouts. The first one stemmed from the debt crisis in the kibbutzim and moshavim, whose low profitability and financial mismanagement left them with a combined debt of $4 billion. Some of the debt was forgiven, and the rest was rescheduled at favorable terms for up to twenty years.[32] The second bailout pertained to the Histadrut company Koor, whose poor management led to a loss of $300 million in 1989 and $1.2 billion in debt. Under threat of default by foreign banks that owned some of the debt, the government was forced to arrange a bailout.

The well-publicized woes of the agricultural settlements and the collapse of Koor triggered a vigorous public discourse. The circle of critics of the socialist economy grew to include a number of pro-market think tanks and the *Jerusalem Post,* whose owner, Canadian tycoon Conrad Black, declared the Israeli economy to be a "basket case."[33] Daniel Doron, a disciple of Milton Friedman and the head the Israel Center for Social and Economic Progress, called socialism and Zionism a "deadly mix."[34] Alvin Rabushka, a scholar at the Institute for Advanced Strategic and Political Studies in Jerusalem, has published an annual *Scorecard on the Israeli Economy* to highlight socialist failures. According to the 1991 *Scorecard,* Israel was rife "with money-losing state enterprises, Histadrut's debt-ridden industrial conglomerates, a huge government bureaucracy, massive public spending consuming three quarters of national income," and "dozens of official monopolies and cartels."[35] The collapse of communism in Eastern Europe bolstered these critics, with many commentators proclaiming the ultimate victory of capitalism.[36]

Perhaps the most compelling reason for restructuring the economy stemmed from the difficulties of absorbing the growing numbers of Russian immigrants, who began arriving in the waning days of the Soviet Union. Some 200,000 entered in 1990 alone, and there was an expectation that one million might come by 1994. Observers pointed out that the

Soviet *aliyah*, boasting a high percentage of skilled workers, could not be absorbed through the old paternalistic channels perfected in the development towns of the 1950s.[37] A 1991 report of the Bank of Israel warned that unless the government carried out fundamental economic changes, most of the newly arrived Jews would leave, jeopardizing Israel's future prospects.[38] Indeed, in 1992 there was a decline in immigration and there were reports that many of the would-be immigrants had adopted a wait-and-see attitude.

The anticipated slowdown in Russian immigration and the threat of emigration—an implied default of the mandate of ingathering of exiles—finally persuaded the government to commit itself to a more serious market reform. In a gesture to this newly found resolve, Jacob Frenkel, a University of Chicago professor and a disciple of Milton Friedman, was appointed to head the Bank of Israel in 1991. Guided by Frenkel, the government promised a balanced budget, more deregulation of the economy, and, most important, an accelerated drive to privatize inefficient state-owned enterprises. In the six years since its inception in 1986, the previous reform netted only about $1.5 billion from the sale of state-owned companies.

Yitzhak Rabin, who led Labor to victory in 1992, vowed to continue the privatization program. Indeed, in 1993 about $1.3 billion worth of companies were sold, but between 1994 and the end of Labor's tenure in mid-1996, privatization contributed only $925 million. Hampered by labor unrest and distracted by the peace process, the Labor government slacked off in its efforts to privatize. Upon his election in 1996, Benjamin Netanyahu, the leader of the Likud, promised a "Thacherite revolution" in Israel. The government announced plans to establish a Privatization Trust Fund to expedite the process, but the beleaguered Likud government was only modestly successful in this. Netanyahu's plan to sell government stakes in Israel's three largest banks and thirteen big companies to raise $1.2 billion in 1997 fell short of target. All in all, between 1985 and 1996, some $3.6 billion worth of companies were sold, a fraction of state holdings. The majority of the privatized companies were small and middle sized, while most of the large monopolistic corporations—such as the utilities, telecommunication, refiners, Israeli Chemical, the national air carrier El Al, the state shipping company Zim, and the Israeli Aircraft Industry are still awaiting action. Compared to Great Britain or Latin America, the pace of the Israeli privatization programs has been slow.[39]

Observers have pointed to a number of obstacles to speedy privatization. Perhaps the most difficult to overcome is the economic culture of Israel which, after decades of paternalism and protectionism, drove a wedge between efforts and rewards and encouraged state relief from personal responsibility. The former hinders economic motivation and the latter teaches individuals (and firms) that they will be "bailed out in case of difficulties arising from their own action."[40] Since a market economy rests on a causal relationship between effort and reward and entails risks that individuals and firms must incur, the economic culture of Israel has worked against privatization. In addition, ideological concerns about the alleged evils of the market economy have not totally disappeared. Defenders of the socialist model have advanced the novel argument that immigration to Palestine/Israel has always involved a certain element of self-selection; those who thrived on market economy emigrated to the West, leaving the state to cater to the less entrepreneurial individuals. The latter are said to be philosophically and psychologically attuned to a relatively sheltered economic existence and seek the state's protection from the vagaries of the free market.[41]

Another major impediment is the Histadrut, which still claims about three-quarters of all wage earners as members and is involved in some 85 percent of all labor negotiations. Through its holding company, Hevrat Ovdim, the Histadrut has continued to control a large number of public enterprises. The Histadrut has used its considerable power to hinder the privatization process, not the least because labor costs in Histadrut-owned firms are higher than in the private sector.[42] Since the public sector unions provide the Histadrut with most of its leverage against the government, the struggle against privatization has become the focal point of its activity. The Histadrut-led general strike in December 1996 put Benjamin Netanyahu on notice that his "Thacherite revolution" might be in trouble. The Histadrut has also tried to undermine some early divestiture efforts; at the privatized Haifa Chemicals, the Histadrut paid the wages of workers striking against a new salary structure. In July 1997, the Histadrut backed a strike by 6,000 Bezek workers who were protesting the sale of 12.5 percent of the company shares to Merrill Lynch. Some 60,000 workers at ten major government-owned companies, including El Al, the utility company, and defense industries, supported the Bezek strike, shutting down the airport and disrupting telephone connections and other services throughout the country.[43]

While the privatization process has faced an uphill struggle, the liberalization of the Israeli economy and the peace process has invigorated the private sector. *The International Country Risk Guide* upgraded Israel's economic rating from 52.5 in 1991 to 74.5 in 1994, propelling Israel from number 79 to 37 among the 126 countries ranked by the guide. Israel received an A+ rating from Standard & Poor, and, in 1994 the Union Bank of Switzerland, which specializes in tracking emergent markets, ranked Israel third among the five nations designated as leaders in future economic competitiveness, right after Korea and China and before Singapore and Japan. The improved ranking boosted Israel's attractiveness as an emerging market for foreign investors.

Israel has two major advantages in attracting foreign investment. The first derives from the structure of the Israeli labor force which, enriched by the Russian immigration, leads the world in per capita scientific skills. At present, 30 out of 10,000 Israelis are engineers and scientists, compared to 25 in the United States. About 10 percent of the country's 50,000 scientific cadres have been directly involved in research and development (R&D). The availability of a highly skilled and relatively cheap labor force has been attractive to high technology manufacturers. The second advantage stems from Israel's unique trading status vis-à-vis the United States, the European Union, and the European Free Trade Association (EFTA). The Free Trade Agreement with the United States and the preferred status accorded by Europeans made Israel an ideal "bridge country" for penetrating these markets. By creating joint ventures with Israeli partners, American, European, and Asian firms could avoid the tariffs imposed on their products in these markets. Israel has also developed economic ties with the Commonwealth of Independent States and other former Soviet republics, as well as with East European countries.

Investing in Israel takes two forms. The first one is Foreign Direct Investment (FDI), with large technology corporations leading the way. Most of the world's top silicon chip producers, such as Intel Corporation, Motorola, National Semiconductor, and Digital Equipment Corporation, created facilities in Israel. Intel, which had a production plant in Jerusalem and a research facility near Haifa, decided, in 1995, to invest $1.5 billion in a new plant in southern Israel to be completed before the turn of the century. Currently, Intel has 2,700 workers and expects to hire 3,000 more to staff its new plant. Other corporations, including Microsoft, Bay Network, America Online, Medtronic, and 3Com Corporation's U.S. Robotics division, have either purchased or bought an interest in Israeli technological companies.

Portfolio investment is another form of foreign capital from which Israel has profited in recent years. The robust growth of Israel's high technology firms did not go unnoticed. Among the leading attractions are health care and information technology. The health care industry offers electromedical devices, pharmaceuticals, biomedical products, and human diagnostics. The information technology ventures focus on cutting-edge software applications such as Check Point, a provider of firewall software for Internet security. In fact, Israel is the second place—after the United States—in the number of high-tech start-up companies; currently, there are some 1,000 start-ups, mostly in software. This impressive growth has been attributed to a shift from defense to civilian use and the government's involvement in promoting technological infrastructure.

The earning potentials of such companies have attracted venture capital and other forms of capital. American investors alone had poured in some $3 billion since the beginning of the decade. By 1995, overseas investors owned about 15 percent of the Tel Aviv stock market. The investment firm of Morgan Stanley included Israel in its Emerging Markets Index and several financial groups have created Israeli indexes in which investors can buy options.

The notion that Israel has become the Silicon Valley of the Middle East has apparently taken root in technological circles. This may make Israel even more attractive to American venture capital that, hampered by the increasing competition in the United States, is ready to look for other regions to invest in.[44] However, the slowdown in the peace process has dampened the enthusiasm of foreign investors, raising the possibility of the return of a high-risk business environment that has hurt Israel in the past.

The existence of a thriving private sector has boosted the overall performance of the Israeli economy. After nearly two decades of stagnation, the average annual growth since 1990 has been on the order of 6 percent, and the GDP per capita has climbed to $17,000. Exports have been up, especially to Asia, where $2 billion in purchases accounted for 20 percent of Israel's total exports in 1997. The inflation rate had dropped to single digits and, according to projections, it will fall to 6 percent by 2001. However, the strict monetary and fiscal restraints needed to keep inflation in check have taken a toll. In 1997, there was a serious slowdown in economic growth; the annual increase in GDP was only 1.9 percent, and the unemployment rate stood at 8 percent. These trends intensified in 1998. The GDP fell to an annualized rate of 1.2 percent in the first quarter of 1998, representing a real contraction in per capita terms, and the joblessness rate exceeded 9 percent.

The economy has suffered from additional problems. The budget deficit in 1995 was 4.2 percent of GDP, as compared to the European Community guidelines of 3 percent, and public expenditure has amounted to some 46 percent of the GDP. The government is still deeply involved in the economy, and extensive subsidies for agriculture, construction, manufacturing, and defense have continued, impeding efficiency and eroding productivity. In fact, because of the "old" subsidized economy, the labor productivity in Israel had decreased in real terms in 1993–94 and increased only by 1 percent in 1995, half the rate of increase for industrial countries. According to some observers, the inability of the government to radically abandon the old socialist principles may imperil the overall economic performance of Israel in the twenty-first century.[45]

Conclusions: The Future of Israel as a Market Economy

While few fear that Israel will reverse its slow transformation into a market economy, major obstacles remain. Probably the most serious one is the redefinition of the national ethos. The goal of the Socialist-Zionist founding fathers was to bring into being a "new" and independent Jew living in an egalitarian society. Critics have pointed out that the economic institutions of the new state created a centralized and authoritarian society that kept individuals shackled in a culture of paternalism and dependency. The vaunted egalitarian ethos was belied by a system of indirect benefits to select individuals and firms and subverted by a large underground economy. What is more, this stagnant social and economic structure has jeopardized the goal of ingathering exiles: Potential immigrants from Western countries have stayed away, and large numbers of Israelis have left in pursuit of better economic opportunities abroad. Nor was Israel, mired for most of its existence in a huge balance-of-trade deficit, able to achieve its declared goal of economic independence.

Whether a new national ethos based on market principles can emerge within the overall Zionist vision is not yet clear. The classic liberal view of the economy in which the individual bears the responsibility for his success or failure is alien to the Jewish values of communalism and shared fate. The pursuit of material wealth as a national goal clashes with deeply ingrained religious values and cultural sentiments. However, the growing integration of Israel into a global market economy may force Israeli society to adjust its values to a new international ethos in the name of national independence.

Notes

1. Yair Aharoni, *The Israeli Economy*, 320.
2. Alex Rubner, *The Economy of Israel*, 33, 35, 70; Mohamed Rabie, *The Politics of Foreign Aid*, 128.
3. Aharoni, *The Israeli Economy*, 326.
4. Levy Eshkol, "Economic Policy."
5. Rubner, *The Economy of Israel*, 106.
6. Aharoni, *The Israeli Economy*, 208.
7. Rubner, *The Economy of Israel*, 114.
8. Ibid., 100.
9. Don Patinkin, *The Israeli Economy*, 35.
10. Ibid., 51.
11. Rubner, *The Economy of Israel*, 20.
12. Yakir Plessner, *The Political Economy of Israel*, 26.
13. Aharoni, *The Israeli Economy*, 216; Yitzhak Tishler, *The White Elephant*, 185; Barry Chamish, *The Fall of Israel* (Edinburgh: Canongate, 1992), 219.
14. Yusuf Shibl, *Essays on the Israeli Economy*, 209.
15. Yoram Ben Porat, *The Israeli Economy: Maturing through Crisis*, 14.
16. Yitzhak Modai, *Eliminating the Zeros* (Tel Aviv: Edanim, 1988), 185.
17. Aharoni, *The Israeli Economy*, 3.
18. Yohanan Bader, "The Individual Versus the State in Economic Life," in *The Israeli Economy*, ed. Joseph Ronen, 28–47; Ezra Sohar, *Israel's Dilemma*, 88.
19. Patinkin, *The Israeli Economy*, 108, 126; Shibl, *Essays on the Israeli Economy*, 199; Tishler, *The White Elephant*, 135.
20. Aharoni, *The Israeli Economy*, 253.
21. Plessner, *The Political Economy of Israel*, 206.
22. Ibid., 11, 23.
23. Ben Porat, *The Israeli Economy*, 1.
24. Aharoni, *The Israeli Economy*, 322.
25. Modai, *Eliminating the Zeros*, 161.
26. Paul Rivlin, *The Israeli Economy* (Boulder: Westview Press, 1992), 15.
27. Plessner, *The Political Economy of Israel*, 233.
28. Aharoni, *The Israeli Economy*, 193.
29. Rivlin, *The Israeli Economy*, 17.
30. Sohar, *Israel's Dilemma*, 130–81.
31. Bruce Bartlett, "The Crisis of Socialism in Israel."
32. Chamish, *The Fall of Israel*, 225–31.
33. Conrad Black, "An Economic Basket Case," *Jerusalem Post*, September 26, 1992.
34. Daniel Doron, "Zionism and Socialism: A Deadly Mix," *Moment* (April 1992): 36–50.
35. *Security Affairs* (April 1991): 5.

36. Hillel Schenker, "Has Capitalism Won," *Israel Horizons* (Summer 1991): 18–19.

37. Stef Wetheimer, "Cheap Political Payoffs versus Real Independence," *Jerusalem Post,* April 4, 1992.

38. Joel Brinkely, "Israeli Economy Is Keeping Many Jews in U.S.S.R," *New York Times,* May 5, 1991.

39. Ofira Seliktar, "The Transition to Market Economy: The Road Half Taken," in *Books on Israel,* vol. 5, ed. Laura Zittrain Eisenberg and Neil Caplan (Albany: State University of New York Press, 1998); Yitzhak Katz, *Privatization,* 189–254; Assaf Razin and Efraim Sadka, *The Economy of Modern Israel,* 198–200.

40. Plessner, *The Political Economy of Israel,* 80–81, 90–91.

41. Baruch Kanari, *Zionist and Socialist-Zionist Planned Economy,* 15.

42. Haim Barkai, "Fifty Years of Labor Economy."

43. Ofira Seliktar, "The Peace Dividend," in *The Middle East Peace Process,* ed. Ilan Peleg.

44. Seliktar, "The Peace Dividend"; Peter Barlas, "Satellite for Silicon Valley? Israel Courts Tech's Giants," *Investors Business Daily,* April 8, 1988.

45. Yitzhak Klein and Daniel Polisar, *Choosing Freedom,* 5–17.

11

The Press and Civil Society in Israel

Michael Keren

"Civil society" is one of the most neglected subjects in Israeli scholarship. Few scholars have given attention to the concept of a civil society, that is, the plurality of groups operating in relative autonomy from the constraints both of the government and of the free market.[1] This neglect has its historical reasons; in a country preoccupied with security and dominated for many years by socialist and nationalist ideologies, the affairs of citizens and the arenas in which they are conducted were of little interest. Academics writing on Israel preferred to focus on the Arab-Israeli conflict or on the peculiarities of the political system rather than on the public sphere in which individuals and groups interact on civil issues such as freedom of speech, public order, quality of life, feminism, or animal rights. To most Israelis, such matters always seemed marginal, and political parties relating to them, such as the civil rights movement, never gained much support in elections. Even studies of the Israeli press mostly focused on press-military relations, with the status of the press vis-à-vis civil society widely neglected.

While historically understandable, this is intellectually inexcusable because the press, in Israel as elsewhere, has played an important role in the public sphere in which the boundaries of the civil society were defined both in relation to the government and to the market. By "public sphere" I refer to Habermas's notion of "the sphere of private people come together as a public."[2] As Habermas explained, the public sphere emerged as part of the evolution of the European bourgeoisie. The liberalization of the market since the High Middle Ages transformed social relations from feudal dependency to individual exchange. Civil society crystallized as a private realm, a process enhanced by new media, such as the newspaper and the literary salon, which allowed individuals to engage in issues exceeding the will of economic patrons, church patriarchs, and state leaders.

The public sphere, composed of private citizens exchanging opinions of public significance, developed under the Absolutist State, which raised the public's awareness of itself. Under absolutism, the public sphere turned into "an organ for the self-articulation of civil society with a state authority corresponding to its needs."[3] It was here that the tradition developed recognizing the universality of civil liberties and constitutional rights.

While this European notion of the public sphere has rarely been mentioned in the Israeli context, it is by no means alien to that context, for Israel was conceived by thinkers many of whom were members in good standing in Europe's intellectual circles of the late nineteenth and early twentieth century. Their thought was deeply rooted in the notions of the Central European bourgeoisie which themselves were, to a large extent, the product of Jewish thinkers. To Theodor Herzl, founder of the Zionist movement, the Jewish society to be formed in Palestine was to be designed after the Central European model, and he all but proposed a constitution for an "aristocratic republic" in which virtue, as defined by Montesquieu, would prevail.[4] Max Nordau, the movement's foremost intellectual, set the stage for the formation of institutions, such as the police, the courts, and the newspapers, which would allow a bourgeois civil society to flourish: "Saint Martin," he wrote, "no longer needs to divide his cloak to give half to a poor shivering man. The public charity commission gives him winter clothes if he cannot afford to buy any. No knights are needed to protect innocence, weakness and humility from oppressors. The oppressed appeal successfully to the policy, the court of justice, or, by writing to the papers, to public opinion."[5]

The main advocate of Zionism as an extension of the Central European bourgeoisie was Vladimir Jabotinsky. As analyzed by Yaacov Shavit,

> the ideal bourgeois type in the eyes of Jabotinsky was an entrepreneur with a civic conscience; someone who from a national point of view combined in himself qualities such as republican values, economic and industrial initiative—one who was capable of moving the wheels of industry and civilization through his industrious and innovative qualities, his brains and his capital. This was the idealized image of the French and British middle class which during the nineteenth century had spearheaded the Industrial Revolution and the struggle for political emancipation, as well as the struggle for national independence in various other countries. This republican entrepreneur was an individualist with a natural dislike for the antiliberal and anti-democratic approach of Marxist and socialist collectivism.[6]

However, Israel did not provide the arena for a flourishing civil society set after the European bourgeois model. The public sphere was constrained by socialist and nationalist ideologies advocating the mobilization of the citizenry to the collective tasks at hand. Particularly effective was socialist leader David Ben-Gurion, who downgraded the bourgeoisie and demanded that the citizenry join in the state-building effort in body and mind. Private initiative was restrained by an elaborate system of bureaucratic controls, favoring Histadrut (General Federation of Labor) enterprises, and private affairs were subordinated to the affairs of state through policies encouraging large families, unifying parochial educational systems, establishing a national draft, and so forth.[7]

Such mobilization left no room for the assertion of a civil society. During the Ben-Gurion era, lasting from 1948 to 1963, the public sphere was dominated by an ideology that cherished the national effort and was intolerant toward the individual challenging the collective, or the voluntary group proposing another way. This ideology was reinforced by the experience of the War of Independence as well as by the massive tasks of security and absorption of immigrants in the 1950s, which led to the aligning of cultural elites participating in the public sphere around a mainstream discourse. As Shlomo Sand has written, "most cultural creation in the first decade of the life of the state consisted in committed nationalistic works that reveled in the birth of the state. The intellectual classes quickly completed the process of conformist integration within the new cultural establishment, and thereby contributed greatly to erasing the borders between state and civil society. Indeed, reducing the separation between the state and civil society was necessary for continuing the rapid consolidation of a new national culture."[8]

Nowhere was the struggle over the public sphere more apparent than in the press. It was here that the boundaries between the civil society, the market, and the state were set. In what follows I analyze this struggle by reference to three ideal types of newspapers classified by their relation to the civil society: "civil society's voice," "his master's voice," and "the imagined community's voice."

Civil Society's Voice

The first ideal type refers to the model of the press set forward by John Stuart Mill and other liberal thinkers to whom society consists of a plurality of groups whose free and equal access to the public sphere assures society's vitality. The press, operating within a system cherishing freedom of expression, reflects a variety of concerns emerging in the civil society and criticizes big government and big business, a function considered to be crucial to the maintenance of public virtue and order.

In order to fulfill this function, the newspaper approximating this ideal type operates in a decent and serious manner. It checks and rechecks its facts before publication, keeps a distinction between facts and interpretations, and takes special care not to offend the objects of criticism. Different opinions are balanced, and peripheral views, unless offensive, subversive, or overly esoteric, are recognized as legitimate contributions to public discourse. Press sensationalism is seen as an infringement upon the journalistic endeavor.

His Master's Voice

The second ideal type refers to the suppression of civil society either by the government or by the market. Firm rules and norms are set by the newspaper's owner—whether a government, a political party, a social movement, a private enterprise, or a media tycoon. Students of journalism emphasize the distinction between public and private ownership of mass media, but from the perspective of civil society this matters less than the degree to which a newspaper reflects a plurality of concerns emerging in civil society or rather is mobilized to pursue limited ones, be they political or commercial.

The suppression of civil society in this ideal type does not have to follow authoritarian lines. To the contrary, the restraining of pluralistic concerns for the sale of limited political or commercial interests may be internalized by committed journalists and pursued by them quite enthusiastically. The main characteristic of the newspaper approximating this ideal type is its unbalanced commentary and its neglect of the distinction between fact and interpretation.

The Imagined Community's Voice

The third ideal type refers to the newspaper catering to a civil society, yet the latter is more imagined than real. This is the newspaper setting for itself, and for its readers, a model community that flourishes mainly in the newspaper itself. Political issues are discussed, economic investigations conducted, and cultural icons built, but these relate to a virtual reality in which some imagined nation, region, or city replaces the existing net of social groups whose real concerns are hardly touched upon.

The newspaper approximating this ideal type is marked by a relative lack of concern with facts, by a degree of sensationalism, and possibly by the "new journalism" style, tolerating the confusion of the real with the imagined and providing the journalists using it with a degree of freedom to invent reality.

The above typology allows us to view the Israeli press, as will now be done, from the point of view of its role in the competition over the public sphere. Obviously, existing newspapers do not match the three ideal types in a perfect manner, and developments in press-society relations are not linear. Moreover, newspapers falling into the respective types often influence each other, and mixed patterns are formed. Keeping these constraints in mind, it may be argued that since the beginning of statehood, a competition over Israel's public sphere has taken place between the three ideal types. And although for a while it seemed that a liberal notion of the press, implied in ideal type 1, might prevail, today this notion is heading toward defeat both by commercial interests replacing political parties in their tight control of newspapers, and by a press losing a genuine concern with the civil society.

Origins

The origins of the Israeli press may be attributed to *Ha'havazelet* and *Ha'levanon,* two Hebrew newspapers founded by Orthodox Jews in Ottoman Palestine in 1863. In the late nineteenth century, Eliezer Ben-Yehuda, composer of the first modern Hebrew dictionary, who settled in Jerusalem, published a Hebrew newspaper named *Hatzvi* (glory—after the biblical denomination of Israel as "land of glory"), similar in its format and approach to the European press. The Ben-Yehuda paper was not only condemned by Orthodox Jewry; it was considered "sensational" by socialist settlers, mainly from Russia, who came at the turn of the century with a puritanical approach and founded their own means of expression, notably the weekly *Ha'poel Hatza'ir* (the young worker).

During World War I, the Ottoman authorities closed down all the Hebrew newspapers, but the British military conquest of Palestine revived the Hebrew press. In 1918, the British military began to publish a news bulletin. In 1919, it was bought by Y. L. Goldberg, a Jewish philanthropist in Russia, and renamed *Ha'aretz* (the land). Bought in 1935 by the Schocken publishing family, it became the main voice of Israel's liberal intelligentsia. In 1919, Ben-Yehuda's son, Itamar Ben-Avi, also founded a newspaper named *Do'ar Hayom* (called and modeled on the *Daily Mail*), whose touch of sensationalism was one of the factors which gave its competitor, *Ha'aretz*, the solid image it carries to the present day. In the 1920s and 1930s, political parties with strong ideological orientations founded their own newspapers, notably *Davar* (statement), founded by the Histadrut in 1925. In 1932, the English-language *Palestine Post* was founded, and in 1939, the evening paper *Yediot Aharonot* (latest news), today the most popular paper in the country.

The Party Press

In 1948, when the State of Israel was established, two dozen dailies were published, most of them owned by political parties. Political parties that did not own newspapers decided to do so after the establishment of the state. Thus, in the 1950s, Mapai published *Ha'dor* (the generation) and practically controlled *Davar;* Mapam published *Al Hamishmar* (on guard); Achdut Ha'avodah—*Lamerchav* (literally: "to the open space"— referring to the party's stand on territorial expansion); the Communist party—*Kol Ha'am* (voice of the people); Herut—*Herut* (liberty); the General Zionists—*Haboker* (this morning); the Progressive party—*Zemanim* (times); and the National Religious party—*Hatzofeh* (the observer).

In an important study of the parties' press, Avraham Wolfenson, himself a party official, described their main characteristics.[9] According to Wolfenson, the party press was created and sustained by the parties' leadership as an instrument of propaganda and as a unifying device within the parties. In most cases, the journalists working for that press, who in the 1950s constituted a majority of journalists in Israel, were expected to comply with the party leadership's line and defend it against political rivals both inside and outside the party. Salient examples of support given to party leaders by their respective newspapers include *Al Hamishmar*'s support of Mapam's leadership in its controversial pro-Stalinist stand in the early 1950s, and *Davar*'s support of Mapai's old guard during the so-called Lavon Affair of the early 1960s. Compliance was manifested in various practices such as the citation of speeches by party leaders, favorite editorials, articles signed in name or in pseudonym by party leaders, tendentious reportage, whitewashing political withdrawals of the party leadership, advertisement of party activities, and so forth.

Wolfenson's study also demonstrates, however, that party newspapers had often diverted from the role of "his master's voice," especially at times of internal struggle within parties. Since political parties were never as cohesive as the "iron law of oligarchy" had implied, party newspapers supported opposition groups within parties in their struggle with party leaders, supported party policy when the leadership deviated from it, and often turned into a "semi-autonomous organization," to the extent of becoming major instruments of political change.[10] Wolfenson concludes that the party press legitimized the positions of party leaders in matters of foreign policy. In such matters, the press could be relied upon to explain and justify the leadership's positions. However, the party press followed a relatively autonomous path in matters concerning interparty politics. He attributes this autonomy to professional standards emerging among journalists as well as to disputes between journalists and their respective newspapers' management.

Israel's journalists, whether or not working for party newspapers, were always quite aware of professional standards, which became an important factor in the decline of the party press in the 1960s. Such standards were debated at length in the *Journalists' Yearbook* and other public forums that served as a check against party and government control of newspapers.[11] Another check was provided by the legal system. On the one hand, the Israeli press operated under British Mandate laws ordering the licensing of newspapers, and had been subjected to military censorship. Newspapers were required to submit to the military censor before the publication of items concerning military affairs, as well as a handful of other "sensitive" matters (mainly those concerning immigration to Israel). Another means to control the Israeli press was frequent meetings between the prime ministers and the editors of the newspapers, in which sensitive information was revealed to them with the understanding that they refrain from publishing it. At the same time, not only did the press learn to evade censorship and become quite free and vibrant, the Supreme Court stood guard against the abuse of the press. In a landmark decision over the closing of *Kol Ha'am* in 1953, the court declared freedom of the press to be a supreme constitutional principle despite the lack of a constitution in Israel. This decision, reaffirmed on many occasions, assured that neither the government nor any political party could violate that principle.

The readers provided yet another check on party control of newspapers. From its inception, *Davar* held a dialogue with its readers, who often objected to the line of party ideologues who served as its editors. From the early 1930s, *Davar* held Friday night feedback sessions with readers in various communities. In her report on those sessions, Anita Shapira reveals that while the anti-British attitude of the paper was accepted, its moderate socialistic approach was not.[12] The paper's editors, Berl Katznelson and Moshe Beilinson, considered *Davar* an educational device in the construction of a social, democratic, reformist, Zionist community, while many of the readers at the time admired the Communist party of the Soviet Union. At one point, the complaint had been raised that *Davar* supported Trotsky's argument against Stalin without letting Stalin have "equal space" in the newspaper. Readers also complained about the mention of religious affairs in their socialist newspaper, for example, the mention of Maimonides's anniversary, while Karl Marx's had been ignored. Socialist activists considered the newspaper too moderate in its approach and demanded that it take a more radical line in matters concerning the centrality of the workers in the state-building effort. Shapira contends that such disagreements between the paper and its readers stemmed from the paper's underestimation of the latter, who were expected to be content with long, argumentative articles by party officials. Only in 1934, for instance, had *Davar* yielded to its readers' demand to include photographs in the paper.

In debates held in the *Journalists' Yearbook* throughout the years over the role of newspapers in the state-building process, party activists acknowledged the need to yield to professional standards as well as to popular demand. They expressed concern, however, that this would lead to cheap journalism of the kind prevailing abroad. In an article celebrating *Al Hamishmar*'s twentieth birthday, editor Yaacov Amit argued that the socialist paper sought to serve as the party's voice in accordance with the glorious tradition set by "socialist fighting literature."[13] He acknowledged the fact that journalism had developed as a profession and was influenced by new journalistic practices in the world. He argued, however, that in order to publish a newspaper that is both appealing to its readers and fulfills its educational function, conscience, faith, and vision must accompany professional knowledge: "Only by the integration of professionalism and ideals can a newspaper be shaped which would be worthy of the great tradition of the people of the book."[14]

Competition over the Public Sphere

Such statements, typical of party ideologues in the early years of statehood, became increasingly anachronistic with the introduction of professional traditions and standards from abroad, which left little room for a party press. This worried party leaders who believed in the educational role of the newspaper. David Ben-Gurion, aiming at the mobilization of society by a devoted vanguard, was particularly worried about a press failing to fulfil its educational function. He took every opportunity to educate journalists, as during his appearance before the annual conference of the Journalists' Association in 1953, where he stressed the difference between his audience's concern with scandal, corruption, and crime and his own concern with "people who do not throw themselves from the third or fourth floor but go by foot every day to their work in the field, the factory, the military camps, the offices, the port or another work-place."[15] He declared he was interested not in issues creating a fuss in the press—lost children, corrupt clerks, teachers demanding a pay raise, military disasters, and so forth—but in kids who go daily to school, clerks who do their work, and the military during routine training.

These ideas, repeated by Ben-Gurion in dozens of speeches, may be seen as part of a competition over the public sphere. Particularly significant was the prime minister's correspondence with *Ha'aretz*'s editor Gershom Schocken. The liberal *Ha'aretz,* with its touch of cosmopolitanism introduced by a staff coming in the 1920s from Russia and in the 1930s from Germany, its high journalistic standards, and its solid headlines and writing, could not be disparaged as the evening papers often were. Its liberal ideology placed free enterprise, the rule of law, and civil rights at center stage and thus posed a true challenge to the prime minister's mobilization efforts. During the struggle against the British Mandate, *Ha'aretz* often supported British policy and was particularly harsh against the use of force in that struggle. In debates within the World Zionist Organization between the moderate line of Chaim Weizman and the more radical line of Ben-Gurion, *Ha'aretz,* although refraining from an explicit partisan line, definitely sided with Weizmann. *Ha'aretz* strongly criticized the strict political and bureaucratic measures by which the Histadrut, operating as an organ of Mapai, controlled the economy. The paper's persistent objection to workers' strikes initiated by the Histadrut was part of its challenge to the labor movement's hegemony over all phases of life.

The correspondence between Ben-Gurion and Schocken reveals the difficulty of reconciling a liberal stance on economic and political matters with the state-building tasks at hand. For instance, in 1958, as a result of *Ha'aretz*'s success in evading military censorship and its revelation of secret contacts between the Israeli defense establishment and Germany, Ben-Gurion wrote Schocken that although the state is formed to serve the individual rather than vice versa, one of the services it is expected to grant is security, which may result in the need to restrain individual liberty. Schocken admitted that the state had a right to limit action by individuals but insisted that freedom of thought and expression cannot be infringed upon, unless security reasons demand it in the most exceptional cases.[16]

It is hard to measure the impact newspapers have on societal change, but one can clearly attribute the privately owned *Ha'aretz, Yediot Aharonot,* and *Ma'ariv* (founded by a group of journalists who split from *Yediot Aharonot*), and a handful of other nonpartisan papers, as playing a role in the process in which the individual came to the forefront in the Israel of the 1960s. In the early 1960s, the dominant Mapai party split between the "old guard" and Ben-Gurion's young disciples, notably Moshe Dayan and Shimon Peres. The fierce struggle, in which *Ma'ariv* played a central role in its unequivocal support of Ben-Gurion's rivals (while *Ha'aretz,* incidentally, sided with Ben-Gurion), signified the demise of Mapai's hegemony and the blooming of a thousand flowers. A new attitude prevailed in literature, the arts, and journalism, with cosmopolitan standards and a culture of open debate developing in student meetings, book clubs, radio shows, and other media through which civil society expresses itself. Under these conditions, no room was left for the hegemony of any one political, economic, or cultural movement. Among the first victims of this new phase in Israeli life were party newspapers, which lost their readers and gradually closed down; today only the Orthodox religious parties own newspapers.

Students of the Israeli press have often referred to the process of transformation from a partisan to a nonpartisan press but have mostly considered it one-directional.[17] This consideration is inaccurate because the struggle for the public sphere was not over with the closing down of party newspapers. Paradoxically, it was *Ha'aretz,* the champion of liberal democracy, which on the eve of the Six-Day War, when Israel perceived itself to be in great danger, led the call for an emergency government. That call, as I have shown at length elsewhere, was accompanied by expressions of regret over the opening up of the public sphere.[18] A well-known example concerns Shabtai Tevet, a *Ha'aretz* journalist, who in 1967 called upon the country's intellectuals to ask Air Force Commander Ezer Weizmann for forgiveness because they had criticized an air force recruitment slogan in the past. Tevet and his associates played a central role in the process in which former chief of staff Dayan was placed as Israel's main decision maker over the fate of the territories occupied by Israel in the war. His dominance of the public sphere in the years ahead matched that of Ben-Gurion two decades earlier, and from 1967 on, generals and politicians had an enormous presence in public debate in Israel. That debate, held since 1968 both in the written press and on television, focused almost exclusively on the fate of the occupied territories, to the extent of neglecting the needs and desires of civil society.

The coming to power in 1977 of a Likud government was seen as the political culmination of the process in which the labor movement had lost its hegemony. Likud's promise that it would lift central economic controls for the sake of "liberalization" raised expectations for further liberalization of the public sphere. Likud had a stronghold in the so-called civil circles (middle-class merchants, shopkeepers, and farmers with a free enterprise orientation) and headed a coalition of bourgeois parties, especially the Democratic Party for Change. In principle, this could encourage public discourse responsive to a civil society liberated from the tiring demands of a socialist state. But no such discourse emerged because, as rightly sensed by Likud's leadership, the Israeli cultural and intellectual elite had its roots in the socialist movement and mostly suspected the new regime. Rather than inspiring a free, open public sphere, the political change of 1977 gave rise to polarized discourse over national issues, with "civil" issues once again pushed aside. After 1977, the press was very critical of the nationalistic policies of the Likud governments, but it was these governments which set the agenda, not the civil society.

Real versus Imagined Civil Society

No account of the Israeli press in its relation to the civil society can ignore the important role of *Ha'olam Hazeh*, a weekly founded by Uri Avnery and Shalom Cohen, two soldiers who fought in the War of Independence in 1948. The weekly was highly critical of the Zionist leaders who founded the state for their failure to solve the Arab-Israeli conflict, and it proposed an alternative to Zionist ideology. It called for the adoption in the Middle East of a new "Semitic" identity; Jews and Arabs would give up their history for the sake of a fresh historical identity as descendants of the glorious forces which operated in the region in ancient times, such as the Assyrians and Babylonians.

Ha'olam Hazeh, disseminating these ideas, did so in the name of young people disappointed by the failures of their Zionist forefathers and seeking a fresh way. No wonder the weekly became very popular among the youth. Avnery claimed that the founders of Jewish nationalism, living in the European Jewish Ghetto, were unable to recognize the existence of an Arab national movement, while the young generation, fighting in the War of Independence, had a different perspective.

Avnery constructed an imagined community of youngsters untouched by the dross of 2,000 years of Jewish life in the diaspora and pointed to the discrepancy between the model state they dreamed about during the War of Independence and the corrupt state emerging in reality.[19] This community was imagined indeed; it was an abstract model rather than a real constituency. A recurrent motive in Avnery's writing was his reminder of a vow he owed to a soldier he encountered in a military hospital in 1948 who was dying at his side when he himself was wounded:

> When in the morning I saw this dead body lying in the bed across from me, I pledged a vow to myself. I pledged that if I come out alive from this room, if my strength is regained, I will devote the rest of my life to two aims: the first that there be no more war; that young people like him no longer have to go to the fields of slaughter; that we would not have to kill and get killed anymore for the existence of our state. The second aim is to fight for the character of the state, so that the state established for such a high price would be deserving of this sacrifice; that it be a pure, clean, free state seeking justice and truth.[20]

The vow pledged by Avnery to a dead soldier in a military hospital in 1948 affected every feature published in his weekly. The paper aimed at the construction of a pure political system that would be worthy of "fallen soldiers."[21] With sensational headlines printed in red long before other papers adopted such techniques, *Ha'olam Hazeh* every week exposed wrongdoings, called for separation of state and church, raised human rights issues, fought for freedom of the press, and brought up the cause of underprivileged families, prisoners, pregnant women, reserve soldiers, war widows, gays, hospital patients, schoolchildren, and so forth.

It is not that Israel had a shortage of underprivileged families, minorities suffering from discrimination, or women denied the right to an abortion by a domineering religious establishment, but rather than catering to these groups, *Ha'olam Hazeh* preoccupied itself with their cause in a platonic way. While Aristotle recognized the need for a balance between the state and the social groups composing it, Plato sought political perfection, and so too did Avnery. At times, the distinction between concern for real versus imaginary social groups was not clear. In 1967, Avnery won a seat in the Knesset, where he proposed legislation favoring a civil society, yet his concern always seemed to transcend the actual groups his legislation related to. When he proposed, for instance, a bill obliging drivers to pick up soldier-hitchhikers, there undoubtedly existed a group that could benefit from it—soldiers waiting at the roadside for a ride. Yet, the bill had not only been highly symbolic, as a bill obliging drivers to stop their cars cannot be expected to pass in a democracy; its initiation had little to do with the actual soldiers who could benefit from it. It was introduced in the name of an abstract group, "the IDF's men and women soldiers," and justified by the debt of honor Avnery owed to comrades in the past, the present, and the future.[22]

Ha'olam Hazeh was never successful in turning the masses over to its "Semitic" ideology, but it did change attitudes toward politics. While *Ha'aretz* provided a highly intellectual liberal alternative to socialist and later to nationalist hegemony, *Ha'olam Hazeh* exposed the entire social and political "establishment" as corrupt. It thus set the stage for developments in press-society relations to come. It was a vanguard of a combative press exposing corruption, inefficiency, and other ills of the political system in a purist way, marked by a concern with a model society but not with the actual groups composing it.

The Latest Phase

The story of the Israeli press in the last two decades is that of a dialectic between the perfectionist tradition set by Avnery and an attempt by civil society to assert itself in the form of a localized, specialized press catering to its concerns. In the 1980s, an upsurge of localized and specialized newspapers took place in Israel. Judging by the diversification of newspapers and television channels catering to local regions and diverse interests, civil society has proven itself to be more vibrant than expected. Hundreds of newspapers in today's Israel cover diverse issues from motorcycle maintenance, through stock market investment, to computers. The business community reads *Globes;* incumbents of the feminist movement read *Nogah,* and teenagers read the cultural supplement of *Ma'ariv.* As many of the special and local papers are published by giant media corporations owned by three families (*Ha'aretz*'s Schocken family, *Ma'ariv*'s Nimrodi family, and *Yediot Aharonot*'s Moses family), they are often found on one's doorstep together with a major newspaper. Thus, Israelis whose public sphere is dominated by national-political issues are exposed to a press referring to far more special and local interests. Such interests are also satisfied in special sections and supplements of the national newspapers.

An important example of diversification may be found in the growth of a press catering to the vast immigration from the Soviet Union. Since the early 1990s, an influx of Russian-speaking immigrants with a high number of educated people has given rise to many Russian-language newspapers. A survey of these newspapers, reported by Avraham Ben-Yaacov, reveals that about one million Russian speakers read 4 dailies, at least 10 weeklies, nearly 20 local papers, and monthlies and periodicals of all types.[23] This volume makes those immigrants the largest consumers in the world of print media. According to Ben-Yaacov, by the fall of 1998, a total of 137 Russian-language newspapers, weeklies, monthlies, and periodicals had been published in Israel, most of them privately owned. The four weeklies, *Vesti,* with its rightist political orientation, as well as *Novosti Nedeli, Nasha Strana,* and *Vremia,* serve as vivid examples of a press emerging as a result of civil groups creating a market demand. The satisfaction of that demand has so far led to a far more autonomous approach to politics among Russian speakers than could be found among immigrant groups in earlier years. While such groups formed foreign-language newspapers—*Yediot Hadashot* in German, *Ujkelet* in Hungarian, and so forth—these were considered means of integration, while the Russian-language press serves as a means to exercise cultural autonomy in a way whose societal and political consequences are still impossible to assess.

Another important example of diversification is the religious press. Although big dailies such as *Hatzofeh, Ha'amodi'a,* and *Yated Neeman* are strictly controlled by political parties, many smaller publications with varying degrees of political control, produced by and oriented to the religious community, provide important means of communication for people protecting themselves from exposure to the outside world, yet seeking information and interpretation about it. An interesting development in this regard are so-called synagogue newspapers—several dozen weeklies produced locally and nationally on Jewish affairs, oriented toward Jewish observers of varying degrees of orthodoxy. These newspapers often have large circulation; *Si'hat Ha'shavu'a* alone, a weekly published by the youth wing of the Habad movement, was described as having a circulation of 190,000, which is equal to the circulation of Tel Aviv's weekly *Ha'ir.*[24] Such newspapers, distributed in synagogues, respond to their readers' urge to preserve their religious heritage as well as to the missionary motives of some of their publishers. These papers include commentary and supplementary material on the weekly portion, reports on religious affairs, questions and answers about Jewish religious law, and so forth. Considering the fact that the Jewish press originated in the seventeenth century in order to satisfy exactly the same concerns, this kind of press may be seen as fulfilling the same function which the traditional sermon fulfilled in the past.[25] Moreover, from a sociological perspective, it may be seen as closing a circle. While the Zionist movement aspired to create a new form of living for Jews in Israel, and the press, from *Davar* through *Ha'aretz* to *Ha'olam Hazeh,* reflected different versions of this aspiration, the wide circulation of synagogue newspapers, or, for that matter, of Russian-language newspapers, reflects the return of Jews in Israel to a loose structure of diverse communities with or without civil consciousness.

Whether or not diverse groups in today's Israel consider themselves part of a civil society or simply stress their unique cultural features, their press is facing competition from an unexpected angle. Local and special newspapers compete over the public sphere with newspapers catering to imagined rather than real civil concerns. This is not an easy distinction because the modern mass media have largely blurred the distinction between the real and the imagined. One can hardly distinguish between reality and its media-created images; as is well known, for many citizens in the United States, the marital problems faced by soap opera stars on the screen seem to constitute a real concern. In Israel, where the soap opera culture is less prevalent, the media have been no less successful in blurring imaginary and real concerns—Israelis follow the careers of politicians and military officers, for instance, with the same devotion with which soap opera fans watch their heroes, and the Habad newspapers spread messianic visions with the same confidence preserved for scientific facts.[26]

And yet, a competition over the public sphere is taking place to the extent that special and local newspapers have difficulty maintaining their initial concerns. Today, one can find a local newspaper in every major city. However, as part of the need to appeal to a large readership, local papers construct press images which exceed reality. A fascinating example concerns Tel Aviv's local paper *Ha'ir* (the city), with its well-known construction of an imagined city.[27] *Ha'ir* is typical of an emerging trend to replace the real for the imagined, creating for its readers the image of a city designed after the model of cosmopolitan Paris or New York. This visionary endeavor, although resembling the vision to build Tel Aviv on sand dunes at the turn of the century, suffers from detachment from reality, as the cosmopolitan community portrayed weekly in *Ha'ir* hardly exists.

It is hard not to feel that this tendency to venture into the sphere of the imagined has been enhanced by economic competition between the two big papers, *Yediot Aharonot* and *Maariv,* as well as between various television channels. Following the line of mass media all over the world, the papers display huge headlines which help sell newspapers but lower the excitement threshold of a whole population and compete in displaying fake events. What distinguishes a fake event from a real one may be judged by its relevance to the daily life of a real, as opposed to an invented, public, and when preference is given to the fake, the press changes course.

This change has been summarized by Israel's master journalist Shalom

Rosenfeld, who wrote that a culture that creates and destroys idols of plastic goes hand-in-hand with several other phenomena no less worrisome: the corruption of the language, the terrible distortion of style and composition, and rank ignorance, and he added:

> Once, only certain local newspapers excelled in this kind of ignorance and superficiality. Today, it is much more widespread. I am grateful every morning if I discover an intelligent article devoid of ignorance and linguistic distortion, or an editorial column of substance which at least attempts to deal seriously with reality. I hasten to add, with satisfaction, that these kinds of pieces do indeed appear, are proliferating, and are qualitative, even if they lack the tone of the old days, which, inevitably, I recall with such nostalgia. But, good God—the ignorance![28]

Conclusion

While in the past, Israel's public sphere was marked by competition between two ideal types of newspapers—"his master's voice" and "civil society's voice"—today the main competition seems to be between press discourse catering to a real versus imagined civil society. Since the competition is far from over, it is hard to draw conclusions, as one is tempted to do, about the nature of the public sphere today and its prospects for the future. What can be said, however, is that the growing concentration of the Israeli press and other media in the hands of giant corporations and the seemingly related trend whereby the press is losing a genuine concern with civil society, catering instead to imagined communities, have severe consequences for Israeli democracy.

The survival of Israeli democracy is strongly related to its capacity to maintain an open public sphere, that is, to prevent the cultural and intellectual hegemony of any one power. In a society facing severe security problems, the probability that a determined political or military force would dominate all spheres of life is very high, and the fact that this did not happen in Israel cannot be understood without reference to the open debate always held in the country. Yet, the neglect of the press to relate to real as opposed to invented concerns may be a hindrance to a free, open, creative discourse. Although journalists often rejoice at their liberation from party control, a press that ignores the real concerns of the citizenry for the sake of sensational news betrays civil society and subsequently the capacity to maintain a viable democracy. Democracy requires a serious, responsible press relating to the concerns of the varied groups in society and serves as a check on infringements upon their freedom.

Notes

1. Dominique Colas, *Civil Society and Fanaticism;* John A. Hall, ed., *Civil Society;* Michael Walzer, "The Civil Society Argument," in *Theorizing Citizenship,* ed. Ronald Beiner (Albany: SUNY, 1995).
2. Jürgen Habermas, *The Structural Transformation of the Public Sphere.*
3. Ibid., 74.
4. Theodor Herzl, *The Jewish State,* 99.
5. Max Nordau, *Morals and the Evolution of Man,* 238.
6. Yaacov Shavit, *Jabotinsky and the Revisionist Movement 1925–1948,* 285.
7. Michael Keren, *Ben-Gurion and the Intellectuals.*
8. Shlomo Sand, "Between the Word and the Land: Intellectuals and the State in Israel," in *Intellectuals in Politics: From the Dreyfus Affair to Salman Rushdie,* ed. Jeremy Jennings and Anthony Kemp-Welch (London: Routledge, 1997), 110.
9. Avraham Wolfenson, "The Party Press in the Political Process" (Ph.D. thesis submitted to the Hebrew University of Jerusalem, 1979), 8.
10. Ibid.
11. Yaacov Shamir, "Israeli Elite Journalists."
12. Anita Shapira, *Berl Katznelson.*
13. Yaacov Amit, "Ledarko Shel 'Al Hamishmar,'" *Journalists' Yearbook* (1963), 40–41.
14. Ibid.
15. David Ben-Gurion, "Ha'itonut Ve'ha'hayim," 193.
16. "Ben-Gurion-Schocken: A Correspondence," *Qesher* 9 (May 1991): 90–95.
17. "Symposium: On the Expiration of Newspapers," *Qesher* 15 (May 1994): 4–18.
18. Michael Keren, *The Pen and the Sword.*
19. Benedict Anderson, *Imagined Communities.*
20. *Ha'olam Hazeh,* September 1, 1985.
21. George L. Mosse, *Fallen Soldiers.*
22. Quoted in Amnon Zichroni, *1 against 119* (Tel Aviv: Daf Hadash, 1969), 355.
23. Avraham Ben-Yaacov, "The Russian-Language Press in Israel."
24. Yoel Rappel, "Synagogue Newspapers in Israel."
25. Menahem Blondheim, "Cultural Media in Transition."
26. Orly Tsarfati, "A Press in the Service of the Messiah."
27. Ehud Graf, "The Universal City of 'The City.'"
28. Shalom Rosenfeld, "From Basel to Sheinkin: The Road from the 'Old-New Land' to 'Freha-Land,'" *Qesher* 23 (May 1998): 7.

12

Epilogue
The 1999 Elections and the Victory of Ehud Barak

Mark Rosenblum

Popular wisdom has it that Ehud Barak inherited the mantle of his fallen commander Yitzhak Rabin, who had groomed him to be his successor. From chief of the Israel Defense Forces to head of the government of Israel, it was assumed that the path had been cleared for another military hero to ride his security credentials into the prime ministership and become Israel's next "General of Peace." In 1999, however, several barriers blocked this ascent to political power—most notably, the incumbent Benjamin Netanyahu, with his reputation as a masterful campaigner, if not a successful statesman. The souring of the "Oslo spirit" and the domestic electoral political environment also seemed to work to the disadvantage of both Barak's candidacy and the quest for peace. The still-unfolding history of Israel's would-be "General of Peace" begins here, with Prime Minister Netanyahu's own peace policies, the unraveling of his government, his unanticipated landslide electoral defeat, and the policy inheritance he eventually bequeathed to Barak.

Netanyahu: "A Maniacal Wrecking Ball"

For nearly three years, Prime Minister Benjamin Netanyahu confounded political pundits with the zigzag course of his peace policies. His opening political gambit of personally boycotting Yasser Arafat in the summer of 1996, plus his middle-of-the-night fiasco opening of the Hasmonean tunnel later that September, convinced some analysts that Netanyahu was an unrepentant ideological hawk bent on sabotaging the Oslo Accords. However, his zag back to the negotiating table, where he signed the Hebron Agreement and endorsed the American-drafted "Note for the

Record" in January 1997, persuaded other analysts that Netanyahu's natural affinity for the cause of "Greater Israel" could be tempered by the forces of realpolitik and, most notably, pressure from Washington.

But the ink on these negotiating documents was barely dry when the prime minister pursued two other policy initiatives that tarnished his newly won image as a centrist. First, without consulting his Palestinian interlocutors, Netanyahu tried to satisfy the first of three "Further Redeployments" (RFDs) that his government had to begin implementing in March 1997 by offering a minuscule amount of land—only 7 percent of area "B," land over which Israel has security control and the Palestinian Authority (PA) has civil authority—to exclusive Palestinian control. More significantly, this offer contained only 2 percent of area "C"—70 percent of the West Bank—which remains solely under Israeli authority and represents the basis for Palestinian aspirations for a territorially contiguous Palestinian state. The prime minister accompanied this negligible withdrawal offer with the decision to construct a controversial new Jewish community in southeastern Jerusalem, Har Homa, thus scuttling negotiations between Israel and the Palestinians for nearly two years.

In October 1998, President Clinton's attempt to revive the by-then moribund Oslo process at the Wye River Plantation afforded Prime Minister Netanyahu one last chance to salvage his reputation as a pragmatic hawk. And seemingly he did. At this second emergency summit in two years, Netanyahu demonstrated that his ideological affinity for "Greater Israel" could temporarily be reconciled by signing, if not entirely implementing, a second agreement, which he helped forge, that amended the Oslo Accords. With his endorsement of the Wye River Memorandum in Washington and his subsequent shepherding of the agreement through the cabinet and Knesset for approval, the prime minister seemed to have recentered his policies to reflect the sentiments of the majority of the Israeli public. Inevitably, he returned to Jerusalem to find the hard-line nationalists he had so assiduously recruited to form his political base feeling betrayed and defiant. Nevertheless, his government and the PA implemented the first of the three phases of Wye.

In December 1998, however, Netanyahu made another volte-face. Claiming that the PA had failed to honor its Wye obligations, he suspended the implementation of further territorial withdrawals as prescribed by Wye until the PA had met a series of conditions. The Arab world and the European Community, the latter having fallen into an acrimonious relationship with him after four years of relative harmony with the Labor party government, were not the only ones to denounce this latest move. The Clinton administration and State Department officials were furious as well and publicly rebuked the Israeli government for raising what it considered to be new conditions that went beyond the terms of Wye. The American condemnation carried significant weight not only because the United States was Israel's strategic ally and economic benefactor, but also because both the Netanyahu government and the PA, as their relationship with each other became poisoned by discord and mistrust, had officially drafted the Americans to play a more intrusive mediating and adjudicating role.

This latest move by the prime minister did not help quell the rebellion brewing within his governing coalition. For the territorial maximalists who had helped being him to power, it was too little, too late. On December 21, 1998, members of Netanyahu's own coalition joined the opposition in a vote that dissolved the Knesset, ushered in an early election for May 17, 1999, and marked June 1 as the date for a second round in the event that no candidate received more than 50 percent of the vote.

But even before this mass defection, Netanyahu's near three years of erratic performance and wild policy swings had already left him virtually deserted. A year and a half earlier, in June 1997, Dan Meridor, a highly respected moderate hawk, resigned after Netanyahu effectively undermined him as finance minister. Foreign Minister David Levy, the disaffected populist politician, stepped down in January 1998. In May 1998, Roni Milo, the mayor of Tel Aviv and long-time Likud parliamentarian, broke with Netanyahu to form a new secular, centrist party. Immediately after the signing of the Wye Agreement, Benny Begin, a champion of the hard-core ideological annexationists, walked out; on the other hand, when Netanyahu refused to implement Wye, the popular moderate defense minister Yitzhak Mordechai resigned in protest.

The remaining senior Likud leadership was in turmoil, with Uzi Landau, Ehud Olmert, and Netanyahu's own political mentor Moshe Arens mounting challenges against him. Yitzhak Shamir, the hard-line former Likud prime minister, added his voice to those of party stalwarts who declared Netanyahu an "angel of destruction" who was unfit to represent Likud and serve the nation as prime minister. In the end, of all the notable senior political leaders of Likud, only Ariel Sharon, former defense minister under Shamir, remained at Netanyahu's side, although Arens later returned to support Netanyahu.

In the autumn of 1998, Netanyahu had recruited Sharon as minister of national infrastructure to help rein in the radical nationalists and perhaps Washington as well, as protracted negotiations on redeployment approached their end-game. While Sharon's presence might have helped sell Wye in the cabinet and Knesset, he could not save the prime minister from the subsequent revolt within the militant nationalist camp that helped bring his government down. Sharon's own standing among the radicals of "Greater Israel" and, consequently, his attempt to dissuade them from bolting Netanyahu's coalition were weakened by the fact that the Wye Plantation Agreement required a withdrawal of 13 percent, not the 9 percent he had earlier declared was Israel's security red line.

Ultimately, Netanyahu failed to mediate the opposing demands of policy—coming to terms with Israel's Palestinian and Arab neighbors and politics—placating the right-wing coalition members who refused to support Wye and dealing with his own ideological proximity to those members. He was personally divided. His head seemed to acknowledge the policy requirements of territorial concession; his heart seemed to beat for the cause of "Greater Israel." To pursue a peace policy successfully, he needed to repress his own emotional commitments and restrain the core annexationist constituency that had initially catapulted him to power.

Unable to do this, he became, in the words of a Likud party activist, a "maniacal wrecking ball swinging back and forth for the better part of three years."[1] In the interests of a peace policy that assuaged the Americans, Egyptians, and Jordanians, he signed the Hebron Agreement in January 1997 and the Wye River Memorandum in October 1998. In the interests of coalition politics and placating his right-wing critics, he began groundbreaking at Har Homa in February 1997 and froze further Wye withdrawals in December 1998.

The prime minister's inability to reconcile peace policies with domestic politics cost him his government. He satisfied virtually no one. The Americans were exhausted by what they perceived to be his personal deceitfulness and policy provocations. The Egyptians, as patrons of the Palestinians and as the first Arab state to make peace with Israel, had lost all hope that Netanyahu had a pragmatic streak that could be nurtured. Even Jordan, the only Arab state sympathetic to Netanyahu during his 1996 election campaign, thinking him to be a more reliable ally than Labor in the joint enterprise of restraining Palestinian territorial ambitions, concluded by the end of 1998 that Netanyahu was "irredeemably unreliable."[2]

A Failed Statesman but a Masterful Campaigner?

Prime Minister Netanyahu's performance may have earned him the label of "serial blunderer" and brought about his government's collapse, but he possessed a remarkable ability to survive his own mishaps.[3] Despite defections that read like a who's who of his government and party and erratic peacemaking efforts that cost him the goodwill of the Clinton administration, few were prepared to write him off as a masterful campaigner. In fact, Netanyahu appeared to enter the electoral battle with such formidable weaponry that many political analysts concluded that the incumbent was the man to beat.[4] His arsenal included: extraordinary communication skills, a seductive public relations campaign against both Arafat and those Israelis he accused of plotting to redivide Jerusalem, a notable decline in terrorism, electoral demographics that decidedly favored him, and two challengers, Ehud Barak and Yitzhak Mordechai, who seemed unable to either organize their parties or inspire their constituencies.

These political advantages were most pronounced at the outset of the campaign. In late February 1999, in anticipation of Israel's second direct election of a prime minister and its fifteenth Knesset elections, a delegation from the Conference of Presidents of Major American Jewish Organizations met with the candidates and analysts. After presentations by and discussions with prime ministerial candidates Ehud Barak, Benny Begin, and Yitzhak Mordechai, the mission culminated in a session with Prime Minister Netanyahu. All of the incumbent's talents and advantages were strikingly revealed. As Netanyahu left the room, one of the leaders of the conservative religious movement characterized his performance, in comparison to his competitors', as that of a "man among boys."[5] Jerry Goodman, a prominent figure in American labor Zionist circles hardly enamored with Netanyahu, countered: "To be more politically correct and more accurate, Bibi is a parent among infants."[6]

This visiting audience concluded that Netanyahu "was on message," focusing with laser beam precision on his strengths and his opponents' vulnerabilities. Memories of Netanyahu's June 1996 electoral triumph, in which he "ran" against Yasser Arafat and Palestinian terrorism in order to defeat Shimon Peres, were projected as a foreshadowing of the May 1999 political contest. Analysts could not forget the only television debate on the eve of that election when Netanyahu hurled accusations at his opponent with sound bite precision: "You have created asylum cities [in the West Bank] while our front line is under bombardment."[7] His one-liners resonated with Israel's swing constituency of security hawks then, and it did not seem farfetched to surmise that they might do so again. In the age of mass communication, many perceived Netanyahu as a telegenic master without rival in Israel.

Prime Minister Netanyahu's campaigning tools extended beyond the sound bite; he modeled himself as "Mr. Security," the man who saved Israel from the "suicidal path" Labor had set it on. He had, after all, prevailed upon Arafat and the Americans to renegotiate important elements of the Oslo Accords not once, but twice—first, in the January 1997 "Hebron Redeployment Protocol" and "Note for the Record," and then again in the October 1998 Wye River Memorandum, creating changes notable enough to earn Oslo a new tag line: The old slogan was "land for peace," now it was "land for security." The symbolic, partisan message Netanyahu was trying to communicate was clear: The Labor party's historic quest of "land for peace" had yielded land to the other side, but with neither the compensatory peace nor security in return. In fact, Labor, or "the left," stood accused of deeming the latter so insignificant as to not even bother including it in their slogans. In contrast, the new prime minister demanded, and won, more detailed and time-specific obligations from the PA in the security realm.

The prime minister had seemingly altered his reputation from that of an ideological hawk to that of a less strident and more pragmatic politician. With this makeover, he could now supersede his previous relentless campaign to label the Oslo Accords as "land for terrorism," with one showing how his amending of the accords had created a new deal—one that even the liberal international media regularly characterized as the "land-for-security" deal. In addition, Netanyahu introduced a corollary term that has since become part of the Oslo lexicon: "reciprocity." The term was invoked whenever the Netanyahu government tried to draw attention to those Oslo obligations it claimed the PA had failed to fulfill and served as shorthand for the prime minister's mantra that, "Israel gives and gives, while the Palestinians take and take."

Netanyahu was determined to make the Palestinians give. Among his demands were that the Palestinian National Council amend its National Charter, which had called for the destruction of Israel. The previous Israeli government, the Clinton administration, and virtually the entire international community, along with Israeli doves, had already accepted Palestinian claims that they had expunged the politicidal articles on April 24, 1996, at a historic gathering in Gaza. However, Netanyahu's persistence paid off.[8] Arafat endorsed the "Note for the Record," a road map of Israeli and Palestinian obligations, in which the first article under the heading of "Palestinian Responsibilities" required the PLO to "complete the process of revising the Palestinian National Charter." Thus, Bibi's unrelenting insistence along with an ambiguous process for rescinding the charter and a dramatic trip to Gaza by President Clinton and the First Lady to witness and support the amendment process officially closed the books on this saga of the Palestinian National Charter.

Prime Minister Netanyahu tried to sell this second and final episode of amending the covenant as a triumph of his hard-nosed reciprocity demands. In the meantime, however, Arafat was marketing it as good business with the Americans. The Palestinians were now in compliance with the American "Note for the Record" as far as completing the process of revising their infamous covenant was concerned, but, more importantly, they had solidified their relationship with Washington. The expanding American role in trying to save Arab-Israeli negotiations now seemed to include serving as midwife in the birthing of a Palestinian state. Netanyahu's victory was a Pyrrhic one.

While Prime Minister Netanyahu's campaign to abrogate the Palestinian Charter had boomeranged, he did compel the PA and the Americans to renegotiate the Oslo Accords, an accomplishment that included more than just creating a paper trail of fresh promises from Arafat to upgrade Palestinian security efforts. The written promises were translated into new realities on Israeli streets: Netanyahu presided over a protracted period of diminished terrorism. Buses were safe, and thus Netanyahu's prime ministership seemed secure—this was a simple political correlation that informed many pundits that Netanyahu was politically invulnerable.

Terrorism: Netanyahu's Win-Win Politics

In fact, the prime minister seemed to have converted the lethal issue of Palestinian terrorism into win-win domestic politics. On the one hand, a resurgence of Palestinian terrorism could be used to justify suspending further Israeli territorial withdrawals and thus salvage the bulk of Greater Israel. On the other hand, a continuation of the relative decline in terrorism would be used to justify the prime minister's tough policies and consolidate his political support from the Israeli center.

In reality, a number of factors other than Netanyahu's "get tough" approach contributed to the relative diminishment of terrorism. The first post-Oslo crackdown on Arafat and the PA security performance had actually occurred under the stewardship of Shimon Peres. During the wave of suicide terrorist attacks in late February and early March 1996, the Peres government specifically conditioned further Israeli withdrawals on a series of reciprocal security-enhancing policies from the PA. These included capturing, arresting, trying, and punishing with the full force of the law the thirteen most wanted military leaders of Hamas and Islamic Jihad.[9] The Labor party-led government also demanded that the Palestinian National Council formally revoke those parts of its charter that violated agreements signed by the PLO and the PA with the Israeli government. The Israeli demands regarding the charter established for the first time a specific date, May 7, 1996, by which the revocation process had to be complete. The Peres government additionally pressured the PA to address the broader problem of the Palestinian public's attitude toward anti-Israeli violence and terrorism. In compliance, Arafat proceeded to monitor and discipline mosques and universities that supported violent anti-Israeli activities, and the PA helped organize demonstrations for the cause of "Yes to Peace, No to Closure" in a number of cities.[10]

Closure was the Labor party-led government's most dramatic and draconian response to the Palestinian terrorist attacks that ravaged Israeli cities. The Peres government's retaliation to the February–March 1996 barrage of suicide terrorist attacks was particularly harsh. A "total closure" was imposed on the West Bank and Gaza, virtually stopping all movement of people and goods into Israel from the self-governing area. In addition, Palestinian access to Egypt and Jordan was dramatically curtailed.[11] While Netanyahu would accuse Peres of "subcontracting" Israeli security to Arafat and the PA, the historical record suggests that by the end of February 1996, Peres had subordinated the peace process to Israelis' personal security. This crackdown on terrorism did not spare Peres from a cliffhanger election defeat, but his own version of reciprocity helped usher in an extended period of reduced terrorism that Netanyahu built upon and benefited from.

Neither Peace nor Terrorism

Although the decline in Palestinian terrorism has its roots in the waning days of the government preceding Netanyahu's, the latter claimed and received credit for creating and sustaining this trend through the early summer of 1999. However, Israeli military and intelligence explanations for this relative relief from Palestinian terrorism are far more complex and emphasize four factors that have little to do with the prime minister's "get tough" stance. Beyond representations of their own vigilance and intervention in hampering terrorist operations, they acknowledge that Palestinian extremists were relatively pleased with the atmosphere of crisis and breakdown that characterized the peace negotiations from March 1996 through the collapse of the Netanyahu government.[12] Put bluntly by a Hamas activist from Gaza, "Netanyahu has been doing our work for us. He is revealing the face of this phony peace. He is our secret weapon. It is a bit ironic that the Israeli prime minister and not our martyrs are exploding the Oslo blasphemy."[13] The former Israeli ambassador to Egypt and Jordan, Shimon Shamir, suggests the same logic: "One of the reasons we did not have much violence from Arabs in the past three years was because the extremists were relatively happy with the situation of a frozen peace process."[14] Conversely, he argues that "it should be understood that a higher level of violence is an indication of genuine progress toward peace. The extremists try to undermine and jeopardize real movement through violence."[15]

A second factor that Israeli security officials believe contributes to the diminished terrorism is the populist tendency of the West Bank/Gaza leadership of Hamas. While an ideological absolutist current runs through the group, one that perceives "Jews as our enemies whom we are destined to combat to the end,"[16] Hamas also has a strong populist strain that is responsive to the will of the Palestinian population.[17] Key segments of the Palestinian public, having paid a steep economic price via closures for acts of Palestinian terrorism in the past, have vented their displeasure at terrorist operations, rather than at Israelis themselves.[18] The commitment of the Hamas leadership, particularly within the West Bank and Gaza, to represent a popular cause that reflects the desires of its people may have had a restraining hand on terrorism.[19]

Thirdly, while Israeli intelligence officials point out that Arafat's refusal to uproot the infrastructure that supports terrorism in the West Bank and Gaza constitutes an egregious security failure, they nevertheless credit him with having improved the security performance of the Palestinian Authority.[20] Even after Netanyahu froze implementation of the Wye Agreement, branches of the Palestinian security and intelligence services continued to cooperate unofficially with the Israeli Defense Forces.[21] In late March 1999, the prime minister gave rare praise to the PA for helping to thwart a major Hamas bombing in Tel Aviv. His praise was very specific and limited: "They took one step. We absolutely praise it. But there are still many things that have not been done. . . . They are not acting systematically and there is still the revolving door phenomenon in which they release murderers of Jews."[22] Although criticism of the PA security performance continued, the PA's increasing intolerance of terrorist attacks emanating from its territories helped reinforce the "inside" Hamas leadership's decision to curtail terrorist activity.[23] This modest success, in part a testimony to Israeli-Palestinian security cooperation, however, produced the negative side effect of inciting an escalation of terrorist threats from the external branches of Hamas and Israeli Palestinian individuals associated with Israel's Islamic Movement.

Finally, Israeli security experts attribute the greater American involvement in Middle East politics and their attempt to salvage Oslo for this period of diminished terrorism.[24] The newly consolidated American-Palestinian relationship, spurred in no small part by President Clinton's political engagement, energized Arafat to intensify the Palestinian Authority's battle against terrorism. At the same time, the CIA, led by its Tel Aviv station chief Stanley Moscovitz, prodded and monitored the PA to enhance its security efforts.

Paradoxically, Israeli security has been a beneficiary of this unusual combination: a breakdown in peace negotiations, which provided Hamas a disincentive to practice terrorism, and a breakthrough in American-Palestinian relations, which provided Arafat an incentive to fight terrorism. Netanyahu seemed to be living in a protective bubble that defied the logic of political detractors such as Shimon Peres. Peres had suggested that there was only one alternative to the "peace and terrorism" that were unhappily coupled during his watch—the nightmare combination of "terrorism without peace."[25] However, Netanyahu seemed to have found a third way, even if it was only a historically transient one: "neither peace nor terrorism."

This was hardly a campaign formula for the prime minister to run and win on. Netanyahu dared not make a virtue out of the protracted stalemate in negotiating peace with Israel's Arab neighbors. Instead, he would give a command performance. He planned a repeat of his 1996 campaign in which he appropriated the peace and security issue and welded together an alliance of ideological hawks, security centrists, anti-Labor ethnic constituencies, and the Orthodox community.

This time, he would also have one other supposed asset to attract the center and the right: a political record to run on. The center would ostensibly be drawn by his capacity to negotiate and implement agreements such as Hebron and Wye (at least in its first phase). To them, he could admit not liking the Oslo Accords but would point out that he had not destroyed them, only improved them. According to Moti Morel, a well-known Israeli political consultant, Netanyahu had a compelling advantage with this swing constituency: "Bibi is perceived not as a non-bargainer but a tough negotiator. Just what the mainstream craves as they anticipate the end-game bargaining over the size and powers of a Palestinian state."[26] On the other hand, the right would be reassured by his reciprocity demands which, when not realized, led to a cessation of Israeli withdrawals. To them, he could concede that the salvational mission of "Greater Israel" had been eclipsed but that the salvaging operation of the Land of Israel was nevertheless a critical, albeit less lofty, goal.

Bibi's People: Electoral Demographics

It was also widely assumed that Netanyahu would receive the majority vote from several key segments of Israeli society. Pundits expected Russian immigrants to once again overwhelmingly cast their ballots against the "territorial defeatists" who would reduce Israel to "dollhouse dimensions." They excluded the possibility of Barak or Mordechai making any appreciable dent in the incumbent's lead in the Russian community.[27] The religious constituencies, including the traditionalist supporters of the Shas party despite its relatively dovish leadership, were perceived as an electoral lock for the prime minister. The demographic composition had also changed since the 1996 vote, creating an additional advantage for Netanyahu. Among the first-time voters from whom Netanyahu was expected to draw overwhelming support were the new immigrants from the former Soviet Union, approximately 2 percent of the voters, and Jewish Israeli youth primarily from the ultra-Orthodox and Sephardic communities who made up about 6 percent.[28] "Saving Bibi from the left and the Arabs" became the rallying cry for mobilizing these voters.

Not all demographic changes were beneficial to Netanyahu. First-time Israeli Arab voters, forming nearly 2 percent of the electorate, would certainly cast their ballots *en masse* against Netanyahu. However, their vote, and the general Israeli Arab population, which constituted approximately 20 percent of the general population but only 10 percent of the electorate, posed less of a threat to Netanyahu than what the numbers would suggest for two reasons. First, if a second-round ballot for the prime minister's race was required on June 1, there were severe doubts that participation rates among Israeli Arab voters, new or veteran, could be sustained. Without the lure of voting for an Israeli Arab party in the Knesset elections, which would be completed on May 17, Arab participation was expected to decline, perhaps even significantly.[29] Second, there was virtually no chance of increasing the already extraordinarily high Israeli Arab turnout—77.6 percent—for the 1996 election, in which Netanyahu defeated Peres. Their participation rate for that election for the first time nearly equaled the rate of Israeli Jews, which stood at 79.3 percent.[30] Hence,

Barak or Mordechai would be accomplishing a Herculean feat if either could match the last election's numbers and come close to getting half of all first-time votes.

This was gruesome news for the Barak camp. His hopes for winning depended on some combination of a massive Arab turnout, a revolt against Netanyahu by Russian voters, and Mordechai dropping out of the race, with his supporters overwhelmingly casting their ballots for Barak. Given the circumstances, it was not unreasonable to anoint Netanyahu the favorite, perhaps even a prohibitive one.

In short, Netanyahu seemed poised to effectively exploit the changing demographics of the electorate and to supplement the emerging national consensus that territorial disengagement from the Palestinians was irreversible with the tough-sounding claim: "It's security, stupid." Why Netanyahu seemed impervious to the slogan: "It's the economy, stupid" puzzled American observers.[31] After all, the prime minister was presiding over the worst economic downturn in a generation.

"Us versus Them": Netanyahu's Politics of Polarization

Israeli analysts provided several explanations as to why economic slogans would not resonate in Israel's political culture. First, they argued that Israeli elections historically are not won or lost on economic issues. Israeli pollsters repeated this mantra over and over as the 1999 election approached. While there is evidence that this is often true—in the elections of 1969, 1988, and 1996 more than 70 percent of electoral respondents indicated that they were more concerned about peace and security issues— there have also been other elections, particularly in 1984, when the predominant issues were domestic.[32] Second, many voters identified the old social and economic statist structure of paternalistic socialism with the Labor party; they viewed Netanyahu as their liberator from this ancient regime.[33] Barak's creation of the One Israel party did not free him from the burden of having to project a new vision of social justice and economic prosperity—one which voters would perceive as independent from the trappings of the old Labor bureaucracy.[34]

A third explanation for Netanyahu's supposed invulnerability to the social and economic fronts stems from the empathy that important segments of the Israeli public held for his embattled prime ministership. In March 1999, Dalya Ya'iri, a Kol Yisrael talk show host, explained: "Stories abound regarding development town workers who have no jobs, no money, and no housing. But they were all invariably voting for Netanyahu. Why? Because they feel the elite won't let him do his job. He is besieged. One of them."[35] She suggested that this identification with Netanyahu reflected an intense cultural dichotomization that the prime minister and his media czar, Arthur Finkelstein, effectively exploited. Ya'iri asserted that an "us" versus "them" Kulturkampf was being played out to the advantage of the prime minister: "It was 'us' (Netanyahu) the strong vs. 'them' the weak, 'us' preserving the Jews vs. 'them' giving away our heritage, 'us' the people vs. 'them' the elites."[36]

Netanyahu intensified this politics of polarization as the campaign went into full swing, subjecting the Israeli public to a blitz of dueling television ads for three weeks prior to the May 17 election. Likud's televised commercials, with the exception of one that focused on socioeconomic issues, pounded away at the theme of security and peace. The prime minister's own ad campaign declared the elections a "referendum about our existence," where he was the sole candidate willing to take Israel down "the only path that would lead to security and real peace."[37] In contrast:

> The left . . . Barak and the people he depends on—Beilin, Sarid, Bishara . . . believe that if we just retreat to the '67 lines, the Arabs will be satisfied with that. They are wrong. They won't be satisfied with that. And their surrenders weaken us so much that they will threaten our existence. In contrast to the left, we will leave the broad security regions in Israel's hands. In this way, we can protect ourselves and protect the peace, because only a strong Israel will achieve peace, and maintain it. This is the whole difference between us and the left. The left wants peace at any price. But we know Israel will pay the whole price and not get the real peace. We will bring the real peace that we can defend.[38]

Anti-Barak ads also tried to de-legitimate their target by associating him with Arafat. One commercial featuring puppets had Arafat "giving birth" to a Palestinian state in a hospital delivery room, while Ahmed Tibi, newly elected Palestinian Israeli Knesset member and former advisor to the Palestinian Authority president, stood at his bedside. A puzzled Tibi asked Arafat why he had recently been so quiet about declaring a Palestinian state. Arafat had been threatening to unilaterally declare a Palestinian state on May 4. The puppet responded, "Believe me, Tibi, Beilin does it much better than me. His Hebrew is much better than mine, too." As canned laughter played in the background, Barak entered the scene, calling Arafat to remind him: "First, you've got to wait with the declaration until after the election. Second, if you declare a state, Bibi gets elected."[39] Arafat assured the candidate, "My friend, just not Bibi!" The ad ended with Arafat's parting statement: "I'm holding back. I'm postponing the birth of the state of Palestine. What's good for Barak is good for Arafat."[40]

Also playing on the theme that a vote for Barak would mean a vote for Arafat, a Likud commercial showed images of the Palestinian Authority president while a voice-over warned: "There is someone who has been waiting three years for the elections. There's someone who finds it very important that Barak get elected. He knows that Barak will give in. And then, the day will come and he can get everything he wants—and he wants a lot. If Barak wins, Israel will lose."[41]

Netanyahu and Finkelstein were targeting what they believed to be a chink in Barak's security armor, despite the fact that he was a decorated former head of the IDF. Not only did they imply Barak was Arafat's "friend," but they used the candidate's own words to indicate a personal identification with Palestinian terrorism. During a February 1998 interview, Israeli journalist Gideon Levy asked Barak what course of action he would have taken had he been born a Palestinian. His response that he would have "joined one of the Palestinian terrorist organizations and struggled"—without attacking civilians—may have been painfully honest, but his standing in public opinion surveys immediately plummeted.[42] Even his allies considered it a setback in his efforts to win over undecided votes.

Netanyahu's campaigners were determined to recycle this rhetorical blunder for the 1999 prime ministerial race. Hence, a Likud television ad displayed the newspaper headline quoting Barak: "If I had been a Palestinian . . . I would have joined a terror organization," with a voice-over declaring: "Deep inside, something's wrong here. A man like this cannot be prime minister. If Barak wins, Israel loses."[43] Netanyahu's team ran this commercial virtually every night of the three-week television campaign.

The attempt to develop the portrait of "a man like this," who had Arafat and the Israeli left as electoral allies and who could identify with Palestinian terrorists, would not be complete without the accusation that such a person was prepared, if not willing, to "surrender Jerusalem." Netanyahu's attack ads linked Barak to the Yossi Beilin–Abu Mazen "Agreement," asserting that "Barak, Beilin and the Labor Party will fold on Jerusalem. Don't let Barak give Israel back to the left."[44]

Barak's Biography: Security Clearance

Barak's camp responded to Netanyahu's attacks with a simple counterplan, one that was more forcefully revealed in a two-minute television ad which his campaign team dubbed "The Biography."[45] "The Biography" served as powerful visual testimony that Barak was not an ideologue of the left but rather the nation's "number one soldier . . . with more decorations for his courage and strength than any other soldier in our history has received."[46] Barak was shown in white overalls standing on the wing of a plane as the narrator explained the circumstances: "When a Sabena airline was hijacked in Tel Aviv, he put on mechanic's clothes and personally led the operation to free hostages and kill the terrorists."[47] Against the backdrop of more dramatic archival footage, the narrative continued, "He penetrated Beirut and brought justice when he killed the perpetrators of the massacre of our athletes in Munich. He was one of the planners and commanders of the Entebbe operation for freeing the kidnapped hostages. In 1991, Ehud Barak, the number one soldier of the State of Israel, was appointed chief of staff. For Ehud Barak, fighting terror, daring operations, and protecting our security are not just words . . . but a way of life. This is Barak's way, and with the same determination, he will bring change to Israel."[48]

"The Biography" became the case statement for establishing Barak's security credentials. He was not to be confused with Shimon Peres. In the 1996 election, the latter had waxed poetic about a new Middle East with "tomatoes bigger than Toyotas" and where "the only generals . . . will be General Motors and General Electric."[49] Instead of painting wistful visions of the future, Barak's military history reassured the floating centrist voters that a vote for him would be a vote for this generation's "Mr. Security."

It was also especially crucial to get the story out to the Russian immigrant population, which might not have been familiar with the exploits of this military hero and, later, chief of staff under Yitzhak Rabin, Israel's former, martyred "Mr. Security." Barak's campaigners distributed a Russian-language version of "The Biography" that specifically took care to differentiate him from the "generals" of the former Soviet Union — undeserving apparatchiks and party commissars whom the party regaled with the title.

The Barak campaign aired two television spots to reinforce the message behind "The Biography," one of personal statements from soldiers who served under Barak and another of the leading generals who commanded with him. In the first ad, each of the former soldiers attested to the general's tenacity, trustworthiness, and character: "When we marched behind Ehud, we knew that we would return safely," "He focuses on the goal, and wins," and "He leads by personal example. He is moral, honest."[50] The ad concluded with the following narration: "The number one fighter with five decorations for heroism and courage, he will never give in to any person or plan that will endanger the state that he has fought for his whole life."[51]

In the second of these security testimonials, four of Israel's most experienced military and security leaders supported and amplified the soldiers' claims. The fact that several of the speakers had been in one way or another connected to the prime minister added even more weight to their endorsements. Yossi Peled, a brigadier general who had joined Likud and supported Netanyahu in 1996, declared, "I know Netanyahu from close up, and Barak as well. In the war for security of the state, I prefer Barak as the leader."[52] Next, Natan Vilnai, the former deputy chief of staff of the IDF, pointed out, "It's no secret that Netanyahu offered me the position of defense minister in his government. I refused because I believe that Ehud Barak is the only man who can bring security."[53] Assad Hefetz, a former head of Israeli police who served under Netanyahu, asserted, "For Ehud Barak, fighting against terror and for security—these are issues where there can be no compromise."[54] Then, Brigadier General Uri Saguy, who had taken a lead role in negotiating with the Syrians, delivered the final security affidavit: "I have seen Ehud Barak on the battlefield and also at the negotiating table with the Syrians. At the negotiating table, he was no less determined than at the battlefield."[55]

Following this barrage of endorsements from citizen-soldiers and the security establishment's top brass was Barak himself, facing the camera for one final security-credentialing ad to be aired through the last week of his television campaign. Addressing the Israeli public, he said: "I want to talk to you about a subject that is very close to my heart: the security of all of us. On Netanyahu's campaign trail, they are trying to mislead you with regard to my security issues and with regard to my ability to stand strong for Israel's security interests. I served in the army for 35 years, and Netanyahu knows it. Netanyahu knows that the only peace agreement that I would bring to Israel is a peace that ensures the security of all citizens." Barak then identified three positions central to his security theme: "Physical separation from the Palestinians, uncompromising war against terrorism, and Jerusalem as our united, eternal capital. There will be no compromise on these issues. I've established a security team that Netanyahu also knows, who are the most experienced and senior people in Israel: Natan Vilnai, Yossi Peled, Danny Yatom, Uri Saguy, and Assad Hefetz. They will be the ones who will design a security policy together with me and will take part in the negotiations on the final status."[56]

Defusing the Electoral Time Bomb: Jerusalem

Barak's campaign had effectively preempted Netanyahu's security offensive. The additional challenge of deflecting Likud's charge that "Barak, Beilin, and the Labor Party will fold on Jerusalem" got help from another unexpected quarter—Likud stalwart and Jerusalem mayor Ehud Olmert. Although Olmert frequently spoke in favor of increasing budgetary allocations for East Jerusalem and developing better infrastructure there, he was nevertheless a staunch advocate of Israel consolidating control over Arab neighborhoods in this part of the city. In the past, he had supported a host of initiatives in East Jerusalem that were championed by the nationalist right, including opening the Hasmonean tunnel, building the new Jewish community at Har Homa, and constructing a new Jewish neighborhood in Ras el-Amud. An authoritative representative of the Israeli hard-line on Jerusalem, Olmert was cast as the star of Barak's spot ad on Jerusalem. The ad began with a voice-over claiming, "The Netanyahu government is stuck on every issue, so Netanyahu is trying to divide the state that is united on the issue of Jerusalem." Olmert, shown at Likud party headquarters, delivered the verbal knockout counterpunch to Netanyahu: "I have no doubt that Ehud Barak is committed to the unity and wholeness of Jerusalem, the capital of Israel. And he will not give a hand in any task that would harm the unity or wholeness of Jerusalem."[57] Barak concluded the ad by proclaiming, "Israel is united around a united Jerusalem, and no one will succeed in dividing the nation on this issue."[58]

Barak not only won surprising political endorsements for his position on Jerusalem, but he was also the beneficiary of an unexpected Israeli Supreme Court ruling that prevented Netanyahu from closing a prominent Palestinian institution—the headquarters for Palestinian activities in East Jerusalem, the Orient House. On the eve of the election, the prime minister ordered the closure of three offices in the Orient House for alleged violations of the Oslo Accords. Netanyahu seemed determined to display a firm hand in Jerusalem, even at the cost of creating potential violent confrontations between Israelis and Palestinians. If this was an electoral gamble to create and exploit an Orient House crisis and send "security hawks" and centrists voting in his favor, it failed.

A group of prominent Israeli residents of Jerusalem filed a petition with the Supreme Court. They claimed that regardless of the legal status of the Orient House, the only reason it had become the focus of attention now was the prime minister's desire to boost his own standing in the polls prior to the balloting.[59] They asked the court to issue an injunction prohibiting the government from taking any steps to enforce the prime minister's order, and that the court not reconsider the case until after the elections.[60] To the surprise of the petitioners, and perhaps the Netanyahu government as well, the Supreme Court agreed.[61] The injunction was issued, and Netanyahu was deprived of one of his last political gambits to rescue his failing campaign.[62]

After deftly sidestepping Netanyahu's one-two punch on Jerusalem and security, Barak campaigners went on the electoral offensive, targeting domestic issues and the social and economic discontent simmering among swing constituencies previously leaning toward the prime minister. They did not have to swing hard—Netanyahu's reelection bid already seemed to be unraveling from within. An internal Kulturkampf was destroying the prime minister's heterogeneous coalition of "outsiders," and his self-centered, divisive responses to each crisis served only to stir more discontent.

Dynamics of a Debacle

The Russian immigrant vote that had been so overwhelmingly for Netanyahu in 1996 (60 percent–38 percent), and whose support in the polls had further solidified only five weeks before the May 17 elections (57 percent–17 percent), was now showing signs of slippage.[63] Netanyahu's broad support among the Russians was not nearly as deep as pollsters had surmised in February and March of 1999. Moti Morel, the public relations expert for Natan Sharansky's party Yisrael b'Aliyah (Israel on the ascent), discovered what he believed to be the one issue that energized the party's activists. It was not unemployment, education, or housing, but the Ministry of the Interior.[64]

The Ministry of the Interior had become the fiefdom of the Shas party, the populist Sephardic ultra-Orthodox party. Shas had blazed into electoral prominence in 1984, gaining four Knesset seats in its first electoral bid, and it had since been steadily expanding its Sephardic Orthodox base to include traditionalist Jews and economically disadvantaged populations which benefited from its network of local social services and its educational system. However, the Russians did not feel that the welcome mat had been rolled out for them. Instead of inclusion in the burgeoning political empire of Shas, Russian immigrants traded stories of systematic exclusion and humiliation. Shas officials raised doubts about the Jewish status of Russian immigrants and strongly implied that Russian immigrant women were ensnaring Jewish men into their prostitution rings.[65]

Russian antipathy toward the Shas-dominated Ministry of Interior found a rhythmic slogan in Russian: "The Ministry of Interior in control of Shas? No! Under our control!" The shorthand, "Nash (Our) Control," in turn became a winning battle cry for Barak, who benefited from this enormous secular Russian backlash vote against the forces of religious orthodoxy—forces associated with Netanyahu and symbolized by Shas.

Netanyahu's political coalition of "the rejected" was breaking apart. He was discovering that the cultural fault lines that splintered Israeli politics ran deep inside his own camp as well. Three constituencies within his coalition of "the rejected"—Russian immigrants from the former Soviet Union, Sephardic Jews, and the ultra-Orthodox—were honing their resentments against one another. Their shared enemy was no longer Barak. Their common ally was no longer Netanyahu. Tribal politics would still pay off handsomely in the fifteenth Knesset election for the Russian, ultra-Orthodox, and Sephardic parties, particularly Shas. However, for the incumbent prime minister, these schisms, most evident in the escalating antagonism between Shas and Yisrael b'Aliyah, were dooming his reelection bid.

Evidence of growing Russian immigrant discontent with Netanyahu had begun to emerge in late March. Four Likud activists from the former Soviet Union announced they were switching their support to Yisrael b'Aliyah. The defectors included Alec Sultanovitch, the former head of the Likud campaign staff for immigrants, Ludmila Tabenchik, the former coordinator of Likud's immigrant campaign in the Negev, and Eli Greenman, a former Likud Central Committee member and deputy mayor of Yehud.[66] Then, Natan Sharansky, Netanyahu's own cabinet member and Knesset member, displayed his displeasure with the prime minister when he helped save the prime ministerial candidacy of hard-liner Benny Begin, who faced disqualification without the nomination of then Knesset members.[67] By nominating Begin and keeping him in the race, Sharansky was making it more difficult for Netanyahu to win the first-round election, as Begin was certain to attract right-wing voters who otherwise would have voted for Bibi.

Relations between Netanyahu and Sharansky became increasingly frayed. In late April, rumors abounded that the prime minister had not only encouraged Sharansky's main rival for the Russian vote, Netanyahu's former chief of staff Avigdor Lieberman of the Yisrael Beiteinu (Israel is our home) party, to run for a seat in the Knesset, but that he had also tapped him to head his campaign in case of a second-round run-off on June 1.[68] On May 5, 1999, Netanyahu called a press conference in order to disassociate himself from Lieberman. He claimed, "I tried various means to persuade Lieberman not to set up a party."[69] Netanyahu's attempt to tack back to Sharansky was to no avail. Sharansky announced that he would not endorse any candidate for prime minister, even for a possible second round, although he was serving in Netanyahu's cabinet.[70] The prime minister was losing one of his most important allies.[71]

Fearing massive Russian desertion, Netanyahu attempted to woo Sharansky back to the fold by sending a letter to Russian immigrants urging them to vote for Sharansky.[72] His tactic backfired. This transparently instrumental use of the Russian immigrant vote for personal political gain—on the one hand, encouraging his former chief of staff to create a second Russian party, Yisrael Beiteinu, and on the other, abruptly calling for support of Sharansky—offended both camps in the Russian community. Not satisfied with backing one candidate at the cost of offending the other, Netanyahu ended up alienating both.

This double-dealing with the Russian vote coincided with the "Nash Control" campaign, a new development in the fight between Yisrael b'Aliyah and Shas. In late April, as Yisrael b'Aliyah's television spots featured the call for "Nash Control," Barak's party was hinting at a post-election relationship with the Russian party.[73] Barak indicated that if elected, he would ensure that the Ministry of the Interior would be run by someone "for whom all those eligible to emigrate to Israel under the Law of Return are equal before the law."[74]

Yisrael b'Aliyah pollster Ron Dermer presciently anticipated the outcome, saying that when his party and Netanyahu "lock horns, both get hurt. . . . The difference is that while we'll lose a mandate in the Knesset, he'll lose the election."[75] On May 17, 1999, Yisrael b'Aliyah lost one seat in the Knesset, and Netanyahu suffered an electoral debacle in his campaign to retain the prime ministership.

To be sure, Netanyahu's embarrassing defeat was partly due to the revolt of Russian voters offended by his alliance with and empowerment of the ultra-Orthodox. The downturn in the economy also diminished his hopes of building upon the decisive Russian majority he had acquired in 1996. With seething cultural grievances and a lighter purse, Russian immigrants sustained their trend of voting against the incumbent regime. For a third time in the decade, they voted for the opposition. Barak, like his mentor Rabin, was the beneficiary of this anti-incumbency backlash.

As important as the Russian electorate was in helping Barak win in a landslide, there were a number of other contributing factors. First, Netanyahu's strategy of extending the election to a second round, where he would have had a better chance of reducing the Israeli Arab turnout while maximizing his own, collapsed. He was counting on Mordechai staying in the race to prevent Barak from a majority victory in the first round. However, with support for Mordechai's election bid plummeting in public opinion polls, from 17 percent in mid-April to an embarrassing 5 percent in mid-May, the candidate withdrew on the eve of the elections.[76] At the same time, the first Israeli Arab to run for prime minister, Azmi Bishara, pulled out. Netanyahu now confronted his nightmare scenario: a face-to-face contest with Barak and the possibility of a first-round knockout.

On May 17, the rout of Netanyahu was under way, with 58 percent of Russians casting their votes for Barak. A massive turnout of Israeli Arabs approached the historic levels of 1996. While there was no doubt over which way Israeli Arabs would vote, the direction of Mordechai's supporters' ballots was less certain—even with his exhortations for them to save the nation and side with Barak. In the end, 80 percent of the Center party supporters did just that.

Another crucial factor in Barak's stunning victory over Netanyahu (56.1 percent–43.9 percent) was his campaign's effective mobilization and integration of its natural and traditional left constituency into its election efforts. "The street belonged to Barak" was a constant refrain throughout the spring of 1999. Plastered throughout the country, posters of Rabin exhorting Israelis to "continue in his path" helped to create a memorial/ electoral atmosphere with a not-so-subtle message: If you mourn Rabin, vote for Barak. In response, "the left," so excoriated by Netanyahu, but not always so enthralled with Rabin's policies when he was prime minister, swelled the ranks of Barak's campaign army. An Israeli peace activist who helped organize One Israel's election campaign in Jerusalem vividly recalled "the lethargy, arrogance and incompetence that characterized the Peres campaign in 1996." She believed history had given Israeli doves a triple reprieve from their past political sins. First, they had a prime minister who was electable. Second, intense consciousness of their own political camp's failures in the 1996 election inoculated them against repeating their mistakes in 1999. This time they were committed to be vigilantly active until the last ballot was cast. Third, during this election, they would not keep Rabin's legacy at bay. This time they would bask in his memory. In the words of this Jerusalem peace activist, "His path would be our way."[77]

The Barak campaign's successful mobilization of the left was no doubt an important, perhaps even necessary, factor in its candidate's first-round landslide; however, as Shevah Weiss and other analysts have suggested, it was the combination of Barak's energizing the left, holding the center, benefiting from a Russian backlash, and making inroads—no matter how modest—into the Orthodox electorate that formed the most credible and comprehensive explanation for his stunning triumph.[78] While the big numbers Barak posted—80 percent of Center party voters, 94 percent of Israeli Arabs, and 58 percent of the Russians—may have turned the most heads, it was also the much smaller numbers culled from Netanyahu's religious heartland—5 percent of Mafdal, eight percent of Shas, and ten percent of Agudah—that helped turn this election into an unexpected pummeling of Netanyahu. The latter were no less a part of the cumulative, decisive thrashing of the incumbent.[79] In part, this may have been because Barak played on the economic theme, with a very effective television ad pointing out Israel's rapidly rising unemployment rate: "100,000 Israelis have lost their jobs under Netanyahu. Should he keep his job?"

In the early hours of May 18, 1999, tens of thousands of Israelis descended on Kikar Rabin, the site of Yitzhak Rabin's assassination on November 4, 1995, in order to celebrate Ehud Barak's landslide victory. Gavri Bargil, a lieutenant colonel and brigade commander in the IDF (Res.), as well as a leader of Peace Now, Israel's oldest and largest extraparliamentary peace movement, joined the festivities in Rabin Square. He reported live via cellular phone to a group of liberal American Jews who anxiously awaited an election briefing: "This is amazing. People are filling the entire square. It's as if the period of sitting shiva for Rabin and for our cause has finally ended. It's as if Rabin's assassination has finally been electorally avenged."[80]

Split Decision: Barak's Tempered Utopia

The euphoria of the evening was tempered by the realization that the electorate had cast a second ballot for a Knesset that was ideologically fractured and polarized along lines that looked agonizingly familiar. While the Israeli public had given Barak a runaway victory by 363,000 votes out of 3 million—a margin twelve times greater than Netanyahu's over Peres in 1996, it had also seemingly voted for a stalemate in the fifteenth Knesset. The three religious parties had increased their representation from 23 to 27, with Shas becoming the third largest party in the Knesset with 17 mandates (MKs)—an increase of seven seats. Shas was one of the two big political party winners. Shinui, a new militantly secularist party headed by media personality Tommi Lapid, was the second parliamentary victor with six seats. The electoral breakthroughs for Shas and Shinui were symbolic of the intensifying secular/religious divide between Israelis. Three Israeli Arab parties succeeded in passing the electoral threshold of 1.5 percent, increasing their parliamentary representation from nine MKs to ten.

Likud and the secular nationalist right lost 11 seats. Although a new political party devoted to the politics of "Greater Israel" called National Unity—an amalgam of a breakaway hard-line Likud faction, the old Moledet party which had two MKs in the previous Knesset, and the radical settler formation Tekuma—won a total of four seats, Likud itself suffered a political meltdown. With their prime minister soundly defeated, their party reduced to 19 seats from 32, and their leadership falling to the aging war horse Ariel Sharon, Likud seemed unfit to either govern or lead an opposition.

Likud's only compensation was that Barak's attempt to present the old Labor party as a new, more inclusive political formation, One Israel, failed. Regardless of how David Levy's Gesher constituency of Sephardic Jews and moderate Orthodox voters associated with Meimad may have helped Barak's personal triumph, it did not help his party avoid a political debacle. Labor lost eight seats, and the One Israel list fell to 26 mandates. Meretz, Labor's left-secular-dovish ally, enhanced its Knesset standing by only a single seat, giving it ten MKs, although Shinui, whose members were predominantly from Labor and Meretz, captured six seats. The Center party, which had begun with extraordinary expectations of becoming Israel's third party, if not better, finished with only six seats. Russian representation in the Knesset increased from seven to ten, as Avigdor Lieberman's new party, Yisrael Beiteinu, captured four seats and Yisrael b'Aliyah lost one, reducing its parliamentary faction to six. Completing the composition of the fifteenth Knesset was One Nation, a party that represented workers and pensioners, making its successful electoral debut with two MKs.

The May 17 elections were a split decision. Voters sent Israel's hybrid political structure—part American presidential system and part European parliamentary arrangement—a mixed message. With one vote, Israelis empowered Barak to transcend the politics of polarization and unify their

Table 2. The Israeli elections

	Final Knesset results	
Political parties	1999	1996
One Israel (Labor)	26	34
Likud	19	32
Shas	17	10
Meretz	10	9
Shinui*	6	-
Yisrael b'Aliyah (Russian)	6	7
Center Party*	6	-
National Religious Party (Mafdal)	5	9
United Torah Judaism (religious)	5	4
United Arab Party (Arab)	5	4
National Union*	4	-
Yisrael Beitenu* (Russian)	4	-
Hadash (Arab)	3	5
Balad* (Arab)	2	-
Am Ehad*	2	-

*Did not exist as a party in the 1996 elections

nation; with their second ballot, they registered their sectarian interests, reproducing the tribal cleavages in Israeli society.

The proliferation of parties had changed the face of the Knesset and further eroded the power which the historically dominant parties, Labor and Likud, had traditionally wielded. For the first time ever, Likud and Labor combined failed to win a majority in the newly realigned parliament. Meanwhile, no less than fifteen parties had won mandates in the Knesset, six of which were new. This was in significant contrast to the total of ten parties that had won representation in 1992 and eleven in 1996.

A Disparate Coalition for Peace?

Barak seemed remarkably nonplussed by his contradictory political inheritance and the fractious Knesset he would be forced to draw his government from. With only 26 mandates, he began the process of constructing a government from the weakest party base any prime minister has had in more than a generation. The dramatic electoral decline of Barak's One Israel required government coalition-building that went beyond his most natural allies: Meretz (10), Mercaz (6), and One Nation (2), and even beyond his potential partner, Yisrael b'Aliyah (6). Barak could have done what no prime minister had ever dared to do: include Israeli Arab parties in his government. If Barak and his coalition partners were predisposed to also include Shinui with its six mandates, this would have created a narrow, secular, centrist-left government. However, the possibility of heading a government with Israeli Arab partners was apparently never more than a theoretical proposition for Barak.

The new prime minister was keenly aware of the deep antidemocratic and anti-Arab sentiment that permeated important sectors of the Jewish Israeli population—ones that had declared Rabin and Peres unfit to pursue any peace policy because they had not won a majority of the Jewish vote. While Barak may have been affronted by such attempts to de-legitimate Arab Israeli voters, he was not about to be the trailblazer who forged a government that included Arab Israeli parties. His senior advisors lamented that chauvinism was rife in Israeli political culture and were reminded that Barak's popularity had taken a steep dive after he suggested he might have engaged in armed struggle had he been born a Palestinian.[81]

But Barak did win a victory that included a majority of the Jewish vote—51.5 percent to 48.5 percent—encompassing about 80 percent of the electorate.[82] As a result, he was determined to create a broad Jewish coalition that he considered to have the best, if not the last, chance to make peace between Israel and the Arabs, as well as among Israeli Jews themselves. For now, the Israeli Arab political parties would have to remain outside the government, even as several individual Israeli Arabs obtained key governmental posts for the first time. One Israel Knesset member Nawf Massalha was appointed deputy foreign minister, and MK Hashem Mahameed became the first Arab to be seated in the Knesset's prestigious Defense and Foreign Affairs Committee.[83]

In the end, Barak fashioned a bulging Jewish coalition of seven parties constituting nearly two-thirds of the Knesset. It included One Israel's natural secular, dovish allies, Meretz and the Center party, as well as centrist Yisrael b'Aliyah and all three religious parties—Shas, the National Religious Party, and United Torah Judaism. Barak could also expect to count on an external safety net provided by Shinui, One Nation, and the three Israeli Arab parties.

By numbers alone, Barak's government looked nearly impregnable.[84] He started out with a government of 75 MKs, with another 18 likely to support it from the outside. Two defections from Yisrael b'Aliyah—who formed a new faction—and United Torah Judaism's decision to leave the coalition whittled the number down to 68. Nevertheless, both remained part of Barak's political safety net. No single coalition partner could threaten the government's parliamentary majority, and on the outside, no opposition to the government existed, aside from a fractured and ideologically muddled Likud, a marginalized remnant of a messianic nationalist party, the National Democratic Alliance, and Yisrael Beitenu. That was because the bulk of the opposition was inside Barak's government.

This is the bold gamble of Prime Minister Ehud Barak. He might not have simply been trying to make the best of a bad hand dealt to him by the Israeli electorate, but rather, these may be the cards he prefers to play. His creation of such a broad, inclusive Jewish coalition was more than a mere tactical attempt to co-opt potential adversaries. Instead, a centrist at heart, Barak believes that this disparate coalition is the real Israel—the one that he had campaigned to reach and was elected to win over and make peace with.

The broad coalition government that Prime Minister Barak assembled and the numerical lock he appears to have in the Israeli Parliament look most impressive when yet untested by the heat of policy making. In reality, the fault lines he has built into his government—right versus left, religious versus secular, Russian versus Sephardic, and hawk versus dove—all require his mediating magic. He did display flashes of the Midas political touch during the grueling four-and-a-half weeks it took him to corral this disparate coalition, while at the same time leaving no doubt as to who was the commander in chief.

From the outset of the protracted coalition negotiations, Barak demonstrated a tenacious commitment to centralizing decision making and protecting his political flanks. First, he ensured that the senior players in the Labor party, with whom he had forged no political alliances nor cultivated any personal friendships, would be unable to mount a leadership challenge. Knesset members Yossi Beilin, Shlomo Ben-Ami, and Chaim Ramon jointly constituted perhaps the most serious alternative axis of power within the party.[85] And although they seethed over Barak's seeming disregard for them when he was cobbling together his government and selecting his cabinet ministers, they eventually settled into the ministries of their second or third choice. With their ambitions thwarted, and consumed by their daily administrative responsibilities, they joined most of the rest of One Israel in being "out of the loop."

Chaim Ramon at least got inside Barak's office where, as minister in the prime minister's Office with Responsibility of Jerusalem Affairs, he serves as both point man on Jerusalem and as Barak's liaison to the Knesset. The rest of the Labor party stalwarts, chafing at being excluded from decision making and wary of Barak's goal to complete the process of overhauling their party into One Israel, mustered only one mini-rebellion: when Barak backed MK Shalom Simhon for the prestigious job of Knesset Speaker, a post that popular senior Labor party parliamentarian Avraham Burg also sought. The Knesset elected Burg, whom the prime minister had previously called "an undermining cub."[86] The other candidate seemed to have possessed only one important qualification that Burg lacked—personal loyalty to Barak

Some Israeli analysts saw ominous signs in Barak's failed sponsorship of Simhon. Ofer Shelah, a columnist for the newspaper *Ma'ariv,* compared the Simhon nomination to the power-mad Roman emperor Caligula's appointment of his horse to the senate.[87] Larry Derfner of the *Jerusalem Post* saw shades of Napoleon, reminding his readers that this was, after all, one of Barak's nicknames.[88]

Caligula and Napoleon are amusing but fanciful comparisons. It is fairer to assess Barak in the context of his own biography. His only organizational training ground has been the Israel Defense Forces. He has been out of uniform for only a relatively short period of time. Once in office, he surrounded himself with tested and trusted career military and intelligence officers. Therefore, it is not surprising that some analysts have observed that beyond insulating himself with an inner sanctum of the military personnel whom he summoned, the prime minister also exudes a "military style of issuing commands and expecting them to be obeyed without dissent."[89]

Barak's modus operandi is not likely to sit well with Avraham Burg, his party cohorts, or the parliament in which he appears to have such an overwhelming majority. Yet, in his first hundred days as prime minister, he effectively combined his military inclination to issue commands with the political dexterity to work out compromises. He succeeded in incorporating Shas into his governing coalition, but on his terms—without Aryeh Deri, the indicted head of the party, and without the Ministry of the Interior. The latter went to Shas's arch rival, Yisrael b'Aliyah. Barak also succeeded in recruiting the National Religious Party, but without their prized Education Ministry, which he handed over to their political nemesis, Meretz. With this coalition of opposites in place, Barak proceeded relentlessly toward the center of the political map, hoping to locate that sweet spot of national consensus—that place from which he could initiate the change and the momentous decisions that he had promised—without imploding his volatile coalition or deepening the divisions that wrack the Israeli public.

Between Barak's Red Lines and the Green Line

This is an imposing challenge—one that Barak has chosen to meet by giving priority to negotiating and implementing peace between Israel and its Arab neighbors. He brings one invaluable political asset in waging peace, his heroic credentials on the battlefield. The biography of Barak and his phalanx of generals and military heroes will undoubtedly help to sell the peace treaty with Syria and the final accords with the Palestinians, both of which he has promised to submit to a national referendum. However, Barak's marketing strengths in selling peace agreements to the Israeli public cannot disguise the uphill battle that lies ahead. He is likely to confront the wrath of his hawkish coalition members, led by the National Religious Party and supported by Yisrael b'Aliyah, particularly if and when the fate of the Golan Heights is negotiated with Syria.[90] Both of these parties have been operating as an internal opposition, joining with Likud, the National Unity party, and Yisrael Beitenu in opposing key elements of Barak's peace policy and laying markers for leaving the coalition. Shas, despite its historically dovish political leadership under Aryeh Deri and Rabbi Ovadia Yosef, cannot be counted on to stand with Barak on questions of peace and security. Their rank and file is relatively hawkish, and party officials have other priorities. They are determined to protect their separate school system and social welfare institutions as well as maintain the power that they and other ultra-Orthodox forces wield over religious affairs and life cycle events, from marriage and conversion to divorce and burial. Shas entered Barak's government embittered by their parliamentary leader's criminal conviction and their denial of the Ministry of the Interior, both of which they blame on the prime minister and his party. The rancor between Shas and Barak's government was further fueled by the demand by the Ministries of Education and Finance that Shas fulfill their commitment to reform their private educational system, Ma'ayan Hahinuch Hatorani, before government funds would be released to rescue the deeply indebted schools.[91] For at least one member of Shas's Council of Torah Sages, Rabbi Shimon Ba'adani, being in the Barak government was the equivalent of "living in Sodom."[92] Whether the Barak government is sufficiently wicked in the eyes of the Shas leaders for their severely indebted party to bring the government down is hard to calculate. Yet in a moment of crisis, with the NRP and Yisrael b'Aliyah bolting the coalition, it is not implausible that Shas might join them in the opposition.

Such a development would force Barak to replace the three mutinous parties and their twenty-eight parliamentarians with the three Jewish dovish parties and their ten MKs who had been supporting the coalition policies from outside the government. This would leave Barak in a position that he desperately wants to avoid: dependence on the Israeli Arab parties to provide him with a blocking majority, either as partners within his government or supporters outside of it. Hence, Barak's bloated government could shrink very quickly in a crisis, the kind of crisis that is likely to accompany a Permanent Agreement with the Palestinians or a peace treaty with Syria.

Ehud Barak has inherited not only Rabin's mantle as a "General of Peace," but also the political reality that his natural parliamentary constituency for peacemaking constitutes a narrow majority, one that includes Israeli Arab legislators. Given these coalitional realities, will Barak unnecessarily compromise his efforts to negotiate on the Palestinian or Syrian fronts? Will Barak's hawkish coalition partners succeed in exercising a veto over his government's peace and security policies? Will Yitzhak Levy's Ministry of Housing be permitted to significantly expand Jewish settlement building in the West Bank as final status negotiations begin? Will Barak's desire to keep Sharansky in his government prevent a peace treaty with Syria? Will Barak realize his aspirations to be the champion of Israel's national consensus? Unlike Netanyahu, he craves to heal his country's wounds as he divides a land over which his nation has fought a hundred years' war. Can this would-be General of Peace create a new map of relations between Israel and its Arab neighbors somewhere between his red lines and the green line of June 4, 1967?[93] Will he find Palestinian and Syrian interlocutors who are willing to agree to these new borders of peace?

Notes

1. Charley J. Levine, "Likud's Best Chance," *Jerusalem Post,* Internet edition, August 24, 1999.

2. Meeting with the Jordanian ambassador to the United States, Marwan Mausher, Washington, D.C., January 10, 1999.

3. The cover story in the *Economist* (October 11, 1997) characterized Netanyahu as a "serial blunderer."

4. Interview with Hanoch Smith, director of the Smith Research Center, Jerusa-

lem, March 2, 1999. Smith ticked off a series of reasons why Netanyahu remained the favorite. Beyond his "natural gift" for campaigning, "he had demographic trends on his side as well as the popular belief that only a Likud-led government could bring peace. In addition, the public viewed his victory as nearly inevitable." Smith was in good company in declaring Netanyahu the favorite. Mina Zemach, director of research for the Dahaf Public Opinion Research Institute, and Ephraim Yuchtman-Yaar, head of Tami Steinmetz Center for Peace Research, concurred. See note 27.

5. Joel Meyers, executive director of the Rabbinical Assembly, at Conference of Presidents of Major American Jewish Organizations' Israel Leadership Mission, Jerusalem, February 22, 1999.

6. Quoted at Conference of Presidents Israel Leadership Mission, February 22, 1999.

7. David Gardner, "Peace Hangs in the Balance," *Financial Times*, May 31, 1996.

8. The issue of the Palestinian National Charter has been one of the most vexing and emotional issues that has poisoned Israeli-Palestinian negotiating efforts. On April 24, 1996, against the backdrop of Israeli retaliatory strikes against Hezbollah in Lebanon and a protracted closure in the West Bank and Gaza, Arafat convened a meeting of the Palestinian National Council (PNC) as promised in the September 1995 Interim Agreement, in order to consider amending the covenant and revoking those articles calling for the destruction of Israel. Prime Minister Peres agreed to allow known terrorists and sworn enemies of Israel to participate in the proceedings in Gaza, as the charter could officially be amended only by a two-thirds vote of its 669 members. By a vote of 504–54 (with 14 abstentions), well over the two-thirds required, the PNC voted to amend the charter by canceling those clauses that contradicted the letters exchanged between the Israeli government and the PLO on September 13, 1993. It also empowered a committee to report back to the council in six months in order to consider adopting a new charter. The Israeli government hailed this as a breakthrough, and the Labor party, in a reciprocal landmark vote the following day, abandoned its longstanding opposition to a Palestinian state, which had been enshrined in its party's platform. This mutual understanding that the infamous covenant had finally been removed as a negotiating obstacle was shattered with the election of Netanyahu. The new Likud-led government claimed that the PLO had not fulfilled its abrogation commitments and succeeded in reviving the issue and having it formally incorporated into the 1997 "Note for the Record." The Wye Agreement included a formula that, in the end, satisfied the Netanyahu government that the covenant issue had once and for all been resolved.

9. "Israel and Palestine: A Matter of Confidence," *Economist*, April 6, 1996, 46.

10. "West Bank and Gaza Closed Down," *Economist*, March 23, 1996, 39.

11. For a brief but lucid description of "total closure," "normal closure," and

"internal closure" and their debilitating impact on the Palestinian economy, see ibid.

12. Shimon Shamir quoted in David Rudge, "Experts: Terror May Reemerge with Peace Talks," *Jerusalem Post,* July 9, 1999, 2.

13. Interview with Ghazi Hamid, a leading activist and intellectual associated with Hamas, Gaza City, February 10, 1998.

14. Shimon Shamir in David Rudge, *Jerusalem Post,* July 9, 1999, 2.

15. Ibid.

16. Interview with Ghazi Hamid, Gaza City, January 23, 1996.

17. Ibid.

18. Interview with Ghazi Hamid, Gaza City, February 10, 1998.

19. Conference of Presidents of Major American Jewish Organizations, meeting with Brigadier General Amos Gilad, deputy chief of intelligence, February 21, 1999. Ziyad Abu Amr, a Palestinian legislator and author of *Islamic Fundamentalism in the West Bank,* concurs that Hamas carefully gauges Palestinian public opinion in the territories before deciding whether or not to embark on military operations. Quoted in Ben Lynfield, "In Hebron, Explosion Prompts Questions about Hamas Tactics," *Jerusalem Post,* Internet edition, August 17, 1999.

20. Ibid.

21. Lamia Lahoud, "Joint Security Committee Resumes Active Role," *Jerusalem Post,* Internet edition, August 19, 1999.

22. Quoted in "Netanyahu Lauds PA for Foiling Bombing," *Jerusalem Post,* Internet edition, March 24, 1999.

23. According to Abu Amr, Hamas's leadership in the West Bank and Gaza has a flexible and "long-range strategy. If it cannot engage in jihad . . . it can postpone it and rely on the idea of preparation. According to its doctrine, working on institutions and organizations is part of the long-term jihad. So there would be no contradiction if they give up violent attacks and resort to social engineering." Quoted in Ben Lynfield, "What Will Hamas Do Now?" *Jerusalem Post,* Internet edition, July 21, 1999.

24. Conference of Presidents of Major American Jewish Organizations meeting with Brigadier General Amos Gilad, Deputy Chief of Intelligence, February 21, 1999.

25. Meeting with Shimon Peres, Jerusalem, July 6, 1995.

26. Conference of Presidents meeting, Moti Morel, February 20, 1999.

27. His widely held assumption was repeated by pollsters and journalists on a panel devoted to "Election Analysis" at the Conference of Presidents, February 20, 1999. Mina Zemach, director of research at the Dahaf Public Opinion Research Institute, and Ephraim Yuchtman-Yaar, professor of sociology, head of the Tami Steinmetz Center for Peace Research, were among those who were skeptical of Barak's capacity to make significant inroads among Russian immigrants. Hanoch Smith, the Israeli pollster, concurred with this sentiment. Interview with Hanoch Smith, Jerusalem, March 3, 1999.

28. Interview with Hanoch Smith, Jerusalem, March 3, 1999.

29. Ibid.

30. Asher Arian, *The Second Republic*, 206.

31. These economic inquiries into Prime Minister Netanyahu's presumed economic liabilities were the subject of extended discussion by American Jewish missions to Israel in the winter and spring of 1999. Typical of the American inquiries, Rabbi Eric Joffe, head of the Reform movement in the United States, asked a panel of Israeli political experts whether Barak's election hopes rested on his social-economic platform. The panelists, who included Dalya Ya'iri, talk show host on Kol Yisrael, Moti Morel, a well-known political consultant, Haim Shibi, political reporter for *Yediot Aharanot*, Mina Zemach, director of research at Dahaf Public Opinion Research Institute, and Ephraim Yuchtman-Yaar, head of the Tami Steinmetz Center for Peace Research, remained doubtful that this would be the issue that would prove to be Netanyahu's downfall. Conference of Presidents of Major American Jewish Organizations' Israel Leadership Mission, Jerusalem, February 20, 1999.

32. Arian, *Second Republic*, 222.

33. Moti Morel, Conference of Presidents Leadership Mission, Jerusalem, February 20, 1999.

34. Ibid.

35. Dalya Ya'iri, Conference of Presidents Leadership Mission, Jerusalem, February 20, 1999.

36. Ibid.

37. The notes in this section of the chapter are based on both the text and the visuals in these dueling ads. This first ad contained the most elaborate text in Likud's television campaign efforts to portray the "left"/Barak as "surrendering" to Assad's and Arafat's final status demands—"complete withdrawal from the Golan Heights up to the shores of the Kinneret and the establishment of an Arab state with its capital in Jerusalem."

38. Ibid.

39. Ibid. Arafat did, in fact, postpone his unilateral declaration of statehood, both out of consideration for the request by the Clinton administration and because Arafat concluded, without Barak having to coach him over the telephone, that such a declaration might help Netanyahu's reelection bid. Following the Israeli elections, Arafat was neither shy in asserting his political partisanship for Barak nor claiming credit for Barak's victory. "I hope Barak remembers I helped him win the elections.... I pressured the Arab's candidate Azmi Bishara to quit the race. That convinced Mordechai to quit and helped [Barak] in winning." *Jerusalem Report*, September 27, 1999.

40. Ibid.

41. Netanyahu's decision to run against Arafat in hopes of defeating Barak worked in 1996. However, he made a fundamental miscalculation in 1999 by refighting the last electoral battle. Netanyahu apparently overestimated Arafat's

268 | Mark Rosenblum

demonic image in Israeli politics and underestimated Barak's capacity to project himself as a heroic soldier against terrorism.

42. Barak's comment during the Gideon Levy interview was considered a setback in his efforts to win over the undecided votes. However, the Barak campaign considered that "an old problem" that had been overcome by successfully presenting him as an unflappable military hero. Interview with Lonnie Rafaeli, Jerusalem, August 4, 1999.

43. Quoted from Likud's Gideon Levy ad.

44. This "understanding" that Yossi Beilin and Abu Mazen helped shepherd through twenty secret meetings culminated in a broad agreement on permanent borders and an approach to resolving the Jerusalem problem. This exercise in final status thinking ended successfully after two years on November 1, 1995, only days before the assassination of Rabin. Beilin argued that these talks demonstrated that a final agreement could be reached within the Israeli national consensus. First, there would be a demilitarized Palestinian state, not "a Palestinian state with an army." Second, the problem of Palestinian refugees would be resolved outside Israel's borders. Israel would agree to family reunification within Palestinian territory. Third, Jerusalem would not be redivided. According to the understanding, a Palestinian capital—"Al-Quds"—would be established in Abu-Dis, outside Jerusalem's municipal jurisdiction. Palestinians would have free access to the Temple Mount (Haram Ash-Shareef) and would have the right to fly a Palestinian flag there. The Old City would be "without sovereignty" but in practice would remain under Israeli jurisdiction and the control of the Jerusalem municipality. There was also an understanding that the issue of sovereignty in East Jerusalem would be deferred for later discussion. Teddy Kollek's "quarters" plan, modeled on the Greater London boroughs system, was to be introduced into Arab neighborhoods in East Jerusalem. When presented with these understandings, neither Arafat nor Peres was fully convinced that they were an adequate basis for negotiations. Ze'ev Schiff, *Ha'aretz*, February 22, 1996. For the full text of the Hirschfeld interview and Prime Minister Peres's and President Arafat's objections to the understanding, see *Mideast Mirror,* Israel section, July 31, 1996, 1–5. Several more recent and fuller revelations on this "understanding" can be found in Yossi Beilin, *Touching Peace: From the Oslo Accord to a Final Agreement* (London, England: Weidenfeld and Nicolson, 1999), 139–89. An interesting alternative interpretation is provided by Khalil Shikaki in *Palestine Report,* Jerusalem Media and Communications Center, September 22, 1999.

45. The full two-minute version of "The Biography" ran on the first and last two nights of the three weeks allotted for television campaign ads. In addition, a one-minute version aired virtually every night. A thirty-second variation was also viewed on several occasions.

46. Quoted from the Barak campaign ad "The Biography."

47. Ibid.

48. Ibid.

49. David Gardner, "Poll Serves as Referendum for Labour Leader's Vision of Peace," *Financial Times,* May 29, 1996, 6.

50. Quoted from the Barak campaign ad "Fighters Tell."

51. Ibid.

52. Quoted from the Barak campaign ad "The Security Forum."

53. Ibid.

54. Ibid.

55. Ibid. Saguy was rumored to be Barak's favored candidate for heading the negotiations with Syria.

56. Ibid.

57. Quoted from the Barak campaign ad "Jerusalem."

58. Ibid.

59. Cited in Americans for Peace Now press release, "Peace Now/Ir Shalem Activists Succeed in Court Case to Keep Orient House Open," May 11, 1999.

60. Ibid.

61. Interview with Daniel Seideman, the lead attorney for Ir Shalem, Jerusalem, May 12, 1999. Seideman expected the court to reject the petition because it was so manifestly political in nature.

62. Joel Marcus offered the following blunt assessment of Netanyahu's Orient House policies on the eve of Israeli elections and the significance of the Supreme Court ruling against him: "Had it not been for the High Court of Justice ruling on Orient House, we might have found ourselves in the midst of bloody clashes, with dead and wounded on both sides. The very thought is enough to send shivers down the spine. If it was said that the affair surrounding the Western Wall Tunnel ('the very rock of our existence'), in which 15 persons [Israeli Jews] lost their lives, was the blunder of a novice prime minister, it is difficult to overcome the heavy-as-lead feeling that the Orient House episode was some cold-blooded macho gimmick to save Bibi's skin at the polls." Joel Marcus, "An Open Letter to Jittery Voters," *Ha'aretz* Internet edition, May 14, 1999. (Note: Fifty-five Arabs also were killed in the fighting following the opening of the tunnel.)

63. Cited in Avishai Margalit, "Israel: Why Barak Won," *New York Review of Books,* August 12, 1999, 47.

64. Moti Morel, Conference of Presidents panel, Jerusalem, February 20, 1999.

65. *Mideast Mirror,* Israel section, May 7, 1999, 3.

66. Amira Segev, "CIS Immigrant Activists Bolt from Likud to Yisrael b'Aliyah," *Ha'aretz,* Internet edition, March 31, 1999. Netanyahu's ineptitude in managing his striking advantage among the Russian immigrants was illustrated in these defections. Netanyahu closed down Likud's immigrant campaign office on March 26, explaining that Avigdor Lieberman was coordinating his campaign among immigrants from the Commonwealth of Independent States. However, after this announcement appeared in the Russian-language newspaper *Vesti,* Netanyahu reversed his decision and reopened Likud's immigrant campaign office under a new director.

67. Amira Segev, "Begin Qualifies for PM Race with Last Minute Help," *Ha'aretz,* Internet edition, March 31, 1999.

68. Yerah Tal, "Lieberman May Head PM Runoff Team; Likud Livid," *Ha'aretz,* Internet edition, April 23, 1999.

69. Nahum Barnea, *Yediot Aharanot,* May 7, 1999. Cited in *Mideast Mirror,* Israel section, May 7, 1999, 3.

70. *Ha'aretz,* Internet edition, April 25, 1999.

71. One of Israel's most insightful political journalists, Nahum Barnea, suggested that Netanyahu had driven Sharansky and Yisrael B'Aliyah into "partial cooperation with Barak." Cited in *Mideast Mirror,* Israel section, May 7, 1999, 3.

72. Netanyahu's last-ditch effort to stem the fear of Russian voters who were moving to Barak included a direct mail appeal to thousands of Russian immigrants who were supporters of Yisrael b'Aliyah. This appeal focused on security: "Your vote will decide whether we can continue to maintain Israel's security or we return to the times when the nation lived in constant fear of terrorism." Netanyahu also indicated that if he was reelected, he would give Yisrael b'Aliyah three ministries: Interior, Housing, and Absorption. Yisrael b'Aliyah's Yuli Edelstein was Netanyahu's minister of immigration and absorption, and they were determined to wrest the Interior and Housing ministries away from the ultra-Orthodox parties. Netanyahu's promise to deliver on this score rang hollow to Yisrael b'Aliyah activists. It was "an insult to our intelligence." Even with a stronger than expected showing of seven or eight seats, party activists knew it did not "stand to reason that we get three ministries." Amira Segev, "PM Tries Direct Mail Blitz to Yisrael b'Aliyah Supporters," *Ha'aretz,* Internet edition, May 14, 1999.

73. Cited in "Israeli Election Insight," Americans for Peace Now, issue 6, April 8, 1999.

74. Ibid.

75. Elli Wohlgelernter, "Rift with Yisrael B'aliya Could Sink Netanyahu," *Ha'aretz,* Internet edition, March 26, 1999.

76. Mordechai's numbers were steadily falling in the run-up to the May 17 election, while Barak's edge over Netanyahu was steadily increasing. Mordechai's 5 percent share of the vote was based on a five-way race, as calculated by the *Jerusalem Post*/Smith Research Center Poll, "Barak's Lead Grows in Latest Poll," *Jerusalem Post,* Internet edition, May 14, 1999.

77. Interview with Irena Sternfield, a peace activist who had worked on One Israel's election campaign in Jerusalem with former deputy chief of staff of the IDF Natan Vilnai, March 3, 1999.

78. Hannah Kim, *Ha'aretz,* September 10, 1999.

79. Ibid.

80. Interview with Gavri Bargil, Jerusalem, May 19, 1999.

81. Interview with Lonnie Rafaeli, Jerusalem, August 4, 1999.

82. Elections Site '99, Internet, http//www.99.netvision.net. Final results con-

firmed by the Central Elections Committee. See also Avishai Margalit in *New York Review of Books.*

83. MK Hashem Mahameed's appointment generated the most controversy for several reasons. First, Massalha was a Labor party MK, while Mahameed was associated with anti-Zionist parties, as the former chair of Hadash (the Israeli communist party) and currently as a member of the United Arab List, an alliance of Arab nationalists like himself and fundamentalist Muslims. Second, Mahameed has made a number of provocative statements including praising Hezbollah as a "national liberation movement." Moshe Arens, former defense minister and a staunch supporter of integrating Israeli Arabs into Israeli society, denounced Mahameed's appointment as heralding "the end of Parliamentary supervision over the defense apparatus," assuming that "security officials can't be expected to report to a committee which contains a member who cannot be trusted with secrets." Aren's criticism was indirectly refuted by the committee's new chairman, Dan Meridor, a Center party MK, with his characterization of the Knesset's most prestigious body: "It monitors the army on behalf of the public—in all its diversity." Yossi Klein Halevi, "Mr. Security," *Jerusalem Report,* August 16, 1999, 18–20.

84. Daniel Block's assessment is typical of this school of thinking: "Barak has almost unparalleled freedom to maneuver because no single political faction can bring down his government. He can move to implement the varied items on his agenda, without fear that any sharp turn will cause his carriage to collapse." Daniel Block, "Mandate for Change," *Jerusalem Post,* July 4, 1999, 6.

85. This trio represented the growing dovish wing of the Labor party that was less hesitant about both the Oslo Accords and embracing a two-state solution as well as more resistant to Barak's apparent plans to displace the Labor party with the prime minister's new creation, One Israel. The Hebrew press reported that Beilin was the originator of "an attempted rebellion" that was precipitated by their unhappiness over cabinet posts offered to them. In the end, Shlomo Ben-Ami was apparently unwilling to join his Labor party colleagues in contesting their appointments. Hannah Kim, Aluf Benn, and Gideon Alon, "Ben-Ami Balked at Revolt with Beilin and Ramon against Barak," *Ha'aretz,* July 9, 1999, 1.

86. Sarah Honig, "Barak Will Call All the Shots," *Jerusalem Post,* July 5, 1999, 1.

87. Larry Derfner, "The Barak Conundrum," *Jerusalem Post,* Internet edition, July 9, 1999.

88. Ibid.

89. Honig, "Barak Will Call All the Shots," 1.

90. Yossi Verter, Mazal Mualem, and Amira Segev, "Two Coalition Parties Pledge to Oppose Golan Withdrawal," *Ha'aretz,* Internet edition, October 4, 1999.

91. Yosef Goell, "Living in Sodom," *Jerusalem Post,* Internet edition, October 4, 1999.

92. Ibid.

93. Barak's "red lines" include that Jerusalem will remain united under Israeli sovereignty; there will be no return to the June 4, 1967, borders; there will be no foreign army west of the Jordan River; most of the settlers will remain under Israeli sovereignty, consolidated into settlement blocks; Palestinian refugees will not be allowed to return to Israel. Barak has also spoken about the need for a defense and settlement presence in the Jordan Rift Valley. These red lines of Barak are consistent with the emergence of a territorially contiguous Palestinian state in most of the West Bank and Gaza. Barak has obviously refrained from publicly clarifying his ideas on the territorial configuration and powers of such a state. Interviews with members of the Barak government suggest that Barak's red lines are in fact "pinkish" with flexibility to at least partially accommodate the compromises in the Beilin/Abu Mazen Understanding. See note 44. Barak's willingness to accommodate a territorially contiguous state is discussed by Shimon Schiffer, *Yediot Aharanot,* December 2, 1999, cited in *Mideast Mirror,* Israel section, December 2, 1999, 1–2. Barak has demonstrated notable flexibility in trying to draw the Syrians back to the negotiating table. He has repeatedly warned the Israeli public that a peace agreement with Syria will require "a very painful compromise." According to reports in the Hebrew press, Barak suggested that there was no great difference between Rabin, Peres, Netanyahu, and himself regarding the terms for negotiating with the Syrians. All of these former prime ministers as well as Barak were prepared to view the June 4, 1967, border as the agreed basis for negotiations if the Syrians were prepared to fulfill their security and normalization obligations associated with a peace treaty. Chemi Shalev, *Ma'ariv,* December 3, 1999, cited in *Mideast Mirror,* Israel section, December 3, 1999, 3–4.

Bibliography

Books

Aharoni, Yair. *The Israeli Economy: Dreams and Realities*. New York: Routledge, 1991.
Anderson, Benedict. *Imagined Communities: Reflections on the Origin and Spread of Nationalism*. London: Verso, 1991.
Arian, Asher. *The Second Republic: Politics in Israel*. Chatham, N.J.: Chatham House, 1998.
Aronoff, Myron J. *Israeli Visions and Divisions: Cultural Change and Political Conflict*. New Brunswick, N.J.: Transaction, 1989.
———. *Power and Ritual in the Israel Labor Party*. Armonk, N.Y.: M. E. Sharpe, 1993.
Arslan, Amir Adil. *Mudhakkirat al-Amir 'Adil Arslan: al-Juz' al-Thani, 1946–1950*, edited by Yusuf Ibish. Beirut: Al-dar al-Taqaddumiyya lil-Nashr, 1983.
Atkinson, Rick. *Crusade: The Untold Story of the Persian Gulf War*. Boston: Houghton Mifflin, 1993.
Avineri, Shlomo. *The Making of Modern Zionism: Intellectual Origins of the Jewish State*. New York: Basic Books, 1981.
Avnery, Arie. *The Defeat: The Disintegration of Likud's Rule*. Tel Aviv: Midot, 1993.
Bar-Siman-Tov, Yaacov. *Linkage Politics in the Middle East: Syria between Domestic and External Conflict, 1961–1970*. Boulder: Westview Press, 1983.
Ben-Gurion, David. "Ha'itonut Ve'ha'hayim." *Journalists' Yearbook*, 1953.
Ben Porat, Yoram. *The Israeli Economy: Maturing through Crisis*. Cambridge: Harvard University Press, 1981.
Ben-Yehuda, Nachman. *The Masada Myth: Collective Memory and Mythmaking in Israel*. Madison: University of Wisconsin Press, 1995.
Berger, Peter L. *The Heretical Imperative: Contemporary Possibilities of Religious Affirmation*. Garden City, N.Y.: Doubleday, 1979.
Brynen, Rex, ed. *Echoes of the Intifada: Regional Repercussions of the Palestinian-Israeli Conflict*. Boulder: Westview Press, 1991.
Caplan, Neil. *Futile Diplomacy*. Vol. 2, *Arab-Zionist Negotiations and the End of the Mandate*. London: Frank Cass, 1986.
Cohen, Naomi W. *American Jews and the Zionist Idea*. Hoboken, N.J.: KTAV, 1975.
Cohen, Steven M. *Ties and Tensions: The 1989 Survey of American Jewish Attitudes toward Israel and Israelis*. New York: Institute on American Jewish-Israeli Relations/American Jewish Committee, July 1989.

Colas, Dominique. *Civil Society and Fanaticism: Conjoined Histories.* Stanford: Stanford University Press, 1997.
Copeland, Miles. *The Game of Nations: The Amorality of Power Politics.* London: Weidenfeld and Nicolson, 1969.
Dagan, Avigdor. *Moscow and Jerusalem.* New York: Abelard-Schuman, 1970.
Dann, Uriel. *King Hussein and the Challenge of Arab Radicalism: Jordan, 1955–1967.* New York: Oxford University Press, 1989.
Dayan, Arye. *The Story of Shas* [Hebrew]. Jerusalem: Keter, 1999.
Dowty, Alan. *The Jewish State: A Century Later.* Berkeley: University of California Press, 1998.
Duverger, Maurice. *Political Parties.* New York: Wiley, 1963.
Festinger, Leon, et al. *When Prophecy Fails.* St. Paul: University of Minnesota Press, 1956.
Flapan, Simcha. *The Birth of Israel: Myths and Realities.* New York: Pantheon, 1987.
Freedman, Lawrence, and Efraim Karsh. *The Gulf Conflict, 1990–1991: Diplomacy and War in the New World Order.* Princeton: Princeton University Press, 1993.
Freedman, Robert O. *Soviet Policy toward the Middle East since 1970.* 3d ed. New York: Praeger, 1982.
———. *Moscow and the Middle East: Soviet Policy since the Invasion of Afghanistan.* London: Cambridge University Press, 1991.
———. *Soviet Policy toward Israel under Gorbachev.* New York: Praeger, 1991.
Freedman, Robert O., ed. *Israel under Rabin.* Boulder: Westview Press, 1995.
Garthoff, Raymond L. *Detente and Confrontation: American-Soviet Relations from Nixon to Reagan.* Washington, D.C.: Brookings, 1985.
Gelber, Yoav. *Jewish-Transjordanian Relations, 1921–1948.* London: Frank Cass, 1997.
Gerner, Deborah J. *One Land, Two Peoples: The Conflict over Palestine.* Boulder: Westview Press, 1991.
Gordon, Michael R., and Bernard E. Trainor. *The General's War: The Inside Story of the Gulf Conflict.* Boston: Little, Brown, 1995.
Gorni, Yosef. *Achdut Ha'avoda 1919–1939: The Ideological Principles and the Political System* [Hebrew]. Ramat Gan: HaKibbutz HaMeuchad, 1973.
———. *Zionism and the Arabs, 1882–1948: A Study of Ideology.* New York: Oxford University Press, 1987.
Habermas, Jürgen. *The Structural Transformation of the Public Sphere: An Inquiry into a Category of Bourgeois Society.* Cambridge: MIT Press, 1994.
Halabi, Rafik. *The West Bank Story.* New York: Harcourt Brace Jovanovich, 1981.
Hall, John A., ed. *Civil Society: Theory, History, Comparison.* Cambridge: Polity Press, 1995.
Harkabi, Yehoshafat. *Arab Strategies and Israel's Response.* New York: Free Press, 1977.

Hattis, Susan. *The Bi-National Idea in Palestine during Mandatory Times*. Haifa: Shikmona, 1970.
Herzl, Theodor. *The Jewish State*. New York: Herzl Press, 1970.
Horowitz, Dan, and Moshe Lissak. *Origins of the Israeli Polity*. Chicago: University of Chicago Press, 1978.
———. *Trouble in Utopia: The Overburdened Polity of Israel*. Albany: State University of New York Press, 1990.
Horowitz, Moshe. *Rabbi Schach* [Hebrew]. Jerusalem: Keter, 1989.
Inbar, Efraim. *War and Peace in Israeli Politics*. Boulder: Lynne Rienner, 1991.
Isaac, Real Jean. *Party and Politics in Israel: Three Visions of the Jewish State*. New York: Longman, 1981.
Kanari, Baruch. *Zionist and Socialist-Zionist Planned Economy*. Ramat Efal: Yad Tabenkin, 1993.
Katz, Yitzhak. *Privatization*. Tel Aviv: Pecker, 1997.
Keren, Michael. *Ben-Gurion and the Intellectuals: Power, Knowledge and Charisma*. De Kalb: Northern Illinois University Press, 1983.
———. *The Pen and the Sword: Israeli Intellectuals and the Making of the Nation-State*. Boulder: Westview Press, 1989.
Kimche, Jon. *Palestine or Israel*. London: Secker and Warburg, 1973.
Kissinger, Henry A. *Years of Upheaval*. Boston: Little, Brown, 1982.
Klein, Yitzhak, and Daniel Polisar. *Choosing Freedom: Economic Policy for Israel, 1997–2000*. Jerusalem: Shalom Center–National Policy Institute, 1997.
Laqueur, Walter, and Barry Rubin, eds. *The Arab-Israel Reader: A Documentary History of the Middle East Conflict*. 4th ed. New York: Facts on File Publications, 1985.
Lesch, Ann Mosely. *Arab Politics in Palestine, 1917–1939: The Frustration of a Nationalist Movement*. Ithaca: Cornell University Press, 1979.
Lieber, Robert J. *No Common Power: Understanding International Relations*. 3d ed. New York: Harper Collins, 1995.
Liebman, Charles S., and Eliezer Don-Yehiya. *Civil Religion in Israel: Traditional Judaism and Politics in the Jewish State*. Berkeley: University of California Press, 1983.
Liebman, Charles S., and Elihu Katz, eds. *The Jewishness of Israelis*. Albany: State University of New York Press, 1997.
Lustick, Ian. *For the Land and the Lord: Jewish Fundamentalism in Israel*. New York: Council on Foreign Relations, 1988.
Luz, Ehud. *Parallels Meet: Religion and Nationalism in the Early Zionist Movement, 1882–1904*. Philadelphia: Jewish Publication Society, 1988.
Medding, Peter. *Mapai in Israel*. Cambridge: Cambridge University Press, 1972.
———. *The Founding of Israeli Democracy, 1949–1965*. New York: Oxford University Press, 1990.
Mishal, Shaul. *The PLO under Arafat: Between Gun and Olive Branch*. New Haven: Yale University Press, 1986.

Mosse, George L. *Fallen Soldiers: Reshaping the Memory of the World Wars.* New York: Oxford University Press, 1990.
Netanyahu, Benjamin. *A Place among the Nations: Israel and the World.* New York: Bantam, 1993.
Nordau, Max. *Morals and the Evolution of Man.* London: Cassell, 1922.
Organski, Kenneth. *The $35 Billion Bargain: Strategy and Politics in U.S. Assistance to Israel.* New York: Columbia University Press, 1990.
Patinkin, Don. *The Israeli Economy: The First Decade.* Jerusalem: The Maurice Falk Institute for Economic Research, 1967.
Peleg, Ilan. *Begin's Foreign Policy, 1977–1983: Israel's Turn to the Right.* New York: Greenwood, 1987.
———. *The Middle East Peace Process: Interdisciplinary Perspectives.* Albany: State University of New York Press, 1998.
Peretz, Don. *Intifada: The Palestinian Uprising.* Boulder: Westview Press, 1990.
Plessner, Yakir. *The Political Economy of Israel: From Ideology to Stagnation.* Albany: State University of New York Press, 1994.
Porath, Yehoshua. *The Palestine Arab National Movement: From Riots to Rebellion.* London: Frank Cass, 1977.
Rabie, Mohamed. *The Politics of Foreign Aid: U.S. Foreign Assistance and Aid to Israel.* New York: Praeger, 1988.
Rabinovich, Itamar. *The Road Not Taken: Early Arab-Israeli Negotiations.* New York: Oxford University Press, 1991.
Rapoport, Louis. *Stalin's War against the Jews.* New York: Free Press, 1990.
Razin, Assaf, and Efraim Sadka. *The Economy of Modern Israel: Malaise and Promise.* Chicago: University of Chicago Press, 1993.
Riley, John F., ed. *American Public Opinion and U.S. Foreign Policy.* Chicago: Council on Foreign Relations, 1995.
Ro'i, Yaacov. *Soviet Decision Making in Practice: The USSR and Israel, 1947–1954.* London: Transaction, 1980.
Rosecrance, Richard, ed. *America as an Ordinary Country.* Ithaca: Cornell University Press, 1976.
Rubner, Alex. *The Economy of Israel: A Critical Account of the First Ten Years.* New York: Praeger, 1960.
Sachar, Howard M. *A History of Israel: From the Rise of Zionism to Our Time.* New York: Knopf, 1979.
Safran, Nadav. *Israel: The Embattled Ally.* Cambridge: Harvard University Press, 1981.
Schiff, Ze'ev, and Ehud Yaari. *Israel's Lebanon War.* New York: Simon and Schuster, 1984.
———. *Security for Peace: Israel's Minimal Security Requirements in Negotiations with the Palestinians.* Washington, D.C.: Institute for Near East Policy, 1989.
Seliktar, Ofira. *New Zionism and the Foreign Policy System of Israel.* London: Croom Helm, 1986.
Shapira, Anita. *Berl Katznelson: A Biography.* Tel Aviv: Am Oved, 1981.

Shapiro, Jonathan. *The Formative Years of the Israeli Labour Party: The Organization of Power, 1919–1930*. London: Sage, 1976.
———. *The Road to Power: The Herut Party in Israel*. Albany: State University of New York Press, 1991.
Shavit, Yaacov. *Jabotinsky and the Revisionist Movement, 1925–1948*. London: Frank Cass, 1988.
el-Shazly, General Saad. *The Crossing of the Suez*. San Francisco: American Mideast Research, 1980.
Shibl, Yusuf. *Essays on the Israeli Economy*. Beirut: Palestine Research Center, 1969.
Shlaim, Avi. *Collusion across the Jordan: King Abdullah, the Zionist Movement, and the Partition of Palestine*. Oxford: Clarendon Press, 1988.
Sohar, Ezra. *Israel's Dilemma: Why Israel Is Falling Apart and How to Put It Back Together*. New York: Shapolsky, 1989.
Spiegel, Steven L. *The Other Arab-Israeli Conflict: Making America's Middle East Policy, from Truman to Reagan*. Chicago: University of Chicago Press, 1985.
Sprinzak, Ehud. *The Ascendance of Israel's Radical Right*. New York: Oxford University Press, 1991.
———. *Brother against Brother: Violence and Extremism in Israeli Politics from the Altalena to the Rabin Assassination*. New York: Free Press, 1999.
Sternhell, Zeev. *The Founding Myths of Israel: Nationalism, Socialism, and the Making of the Jewish State*. Princeton: Princeton University Press, 1998.
Tessler, Mark. *A History of the Israeli-Palestinian Conflict*. Bloomington: Indiana University Press, 1994.
Tishler, Yitzhak. *The White Elephant*. Tel Aviv: Dvir, 1988.
Yaniv, Avner. *Dilemmas of Security: Politics, Strategy, and the Israeli Experience in Lebanon*. New York: Oxford University Press, 1987.

Articles and Chapters in Books

Arian, Asher, and Michal Shamir. "The Primarily Political Functions of the Left-Right Continuum." *Comparative Politics* 1 (1983): 139–58.
Aronoff, Myron J. "Political Polarization: Contradictory Interpretations of Reality." In *Cross-Currents in Israeli Culture and Politics: Political Anthropology*, ed. Myron J. Aronoff, 4: 1–23. New Brunswick, N.J.: Transaction, 1984.
———. "Better Late Than Never: Democratization in the Labor Party." In *Israel after Begin*, ed. Gregory Mahler, 257–71. Albany: State University of New York Press, 1990.
———. "Myths, Symbols, and Rituals of the Emerging State." In *New Perspectives on Israeli History: The Early Years of the State*, ed. Laurence J. Silberstein, 175–92. New York: New York University Press, 1991.
———. "The Origins of Israeli Political Culture." In *Israeli Democracy under Stress*, ed. Ehud Sprinzak and Larry Diamond, 47–63. Boulder, Colo.: Lynne Rienner, 1993.

———. "Labor in the Second Rabin Era: The First Year of Leadership." In *Israel under Rabin*, ed. Robert O. Freedman, 129–42. Boulder: Westview Press, 1995.

Aronoff, Myron J., and Yael S. Aronoff. "Explaining Domestic Influences on Current Israeli Foreign Policy: The Peace Negotiations." *Brown Journal of World Affairs* 3, no. 2 (Summer–Fall 1996): 83–111.

———. "Domestic Determinants of Israeli Foreign Policy: The Peace Process from the Declaration of Principles to the Oslo II Interim Agreement." In *The Middle East Peace Process: The Impact of the Oslo Accords*, ed. Robert O. Freedman, 11–34. Gainesville: University Press of Florida, 1998.

Aronoff, Myron J., and Pierre Atlas. "The Peace Process and Competing Challenges to the Dominant Zionist Discourse." In *The Middle East Peace Process*, ed. Ilan Peleg. Albany: State University of New York Press, 1998.

Barkai, Haim. "Fifty Years of Labor Economy: Growth, Performance and the Present Challenge." *Jerusalem Quarterly* 50 (Spring 1989): 81–109.

Bartlett, Bruce. "The Crisis of Socialism in Israel." *Orbis* 35, no. 1 (Winter 1991): 53–69.

Barzilai, Gad, and Ilan Peleg. "Israel and Future Borders: Assessment of a Dynamic Process." *Journal of Peace Research* 31, no. 1 (1994): 59–71.

Beilin, Yossi. "Dominant Party in Opposition: The Israel Labor Party, 1977–1981." *Middle East Review* 17, no. 4 (Summer 1985): 34–44.

Ben-Yaacov, Avraham. "The Russian-Language Press in Israel." *Qesher* 24 (November 1998): 2–15.

Bialer, Uri. "David Ben-Gurion and Moshe Sharett: The Crystallization of Two Political/Military Orientations in the Israeli Society." *Medina Umimshal* 1, no. 2 (Fall 1977): 71–84.

Blondheim, Menahem. "Cultural Media in Transition: From the Traditional Sermon to the Jewish Press." *Qesher* 21 (May 1997): 63–79.

Don-Yehiya, Eliezer. "Religion, Ethnicity and Electoral Reform." *Israel Affairs* 4, no. 1 (Autumn 1997): 73–102.

Doron, Gideon. "Labor's Return to Power in Israel." *Current History* (January 1993): 27–31.

Eshkol, Levy. "Economic Policy." In *Israeli Economy: Theory and Practice*, ed. Joseph Ronen, 4–27. Tel-Aviv: Dvir, 1963.

Freedman, Robert O. "The Partition of Palestine: Conflicting Nationalism and Great Power Rivalry." In *The Problem of Partition: Peril to World Peace*, ed. Thomas E. Hachey, 175–212. Chicago: Rand McNally, 1972.

———. "Soviet Jewry and Soviet-American Relations: A Historical Analysis." In *Soviet Jewry in the Decisive Decade 1971–1980*, ed. Robert O. Freedman. Durham: Duke University Press, 1984.

———. "Soviet Jewry as a Factor in Soviet-Israeli Relations." In *Soviet Jewry in the 1980s*, ed. Robert O. Freedman. Durham: Duke University Press, 1989.

———. "Soviet-Israel Relations in the Gorbachev Era." In *Legacy of the Soviet*

Bloc, ed. Jane Shapiro Zacek and Ilpyong J. Kim, 218–40. Gainesville: University Press of Florida, 1997.

———. "Russia and Israel under Yeltsin." *Israel Studies* 3, no. 1 (Spring 1998): 140–69.

———. "Russia's Middle East Ambitions." *Middle East Quarterly* 5, no. 3 (September 1998): 31–40.

Garfinkle, Adam. "Israel and Palestine: A Precarious Partnership." *Washington Quarterly* 20, no. 3 (1997): 3–22.

Goldberg, Giora, Gad Barzilai, and Efraim Inbar. "The Impact of Intercommunal Conflict: The Intifada and Israeli Public Opinion." Policy Studies of the Leonard Davis Institute, Hebrew University of Jerusalem, no. 43. February 1991.

Graf, Ehud. "The Universal City of 'The City.'" *Qesher* 10 (November 1991): 101–8.

Grossman, Lawrence. "Jewish Communal Affairs." In *American Jewish Yearbook,* pp. 109–49. New York: American Jewish Committee, 1998.

Gruen, George. "The Not-So-Silent Partnership: Emerging Trends in American Jewish-Israeli Relations." New York: American Jewish Committee, September 1988, 5–8.

———. "Impact of the Intifada on American Jews and the Reaction of the American Public and Israeli Jews." In *The Intifada: Its Impact on Israel, the Arab World, and the Superpowers,* ed. Robert O. Freedman, 228–31. Gainesville: University Press of Florida, 1991.

———. "American Jewish Attitudes toward Israel: Continued Support in the Face of Dramatic Change." In *Israel under Rabin,* ed. Robert O. Freedman, 53–70. Boulder: Westview Press, 1995.

Haass, Richard N. "The Middle East: No More Treaties." *Foreign Affairs* 75, no. 5 (September–October 1996): 53–63.

Kolatt, Israel. "The Zionist Movement and the Arabs." *Studies in Zionism* 5 (April 1982): 129–57.

Korey, William. "The Soviet Public Anti-Zionist Committee: An Analysis." In *Soviet Jewry in the 1980s,* ed. Robert O. Freedman, 26–50. Durham: Duke University Press, 1991.

Lewis, Arnold. "Ethnic Politics and the Foreign Policy Debate in Israel." *Cross-Currents in Israeli Culture and Politics: Political Anthropology* 4 (1984): 25–38.

Lieber, Robert. "Eagle without a Cause: Making Foreign Policy without the Soviet Threat." In *Eagle Adrift: American Foreign Policy at the End of the Century,* ed. Robert Lieber, 3–25. New York: Longman, 1997.

Milson, Menachem. "How to Make Peace with the Palestinians." *Commentary,* May 1981, 25–35.

Mufti, Malik. "The United States and Nasserist Pan-Arabism." In *The Middle East and the United States: A Historical and Political Reassessment,* ed. David W. Lesch, 167–86. Boulder: Westview Press, 1996.

Ozacky-Lazar, Sarah, and As'ad Ghanem. "The Arab Vote in the Elections to the 14th Knesset, May 29, 1996." *Data and Analysis,* no. 5, Tel Aviv: Program on Arab Politics in Israel, Tel Aviv University, 1997; first published in Hebrew by the Institute for Peace Research, Givat Haviva, 1996.

Peleg, Ilan. "The Likud under Rabin II: Between Ideological Purity and Pragmatic Readjustment." In *Israel under Rabin,* ed. Robert O. Freedman, 143–67. Boulder: Westview Press, 1995.

Postel, Theodore A. "Lessons of the Gulf War Experience with the Patriot." *International Security* 16, no. 3 (Winter 1991–92): 119–71.

Rappel, Yoel. "Synagogue Newspapers in Israel." *Qesher* 10 (November 1991): 109–11.

Rekhess, Elie. "Resurgent Islam in Israel." *Asian and Algerian Studies* 27, nos. 1 and 2 (March–July 1993): 189–206.

———. "Israel's Arab Citizens and the Peace Process." In *Israel under Rabin,* ed. Robert O. Freedman, 189–204. Boulder: Westview Press, 1995.

———. "The Islamic Movement in Israel: The Internal Debate over Representation in the Knesset." *Data and Analysis,* no. 2, Tel Aviv Program on Arab Politics in Israel, Tel Aviv University, 1996.

Rosenfield, Geraldine. "U.S. Public Opinion Polls and the Lebanon War." *American Jewish Yearbook, 1984,* 106–16.

Satloff, Robert B. "The Jordan-Israel Peace Treaty: A Remarkable Document." *Middle East Quarterly* 2, no. 1 (March 1995): 47–51.

Schiff, Ze'ev. "Green Light, Lebanon." *Foreign Policy* 50 (Spring 1983): 73–85.

Shamir, Yaacov. "Israeli Elite Journalists: Views on Freedom and Responsibility." *Jerusalem Quarterly* 65 (1988): 589–94.

Slater, Jerome. "Netanyahu, a Palestinian State, and Israeli Security Reassessed." *Political Science Quarterly* 112, no. 4 (1997–98): 675–89.

Sprinzak, Ehud. "Netanyahu's Safety Belt." *Foreign Affairs* (July–August 1998): 18–28.

Tessler, Mark. "Israel at Peace with the Arab World." Abu Dhabi: Occasional Papers of the Emirates Center for Strategic Studies and Research, 1995.

Tsarfati, Orly. "A Press in the Service of the Messiah." *Qesher* 24 (November 1998): 16–27.

Waxman, Chaim I. "The Haredization of American Orthodox Jewry." *Jerusalem Letter/Viewpoints,* no. 376, Jerusalem Center for Public Affairs, February 15, 1998.

Weisbrod, Lilly. "From Labour Zionism to New Zionism: Ideological Change in Israel." *Theory and Society* 10 (1981): 777–803.

Yaniv, Avner, and Robert Lieber. "Personal Whim or Strategic Imperative? The Israeli Invasion of Lebanon." *International Security* 8, no. 2 (Fall 1983): 117–42.

Contributors

Myron J. Aronoff is professor of political science and anthropology at Rutgers University. He is the author of numerous books on Israel, including *Frontiertown: The Politics of Community Building in Israel; Power and Ritual in the Israel Labor Party;* and *Israeli Visions and Divisions.*

Robert O. Freedman is Peggy Meyerhoff Pearlstone Professor of political science and president of Baltimore Hebrew University. He is the author of four books and the editor of twelve books on Israel, Middle East politics, Soviet Jewry, and the foreign policy of the former Soviet Union. His most recent books are *The Middle East and the Peace Process* and *Moscow and the Middle East.*

George E. Gruen, former director of Israel and Middle East Studies of the American Jewish Committee, is adjunct professor of international relations at Columbia University. He is the author of numerous publications on the Middle East, including *The Not-So-Silent Partnership: Emerging Trends in American Jewish-Israeli Relations* and *Turkey, Israel and the Peace Process.*

Michael Keren is professor of political science and director of the Institute for the Study of the Jewish Press and Communications at Tel Aviv University. Among his numerous publications are *The Pen and the Sword: Israeli Intellectuals and the Making of the Nation-State* and *Ben-Gurion and the Intellectuals.*

Robert J. Lieber is professor of political science at Georgetown University. Among his numerous publications on foreign policy are *Eagle in a New World: American Grand Strategy in the Post–Cold War Era* and *No Common Power: Understanding International Relations.*

Malik Mufti is professor of political science at Tufts University. He is the author of numerous studies of intra-Arab politics, including *Sovereign Creations: Pan Arabism and Political Order in Syria and Iraq.*

Ilan Peleg is the Charles A. Dana Professor of social sciences and the head of the Department of Government and Law at Lafayette College. He is the author or editor of numerous books, including *Begin's Foreign Policy, 1977–1983: Israel's Turn to the Right* and *The Emergence of a Binational Israel: The Second Republic in the Making.*

Elie Rekhess is senior research associate at the Moshe Dayan Center for Middle East Studies at Tel Aviv University and was senior consultant on Arab minority affairs to Prime Minister Rabin. His most recent book is *The Israeli Communist Party and the Arab Minority in Israel: Between Communism and Arab Nationalism.*

Mark Rosenblum is professor of history at Queens College of the City University of New York, where he is the director of the Michael Harrington Center and chair of its Middle East Project. Among his publications on the Middle East are *Israel and the PLO: From Negotiating a "Piece of Paper" to Implementing "Peace on the Ground"* and *Euphoria with the King, Angst with Arafat, Anticipation with Assad: Hope without Delusion.*

Ofira Seliktar is professor of political science at Gratz College. Among her numerous publications on the Middle East are "The Transition to Market Economy: The Road Half Taken," in *Books on Israel*, vol. 5, and *The New Zionism and the Foreign Policy System of Israel.*

Mark Tessler is director of the Center for Middle Eastern Studies at the University of Arizona. He is the author of numerous books and articles on the Middle East and the Arab-Israeli conflict, including *A History of the Israeli-Palestinian Conflict* and "Israel at Peace with the Arab World."

Chaim I. Waxman is professor of sociology at Rutgers University. He is the author of numerous books and articles on religion and politics in Israel, including "The Haredization of American Orthodox Jewry" and *Israel as a Religious Reality.*

Index

Abbas, Mahmud (Abu Mazen) 126, 249, 268n
Abdullah, ibn Hussein ibn Talal (king) 57
Abdullah, Ibn-Sherif Hussein (king) 68–72, 81
Abu Mazen. *See* Mahmud Abbas
Achdut Ha'avodah 121, 224
Afghanistan 5, 7, 8, 11
Agudat Israel party 36, 164, 166, 169, 170, 172, 175, 177–78
Ahad Ha'am 99, 139
Albright, Madeline 40, 54
Algeria 3, 19, 97
Al Hamishmar 224, 226
Aliyah. *See* Immigration
Allon Plan 84, 86, 107, 109
Aloni, Shulamit 125
Al-Sana, Talib 191
Alter, Simha 166
American-Israel Public Affairs Committee (AIPAC) 22, 61, 62
American Jewish Committee 37, 46
Amit, Yaacov 226
Amital, Yehudah 174–75
Aqaba, Gulf of. *See* Straits of Tiran
Arab Local Councils 187–89
Arab Mayors' Forum 183
Arab United List Party 189, 191, 193
Arafat, Yasser 17, 25, 50–51, 53–55, 58, 89–90, 105, 114, 116, 154, 184, 241, 244–45, 248–49
Arens, Moshe 238
Aridor, Yoram 208–9
Ashkenazim 30, 164, 166
Assad, Hafiz 7, 85, 87, 92
Avnery, Uri 229–30

Ba'adani, Shimon 263
Baghdad Pact 3, 11

Baker, James 23
Balad Party 193
Balfour Declaration 96, 109
Bank Shares Scandal 209
Barak, Ehud 13, 17, 26, 57–62, 116, 127, 130–31, 158–59, 166, 192–93, 236–72
Baram, Uzi 128
Bargil, Gavri 257
Bar-Ilan, Meir 167
Begin, Benjamin Ze'ev 130, 135n, 152, 168, 238, 240, 254
Begin, Menachem 44, 80, 86–87, 121–24, 133, 143–45, 148, 150, 152–54, 158
Beilin, Yossi 125, 127, 129, 131, 133, 248–49, 268n
Beilin–Abu Mazen Understanding 268n
Beilinson, Moshe 225
Belkind, Israel 99
Bene Israel 172
Ben-Eliezer, Benyamin 110, 128
Ben-Gurion, David 16, 20, 37–38, 41, 70, 72–75, 81, 86, 106, 147, 170–71, 221, 226–28
Ben-Tzvi, Yitzhak 101, 106
Ben-Yehudah, Eliezer 139, 223
Berger, Sandy 40
Bevin, Ernest 18
Bezek 213
Birthright Israel Project 47–48
Bishara, Azmi 190, 256
Blair, Tony 130
Blaustein, Jacob 37–38, 41
Bnai Brak 164, 178
Borochov, Dov Ber 99
Bosnia 17
Brandeis, Louis 37
Brezhnev, Leonid 4–6, 10, 12

Britain 2, 17–18, 22, 24, 26, 37, 72, 198, 212, 227
Brit Shalom 111
Bronfman, Charles 47–48
Brother Daniel Case 172
Bund 36
Burg, Avi 128
Bush, George 25–26, 150
Bush, George W. 58

Camp David Agreements (1978) 23, 86, 149
Carter, Jimmy 23
Carville, James 130
Center Party (Mercaz) 256–58, 260
Chernobyl 6
China 4, 6, 16, 17
Chirac, Jacques 26
Clayman, David 46–47
Clifford, Clark 18
Clinton, Bill 16, 26, 50–51, 53–54, 58, 129, 157, 238
Clinton, Hilary 58
Cohen, Shalom 229
Cohen-Orgad, Yigal 209
Conference of Presidents of Major American Jewish Organizations 38, 61
Conservative Judaism 30, 32–34, 51, 173
Cook, Robin 26
Cyprus 31, 62n
Czechoslovakia 2, 3, 74
Czech Republic 22

Dahamsha, Abd al-Malik 191
Darawsha, Abd al-Wahab 191
Darwish, Sheikh Abdallah Nimr 188, 190–91
Davar 224–26, 232
Dayan, Moshe 71, 73–74, 85, 106, 148–49, 228
Dead Sea 201
Declaration of Principles. *See* Oslo I Agreement
Degel HaTorah Party 169, 175

Democratic Movement (Party) for Change 229
Deri, Aryeh 166
Development towns 202, 208, 212
Dinitz, Simha 206–8
Do'ar Hayom 223–24
Dulles, John Foster 18–20

Eban, Abba 83, 106
EC. *See* European Community
Economic Stabilization Plan 210–11
EFTA. *See* European Free Trade Area
Egypt 2–4, 72, 75, 78, 97, 103
    relations with Israel. *See* Israel, relations with Egypt
    relations with the United States 72, 73–75, 83–84, 86, 89
    relations with the USSR 4–5, 24, 74, 77, 84
Eisenhower, Dwight 18–20
Eitan, Rafael 38, 149–50, 153
Eldad, Israel 153
Emigration (Yerida) from Israel 203–4, 212, 216
Emigration of Soviet and former Soviet Jews to Israel 2, 4–7, 9, 12, 132, 151, 158, 171, 211–12, 214, 231–32, 246–47, 250, 253–57
Epstein, Yitzhak 99–100
Eshkol, Levi 78, 148, 199–200, 203–4
Ethiopia 76
Etzion Bloc. *See* Gush Etzion
European Community (European Union) (EC) 24, 204, 214
European Free Trade Area (EFTA) 214
European Union. *See* European Community

Faisal, Ibn Husein (king) 68, 98
Faruq, King 69
Fatah 106
Finkelstein, Arthur 248–49
Fishman-Maimon, Rabbi Yehudah Leib 170

France 3, 19, 24–26, 29
Frankfurter, Felix 68
Frenkel, Jacob 212
Friedman, Milton 206–7, 212

Gahal Party 107, 108, 141, 146–49
Gaza Strip 103, 105–6, 114–15, 139, 149, 151, 153, 158, 184, 192, 244
Gemayel, Bashir 88
General Zionists 203, 206, 224
Germany 22, 24, 147–48, 202–3, 227
Gesher Faction 129, 131, 158, 258
Glasnost 7
Globes 231
Golan Heights 59, 60, 71, 82, 85, 87, 140, 149, 158, 192, 263
Goodman, Jerry 240
Gorbachev, Mikhail 6–8
Gore, Al 58
Goren, Rabbi Shlomo 164
Greater Land of Israel Movement 146, 149, 153, 155, 237, 239, 242, 246
Greater Syria 97
Greenberg, Stanley 130
Greenman, Eli 254
Gruenbaum, Yitzhak 170
Gulf of Aqaba. *See* Straits of Tiran
Gulf War 8, 23, 25
Gur Hasidim 166
Gush Emunim 123, 167–68
Gush Etzion (Etzion Bloc) 108

Ha'amodi'a 232
Ha'aretz 223, 227–28, 231–32
Habad. *See* Lubavich Hasidism
Haboker 224
Hadash Party (Democratic Front for Peace and Equality) 189, 191, 193
Ha'dor 224
Ha'havazelet 223
Haig, Alexander 25, 88
Ha'ir 232–33
Ha'levanon 223
Hamas 51, 126, 137n, 243–45

Ha'olam Hazeh 229–32
Hapoel Hamizrahi 167
Ha'poel Hatza'ir 223
Haredim (Ultra Orthodox Jews) 120, 132, 158, 162, 166, 169–71, 175, 257, 263
Har Homa 155, 237, 252
Hasmonean Tunnel 184, 236, 252, 269n
Hatzofeh 232
Hatzvi 223
Hebron 95, 154, 184, 188
Hebron Agreement 236, 239, 241, 245
Hefetz, Assad 251–52
Herut 108, 141, 147–48, 208, 224
Herzburg, Arthur 44
Herzl, Theodore 24, 99, 139, 220
Hevrat Ovdim 213
Hezbollah 10
Hirschfeld, Yair 125–26
Histadrut 126–127, 201, 203, 211, 213, 221, 224, 227
Holocaust 18, 36–37, 43, 53, 112, 143, 153
Horwitz, Yigal 208
Hungary 22
Hussein, King Ibn Talal 14, 57, 68, 78–79, 80–81, 83–84, 87–90, 107
Hussein, Saddam 89, 91
Husseini, Faisal 89

IDF. *See* Israel Defense Forces
Immigration (aliya) 198, 203, 206, 211–13, 216, 221, 225
Indyk, Martin 40
Intel Corporation 214
Inter-Arab Diplomacy 67–94
Intifada 7, 45, 51, 88–89, 113, 129, 151
Iran 5, 9, 76
Iran-Iraq War 11
Iraq 2–4, 9, 20, 75–76, 78, 91
  invasion of Kuwait 89–90
  relations with Israel 25
  relations with U.S. 59, 88–89
  relations with USSR 14, 87
Irgun 126, 144, 147

Ir Shalem 269n
Islamic Jihad 126, 243, 245
Islamic Movement (of Israeli Arabs) 188, 190
Israel
　Arabs in. *See* Israeli Arabs
　civil society in 219-35
　economy of 58, 198-218, 247, 255, 257
　immigration to (Aliyah) 2, 4-7, 9, 12, 30, 41
　religious issues in 30-35, 49, 52, 56, 58, 121, 131, 133, 162-179, 230, 263
—relations with
　　American Jews 22, 29-66, 166, 202
　　Egypt 3, 5, 24-25, 42-44, 70, 72-73, 78, 80-83, 85-86, 90-91, 149, 157, 207, 239
　　Iraq 25
　　Jordan 23, 42-43, 57, 69-71, 73, 78-79, 81-83, 86, 90-92, 107-8, 126, 151, 157, 239
　　Lebanon 10, 43, 57-58, 87-88, 149
　　Palestinians 24, 43, 45, 57, 86, 95-118, 124, 132-33, 143, 145, 151-52, 154, 159, 182, 194, 237-39, 241-46, 263-64
　　Russia and the Soviet Union 1-15, 21, 151
　　Syria 5, 7, 24-25, 42-43, 57-60, 69-70, 73, 78-79, 81-82, 85-88, 90-91, 133, 149, 263-64
　　United States 1-3, 16-28, 38-40, 54, 58, 73-78, 83-84, 86, 88, 150, 151, 156-57, 202-3, 214, 236-39, 241-42
—wars of
　　1948 War of Independence 2, 11, 103, 180-81, 221, 230
　　1956 Suez War 3, 18-19, 75, 104
　　1967 Six-Day War 4, 11, 21, 29, 42-43, 104, 182, 204, 228
　　1973 Yom Kippur War 5, 11, 21, 23-24, 29, 43-44, 85, 203

　　1982 Lebanese War (Operation Peace for the Galilee) 44-45, 87-88, 149-50, 159, 208
Israel Aviation Industry 201, 212
Israel Defense Forces (IDF) 124
Israeli Arabs 132, 180-96, 199, 246, 256-58, 260-64
Israeli-Egyptian Peace Treaty (1979) 21, 23, 149, 207
Israeli-Jordanian Peace Treaty (1994) 23, 126
Israel Policy Forum 53, 57-58, 61
Italy 24

Jaaring, Gunnar 84
Jabotinsky, Valdimir Ze'ev 102, 123, 139, 142-46, 152, 154, 220
Jerusalem 26, 43, 58-59, 69, 79, 83, 95, 97, 192, 249, 251-53
Jerusalem Post 211
Jerusalem Tunnel. *See* Hasmonean Tunnel
Jewish Agency 32-33
Jewish National Fund 96
Jewish Theological Seminary 33
Johnson, Lyndon 19, 25, 79
Jordan 20, 51, 68, 75-76, 83-84, 87, 97, 103
　relations with Israel. *See* Israel, relations with Jordan
　relations with Palestinians 71, 82-84, 88-89
Jordanian Option 107-108, 112
Jordanian Valley 108
Jordan River 71
Josef, Dov 203
Judea and Samaria. *See* West Bank

Kaplan, Lionel 61
Kassem, Abdul Karim 3-4
Kastner, Israel 147-48
Katzav, Moshe 187
Katznelson, Berl 225
Kennedy, John F. 16, 19, 177
Khartoum Arab Summit (1967) 44

Khatib, Sheikh Kamal 191
Khatib, Tawfiq 191
Khrushchev, Nikita 3–4, 12
Kibbutz 199–200
King Hussein. *See* Hussein Ibn Talal
Kissinger, Henry 5, 24, 85–86
Klein, Morton 61
Kohr, Howard 61
Kol Ha'am 224–25
Kollek, Teddy 38
Kook, Rabbi Avraham Yitzhak 167, 174
Kook, Rabbi Zvi Yehuda 167
Koor 201, 211
Kosovo 13
Kulik, Gil 32
Kulturkampf 140, 174, 178, 248, 253
Kurtzer, Dan 40

Labor Party (One Israel) 57, 87, 90, 106–107, 112, 114, 119–38, 142, 150–51, 163, 189, 192, 195, 197, 206–7, 210, 229, 237, 241, 243, 247, 258–60
Lahat, Shlomo 114
Lamerchav 224
Landau, Uzi 131, 238
Land of Israel Movement. *See* Greater Land of Israel Movement
Lapid, Tommi 258
Lauder, Ronald 61
Lausanne Conference 69
Lautman, Dov 56
Lavon Affair 224
Law of Return 193
Lebanon 20, 75, 87, 103
  relations with Israel. *See* Israel, relations with Lebanon
  relations with Syria 87–88
Lekem 38
Levy, David 128–30, 158, 239, 258
Levy, Yitzhak 264
Lewinsky, Monica 54
Liba'i, David 131
Liberal Party 206, 208
Libya 9, 97
Lieberman, Avigdor 255

Likud Party 44, 57, 61, 88, 107, 108, 112, 114, 122–24, 126, 131–33, 139–61, 163, 186, 191, 197, 206–7, 209–10, 229, 258–59
Lipkin-Shahak, Amnon 130
Lubavich (Habad) Hasidism 173, 175, 232–33
Luria, Yosef 99–100

Ma'ariv 228, 233
Ma'ayan Hahinuch Hatorani 263
Madrid Peace Conference 8, 23
Mafdal. *See* National Religious Party
Mahameed, Hashem 260
Malenkov, Georgi 3
Malul, Nissim 99–100
Mapai 120–21, 147, 198, 203, 227–28
Marshall, George 18
Mashal, Khaled 157
Massalha, Nawaf 260
Meimad Party 130–31, 158, 174–75, 258
Meir, Golda 2, 77, 105–7, 148–49
Mendes-France, Pierre 29
Mercaz. *See* Center Party
Meretz party 112, 125, 158, 163, 166, 189, 191–92, 258, 260
Meridor, Dan 130, 238
Millet System 30
Milo, Roni 130, 151, 238
Milson, Menachem 110
Mizrahim. *See* Sephardim
Mizrahi Movement and Party 167
Moda'i, Yitzhak 209
Modern Orthodox Jews 162. *See also* Mizrahi; National Religious Party
Moledet party 168, 258
Mordechai, Yitzhak 130, 238, 240, 247, 256
Moshav 199, 201
Moslem Brotherhood 188
Myers, Rabbi Joel 265n

Nasha Strana 232
Nasser, Gamal 3–4, 19, 67, 72–77, 79–81, 83, 86, 91

National Democratic Alliance 190
National Religious Party (NRP) (Mafdal) 158, 163–64, 167–68, 170, 191, 252, 260, 263–64
National Unity Party 130, 168, 258, 263
NATO 3, 11, 13, 22
Ne'eman, Ya'akov 33–34
Ne'eman Committee 33–34
Netanyahu, Binyamin 10, 13, 22, 26, 31, 34, 38–40, 47–50, 53–59, 61, 115, 123, 128–30, 132–33, 143–46, 152–59, 184, 186, 190, 192–93, 212–13, 236, 237–57
Netivot Shalom Movement 174
New Economic Policy 204
New Israel Fund 32
Nixon, Richard 5, 24
Nogah 231
Nordau, Max 99, 220
North Korea 2
Novosti Nedeli 232
NRP. *See* National Religious Party

Olmert, Ehud 55, 128, 159, 238, 252
One Nation Party 258
OPEC 85
Oriental Jews. *See* Sephardim
Orient House 252–53
Orr, Uri 128
Orthodox Jews 30–31, 34, 36, 45–48, 52–53, 59, 170, 245, 254, 257–58
Oslo I Agreement (Declaration of Principles) 40, 50–51, 90, 112, 126, 152, 154, 159, 183, 192, 195, 237, 241, 244
Oslo II Agreement 126–27
Oz Veshalom Movement 174

Palestine Liberation Organization (PLO) 87–90, 105, 107–8, 110, 112–13, 126, 132, 145, 182, 184
Palestine National Council 113, 241
Palestine Post 224
Palestinians 22, 51, 56, 70, 86, 103, 132, 241–47

National Charter (Covenant) 241–43
  relations with the United States. *See* United States, relations with Palestinians
  See also Arafat, Yasser; Israel, relations with Palestinians); Palestine Liberation Organization
Patam (Foreign Exchanged Indexed) Bank Accounts 207
Patriot missiles 26
Peace Now 257
Peel Commission 68, 90, 102, 103
Peled, Yossi 251–52
Peres, Shimon 9, 50, 61, 90, 124–28, 133, 153, 175, 190, 192, 209, 228, 240, 242–43, 250, 256, 260
Perestroika 7
PLO. *See* Palestine Liberation Organization
Poland 22
Pollard, Jonathan 38–40
Porat, Hanan 168
Porush, Meir 169
Porush, Rabbi Menahem 169
Primakov, Yevgeny 1, 10, 12–13
Pundak, Ron 125–26

Quwwatli, Shukri 68

Rabin, Yitzhak 9, 26, 31, 50, 61, 80, 85–87, 89, 114, 124–26, 133, 153–55, 157, 184–86, 189, 212, 236, 250, 256–57, 260, 264
Ramon, Chaim 126–27, 129, 131, 133
Raslan, Rana 195
Reagan, Ronald 7, 16, 23, 210
Reagan Plan (1982) 23, 88
Reconstructionist Judaism 30, 33
Reform Judaism 30, 32–34, 36, 46–47, 51–52, 59, 173
Regev, Uri 34–35
Reich, Jerome 48
Reines, Rabbi Isaac Jacob 167
Religious Councils 34–35

Religious Zionism. *See* Mizrahi; National Religious Party
Revisionism 139, 142, 146
Rogers, William 23
Rogers Plan 23
Rosenfeld, Shalom 233–34
Ross, Dennis 40
Rothenberg, Alan 31–32
Rugh, William 40
Ruppin. Arthur 100–101, 111
Rusk, Dean 83
Russia (USSR) 1–14
  antisemitism in 1, 10, 12–14

Sabra 45, 159
Sadat, Anwar 4–5, 84–87, 90
Safed 95
Saguy, Uri 251–52
Said, Nuri 3–4
Salah, Ra'id 191
Sapir, Pinhas 202, 204
Satmar Chasidim 46
Saudi Arabia 97
Schneerson, Rabbi Menahem Mendel 173, 175
Schorsch, Chancellor Ismar 33
SEATO 3, 11
Seidman, Daniel 269n
Sephardim (Mizrahim, Oriental Jews) 30, 122, 127–28, 132, 163–64, 166, 208, 245–46, 253–54
Settlements (Jewish) in occupied territories. *See* Gaza Strip; West Bank
Shach, Rabbi Eliezer 166, 175
Shamir, Yitzhak 26, 42, 123–24, 143–44, 149–54, 238
Sharansky, Natan (Anatoly) 10, 254–55, 264
Sharon, Ariel 13, 25, 38, 50, 58, 87–88, 149, 159, 208, 238–39, 258
Shas Party 13, 125–26, 129, 158, 163–64, 191, 246, 253–55, 257–58, 260, 263–64
Shatilla 45, 159
Shetreet, Shimon 128

Shinui Party 166, 258
Shitreet, Meir 159
Shochat, Avraham 128
Shocken, Gerson 227
Shrum, Robert 130
Sidqi, Ismail 68
Si'hat Ha'shavu'a 232
Simsolo, Rami 187
Sinai Peninsula 18–19, 75, 82, 84–85, 87, 139, 207
Six-Day War. *See* Israel, wars
Smilansky, Moshe 100
Sohar, Ezra 210
Sonnenfeldt, Michael 61
South Korea 2
Soviet Jews. *See* Emigration of Soviet and former Soviet Jews to Israel
Stalin, Josef 1–2, 11–12, 226
Status Quo Agreement (1947) 170–74. *See also* Israel, religious issues in)
Steinhardt, Michael 47, 49
Straits of Tiran (Sharm el-Sheikh) (Gulf of Aqaba) 3, 25, 80
Suez Canal 3, 74, 76, 82, 84–85
Sultanovich, Alec 254
Syria 4, 9, 59, 75–76, 78, 83, 97
  relations with Israel. *See* Israel, relations with Syria
  relations with Lebanon 87–88
  relations with Russia 14, 87
  relations with the United States 59, 88–89

Tabenchik, Ludmila 254
Taibe 186
Tekuma Party 168, 258
Tel Aviv 233
Tenet, George 39
Terrorism 43, 50, 57–58, 73, 88, 112, 115, 126, 138, 242–45, 249–51
Tevet, Shabtai 228
Tiberias 95
Tibi, Ahmed 248
Tochnit Dalet 103

Tozeret Ha'aretz (Import Substitution) Program 203
Trotsky, Leon 226
Truman, Harry 18–19
Tsena (Austerity) Program 203
Tsomet party 153, 158
Turkey 29, 75–76

Ujkelet 232
Ultra-Orthodox Jews. *See* Haredim
Um al Fahm 191
United Israel Appeal 32
United Jewish Appeal 31–33, 47, 49, 55
United Nations 1, 5, 24, 37, 79, 103, 105, 113
United Nations Expeditionary Force (UNEF) 25
United Nations General Assembly resolutions
  partition resolution (1947) 68
  "Zionism Is Racism" (1975) 5, 8, 111
United Nations Security Council
  resolution 242 83, 115
  resolution 338 85, 115
United States
  relations with Israel. *See* Israel, relations with United States
  relations with the Palestinians 39, 242–45
  relations with the USSR/Russia 3–7, 12
United Torah Judaism party 164, 169, 260–61. *See also* Agudat Israel

Vesti 232
Village Leagues 210
Vilnai, Natan 251–52
Vremia 232

War of Attrition (1969–70) 83, 148–49
Warsaw Pact 8
Weismann, Chaim 98–99, 102, 227
Weizman, Ezer 149, 228

West Bank (Judea and Samaria) 42, 44, 54, 81–82, 86, 103, 105–8, 114–15, 137, 145, 153, 158, 184, 192
  Jewish settlements in 60, 90–91, 106–9, 123, 149–50, 154, 169, 208, 264
Wexler, Richard 32, 33, 49
White Paper (1939) 37, 68
"Who is a Jew?" issue 171–73
World Bank 204
World Zionist Organization 227
Wye River Plantation Agreement 38–39, 50, 53, 56–57, 59, 129, 132, 137n, 157, 237, 239, 241, 245

Yated Neeman 232
Yatom, Danny 252
Yediot Aharonot 224, 228, 233
Yefiot Hadashot 232
Yellin, David 99
Yeltsin, Boris 1, 8–10, 12–14
Yehud 254
Yemen 77, 79–80
Yerida. *See* Emigration
Yishuv 2, 29, 96, 98–102, 120–21, 147–48, 199–200, 204
Yisrael Ba'aliyah Party 10, 13, 253, 258, 260, 263–64
Yisrael Beiteinu Party 255, 258
Yom Kippur War (1973). *See* Israel, wars of
Yosef, Rabbi Ovadia 164, 166, 175, 263

Zadok, Chaim 131
Zaim, Hosni 69
Zeevi, Rehavam 168
Zemanim 224
Zionism 1, 35–37, 43, 68, 71, 95–102, 120, 126, 139, 181, 197, 203, 216, 220, 226–27, 229
Zuabi, Abdel Rahman 194
Zuebi, Abd al-Aziz 185